PEARSON CUSTOM
BUSINESS RESOURCES

Introduction to Process Analytics

PEARSON

Cover Art: Courtesy of EyeWire/Getty Images and PhotoDisc/Getty Images. Photodisc, "Globe surrounded by business people on computer monitors," courtesy of Photodisc/Getty Images. Dave Cutler (Artist), "Man Dropping Coins Into Glass Jar," courtesy of David Cutler/Images.com. Dave Cutler (Artist), "Three Coins in Glass Jar," courtesy of David Cutler/Images.com. Dean Turner, "Stock Vector: Global Finance" Courtesy of Dean Turner/iStockphoto. Hal Bergman, "Refinery Silhouette" Courtesy of Hal Bergman/iStockphoto. Dan Barnes, "Cargo Container Ship Aerial View" Courtesy of Dan Barnes/iStockphoto. Franc Podgorsek, "Stock Numbers" Courtesy of Franc Podgorsek/ iStockphoto. "Customer in Line at Grocery Store" Courtesy of Digital Vision Photography/Veer Inc. Owaki-Kulla, "Pumping Gas" Courtesy of Flirt Photography/Veer Inc. Lynn Johnson, "Yunnan Province, People's Republic of China" Courtesy of Lynn Johnson/Getty Images, Inc. Thomas Bendy, "Student Typing" Courtesy of Thomas Bendy/iStockphoto. Additional images courtesy of Photodisc, DigitalVision/Getty Images, Stockbyte/Getty Images, Photodisc/Getty Images, Eyewire/Getty Images, Digital Vision, Rubberball Productions/Getty Images, brandXpictures.

Copyright © 2013 by Pearson Learning Solutions
All rights reserved.

Permission in writing must be obtained from the publisher before any part of this work may be reproduced or transmitted in any form or by any means, electronic or mechanical, including photocopying and recording, or by any information storage or retrieval system.

Additional copyright information is included, where applicable, as a footnote at the beginning of each chapter.

20   17

This special edition published in cooperation with Pearson Learning Solutions.

Printed in the United States of America.

Please visit our website at *www.pearsonlearningsolutions.com*.

Attention bookstores: For permission to return any unsold stock, contact us at *pe-uscustomreturns@pearson.com*.

Pearson Learning Solutions, 501 Boylston Street, Suite 900, Boston, MA 02116
A Pearson Education Company
www.pearsoned.com

 ISBN 10: 1-269-23578-8
ISBN 13: 978-1-269-23578-5

EDITORIAL ADVISORY BOARD

Steven R. Kursh, Ph.D., CSDP
College of Business Administration
Northeastern University
Finance/MIS

Theresa K. Lant, Ph.D.
Lubin School of Business
Pace University
Management – Strategy

Karl D. Majeske, Ph.D.
School of Business Administration
Oakland University
Decision Science

James M. Olver, Ph.D.
Mason School of Business
The College of William and Mary
Marketing

Robert Plant, Ph.D.
School of Business Administration
University of Miami
MIS/CIS

PEARSON

Table of Contents

PROJECT
MANAGEMENT

Two boys slug it out in an Xbox 360 wrestling game at the 2011 IT Show in Singapore.

XBOX 360

Four years after the introduction of Xbox, Microsoft needed to quickly design, develop, and produce a new product. Sony's PlayStation 2 was dominating the video game market and Microsoft needed a new product to compete with the impending release of PlayStation 3. Developing such a product is a project of massive proportions. The project consisted of four phases: (1) design, (2) analysis, (3) development, and (4) launch. The result was Xbox 360.

Design

The design of the Xbox 360 was a collaborative effort between Microsoft and many other firms, including Astro Studios in San Francisco, which designed the overall console and controller; IBM, which designed the processor chip; ATI, which designed the graphics chip; and a host of game design firms to develop games for the new product. A key element of the new product was the built-in Internet access that allowed gamers to access online games, buy game add-ons, and access multiplayer games developed exclusively for Xbox 360. Microsoft also included its primary manufacturers, Flextronics and Wistron, in the design process to optimize the production and assembly of the more than 1,000 parts contained in an Xbox 360.

Analysis

Getting an estimate of future sales for a new product is always difficult; however, in this case, the historic patterns for PlayStation 1, PlayStation 2, and Xbox

From Chapter 2 of *Operations Management: Processes and Supply Chains*, Tenth Edition. Lee J. Krajewski, Larry P. Ritzman, Manoj K. Malhotra. Copyright © 2013 by Pearson Education, Inc. All rights reserved.

were useful. Analysts found that the peak year for a PlayStation product was 4 years after its introduction and that the life cycle for those products is about 11 years. This information provided a basis for estimating the sales potential of Xbox 360, although actual sales may be limited due to supply constraints. Nonetheless, Microsoft realized that the potential was there to open a new generation of game consoles well ahead of the market.

Development

Microsoft worked closely with Flextronics, Wistron, and the various design firms to iron out manufacturing problems in the early phases of Xbox 360 production. Once initial production was underway, Microsoft brought on Celestica to add production capacity. The decision was made to focus manufacturing operations in China. All told, 10,000 workers in China would be involved in Xbox 360 production.

Launch

Microsoft's Xbox 360 gained an early lead in terms of market share due, in part, to its early launch date, which was one year ahead of its rivals PlayStation 3 and Wii. All told, the product was released in 36 countries in the first year of production, a Herculean effort requiring extensive coordination and a high level of project management skill. Sales of the Xbox 360 exceeded expectations with more than 10 million units sold in the first year alone. Nonetheless, Microsoft experienced difficulties in getting the supply chain to meet customer demands in a timely fashion. The lesson to be learned is that projects can be planned and executed properly; however, the underlying infrastructure that delivers the product is equally important in the ultimate success of the venture.

Source: David Holt, Charles Holloway, and Hau Lee, "Evolution of the Xbox Supply Chain," Stanford Graduate School of Business, Case: GS-49, (April 14, 2006); "Xbox 360," Wikipedia, the free encyclopedia, **http://en.wikipedia.org/wiki/Xbox_360**.

LEARNING GOALS *After reading this chapter, you should be able to:*

1. Define the major activities associated with defining, organizing, planning, monitoring, and controlling projects.

2. Diagram the network of interrelated activities in a project.

3. Identify the sequence of critical activities that determines the duration of a project.

4. Explain how to determine a minimum-cost project schedule.

5. Describe the considerations managers make in assessing the risks in a project and calculate the probability of completing a project on time.

6. Define the options available to alleviate resource problems.

---

project

An interrelated set of activities with a definite starting and ending point, which results in a unique outcome for a specific allocation of resources.

Companies such as Microsoft are experts at managing projects such as Xbox 360. They master the ability to schedule activities and monitor progress within strict time, cost, and performance guidelines. A **project** is an interrelated set of activities with a definite starting and ending point, which results in a unique outcome for a specific allocation of resources.

Projects are common in everyday life as well as in business. Planning weddings, remodeling bathrooms, writing term papers, and organizing surprise parties are examples of small projects in everyday life. Conducting company audits, planning mergers, creating advertising campaigns, re-engineering processes, developing new services or products, and establishing a strategic alliance are examples of large projects in business.

The three main goals of any project are (1) complete the project on time or earlier, (2) do not exceed the budget, and (3) meet the specifications to the satisfaction of the customer. When we must undertake projects with some uncertainty involved, it does not hurt to have flexibility with respect to resource availability, deadlines, and budgets. Consequently, projects can be complex and challenging to manage. **Project management**, which is a systemized, phased approach to defining, organizing, planning, monitoring, and controlling projects, is one way to overcome that challenge.

Projects often cut across organizational lines because they need the skills of multiple professions and organizations. Furthermore, each project is unique, even if it is routine, requiring new combinations of skills and resources in the project process. For example, projects for adding a new branch office, installing new computers in a department, or developing a sales promotion may be initiated several times a year. Each project may have been done many times before; however, differences arise with each replication. Uncertainties, such as the advent of new technologies or the activities of competitors, can change the character of projects and require responsive countermeasures. Finally, projects are temporary because personnel, materials, and facilities are organized to complete them within a specified time frame and then are disbanded.

Projects, and the application of project management, facilitate the implementation of strategy. However, the power of this approach goes beyond the focus on one project. Operations strategy initiatives often require the coordination of many interdependent projects. Such a collection of projects is called a **program**, which is an interdependent set of projects with a common strategic purpose. As new project proposals come forward, management must assess their fit to the current operations strategy and ongoing initiatives and have a means to prioritize them because funds for projects are often limited. Projects can be also used to implement changes to processes and supply chains. For example, projects involving the implementation of major information technologies may affect all of a firm's core processes and supporting processes as well as some of their suppliers' and customers' processes. As such, projects are a useful tool for improving processes and supply chains.

Project Management across the Organization

Even though a project may be under the overall purview of a single department, other departments likely should be involved in the project. For example, consider an information systems project to develop a corporate customer database at a bank. Many of the bank's customers are large corporations that require services spanning several departments at the bank. Because no department at the bank knows exactly what services a corporate customer is receiving from other departments, the project would consolidate information about corporate customers from many areas of the bank into one database. From this information, corporate banking services could be designed not only to better serve the corporate customers, but also to provide a basis for evaluating the prices that the bank charges. Marketing is interested in knowing all the services a customer is receiving so that it can package and sell other services that the customer may not be aware of. Finance is interested in how profitable a customer is to the bank and whether the provided services are appropriately priced. The project team, led by the information systems department, should consist of representatives from the marketing and finance departments who have a direct interest in corporate clients. All departments in a firm benefit from sound project management practices, even if the projects remain within the purview of a single department.

Defining and Organizing Projects

A clear understanding of a project's organization and how personnel are going to work together to complete the project are keys to success. In this section, we will address (1) defining the scope and objectives, (2) selecting the project manager and team, and (3) recognizing the organizational structure.

Defining the Scope and Objectives of a Project

A thorough statement of a project's scope, time frame, and allocated resources is essential to managing the project. This statement is often referred to as the *project objective statement*. The scope provides a succinct statement of project objectives and captures the essence of the desired project

project management
A systemized, phased approach to defining, organizing, planning, monitoring, and controlling projects.

program
An interdependent set of projects that have a common strategic purpose.

Creating Value through Operations Management

Using Operations to Compete
Project Management

Managing Processes

Process Strategy
Process Analysis
Quality and Performance
Capacity Planning
Constraint Management
Lean Systems

Managing Supply Chains

Supply Chain
Inventory Management
Supply Chain Design
Supply Chain Location Decisions
Supply Chain Integration
Supply Chain Sustainability and Humanitarian Logistics
Forecasting
Operations Planning and Scheduling
Resource Planning

outcomes in the form of major deliverables, which are concrete outcomes of the project. Changes to the scope of a project inevitably increase costs and delay completion. Collectively, changes to scope are called *scope creep* and, in sufficient quantity, are primary causes of failed projects. The time frame for a project should be as specific as possible, as in "the project should be completed by January 1, 2014." Finally, although specifying an allocation of resources to a project may be difficult during the early stages of planning, it is important for managing the project. The allocation should be expressed as a dollar figure or as full-time equivalents of personnel time. A specific statement of allocated resources makes it possible to make adjustments to the scope of the project as it proceeds.

Selecting the Project Manager and Team

Once the project is selected, a project manager must be chosen. The qualities of a good project manager should be well aligned with the roles a project manager must play.

- *Facilitator.* The project manager often must resolve conflicts between individuals or departments to ensure that the project has the appropriate resources for the job to be completed. Successful project managers have good leadership skills and a *systems view*, which encompasses the interaction of the project, its resources, and its deliverables with the firm as a whole.
- *Communicator.* Project progress and requests for additional resources must be clearly communicated to senior management and other stakeholders in a project. The project manager must also frequently communicate with the project team to get the best performance.
- *Decision Maker.* Good project managers will be sensitive to the way the team performs best and be ready to make tough decisions, if necessary. The project manger must organize the team meetings, specify how the team will make decisions, and determine the nature and timing of reports to senior management.

Selecting the project team is just as important as the selection of the project manager. Several characteristics should be considered.

- *Technical Competence.* Team members should have the technical competence required for the tasks to which they will be assigned.
- *Sensitivity.* All team members should be sensitive to interpersonal conflicts that may arise. Senior team members should be politically sensitive to help mitigate problems with upper-level management.
- *Dedication.* Team members should feel comfortable solving project problems that may spill over into areas outside their immediate expertise. They should also be dedicated to getting the project done, as opposed to maintaining a comfortable work schedule.

Recognizing Organizational Structure

The relationship of the project manager to the project team is determined by the firm's organizational structure. Each of the three types of organizational structure described below has its own implications for project management.

- *Functional.* The project is housed in a specific department or functional area, presumably the one with the most interest in the project. Assistance from personnel in other functional areas must be negotiated by the project manager. In such cases, the project manager has less control over project timing than if the entire scope of the project fell within the purview of the department.
- *Pure Project.* The team members work exclusively for the project manager on a particular project. This structure simplifies the lines of authority and is particularly effective for large projects that consist of enough work for each team member to work full time. For small projects, it could result in significant duplication of resources across functional areas.
- *Matrix.* The matrix structure is a compromise between the functional and pure project structures. The project managers of the firm's projects all report to a "program manager" who coordinates resource and technological needs across the functional boundaries. The matrix structure allows each functional area to maintain control over who works on a project and the technology that is used. However, team members, in effect, have two bosses: the project manager and the department manager. Resolving these "line of authority" conflicts requires a strong project manager.

The construction of the 2012 Olympic Stadium in Stratford, East London, required the coordination of materials, equipment, and personnel. Project management techniques played a major role.

Justin Kase z10z/Alamy

Planning Projects

After the project is defined and organized, the team must formulate a plan that identifies the specific work to be accomplished and a schedule for completion. Planning projects involves five steps: (1) defining the work breakdown structure, (2) diagramming the network, (3) developing the schedule, (4) analyzing cost–time trade-offs, and (5) assessing risks.

Defining the Work Breakdown Structure

The **work breakdown structure (WBS)** is a statement of all work that has to be completed. Perhaps, the single most important contributor to delay is the omission of work that is germane to the successful completion of the project. The project manager must work closely with the team to identify all activities. An **activity** is the smallest unit of work effort consuming both time and resources that the project manager can schedule and control. Typically, in the process of accumulating activities, the team generates a hierarchy to the work breakdown. Major work components are broken down to smaller tasks that ultimately are broken down to activities that are assigned to individuals. Figure 1 shows a WBS for a major project involving the relocation of a hospital. In the interest of better serving the surrounding community, the board of St. John's Hospital has decided to move to a new location. The project involves constructing a new hospital and making it operational. The work components at level 1 in the WBS can be broken down into smaller units of work in level 2 that could be further divided at level 3, until the project manager gets to activities at a level of detail that can be scheduled and controlled. For example, "Organizing and Site Preparation" has been divided into six activities at level 2 in Figure 1. We have kept our example simple so that the concept of the WBS can be easily understood. If our activities in the example are divided into even smaller units of work, it is easy to see that the total WBS for a project of this size may include many more than 100 activities. Regardless of the project, care must be taken to include all important activities in the WBS to avoid project delays. Often overlooked are the activities required to plan the project, get management approval at various stages, run pilot tests of new services or products, and prepare final reports.

Each activity in the WBS must have an "owner" who is responsible for doing the work. *Activity ownership* avoids confusion in the execution of activities and assigns responsibility for timely completion. The team should have a defined procedure for assigning activities to team members, which can be democratic (consensus of the team) or autocratic (assigned by the project manager).

work breakdown structure (WBS)

A statement of all work that has to be completed.

activity

The smallest unit of work effort consuming both time and resources that the project manager can schedule and control.

5

▶ FIGURE 1

Work Breakdown Structure for
the St. John's Hospital Project

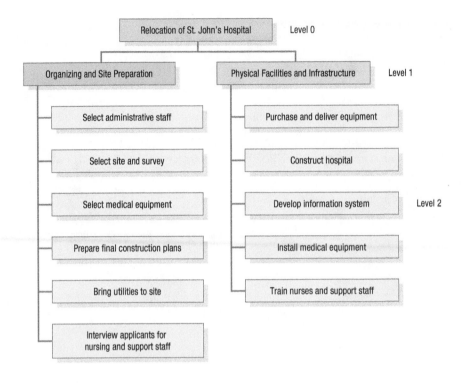

Diagramming the Network

network diagram

A network planning method,
designed to depict the relationships between activities, that
consists of nodes (circles) and
arcs (arrows).

Network planning methods can help managers monitor and control projects. These methods treat a project as a set of interrelated activities that can be visually displayed in a **network diagram**, which consists of nodes (circles) and arcs (arrows) that depict the relationships between activities. Two network planning methods were developed in the 1950s. The **program evaluation and review technique (PERT)** was created for the U.S. Navy's Polaris missile project, which involved 3,000 separate contractors and suppliers. The **critical path method (CPM)** was developed as a means of scheduling maintenance shutdowns at chemical-processing plants. Although early versions of PERT and CPM differed in their treatment of activity time estimates, today the differences are minor. For purposes of our discussion, we refer to them collectively as PERT/CPM. These methods offer several benefits to project managers, including the following:

program evaluation and review
technique (PERT)

A network planning method created for the U.S. Navy's Polaris
missile project in the 1950s,
which involved 3,000 separate
contractors and suppliers.

1. Considering projects as networks forces project teams to identify and organize the data required and to identify the interrelationships between activities. This process also provides a forum for managers of different functional areas to discuss the nature of the various activities and their resource requirements.

2. Networks enable project managers to estimate the completion time of projects, an advantage that can be useful in planning other events and in conducting contractual negotiations with customers and suppliers.

3. Reports highlight the activities that are crucial to completing projects on schedule. They also highlight the activities that may be delayed without affecting completion dates, thereby freeing up resources for other, more critical activities.

critical path method (CPM)

A network planning method developed in the 1950s as a means
of scheduling maintenance shutdowns at chemical-processing
plants.

4. Network methods enable project managers to analyze the time and cost implications of resource trade-offs.

Diagramming the project network involves establishing precedence relationships and estimating activity times.

Establishing Precedence Relationships   A **precedence relationship** determines a sequence for undertaking activities; it specifies that one activity cannot start until a preceding activity has been completed. For example, brochures announcing a conference for executives must first be designed by the program committee (activity A) before they can be printed (activity B). In other words, activity A must *precede* activity B. For large projects, establishing precedence relationships is essential because incorrect or omitted precedence relationships will result in costly delays. The precedence relationships are represented by a network diagram.

precedence relationship

A relationship that determines a
sequence for undertaking activities; it specifies that one activity
cannot start until a preceding
activity has been completed.

Estimating Activity Times   When the same type of activity has been done many times before, time estimates will have a relatively high degree of certainty. Several ways can be used to get time estimates in such an environment. First, statistical methods can be used if the project team has access to data on actual activity times experienced in the past (see MyOMLab Supplement H, "Measuring Output Rates,"). Second, if activity times improve with the number of replications, the times can be estimated using learning curve models (see Supplement I, "Learning Curve Analysis," in MyOMLab). Finally, the times for first-time activities are often estimated using managerial opinions based on similar prior experiences. If the estimates involve a high degree of uncertainty, probability distributions for activity times can be used. We discuss how to incorporate uncertainty in project networks when we address risk assessment later in this chapter. For now, we assume that the activity times are known with certainty.

Using the Activity-On-Node Approach   The diagramming approach we use in this text is referred to as the **activity-on-node (AON) network**, in which nodes represent activities and arcs represent the precedence relationships between them. Some diagramming conventions must be used for AON networks. In cases of multiple activities with no predecessors, it is usual to show them emanating from a common node called *start*. For multiple activities with no successors, it is usual to show them connected to a node called *finish*. Figure 2 shows how to diagram several commonly encountered activity relationships.

MyOMLab

activity-on-node (AON) network

An approach used to create a network diagram, in which nodes represent activities and arcs represent the precedence relationships between them.

◀ **FIGURE 2**
Diagramming Activity Relationships

AON	Activity Relationships
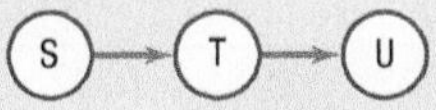 S → T → U	S precedes T, which precedes U.
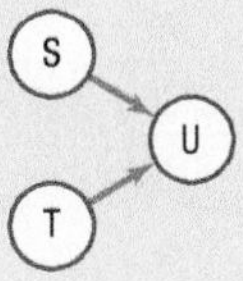 S, T → U	S and T must be completed before U can be started.
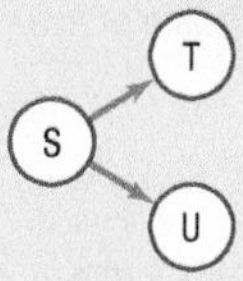 S → T, U	T and U cannot begin until S has been completed.
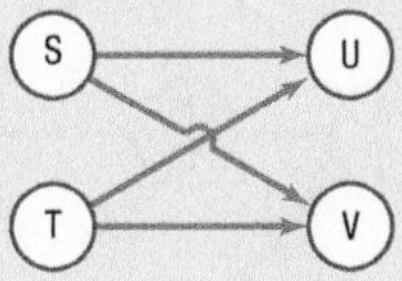 S, T → U, V	U and V cannot begin until both S and T have been completed.
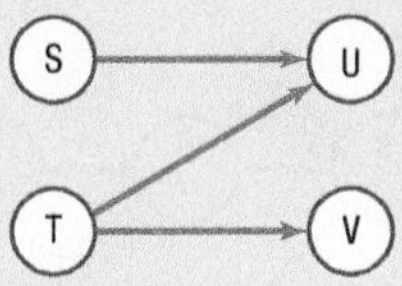 S, T → U, V	U cannot begin until both S and T have been completed; V cannot begin until T has been completed.
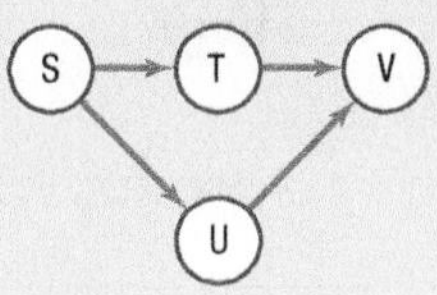 S → T → V, U	T and U cannot begin until S has been completed and V cannot begin until both T and U have been completed.

EXAMPLE 1 **Diagramming the St. John's Hospital Project**

Judy Kramer, the project manager for the St. John's Hospital project, divided the project into two major modules. She assigned John Stewart the overall responsibility for the Organizing and Site Preparation module and Sarah Walker the responsibility for the Physical Facilities and Infrastructure module. Using the WBS shown in Figure 1, the project team developed the precedence relationships, activity time estimates, and activity responsibilities shown in the following table:

Activity	Immediate Predecessors	Activity Times (wks)	Responsibility
ST. JOHN'S HOSPITAL PROJECT			Kramer
START		0	
ORGANIZING and SITE PREPARATION			Stewart
A. Select administrative staff	Start	12	Johnson
B. Select site and survey	Start	9	Taylor
C. Select medical equipment	A	10	Adams
D. Prepare final construction plans	B	10	Taylor
E. Bring utilities to site	B	24	Burton
F. Interview applicants for nursing and support staff	A	10	Johnson
PHYSICAL FACILITIES and INFRASTRUCTURE			Walker
G. Purchase and deliver equipment	C	35	Sampson
H. Construct hospital	D	40	Casey
I. Develop information system	A	15	Murphy
J. Install medical equipment	E, G, H	4	Pike
K. Train nurses and support staff	F, I, J	6	Ashton
FINISH	K	0	

For purposes of our example, we will assume a work week consists of five work days. Draw the network diagram for the hospital project.

SOLUTION

The network diagram, activities, and activity times for the hospital project are shown in Figure 3. The diagram depicts activities as circles, with arrows indicating the sequence in which they are to be performed. Activities A and B emanate from a *start* node because they have no immediate predecessors. The arrows connecting activity A to activities C, F, and I indicate that all three require completion of activity A before they can begin. Similarly, activity B must be completed before activities D and E can begin, and so on. Activity K connects to a *finish* node because no activities follow it. The start and finish nodes do not actually represent activities; they merely provide beginning and ending points for the network.

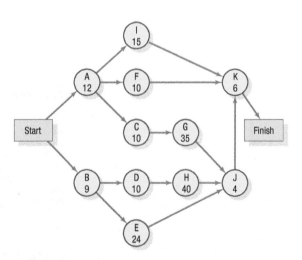

▲ **FIGURE 3**
Network Showing Activity Times for the St. John's Hospital Project

Developing the Schedule

A key advantage of network planning methods is the creation of a schedule of project activities that will help managers achieve the objectives of the project. Managers can (1) estimate the completion time of a project by finding the critical path, (2) identify the start and finish times for each activity for a project schedule, and (3) calculate the amount of slack time for each activity.

Critical Path   A crucial aspect of project management is estimating the time of completion of a project. If each activity in relocating the hospital were done in sequence, with work proceeding on only one activity at a time, the time of completion would equal the sum of the times for all the activities, or 175 weeks. However, Figure 3 indicates that some activities can be carried on simultaneously given adequate resources. We call each sequence of activities between the project's start and finish a **path**. The network describing the hospital relocation project has five paths: (1) A–I–K, (2) A–F–K, (3) A–C–G–J–K, (4) B–D–H–J–K, and (5) B–E–J–K. The **critical path** is the sequence of activities between a project's start and finish that takes the longest time to complete. Thus, the activities along the critical path determine the completion time of the project; that is, if one of the activities on the critical path is delayed, the entire project will be delayed. The estimated times for the paths in the hospital project network are

Path	Estimated Time (weeks)
A–I–K	33
A–F–K	28
A–C–G–J–K	67
B–D–H–J–K	69
B–E–J–K	43

The activity string B–D–H–J–K is estimated to take 69 weeks to complete. As the longest, it constitutes the critical path. Because the critical path defines the completion time of the project, Judy Kramer and the project team should focus on these activities and any other path that is close in length to the critical path.

Project Schedule   The typical objective is to finish the project as early as possible as determined by the critical path. The project schedule is specified by the start and finish times for each activity. For any activity, managers can use the earliest start and finish times, the latest start and finish times (and still finish the project on time), or times in between these extremes.

- **Earliest Start and Earliest Finish Times** The earliest start and earliest finish times are obtained as follows:

  1. The **earliest finish time (EF)** of an activity equals its earliest start time plus its estimated duration, t, or $EF = ES + t$.

     The **earliest start time (ES)** for an activity is the earliest finish time of the immediately preceding activity. For activities with more than one preceding activity, ES is the latest of the earliest finish times of the preceding activities.

     To calculate the duration of the entire project, we determine the EF for the last activity on the critical path.

- **Latest Start and Latest Finish Times** To obtain the latest start and latest finish times, we must work backward from the finish node. We start by setting the latest finish time of the project equal to the earliest finish time of the last activity on the critical path.

  1. The **latest finish time (LF)** for an activity is the latest start time of the activity that immediately follows. For activities with more than one activity that immediately follow, LF is the earliest of the latest start times of those activities.

  2. The **latest start time (LS)** for an activity equals its latest finish time minus its estimated duration, t, or $LS = LF - t$.

path
The sequence of activities between a project's start and finish.

critical path
The sequence of activities between a project's start and finish that takes the longest time to complete.

earliest finish time (EF)
An activity's earliest start time plus its estimated duration, t, or $EF = ES + t$.

earliest start time (ES)
The earliest finish time of the immediately preceding activity.

latest finish time (LF)
The latest start time of the activity that immediately follows.

latest start time (LS)
The latest finish time minus its estimated duration, t, or $LS = LF - t$.

Aircraft construction is an example of a large project that requires a sound project schedule because of the capital involved. Here several 747s are under construction at Boeing's plant in Everett, Washington.

George Hall/Corbis

EXAMPLE 2	Calculating Start and Finish Times for the Activities

Calculate the ES, EF, LS, and LF times for each activity in the hospital project. Which activity should Kramer start immediately? Figure 3 contains the activity times.

SOLUTION

To compute the early start and early finish times, we begin at the start node at time zero. Because activities A and B have no predecessors, the earliest start times for these activities are also zero. The earliest finish times for these activities are

$$EF_A = 0 + 12 = 12 \text{ and } EF_B = 0 + 9 = 9$$

Because the earliest start time for activities I, F, and C is the earliest finish time of activity A,

$$ES_I = 12, ES_F = 12, \text{ and } ES_C = 12$$

Similarly,

$$ES_D = 9 \text{ and } ES_E = 9$$

After placing these ES values on the network diagram (see Figure 4), we determine the EF times for activities I, F, C, D, and E:

$$EF_I = 12 + 15 = 27, EF_F = 12 + 10 = 22, EF_C = 12 + 10 = 22,$$
$$EF_D = 9 + 10 = 19, \text{ and } EF_E = 9 + 24 = 33$$

The earliest start time for activity G is the latest EF time of all immediately preceding activities. Thus,

$$ES_G = EF_C = 22, ES_H = EF_D = 19$$
$$EF_G = ES_G + t = 22 + 35 = 57, EF_H = ES_H + t = 19 + 40 = 59$$

▶ **FIGURE 4**

Network Diagram Showing
Start and Finish Times and
Activity Slack

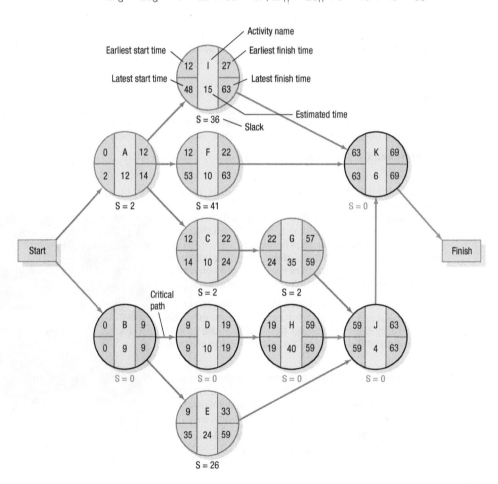

The project team can now determine the earliest time any activity can be started. Because activity J has several predecessors, the earliest time that activity J can begin is the latest of the EF times of any of its preceding activities: EF_G, EF_H, or EF_E. Thus, $EF_J = 59 + 4 = 63$. Similarly, $ES_K = 63$ and $EF_K = 63 + 6 = 69$. Because activity K is the last activity on the critical path, the earliest the project can be completed is week 69. The earliest start and finish times for all activities are shown in Figure 4.

To compute the latest start and latest finish times, we begin by setting the latest finish activity time of activity K at week 69, which is its earliest finish time as determined in Figure 4. Thus, the latest start time for activity K is

$$LS_K = LF_K - t = 69 - 6 = 63$$

If activity K is to start no later than week 63, all its predecessors must finish no later than that time. Consequently,

$$LF_I = 63, LF_F = 63, \text{ and } LF_J = 63$$

The latest start times for these activities are shown in Figure 4 as

$$LS_I = 63 - 15 = 48, LS_F = 63 - 10 = 53, \text{ and } LS_J = 63 - 4 = 59$$

After obtaining LS_J, we can calculate the latest start times for the immediate predecessors of activity J:

$$LS_G = 59 - 35 = 24, LS_H = 59 - 40 = 19, \text{ and } LS_E = 59 - 24 = 35$$

Similarly, we can now calculate the latest start times for activities C and D:

$$LS_C = 24 - 10 = 14 \text{ and } LS_D = 19 - 10 = 9$$

Activity A has more than one immediately following activity: I, F, and C. The earliest of the latest start times is 14 for activity C. Thus,

$$LS_A = 14 - 12 = 2$$

Similarly, activity B has two immediate followers: D and E. Because the earliest of the latest start times of these activities is 9,

$$LS_B = 9 - 9 = 0$$

DECISION POINT

The earliest or latest start times can be used for developing a project schedule. For example, Kramer should start activity B immediately because the latest start time is 0; otherwise, the project will not be completed by week 69. When the LS is greater than the ES for an activity, that activity could be scheduled for any date between ES and LS. Such is the case for activity E, which could be scheduled to start anytime between week 9 and week 35, depending on the availability of resources. The earliest start and earliest finish times and the latest start and latest finish times for all activities are shown in Figure 4.

Activity Slack The maximum length of time that an activity can be delayed without delaying the entire project is called **activity slack**. Consequently, *activities on the critical path have zero slack.* Information on slack can be useful because it highlights activities that need close attention. In this regard, activity slack is the amount of schedule slippage that can be tolerated for an activity before the entire project will be delayed. Slack at an activity is reduced when the estimated time duration of an activity is exceeded or when the scheduled start time for the activity must be delayed because of resource considerations. Activity slack can be calculated in one of two ways for any activity:

$$S = LS - ES \text{ or } S = LF - EF$$

Computers calculate activity slack and prepare periodic reports for large projects, enabling managers to monitor progress. Using these reports, managers can sometimes manipulate slack to overcome scheduling problems. When resources can be used on several different activities in a project, they can be taken from activities with slack and given to activities that are behind schedule until the slack is used up. The slack for each activity in the hospital project is shown in Figure 4.

Gantt Chart The project manager, often with the assistance of computer software, creates the project schedule by superimposing project activities, with their precedence relationships and

activity slack

The maximum length of time that an activity can be delayed without delaying the entire project, calculated as $S = LS - ES$ or $S = LF - EF$.

MyOMLab

Active Model 2.1 in MyOMLab provides additional insight on Gantt charts and their uses for the St. John's Hospital project.

	Task Name	Duration	Start	Finish	Predecessors
1	⊟ St John's Hospital Project	69 wks	Mon 9/12/11	Fri 1/4/13	
2	Start	0 wks	Mon 9/12/11	Mon 9/12/11	
3	⊟ Organizing and Site Prep	33 wks	Mon 9/12/11	Fri 4/27/12	
4	A. Select Staff	12 wks	Mon 9/12/11	Fri 12/2/11	2
5	B. Select Site	9 wks	Mon 9/12/11	Fri 11/11/11	2
6	C. Select Equipment	10 wks	Mon 12/5/11	Fri 2/10/12	4
7	D. Construction Plans	10 wks	Mon 11/14/11	Fri 1/20/12	5
8	E. Utilities	24 wks	Mon 11/14/11	Fri 4/27/12	5
9	F. Interviews	10 wks	Mon 12/5/11	Fri 2/10/12	4
10	⊟ Facilities and Infrastructure	57 wks	Mon 12/5/11	Fri 1/4/13	
11	G. Purchase Equipment	35 wks	Mon 2/13/12	Fri 10/12/12	6
12	H. Construct Hospital	40 wks	Mon 1/23/12	Fri 10/26/12	7
13	I. Information System	15 wks	Mon 12/5/11	Fri 3/16/12	4
14	J. Install Equipment	4 wks	Mon 10/29/12	Fri 11/23/12	8,11,12
15	K. Train Staff	6 wks	Mon 11/26/12	Fri 1/4/13	9,13,14
16	Finish	0 wks	Fri 1/4/13	Fri 1/4/13	15

▲ **FIGURE 5**

MS Project Gantt Chart for the St. John's Hospital Project Schedule

Gantt chart

A project schedule, usually created by the project manager using computer software, that superimposes project activities, with their precedence relationships and estimated duration times, on a time line.

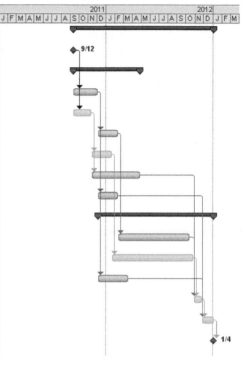

Excavators work on the new Panama Canal project, which has international implications and massive costs.

Mark Eveleigh/Alamy

estimated duration times, on a time line. The resulting diagram is called a **Gantt chart**. Figure 5 shows a Gantt chart for the hospital project created with Microsoft Project, a popular software package for project management. The critical path is shown in red. The chart clearly shows which activities can be undertaken simultaneously and when they should be started. Figure 5 also shows the earliest start schedule for the project. Microsoft Project can also be used to show the latest start schedule or to change the definition of the work week to declare Saturday and Sunday as work days, for example. Gantt charts are popular because they are intuitive and easy to construct.

Analyzing Cost–Time Trade-Offs

Keeping costs at acceptable levels is almost always as important as meeting schedule dates. In this section, we discuss the use of PERT/CPM methods to obtain minimum-cost schedules.

The reality of project management is that there are always cost–time trade-offs. For example, a project can often be completed earlier than scheduled by hiring more workers or running extra shifts. Such actions could be advantageous if savings or additional revenues accrue from completing the project early. *Total project costs* are the sum of direct costs, indirect costs, and penalty costs. These costs are dependent either on activity times or on project completion time. *Direct costs* include labor, materials, and any other costs directly related to project activities. *Indirect costs* include administration, depreciation, financial, and other variable overhead costs that can be avoided by reducing total project time: The shorter the duration of the project, the lower the indirect costs will be. Finally, a project may incur *penalty costs* if it extends beyond some specific date, whereas *an incentive* may be provided for early completion. Managers can shorten individual activity times by using additional direct resources, such as overtime, personnel, or equipment. Thus, a project manager may consider *crashing*, or expediting, some activities to reduce overall project completion time and total project costs.

Cost to Crash   To assess the benefit of crashing certain activities—from either a cost or a schedule perspective—the project manager needs to know the following times and costs:

1. The **normal time (NT)** is the time necessary to complete an activity under normal conditions.

2. The **normal cost (NC)** is the activity cost associated with the normal time.

3. The **crash time (CT)** is the shortest possible time to complete an activity.

4. The **crash cost (CC)** is the activity cost associated with the crash time.

Our cost analysis is based on the assumption that direct costs increase linearly as activity time is reduced from its normal time. This assumption implies that for every week the activity time is reduced, direct costs increase by a proportional amount. For example, suppose that the normal time for activity C in the hospital project is 10 weeks and is associated with a direct cost of $4,000. Also, suppose that we can crash its time to only 5 weeks at a total cost of $7,000; the net time reduction is 5 weeks at a net cost increase of $3,000. We assume that crashing activity C costs $3,000/5 = $600 per week—an assumption of linear marginal costs that is illustrated in Figure 6. Thus, if activity C were expedited by 2 weeks (i.e., its time reduced from 10 weeks to 8 weeks), the estimated direct costs would be $4,000 + 2($600) = $5,200. For any activity, the cost to crash an activity by one week is

$$\text{Cost to crash per period} = \frac{CC - NC}{NT - CT}$$

Table 1 contains direct cost and time data, as well as the costs of crashing per week for the activities in the hospital project.

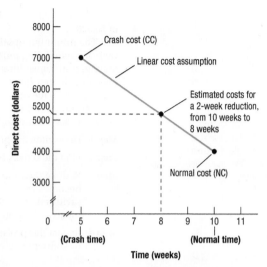

▲ **FIGURE 6**
Cost-Time Relationships in Cost Analysis

normal time (NT)

In the context of project management, the time necessary to complete an activity under normal conditions.

normal cost (NC)

The activity cost associated with the normal time.

crash time (CT)

The shortest possible time to complete an activity.

crash cost (CC)

The activity cost associated with the crash time.

TABLE 1 | DIRECT COST AND TIME DATA FOR THE ST. JOHN'S HOSPITAL PROJECT

Activity	Normal Time (NT) (weeks)	Normal Cost (NC) ($)	Crash Time (CT) (weeks)	Crash Cost (CC) ($)	Maximum Time Reduction (week)	Cost of Crashing per Week ($)
A	12	$12,000	11	13,000	1	1,000
B	9	50,000	7	64,000	2	7,000
C	10	4,000	5	7,000	5	600
D	10	16,000	8	20,000	2	2,000
E	24	120,000	14	200,000	10	8,000
F	10	10,000	6	16,000	4	1,500
G	35	500,000	25	530,000	10	3,000
H	40	1,200,000	35	1,260,000	5	12,000
I	15	40,000	10	52,500	5	2,500
J	4	10,000	1	13,000	3	1,000
K	6	30,000	5	34,000	1	4,000
	Totals	$1,992,000		$2,209,500		

Minimizing Costs   The objective of cost analysis is to determine the project schedule that minimizes total project costs. Suppose that project indirect costs are $8,000 per week. Suppose also that, after week 65, the Regional Hospital Board imposes on St. John's a penalty cost of $20,000 per week if the hospital is not fully operational. With a critical path completion time of 69 weeks, the hospital faces potentially large penalty costs unless the schedule is changed. For every week that the project is shortened—to week 65—the hospital saves one week of penalty *and* indirect costs, or $28,000. For reductions beyond week 65, the savings are only the weekly indirect costs of $8,000.

The minimum possible project duration can be found by using the crash times of each activity for scheduling purposes. However, the cost of that schedule could be prohibitive. Project managers are most interested in minimizing the costs of their projects so that budgets are not exceeded. In determining the **minimum-cost schedule**, we start with the normal time schedule and crash activities along the critical path, whose length equals the length of the project. We want to determine how much we can add in crash costs without exceeding the savings in indirect and penalty costs. The procedure involves the following steps:

minimum-cost schedule

A schedule determined by starting with the normal time schedule and crashing activities along the critical path, in such a way that the costs of crashing do not exceed the savings in indirect and penalty costs.

Step 1. Determine the project's critical path(s).

Step 2. Find the activity or activities on the critical path(s) with the lowest cost of crashing per week.

Step 3. Reduce the time for this activity until (a) it cannot be further reduced, (b) another path becomes critical, or (c) the increase in direct costs exceeds the indirect and penalty cost savings that result from shortening the project. If more than one path is critical, the time for an activity on each path may have to be reduced simultaneously.

Step 4. Repeat this procedure until the increase in direct costs is larger than the savings generated by shortening the project.

| EXAMPLE 3 | **Find a Minimum-Cost Schedule** |

Determine the minimum-cost schedule for the St. John's Hospital project. Use the information provided in Table 1 and Figure 4.

MyOMLab

Active Model 2.2 in MyOMLab provides additional insight on cost analysis for the St. John's Hospital project.

SOLUTION

The projected completion time of the project is 69 weeks. The project costs for that schedule are $1,992,000 in direct costs, 69($8,000) = $552,000 in indirect costs, and (69 − 65) ($20,000) = $80,000 in penalty costs, for total project costs of $2,624,000. The five paths in the network have the following normal times:

A–I–K:	33 weeks
A–F–K:	28 weeks
A–C–G–J–K:	67 weeks
B–D–H–J–K:	69 weeks
B–E–J–K:	43 weeks

It will simplify our analysis if we can eliminate some paths from further consideration. If all activities on A–C–G–J–K were crashed, the path duration would be 47 weeks. Crashing all activities on B–D–H–J–K results in a project duration of 56 weeks. Because the *normal* times of A–I–K, A–F–K, and B–E–J–K are less than the minimum times of the other two paths, we can disregard those three paths; they will never become critical regardless of the crashing we may do.

STAGE 1

Step 1. The critical path is B–D–H–J–K.

Step 2. The cheapest activity to crash per week is J at $1,000, which is much less than the savings in indirect and penalty costs of $28,000 per week.

Step 3. Crash activity J by its limit of three weeks because the critical path remains unchanged. The new expected path times are

A–C–G–J–K: 64 weeks and B–D–H–J–K: 66 weeks

The net savings are 3 ($28,000) − 3($1,000) = $81,000. The total project costs are now $2,624,000 − $81,000 = $2,543,000.

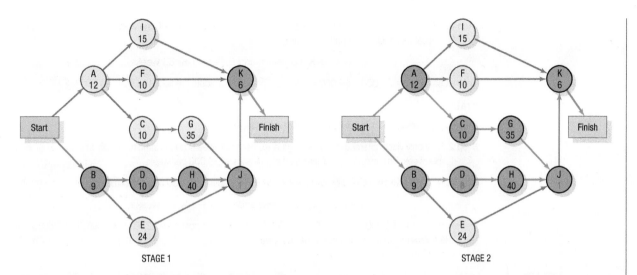

STAGE 1   STAGE 2

STAGE 2

Step 1. The critical path is still B–D–H–J–K.

Step 2. The cheapest activity to crash per week is now D at $2,000.

Step 3. Crash D by two weeks. The first week of reduction in activity D saves $28,000 because it eliminates a week of penalty costs, as well as indirect costs. Crashing D by a second week saves only $8,000 in indirect costs because, after week 65, no more penalty costs are incurred. These savings still exceed the cost of crashing D for a second week. Updated path times are

A–C–G–J–K: 64 weeks and B–D–H–J–K: 64 weeks

The net savings are $28,000 + $8,000 − 2($2,000) = $32,000. Total project costs are now $2,543,000 − $32,000 = $2,511,000.

STAGE 3

Step 1. After crashing D, we now have two critical paths. *Both* critical paths must now be shortened to realize any savings in indirect project costs. If one is shortened and the other is not, the length of the project remains unchanged.

Step 2. Our alternatives are to crash one of the following combinations of activities—(A, B); (A, H); (C, B); (C, H); (G, B); (G, H)—or to crash activity K, which is on both critical paths (J has already been crashed). We consider only those alternatives for which the cost of crashing is less than the potential savings of $8,000 per week. The only viable alternatives are (C, B) at a cost of $7,600 per week and K at $4,000 per week. We choose activity K to crash.

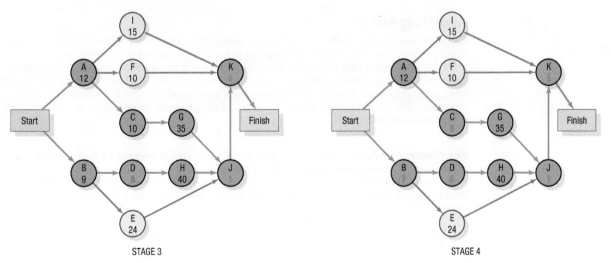

STAGE 3   STAGE 4

Step 3. We crash activity K to the greatest extent possible—a reduction of one week—because it is on both critical paths. Updated path times are

A–C–G–J–K: 63 weeks and B–D–H–J–K: 63 weeks

The net savings are $8,000 − $4,000 = $4,000. Total project costs are $2,511,000 − $4,000 = $2,507,000.

STAGE 4

Step 1. The critical paths are B–D–H–J–K and A–C–G–J–K.

Step 2. The only viable alternative at this stage is to crash activities B and C simultaneously at a cost of $7,600 per week. This amount is still less than the savings of $8,000 per week.

Step 3. Crash activities B and C by two weeks, the limit for activity B. Updated path times are

A–C–G–J–K: 61 weeks and B–D–H–J–K: 61 weeks

Net savings are 2($8,000) − 2($7,600) = $800. Total project costs are $2,507,000 − $800 = $2,506,200. The following table summarizes the analysis:

Stage	Crash Activity	Time Reduction (weeks)	Resulting Critical Path(s)	Project Duration (weeks)	Project Direct Costs, Last Trial ($000)	Crash Cost Added ($000)	Total Indirect Costs ($000)	Total Penalty Costs ($000)	Total Project Costs ($000)
0	—	—	B–D–H–J–K	69	1,992.0	—	552.0	80.0	2,624.0
1	J	3	B–D–H–J–K	66	1,992.0	3.0	528.0	20.0	2,543.0
2	D	2	B–D–H–J–K A–C–G–J–K	64	1,995.0	4.0	512.0	0.0	2,511.0
3	K	1	B–D–H–J–K A–C–G–J–K	63	1,999.0	4.0	504.0	0.0	2,507.0
4	B,C	2	B–D–H–J–K A–C–G–J–K	61	2,003.0	15.2	488.0	0.0	2,506.2

DECISION POINT

Because the crash costs exceed weekly indirect costs, any other combination of activities will result in a net increase in total project costs. The minimum-cost schedule is 61 weeks, with a total cost of $2,506,200. To obtain this schedule, the project team must crash activities B, D, J, and K to their limits and activity C to eight weeks. The other activities remain at their normal times. This schedule costs $117,800 less than the normal-time schedule.

Assessing Risks

Risk is a measure of the probability and consequence of not reaching a defined project goal. Risk involves the notion of uncertainty as it relates to project timing and costs. Often, project teams must deal with uncertainty caused by labor shortages, weather, supply delays, or the outcomes of critical tests. In this section, we discuss risk management plans and the tools managers can use to analyze the risks, such as simulation and statistical analysis, which enable managers to estimate the probability of completing a project on time and the potential for near-critical paths to affect the project completion time.

risk-management plan

A plan that identifies the key risks to a project's success and prescribes ways to circumvent them.

Risk-Management Plans　A major responsibility of the project manager at the start of a project is to develop a **risk-management plan**, which identifies the key risks to a project's success and prescribes ways to circumvent them. A good risk-management plan will quantify the risks, predict their impact on the project, and provide contingency plans. Project risk can be assessed by examining four categories:

■ **Strategic Fit** The project may not be a good strategic fit in that it may not be clearly linked to the strategic goals of the firm.

- **Service/Product Attributes** If the project involves the development of a new service or product, there may be market, technological, or legal risks. There is a chance that competitors may offer a superior product, or a technological discovery may render the service or product obsolete before it even hits the market. There may also be a legal risk of potential lawsuits or liability that could force a design change after product development has begun.

- **Project Team Capability** The project team may not have the capability to complete the project successfully because of the size and complexity of the project or the technology involved.

- **Operations** There may be an operations risk because of poor information accuracy, lack of communication, missing precedence relationships, or bad estimates for activity times.

These risks should be identified and the significant ones should have contingency plans in case something goes wrong. The riskier a project is, the more likely the project will experience difficulties as Managerial Practice 1 shows.

Simulation PERT/CPM networks can be used to quantify risks associated with project timing. Often, the uncertainty associated with an activity can be reflected in the activity's time duration. For example, an activity in a new product development project might be developing the enabling

---

MANAGERIAL PRACTICE 1 — Boston's Big Dig Project Poses Many Challenges

Boston, Massachusetts, has many noteworthy attractions: the world champion Boston Red Sox baseball team, the Freedom Trail, depicting many historic buildings and sights dating back to the 1600s, and the most ambitious road infrastructure project attempted in the United States. The six-lane elevated highway that ran through the center of the city was designed for 75,000 cars per day, but was forced to accommodate close to 200,000 cars per day. The highway was congested for 10 hours a day; congestion was expected to increase to 16 hours a day by 2010. It was costing residents and businesses $500 million a year in accidents, fuel, and late delivery charges.

Solving the traffic problem would take more than adding a few lanes to the existing highway, which was built in 1953 and whose elevated superstructure was rapidly deteriorating. Rather than fixing the old highway, the decision was made to build an 8-to-10-lane underground highway directly beneath the existing road, culminating at the north end of the city in a 14-lane, 2-bridge crossing of the Charles River. On the south end, a four-lane tunnel was built under South Boston and the Boston Harbor to Logan Airport, leaving no doubt how the project got its "Big Dig" nickname; the project spans 7.8 miles of highway with half in tunnels under a major city and harbor! Planning for the project began in 1983, construction began in 1991, and in spring 2007 it was declared 99 percent complete.

Was the project successful? The answer might depend on whom you ask. The residents of Boston have a much more efficient transportation network that allows for growth for many years into the future. However, from a project management perspective, it missed the three goals of every project: (1) on time, (2) under budget, and (3) meet the specifications. The Big Dig was 9 years late (originally scheduled for completion in 1998), more than $10 billion over the budget (originally projected to be about $4 billion in today's dollars), and required significant repairs for leaks shortly after the tunnels were opened. Much negative publicity in summer 2006 resulted from the failure of ceiling panels in the Seaport Access Tunnel, which fell to the roadway and onto a passing vehicle, resulting in the tragic loss of life. Because the project was funded with taxpayer dollars, it is no wonder that the project is the subject of much debate and controversy.

Why did this project experience problems? The Big Dig is an example of a risky project because it was huge and complex. It was called one of the most complex and controversial engineering projects in human history, rivaling the likes of the Panama Canal, the English Channel Tunnel, and the

A great deal of controversy surrounded the "Big Dig," a massive highway tunnel built under the city of Boston and Boston Harbor. By the time the Big Dig was completed, it was over budget, late, and did not meet the specifications—in part, because no one had ever undertaken such a complex project before.

Trans-Alaska Pipeline. Project managers held many meetings with environmental and permitting agencies, community groups, businesses, and political leaders to gain consensus on how the project would be built. Because of meetings such as these the project scope was modified over time, thereby causing the project plan to change. From an operational perspective, most of the construction companies involved in the project had never done anything of this size and scope before and had difficulty providing good time estimates for their pieces of the project. Delays and cost overruns were inevitable. Further, quality was difficult to achieve because so many contractors were involved in such a complex project. Projects of this size and complexity are inherently risky; contingency plans should cover the most likely disruptions. Schedule and budget problems are not unusual; however, the job of project managers is to manage the risks and minimize the deviations.

Sources: http://en.wikipedia.org/wiki/Big_Dig (2010); www.massturnpike.com/bigdig/updates (2007); Seth Stern, "$14.6 Billion Later, Boston's Big Dig Wraps Up," *Christian Science Monitor* (December 19, 2003); "The Big Dig, Boston, MA, USA," www.roadtraffic-technology.com (2005); "Big Dig Tunnel Is Riddled with Leaks," *Associated Press,* http://abcnews.go.com (November 19, 2004); Michael Roth, "Boston Digs the Big Dig," *Rental Equipment Register* (November 1, 2000), http://rermag.com/ar (2005).

technology to manufacture it, an activity that may take from eight months to a year. To incorporate uncertainty into the network model, probability distributions of activity times can be calculated using two approaches: (1) computer simulation and (2) statistical analysis. With simulation, the time for each activity is randomly chosen from its probability distribution (see MyOMLab Supplement E, "Simulation"). The critical path of the network is determined and the completion date of the project computed. The procedure is repeated many times, which results in a probability distribution for the completion date. We will have more to say about simulation when we discuss near critical paths later in this chapter.

Statistical Analysis   The statistical analysis approach requires that activity times be stated in terms of three reasonable time estimates:

1. The **optimistic time** (*a*) is the shortest time in which an activity can be completed, if all goes exceptionally well.

2. The **most likely time** (*m*) is the probable time required to perform an activity.

3. The **pessimistic time** (*b*) is the longest estimated time required to perform an activity.

With three time estimates—the optimistic, the most likely, and the pessimistic—the project manager has enough information to estimate the probability that an activity will be completed on schedule. To do so, the project manager must first calculate the mean and variance of a probability distribution for each activity. In PERT/CPM, each activity time is treated as though it were a random variable derived from a beta probability distribution. This distribution can have various shapes, allowing the most likely time estimate (*m*) to fall anywhere between the pessimistic (*b*) and optimistic (*a*) time estimates. The most likely time estimate is the *mode* of the beta distribution, or the time with the highest probability of occurrence. This condition is not possible with the normal distribution, which is symmetrical, because the normal distribution requires the mode to be equidistant from the end points of the distribution. Figure 7 shows the difference between the two distributions.

MyOMLab

optimistic time (*a*)

The shortest time in which an activity can be completed, if all goes exceptionally well.

most likely time (*m*)

The probable time required to perform an activity.

pessimistic time (*b*)

The longest estimated time required to perform an activity.

▶ **FIGURE 7**
Differences Between Beta and Normal Distributions for Project Risk Analysis

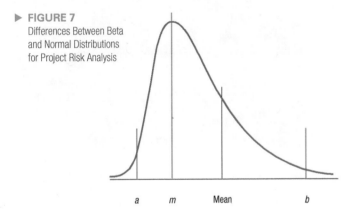

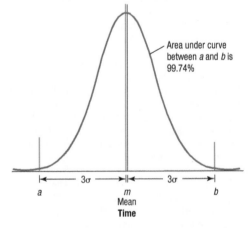

(a) **Beta distribution:** The most likely time (*m*) has the highest probability and can be placed anywhere between the optimistic (*a*) and pessimistic (*b*) times.

(b) **Normal distribution:** The mean and most likely times must be the same. If *a* and *b* are chosen to be 6σ apart, there is a 99.74% chance that the actual activity time will fall between them.

Analysis

Two key assumptions are required. First, we assume that *a*, *m*, and *b* can be estimated accurately. The estimates might best be considered values that define a reasonable time range for the activity duration negotiated between the project manager and the team members responsible for the activities. Second, we assume that the standard deviation, σ, of the activity time is one-sixth the range *b* − *a*. Thus, the chance that actual activity times will fall between *a* and *b* is high. Why does this assumption make sense? If the activity time followed the normal distribution, six standard deviations would span approximately 99.74 percent of the distribution.

Even with these assumptions, derivation of the mean and variance of each activity's probability distribution is complex. These derivations show that the mean of the beta distribution can be estimated by using the following weighted average of the three time estimates:

$$t_e = \frac{a + 4m + b}{6}$$

Note that the most likely time has four times the weight of the pessimistic and optimistic estimates.

The variance of the beta distribution for each activity is

$$\sigma^2 = \left(\frac{b - a}{6}\right)^2$$

The variance, which is the standard deviation squared, increases as the difference between b and a increases. This result implies that the less certain a person is in estimating the actual time for an activity, the greater will be the variance.

EXAMPLE 4	**Calculating Means and Variances**

Suppose that the project team has arrived at the following time estimates for activity B (Select site and survey) of the St. John's Hospital project:

$$a = 7 \text{ weeks}, m = 8 \text{ weeks, and } b = 15 \text{ weeks}$$

a. Calculate the expected time and variance for activity B.

b. Calculate the expected time and variance for the other activities in the project.

SOLUTION

a. The expected time for activity B is

$$t_e = \frac{7 + 4(8) + 15}{6} = \frac{54}{6} = 9 \text{ weeks}$$

Note that the expected time (9 weeks) does not equal the most likely time (8 weeks) for this activity. These times will be the same only when the most likely time is equidistant from the optimistic and pessimistic times. We calculate the variance for activity B as

$$\sigma^2 = \left(\frac{15 - 7}{6}\right)^2 = \left(\frac{8}{6}\right)^2 = 1.78$$

b. The following table shows expected activity times and variances for the activities listed in the project description.

	TIME ESTIMATES (WEEKS)			ACTIVITY STATISTICS	
Activity	Optimistic (*a*)	Most Likely (*m*)	Pessimistic (*b*)	Expected Time (t_e)	Variance (σ^2)
A	11	12	13	12	0.11
B	7	8	15	9	1.78
C	5	10	15	10	2.78
D	8	9	16	10	1.78
E	14	25	30	24	7.11
F	6	9	18	10	4.00
G	25	36	41	35	7.11
H	35	40	45	40	2.78
I	10	13	28	15	9.00
J	1	2	15	4	5.44
K	5	6	7	6	0.11

DECISION POINT

The project team should notice that the greatest uncertainty lies in the time estimate for activity I, followed by the estimates for activities E and G. These activities should be analyzed for the source of the uncertainties and actions should be taken to reduce the variance in the time estimates.

Analyzing Probabilities Because time estimates for activities involve uncertainty, project managers are interested in determining the probability of meeting project completion deadlines. To develop the probability distribution for project completion time, we assume that the duration time of one activity does not depend on that of any other activity. This assumption enables us to estimate the mean and variance of the probability distribution of the time duration of the entire project by summing the duration times and variances of the activities along the critical path. However, if one work crew is assigned two activities that can be done at the same time, the activity times will be interdependent and the assumption is not valid. In addition, if other paths in the network have small amounts of slack, one of them might become the critical path before the project is completed; we should calculate a probability distribution for those paths as well.

Because of the assumption that the activity duration times are independent random variables, we can make use of the central limit theorem, which states that the sum of a group of independent, identically distributed random variables approaches a normal distribution as the number of random variables increases. The mean of the normal distribution is the sum of the expected activity times on the path. In the case of the critical path, it is the earliest expected finish time for the project:

$$T_E = \Sigma \ (\text{Expected activity times on the critical path}) = \text{Mean of normal distribution}$$

Similarly, because of the assumption of activity time independence, we use the sum of the variances of the activities along the path as the variance of the time distribution for that path. That is, for the critical path,

$$\sigma_P^2 = \Sigma \ (\text{Variances of activities on the critical path})$$

To analyze probabilities of completing a project by a certain date using the normal distribution, we focus on the *critical path* and use the *z*-transformation formula:

$$z = \frac{T - T_E}{\sigma_P}$$

where

$$T = \text{due date for the project}$$

Given the value of *z*, we use the Normal Distribution appendix to find the probability that the project will be completed by time *T*, or sooner. An implicit assumption in this approach is that no other path will become critical during the time span of the project. Example 5, part (a), demonstrates this calculation for the St. John's Hospital project.

The procedure for assessing the probability of completing any activity in a project by a specific date is similar to the one just discussed. However, instead of the critical path, we would use the longest time path of activities from the start node to the activity node in question.

Near-Critical Paths A project's duration is a function of its critical path. However, paths that are close to the same duration as the critical path may ultimately become the critical path over the life of the project. In practice, at the start of the project, managers typically do not know the activity times with certainty and may never know which path was the critical path until the actual activity times are known at the end of the project. Nonetheless, this uncertainty does not reduce the usefulness of identifying the probability of one path or another causing a project to exceed its target completion time; it helps to identify the activities that need close management attention. To assess the chances of near-critical paths delaying the project completion, we can focus on the longest paths in the project network keeping in mind that both duration and variance along the path must be considered. Shorter paths with high variances could have just as much a chance to delay the project as longer paths with smaller variances. We can then estimate the probability that a given path will exceed the project target completion time. We demonstrate that approach using statistical analysis in Example 5, part (b).

Alternatively, simulation can be used to estimate the probabilities. The advantage of simulation is that you are not restricted to the use of the beta distribution for activity times. Also, activity or path dependencies, such as decision points that could involve different groups of activities to be undertaken, can be incorporated in a simulation model much more easily than with the statistical analysis approach. Fortunately, regardless of the approach used, it is rarely necessary to evaluate every path in the network. In large networks, many paths will have both short durations and low variances, making them unlikely to affect the project duration.

EXAMPLE 5	Calculating the Probability of Completing a Project by a Given Date

Calculate the probability that St. John's Hospital will become operational in 72 weeks, using (a) the critical path and (b) near-critical path A–C–G–J–K.

MyOMLab

Active Model 2.3 in MyOMLab provides additional insight on probability analysis for the St. John's Hospital project.

SOLUTION

a. The critical path B–D–H–J–K has a length of 69 weeks. From the table in Example 4, we obtain the variance of path B–D–H–J–K: $\sigma_P^2 = 1.78 + 1.78 + 2.78 + 5.44 + 0.11 = 11.89$. Next, we calculate the z-value:

$$z = \frac{72 - 69}{\sqrt{11.89}} = \frac{3}{3.45} = 0.87$$

Using the Normal Distribution appendix, we go down the left-hand column until we arrive at the value 0.8, and then across until we arrive at the 0.07 column, which shows a tabular value of 0.8078. Consequently, we find that the probability is about 0.81 that the length of path B–D–H–J–K will be no greater than 72 weeks. Because this path is the critical path, there is a 19 percent probability that the project will take longer than 72 weeks. This probability is shown graphically in Figure 8.

b. From the table in Example 4, we determine that the sum of the expected activity times on path A–C–G–J–K is 67 weeks and that $\sigma_P^2 = 0.11 + 2.78 + 7.11 + 5.44 + 0.11 = 15.55$. The z-value is

$$z = \frac{72 - 67}{\sqrt{15.55}} = \frac{5}{3.94} = 1.27$$

The probability is about 0.90 that the length of path A–C–G–J–K will be no greater than 72 weeks.

Length of critical path

Normal distribution: Mean = 69 weeks; σ_p = 3.45 weeks

Probability of meeting the schedule is 0.8078

Probability of exceeding 72 weeks is 0.1922

69 72

Project duration (weeks)

▲ FIGURE 8
Probability of Completing the St. John's Hospital Project on Schedule

DECISION POINT

The project team should be aware of the 10 percent chance that path A–C–G–J–K will exceed the target completion date of week 72. Although the probability is not high for that path, activities A, C, and G bear watching during the first 57 weeks of the project to make sure no more than 2 weeks of slippage occurs in their schedules. This attention is especially important for activity G, which has a high time variance.

Monitoring and Controlling Projects

Once project planning is over, the challenge becomes keeping the project on schedule within the budget of allocated resources. In this section, we discuss how to monitor project status and resource usage. In addition, we identify the features of project management software useful for monitoring and controlling projects.

Monitoring Project Status

A good tracking system will help the project team accomplish its project goals. Effective tracking systems collect information on three topics: (1) open issues, (2) risks, and (3) schedule status.

Open Issues and Risks One of the duties of the project manager is to make sure that issues that have been raised during the project actually get resolved in a timely fashion. The tracking system should remind the project manager of due dates for open issues and who was responsible for seeing that they are resolved. Likewise, it should provide the status of each risk to project delays specified in the risk management plan so that the team can review them at each meeting. To be effective, the tracking system requires team members to update information periodically regarding their respective responsibilities.

Schedule Status Even the best laid project plans can go awry. A tracking system that provides periodic monitoring of slack time in the project schedule can help the project manager control activities along the critical path. Periodic updating of the status of ongoing activities in the project allows the tracking system to recalculate activity slacks

Monitoring and controlling shipbuilding projects is critical to keeping these complex projects on schedule. Here a propeller is attached to an ocean-going vessel.

Visual & Written/SuperStock

and indicate those activities that are behind schedule or are in danger of using up all of their slack. Management can then focus on those activities and reallocate resources as needed.

Monitoring Project Resources

Experience has shown that the resources allocated to a project are consumed at an uneven rate that is a function of the timing of the schedules for the project's activities. Projects have a *life cycle* that consists of four major phases: (1) definition and organization, (2) planning, (3) execution, and (4) close out. Figure 9 shows that each of the four phases requires different resource commitments.

We have already discussed the activities associated with the project definition and organization and project planning phases. The phase that takes the most resources is the *execution phase*, during which managers focus on activities pertaining to deliverables. The project schedule becomes very important because it shows when each resource devoted to a given activity will be required. Monitoring the progress of activities throughout the project is important to avoid potential overloading of resources. Problems arise when a specific resource, such as a construction crew or staff specialist, is required on several activities with overlapping schedules. Project managers have several options to alleviate resource problems, including the following:

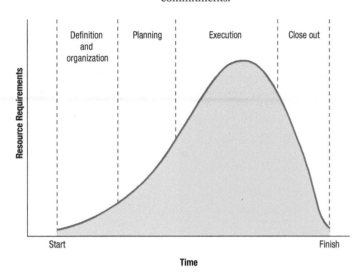

▲ FIGURE 9
Project Life Cycle

- *Resource Leveling.* The attempt to reduce the peaks and valleys in resource needs by shifting the schedules of conflicting activities within their earliest and latest start dates. Software packages such as MS Project have algorithms that move activities to avoid violating resource constraints.

- *Resource Allocation.* The assignment of resources to the most important activities. Most popular project management software packages have a few priority rules that can be used to decide which activity a critical resource should be scheduled to perform when conflicts arise. For example, for all the activities requiring a given resource, assign the resource to the one with the earliest start time. An activity slack report identifies potential candidates for resource shifting—shift resources from high slack activities to those behind schedule.

- *Resource Acquisition.* The addition of more of an overloaded resource to maintain the schedule of an activity. Obviously, this tactic is constrained by the project budget.

Controlling Projects

Project managers have the responsibilities of accounting for the effective use of the firm's resources as well as managing the activities to achieve the time and quality goals of the project. The firm's assets include the physical assets, human resources, and financial resources. Physical assets are controlled by the timely maintenance of machines and equipment so that their failure does not delay the project. Inventories must be received, stored for future use, and replenished. Project managers are also responsible for human resource development. Projects provide a rich environment to develop future leaders; project managers can take advantage of the situation by assigning team members important activities to aid in their managerial development. Last, but not least, project managers must control the expenditures of the firm's financial resources. Most project management software packages contain accounting reports, budget reports, capital investment controls, and cash flow reports. Deviations from the project plan, often referred to as variances, must be periodically reported and analyzed for their causes.

Monitoring and controlling projects are ongoing activities throughout the execution phase of the project life cycle. The project **close out**, however, is an activity that many project managers forget to include in their consideration of resource usage. The purpose of this final phase in the project life cycle is to write final reports and complete remaining deliverables. An important aspect of this phase, however, is compiling the team's recommendations for improving the project process of which they were a part. Many team members will be assigned to other projects where they can apply what they learned.

close out

An activity that includes writing final reports, completing remaining deliverables, and compiling the team's recommendations for improving the project process.

LEARNING GOALS IN REVIEW

1 **Define the major activities associated with defining, organizing, planning, monitoring, and controlling projects.** The entire outline of this Chapter revolves around these five very important activities. Nonetheless, be sure to read the opener to the chapter, which shows the four major phases of the project to introduce the new XBOX 360 product, the introduction to the chapter, and the section "Defining and Organizing Projects,".

2 **Diagram the network of interrelated activities in a project.** See "Defining the Work Breakdown Structure," and "Diagramming the Network,". Figure 2 and Example 1 are important for achieving this learning goal.

3 **Identify the sequence of critical activities that determines the duration of a project.** Study the section "Developing the Schedule," and Example 2 for an understanding of the critical path.

4 **Explain how to determine a minimum-cost project schedule.** The section "Analyzing Cost-Time Tradeoffs," and Example 3 demonstrate how the relevant costs must be considered to minimize costs. Figure 6 explains a key assumption in the analysis. Solved Problem 1 contains a detailed solution.

5 **Describe the considerations managers make in assessing the risks in a project and calculate the probability of completing a project on time.** See the section "Assessing Risks," which explains the risks faced by project managers. The section "Analysis," shows how to compute probabilities. Be sure to understand Examples 4 and 5 and Solved Problem 2.

6 **Define the options available to alleviate resource problems.** See the section "Monitoring and Controlling Projects".

MyOMLab helps you develop analytical skills and assesses your progress with multiple problems on identifying the critical path, calculating an activity's slack, expected time, variance, the project's expected completion time, probability of completing it by a certain date, and minimum-cost schedule.

MyOMLab Resources	Titles	Link to the Book
Video	Project Management at the Phoenician Nantucket Nectars: ERP	Entire chapter. Defining and Organizing Projects
Active Model Exercise	2.1 Gantt Chart 2.2 Cost Analysis 2.3 Probability Analysis	Developing the Schedule; Active Model Example Analyzing Cost-Time Trade-Offs; Example 3 Assessing Risks; Exercise 5
OM Explorer Solvers	Single Time Estimates Three Time Estimates Project Budgeting	Developing the Schedule; Example 2 Assessing Risks; Example 4; Solved Problem 2 Monitoring and Controlling Projects
POM for Windows	Single Time Estimates Triple Time Estimates Crashing Cost Budgeting Mean/Standard Deviation Given	Developing the Schedule; Example 2 Assessing Risks; Example 4; Solved Problem 2 Analyzing Cost-Time Trade-Offs; Example 3; Solved Problem 1 Monitoring and Controlling Projects Assessing Risks
SimQuick Simulation Exercises	Software development company	Assessing Risks
Microsoft Project	*Free Trial*	Planning Projects; Figure 5
SmartDraw	*Free Trial*	Diagramming the Network
Virtual Tours	Reiger Orgelbau Pipe Organ Factory and Alaskan Way Viaduct	Planning Projects Assessing Risks; Monitoring and Controlling Projects
MyOMLab Supplements	E. Simulation H. Measuring Output Rates I. Learning Curve Analysis	Assessing Risks Diagramming the Network Diagramming the Network
Internet Exercises	Olympic Movement, London 2012, and Ch2M Hill	Planning Projects Defining and Organizing Projects
Key Equations		
Image Library		

Key Equations

1. Start and finish times:

   t = estimated time duration of the activity

   ES = latest of the EF times of all activities immediately preceding activity

   EF = ES + t

   LF = earliest of the LS times of all activities immediately following activity

   LS = LF − t

2. Activity slack:

   S = LS − ES or S = LF − EF

3. Project costs:

   $$\text{Crash cost per period} = \frac{\text{Crash cost} - \text{Normal cost}}{\text{Normal time} - \text{Crash time}}$$

   $$= \frac{CC - NC}{NT - CT}$$

4. Activity time statistics:

   t_e = mean of an activity's beta distribution

   $$t_e = \frac{a + 4m + b}{6}$$

   σ^2 = variance of the activity time

   $$\sigma^2 = \left(\frac{b - a}{6}\right)^2$$

5. z-transformation formula:

   $$z = \frac{T - T_E}{\sigma_P}$$

   where

   T = due date for the project

   $T_E = \Sigma$ (expected activity times on the critical path)

   = mean of normal distribution of critical path time

   σ_P = standard deviation of critical path time distribution

Key Terms

activity	Gantt chart	pessimistic time (*b*)
activity-on-node (AON) network	latest finish time (LF)	precedence relationship
activity slack	latest start time (LS)	program
close out	minimum-cost schedule	program evaluation and review
crash cost (CC)	most likely time (*m*)	technique (PERT)
crash time (CT)	network diagram	project
critical path	normal cost (NC)	project management
critical path method (CPM)	normal time (NT)	risk-management plan
earliest finish time (EF)	optimistic time (*a*)	work breakdown structure
earliest start time (ES)	path	(WBS)

Solved Problem 1

Your company has just received an order from a good customer for a specially designed electric motor. The contract states that, starting on the thirteenth day from now, your firm will experience a penalty of $100 per day until the job is completed. Indirect project costs amount to $200 per day. The data on direct costs and activity precedence relationships are given in Table 2.

TABLE 2 | ELECTRIC MOTOR PROJECT DATA

Activity	Normal Time (days)	Normal Cost ($)	Crash Time (days)	Crash Cost ($)	Immediate Predecessor(s)
A	4	1,000	3	1,300	None
B	7	1,400	4	2,000	None
C	5	2,000	4	2,700	None
D	6	1,200	5	1,400	A
E	3	900	2	1,100	B
F	11	2,500	6	3,750	C
G	4	800	3	1,450	D, E
H	3	300	1	500	F, G

a. Draw the project network diagram.

b. What completion date would you recommend?

SOLUTION

a. The network diagram, including normal activity times, for this procedure is shown in Figure 10. Keep the following points in mind while constructing a network diagram.

1. Always have start and finish nodes.
2. Try to avoid crossing paths to keep the diagram simple.
3. Use only one arrow to directly connect any two nodes.
4. Put the activities with no predecessors at the left and point the arrows from left to right.
5. Be prepared to revise the diagram several times before you come up with a correct and uncluttered diagram.

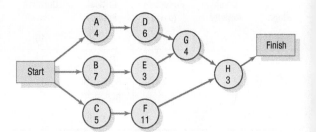

▲ FIGURE 10
Network Diagram for the Electric Motor Project

b. With these activity durations, the project will be completed in 19 days and incur a $700 penalty. Determining a good completion date requires the use of the minimum-cost schedule procedure. Using the data provided in Table 2, you can determine the maximum crash-time reduction and crash cost per day for each activity. For example, for activity A

$$\text{Maximum crash time} = \text{Normal time} - \text{Crash time} = 4 \text{ days} - 3 \text{ days} = 1 \text{ day}$$

$$\text{Crash cost per day} = \frac{\text{Crash cost} - \text{Normal cost}}{\text{Normal time} - \text{Crash time}} = \frac{\text{CC} - \text{NC}}{\text{NT} - \text{CT}} =$$

$$\frac{\$1,300 - \$1,000}{4 \text{ days} - 3 \text{ days}} = \$300$$

Activity	Crash Cost per Day ($)	Maximum Time Reduction (days)
A	300	1
B	200	3
C	700	1
D	200	1
E	200	1
F	250	5
G	650	1
H	100	2

Table 3 summarizes the analysis and the resultant project duration and total cost. The critical path is C–F–H at 19 days, which is the longest path in the network. The cheapest of these acvtivities to crash is H, which costs only an extra $100 per day to crash. Doing so saves $200 + $100 = $300 per day in indirect and penalty costs. If you crash this activity for two days (the maximum), the lengths of the paths are now

A–D–G–H: 15 days, B–E–G–H: 15 days, and C–F–H: 17 days

The critical path is still C–F–H. The next cheapest critical activity to crash is F at $250 per day. You can crash F only two days because at that point you will have three critical paths. Further reductions in project duration will require simultaneous crashing of more than one activity (D, E, and F). The cost to do so, $650, exceeds the savings, $300. Consequently, you should stop. Note that every activity is critical. The project costs are minimized when the completion date is day 15. However, some goodwill costs may be associated with disappointing a customer who wants delivery in 12 days.

TABLE 3 | PROJECT COST ANALYSIS

Stage	Crash Activity	Time Reduction (days)	Resulting Critical Path(s)	Project Duration (days)	Project Direct Costs, Last Trial ($)	Crash Cost Added ($)	Total Indirect Costs ($)	Total Penalty Costs ($)	Total Project Costs ($)
0	—	—	C–F–H	19	10,100	—	3,800	700	14,600
1	H	2	C–F–H	17	10,100	200	3,400	500	14,200
2	F	2	A–D–G–H B–E–G–H C–F–H	15	10,300	500	3,000	300	14,100

Solved Problem 2

An advertising project manager developed the network diagram shown in Figure 11 for a new advertising campaign. In addition, the manager gathered the time information for each activity, as shown in the accompanying table.

Activity	TIME ESTIMATES (WEEKS)			Immediate Predecessor(s)
	Optimistic	Most Likely	Pessimistic	
A	1	4	7	—
B	2	6	7	—
C	3	3	6	B
D	6	13	14	A
E	3	6	12	A, C
F	6	8	16	B
G	1	5	6	E, F

▼ FIGURE 11
Network Diagram for the Advertising Project

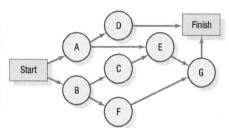

a. Calculate the expected time and variance for each activity.

b. Calculate the activity slacks and determine the critical path, using the expected activity times.

c. What is the probability of completing the project within 23 weeks?

SOLUTION

a. The expected time and variance for each activity are calculated as follows:

$$t_e = \frac{a + 4m + b}{6}$$

Activity	Expected Time (weeks)	Variance (σ^2)
A	4.0	1.00
B	5.5	0.69
C	3.5	0.25
D	12.0	1.78
E	6.5	2.25
F	9.0	2.78
G	4.5	0.69

b. We need to calculate the earliest start, latest start, earliest finish, and latest finish times for each activity. Starting with activities A and B, we proceed from the beginning of the network and move to the end, calculating the earliest start and finish times:

Activity	Earliest Start (weeks)	Earliest Finish (weeks)
A	0	0 + 4.0 = 4.0
B	0	0 + 5.5 = 5.5
C	5.5	5.5 + 3.5 = 9.0
D	4.0	4.0 + 12.0 = 16.0
E	9.0	9.0 + 6.5 = 15.5
F	5.5	5.5 + 9.0 = 14.5
G	15.5	15.5 + 4.5 = 20.0

Based on expected times, the earliest finish for the project is week 20, when activity G has been completed. Using that as a target date, we can work backward through the network, calculating the latest start and finish times (shown graphically in Figure 12):

Activity	Latest Start (weeks)	Latest Finish (weeks)
G	15.5	20.0
F	6.5	15.5
E	9.0	15.5
D	8.0	20.0
C	5.5	9.0
B	0.0	5.5
A	4.0	8.0

▶ FIGURE 12
Network Diagram with
All Time Estimates Needed
to Compute Slack

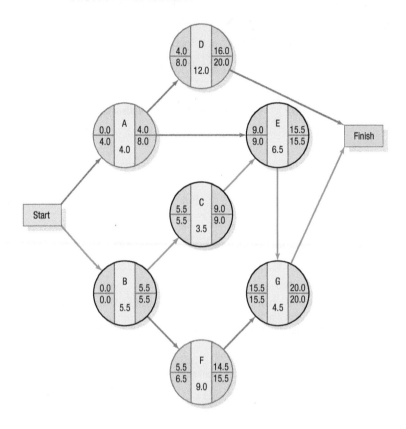

We now calculate the activity slacks and determine which activities are on the critical path:

	START (WEEKS)		FINISH (WEEKS)			
Activity	Earliest	Latest	Earliest	Latest	Slack	Critical Activity
A	0.0	4.0	4.0	8.0	4.0	No
B	0.0	0.0	5.5	5.5	0.0	Yes
C	5.5	5.5	9.0	9.0	0.0	Yes
D	4.0	8.0	16.0	20.0	4.0	No
E	9.0	9.0	15.5	15.5	0.0	Yes
F	5.5	6.5	14.5	15.5	1.0	No
G	15.5	15.5	20.0	20.0	0.0	Yes

The paths, and their total expected times and variances, are

Path	Total Expected Time (weeks)	Total Variance (σ_P^2)
A–D	4 + 12 = 16	1.00 + 1.78 = 2.78
A–E–G	4 + 6.5 + 4.5 = 15	1.00 + 2.25 + 0.69 = 3.94
B–C–E–G	5.5 + 3.5 + 6.5 + 4.5 = 20	0.69 + 0.25 + 2.25 + 0.69 = 3.88
B–F–G	5.5 + 9 + 4.5 = 19	0.69 + 2.78 + 0.69 = 4.16

The critical path is B–C–E–G, with a total expected time of 20 weeks. However, path B–F–G is 19 weeks and has a large variance.

c. We first calculate the z-value:

$$z = \frac{T - T_E}{\sigma_P} = \frac{23 - 20}{\sqrt{3.88}} = 1.52$$

Using the Normal Distribution appendix, we find that the probability of completing the project in 23 weeks or fewer is 0.9357. Because the length of path B–F–G is close to that of the critical path and has a large variance, it might well become the critical path during the project.

Discussion Questions

1. One of your colleagues comments that software is the ultimate key to project management success. How would you respond?

2. Explain how to determine the slack for each activity in a project. Why is it important for managers to know where the slack is in their projects?

3. Define risk as it applies to projects. What are the major sources of risk in a project?

Problems

The OM Explorer and POM for Windows software is available to all students using the 10th edition of this text. Go to **www.pearsonhighered.com/krajewski** to download these computer packages. If you purchased MyOMLab, you also have access to Active Models software and significant help in doing the following problems. Check with your instructor on how best to use these resources. In many cases, the instructor wants you to understand how to do the calculations by hand. At the least, the software provides a check on your calculations. When calculations are particularly complex and the goal is interpreting the results in making decisions, the software replaces entirely the manual calculations.

1. Consider the following data for a project:

Activity	Activity Time (days)	Immediate Predecessor(s)
A	2	—
B	4	A
C	5	A
D	2	B
E	1	B
F	8	B, C
G	3	D, E
H	5	F
I	4	F
J	7	G, H, I

a. Draw the network diagram.

b. Calculate the critical path for this project.

c. How much slack is in each of the activities G, H, and I?

2. The following information is known about a project.

Activity	Activity Time (days)	Immediate Predecessor(s)
A	7	—
B	2	A
C	4	A
D	4	B, C
E	4	D
F	3	E
G	5	E

a. Draw the network diagram for this project.

b. Determine the critical path and project duration.

c. Calculate the slack for each activity.

3. A project for improving a billing process has the following precedence relationships and activity times:

Activity	Activity Time (weeks)	Immediate Predecessor(s)
A	3	—
B	11	—
C	7	A
D	13	B, C
E	10	B
F	6	D
G	5	E
H	8	F, G

a. Draw the network diagram.

b. Calculate the slack for each activity. Which activities are on the critical path?

4. The following information is available about a project:

Activity	Activity Time (days)	Immediate Predecessor(s)
A	3	—
B	4	—
C	5	—
D	4	—
E	7	A
F	2	B, C, D
G	4	E, F
H	6	F
I	4	G
J	3	G
K	3	H

    a. Draw the network diagram.

    b. Find the critical path.

5. The following information has been gathered for a project:

Activity	Activity Time (weeks)	Immediate Predecessor(s)
A	4	—
B	7	A
C	9	B
D	3	B
E	14	D
F	10	C, D
G	11	F, E

    a. Draw the network diagram.

    b. Calculate the slack for each activity and determine the critical path. How long will the project take?

6. Consider the following information for a project to add a drive-thru window at Crestview Bank.

Activity	Activity Time (weeks)	Immediate Predecessor(s)
A	5	—
B	2	—
C	6	—
D	2	A, B
E	7	B
F	3	D, C
G	9	E, C
H	11	F, G

    a. Draw the network diagram for this project.

    b. Specify the critical path.

    c. Calculate the slack for activities A and D.

7. Barbara Gordon, the project manager for Web Ventures, Inc., compiled a table showing time estimates for each of the activities of a project to upgrade the company's Web page, including optimistic, most likely, and pessimistic.

    a. Calculate the expected time, t_e, for each activity.

    b. Calculate the variance, σ^2, for each activity.

Activity	Optimistic (days)	Most Likely (days)	Pessimistic (days)
A	3	8	19
B	12	15	18
C	2	6	16
D	4	9	20
E	1	4	7

8. Recently, you were assigned to manage a project for your company. You have constructed a network diagram depicting the various activities in the project (Figure 13). In addition, you have asked your team to estimate the amount of time that they would expect each of the activities to take. Their responses are shown in the following table:

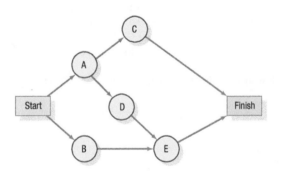

▲ **FIGURE 13**

Network Diagram for Your Company

	TIME ESTIMATES (DAYS)		
Activity	Optimistic	Most Likely	Pessimistic
A	5	8	11
B	4	8	11
C	5	6	7
D	2	4	6
E	4	7	10

a. What is the expected completion time of the project?

b. What is the probability of completing the project in 21 days?

c. What is the probability of completing the project in 17 days?

9. In Solved Problem 2, estimate the probability that the noncritical path B–F–G will take more than 20 weeks. *Hint:* Subtract from 1.0 the probability that B–F–G will take 20 weeks or less.

10. Consider the following data for a project never before attempted by your company:

Activity	Expected Time t_e (weeks)	Immediate Predecessor(s)
A	5	—
B	3	—
C	2	A
D	5	B
E	4	C, D
F	7	D

a. Draw the network diagram for this project.

b. Identify the critical path and estimate the project's duration.

c. Calculate the slack for each activity.

11. The director of continuing education at Bluebird University just approved the planning for a sales training seminar. Her administrative assistant identified the various activities that must be done and their relationships to each other, as shown in Table 4.

TABLE 4 | ACTIVITIES FOR THE SALES TRAINING SEMINAR

Activity	Description	Immediate Predecessor(s)
A	Design brochure and course announcement	—
B	Identify prospective teachers	—
C	Prepare detailed outline of course	—
D	Send brochure and student applications	A
E	Send teacher applications	B
F	Select teacher for course	C, E
G	Accept students	D
H	Select text for course	F
I	Order and receive texts	G, H
J	Prepare room for class	G

Because of the uncertainty in planning the new course, the assistant also has supplied the following time estimates for each activity:

	TIME ESTIMATES (DAYS)		
Activity	Optimistic	Most Likely	Pessimistic
A	5	7	8
B	6	8	12
C	3	4	5
D	11	17	25
E	8	10	12
F	3	4	5
G	4	8	9
H	5	7	9
I	8	11	17
J	4	4	4

The director wants to conduct the seminar 47 working days from now. What is the probability that everything will be ready in time?

12. Table 5 contains information about an environmental clean-up project. Shorten the project three weeks by finding the minimum-cost schedule. Assume that project indirect costs and penalty costs are negligible. Identify activities to crash while minimizing the additional crash costs.

TABLE 5 | ENVIRONMENTAL PROJECT DATA

Activity	Normal Time (weeks)	Crash Time (weeks)	Cost to Crash ($ per week)	Immediate Predecessor(s)
A	7	6	200	None
B	12	9	250	None
C	7	6	250	A
D	6	5	300	A
E	1	1	—	B
F	1	1	—	C, D
G	3	1	200	D, E
H	3	2	350	F
I	2	2	—	G

13. The Advanced Tech Company has a project to design an integrated information database for a major bank. Data for the project are given in Table 6. Indirect project costs amount to $300 per day. The company will incur a $150 per day penalty for each day the project lasts beyond day 14.

a. What is the project's duration if only normal times are used?

b. What is the minimum-cost schedule?

c. What is the critical path for the minimum-cost schedule?

TABLE 6 | DATABASE DESIGN PROJECT DATA

Activity	Normal Time (days)	Normal Cost ($)	Crash Time (days)	Crash Cost ($)	Immediate Predecessor(s)
A	6	1,000	5	1,200	—
B	4	800	2	2,000	—
C	3	600	2	900	A, B
D	2	1,500	1	2,000	B
E	6	900	4	1,200	C, D
F	2	1,300	1	1,400	E
G	4	900	4	900	E
H	4	500	2	900	G

14. You are the manager of a project to improve a billing process at your firm. Table 7 contains the data you will need to conduct a cost analysis of the project. Indirect costs are $1,600 per week, and penalty costs are $1,200 per week after week 12.

    a. What is the minimum-cost schedule for this project?

    b. What is the difference in total project costs between the earliest completion time of the project using "normal" times and the minimum-cost schedule you derived in part (a)?

15. Table 8 contains data for the installation of new equipment in a manufacturing process at Excello Corporation. Your company is responsible for the installation project. Indirect costs are $15,000 per week, and a penalty cost of $9,000 per week will be incurred by your company for every week the project is delayed beyond week 9.

    a. What is the shortest time duration for this project regardless of cost?

    b. What is the minimum total cost associated with completing the project in 9 weeks?

    c. What is the total time of the minimum-cost schedule?

TABLE 7 | DATA FOR THE BILLING PROCESS PROJECT

Activity	Immediate Predecessor(s)	Normal Time (weeks)	Crash Time (weeks)	Normal Cost ($)	Crash Cost ($)
A	—	4	1	5,000	8,000
B	—	5	3	8,000	10,000
C	A	1	1	4,000	4,000
D	B	6	3	6,000	12,000
E	B, C	7	6	4,000	7,000
F	D	7	6	4,000	7,000

TABLE 8 | DATA FOR THE EQUIPMENT INSTALLATION PROJECT

Activity	Immediate Predecessor(s)	Normal Time (weeks)	Crash Time (weeks)	Normal Cost ($)	Crash Cost ($)
A	—	2	1	7,000	10,000
B	—	2	2	3,000	3,000
C	A	3	1	12,000	40,000
D	B	3	2	12,000	28,000
E	C	1	1	8,000	8,000
F	D, E	5	3	5,000	15,000
G	E	3	2	9,000	18,000

16. Gabrielle Kramer, owner of Pet Paradise, is opening a new store in Columbus, Ohio. Her major concern is the hiring of a manager and several associates who are animal lovers. She also has to coordinate the renovation of a building that was previously owned by a chic clothing store. Kramer has gathered the data shown in Table 9.

   a. How long is the project expected to take?

   b. Suppose that Kramer has a personal goal of completing the project in 14 weeks. What is the probability that it will happen this quickly?

17. The diagram in Figure 14 was developed for a project that you are managing. Suppose that you are interested in finding ways to speed up the project at minimal additional cost. Determine the schedule for completing the project in 25 days at minimum cost. Penalty and project-overhead costs are negligible. Time and cost data for each activity are shown in Table 10.

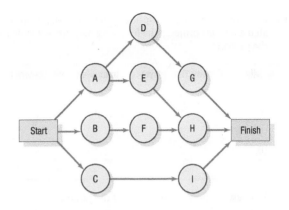

▲ FIGURE 14
Network Diagram for Problem 17

TABLE 9 | DATA FOR THE PET PARADISE PROJECT

Activity	Description	Immediate Predecessor(s)	TIME (WEEKS) a	m	b
A	Interview for new manager	—	1	3	6
B	Renovate building	—	6	9	12
C	Place ad for associates and interview applicants	—	6	8	16
D	Have new manager prospects visit	A	2	3	4
E	Purchase equipment for new store and install	B	1	3	11
F	Check employee applicant references and make final selection	C	5	5	5
G	Check references for new manager and make final selection	D	1	1	1
H	Hold orientation meetings and do payroll paperwork	E, F, G	3	3	3

TABLE 10 | PROJECT ACTIVITY AND COST DATA

Activity	NORMAL Time (days)	Cost ($)	CRASH Time (days)	Cost ($)
A	12	1,300	11	1,900
B	13	1,050	9	1,500
C	18	3,000	16	4,500
D	9	2,000	5	3,000
E	12	650	10	1,100
F	8	700	7	1,050
G	8	1,550	6	1,950
H	2	600	1	800
I	4	2,200	2	4,000

18. Paul Silver, owner of Sculptures International, just initiated a new art project. The following data are available for the project:

Activity	Activity Time (days)	Immediate Predecessor(s)
A	4	—
B	1	—
C	3	A
D	2	B
E	3	C, D

   a. Draw the network diagram for the project.

   b. Determine the project's critical path and duration.

   c. What is the slack for each activity?

19. Reliable Garage is completing production of the J2000 kit car. The following data are available for the project:

Activity	Activity Time (days)	Immediate Predecessor(s)
A	2	—
B	6	A
C	4	B
D	5	C
E	7	C
F	5	C
G	5	F
H	3	D, E, G

a. Draw the network diagram for the project.

b. Determine the project's critical path and duration.

c. What is the slack for each activity?

20. The following information concerns a new project your company is undertaking:

Activity	Activity Time (days)	Immediate Predecessor(s)
A	10	—
B	11	—
C	9	A, B
D	5	A, B
E	8	A, B
F	13	C, E
G	5	C, D
H	10	G
I	6	F, G
J	9	E, H
K	11	I, J

a. Draw the network diagram for this project.

b. Determine the critical path and project completion time.

Advanced Problems

21. The project manager of Good Public Relations gathered the data shown in Table 11 for a new advertising campaign.

   a. How long is the project likely to take?

b. What is the probability that the project will take more than 38 weeks?

c. Consider the path A–E–G–H–J. What is the probability that this path will exceed 38 weeks?

TABLE 11 | ACTIVITY DATA FOR ADVERTISING PROJECT

Activity	TIME ESTIMATES (WEEKS)			Immediate Predecessor(s)
	Optimistic	Most Likely	Pessimistic	
A	8	10	12	START
B	5	8	17	START
C	7	8	9	START
D	1	2	3	B
E	8	10	12	A, C
F	5	6	7	D, E
G	1	3	5	D, E
H	2	5	8	F, G
I	2	4	6	G
J	4	5	8	H
K	2	2	2	H

22. Consider the office renovation project data in Table 12. A "zero" time estimate means that the activity could take a very small amount of time and should be treated as a numeric zero in the analysis.

a. Based on the critical path, find the probability of completing the office renovation project by 39 days.

b. Find the date by which you would be 90 percent sure of completing the project.

TABLE 12 | DATA FOR THE OFFICE RENOVATION PROJECT

Activity	TIME ESTIMATES (DAYS)			Immediate Predecessor(s)
	Optimistic	Most Likely	Pessimistic	
START	0	0	0	—
A	6	10	14	START
B	0	1	2	A
C	16	20	30	A
D	3	5	7	B
E	2	3	4	D
F	7	10	13	C
G	1	2	3	D
H	0	2	4	G
I	2	2	2	C, G
J	2	3	4	I
K	0	1	2	H
L	1	2	3	J, K
FINISH	0	0	0	E, F, L

23. You are in charge of a project at the local community center. The center needs to remodel one of the rooms in time for the start of a new program. Delays in the project mean that the center must rent other space at a nearby church at additional cost. Time and cost data for your project are contained in Table 13. Your interest is in minimizing the cost of the project to the community center.

a. Using the *normal times* for each activity, what is the earliest date you can complete the project?

b. Suppose the variable overhead costs are $50 per day for your project. Also, suppose that the center must pay $40 per day for a temporary room on day 15 or beyond. Find the minimum-cost project schedule.

TABLE 13 | DATA FOR THE COMMUNITY CENTER PROJECT

Activity	Normal Time (days)	Normal Cost ($)	Crash Time (days)	Crash Cost ($)	Immediate Predecessor(s)
START	0	0	0	0	—
A	10	50	8	150	START
B	4	40	2	200	START
C	7	70	6	160	B
D	2	20	1	50	A, C
E	3	30	3	30	A, C
F	8	80	5	290	B
G	5	50	4	180	D
H	6	60	3	180	E, F
FINISH	0	0	0	0	G, H

24. The information in Table 14 is available for a large fund-raising project.

    a. Determine the critical path and the expected completion time of the project.

    b. Plot the total project cost, starting from day 1 to the expected completion date of the project, assuming the earliest start times for each activity. Compare that result to a similar plot for the latest start times. What implication does the time differential have for cash flows and project scheduling?

25. You are the project manager of the software installation project in Table 15. You would like to find the minimum-cost schedule for your project. There is a $1,000-per-week penalty for each week the project is delayed beyond week 25. In addition, your project team determined that indirect project costs are $2,500 per week.

    a. What would be your target completion week?

    b. How much would you save in total project costs with your schedule?

TABLE 14 | FUND-RAISING PROJECT DATA

Activity	Activity Time (days)	Activity Cost ($)	Immediate Predecessor(s)
A	3	100	—
B	4	150	—
C	2	125	A
D	5	175	B
E	3	150	B
F	4	200	C, D
G	6	75	C
H	2	50	C, D, E
I	1	100	E
J	4	75	D, E
K	3	150	F, G
L	3	150	G, H, I
M	2	100	I, J
N	4	175	K, M
O	1	200	H, M
P	5	150	N, L, O

TABLE 15 | DATA FOR SOFTWARE INSTALLATION PROJECT

Activity	Immediate Predecessors	Normal Time (weeks)	Normal Cost ($)	Crash Time (weeks)	Crash Cost ($)
A	—	5	2,000	3	4,000
B	—	8	5,000	7	8,000
C	A	10	10,000	8	12,000
D	A, B	4	3,000	3	7,000
E	B	3	4,000	2	5,000
F	D	9	8,000	6	14,000
G	E, F	2	2,000	2	2,000
H	G	8	6,000	5	9,000
I	C, F	9	7,000	7	15,000

26. Consider the project described in Table 16.

a. If you start the project immediately, when will it be finished?

b. You are interested in completing your project as soon as possible. You have only one option. Suppose you could assign Employee A, currently assigned to activity G, to help Employee B, currently assigned to activity F. Each week that Employee A helps Employee B will result in activity G increasing its time by one week and activity F reducing its time by one week. How many weeks should Employee A work on activity F?

TABLE 16 | PROJECT DATA FOR PROBLEM 26

Activity	Activity Time (weeks)	Immediate Predecessor(s)
START	0	—
A	3	START
B	4	START
C	4	B
D	4	A
E	5	A, B
F	6	D, E
G	2	C, E
FINISH	0	F, G

Active Model Exercise

This Active Model appears in MyOMLab. It allows you to evaluate the sensitivity of the project time to changes in activity times and activity predecessors.

QUESTIONS

1. Activity B and activity K are critical activities. Describe the difference that occurs on the graph when you increase activity B versus when you increase activity K.

2. Activity F is not critical. Use the scroll bar to determine how many weeks you can increase activity F until it becomes critical.

3. Activity A is not critical. How many weeks can you increase activity A until it becomes critical? What happens when activity A becomes critical?

4. What happens when you increase activity A by one week after it becomes critical?

5. Suppose that building codes may change and, as a result, activity C would have to be completed before activity D could be started. How would this affect the project?

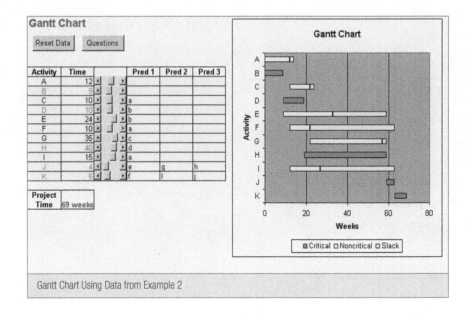

Gantt Chart Using Data from Example 2

VIDEO CASE | Project Management at the Phoenician

The Phoenician in Phoenix, Arizona, is part of Starwood's Luxury Collection and its only AAA Five Diamond Award resort in the southwestern United States. Sophistication, elegance, and excellence only begin to describe the guest experience at the hotel. Guests can dine in one of nine restaurants, relax poolside, play tennis, take in 27 holes of golf on three 9-hole courses, or relax with a variety of soothing spa treatments at the 22,000-square-foot Centre for Well-Being.

The Phoenician recently embarked on an ambitious $38 million spa and golf renovation program. The resort's golf and spa programs historically earned high marks from surveys in their industries over the years, but the environment was changing. Evidence of this change was seen in the explosive growth of new golf courses and spas in the Southwest region. Phoenix alone has over 275 golf courses, and the Southwest boasts the largest concentration of new luxury spas anywhere. The Phoenician's facilities, while world-class and highly rated, were more than 15 years old. The hotel's recently awarded Five Diamond status renewed emphasis on bringing every process and service at the property up to Five Diamond level.

The decision to renovate the golf course and existing spa became not a question of *whether* to undertake the projects, but *to what degree* they needed to be pursued. Key considerations centered on (1) whether to build basic facilities or commit to the grandiose luxury level, (2) having a domestic versus international reputation, and (3) developing creative packaging of the new facilities to attract loyal guests, such as a spa and golf "country club-like" membership program. Such a program would be limited to about 600 spa/golf memberships, with a one-time fee of $65,000 each.

The company's senior management considered three options for the Centre for Well-Being spa. First, the existing space in the heart of the resort could be renovated. This option would require relocating the spa to another part of the resort and offering limited treatments during this time, thereby reducing spa revenues significantly. With option 2, hilly terrain directly behind the resort could be carved out to create a new mountainside facility with sweeping vistas. This option meant the closure of one of the hotel's buildings housing 60 guest rooms and suites during the construction period. The existing spa could remain open, however. Under option 3, a parking structure on existing hotel property could be used, having the least impact on revenues. The first option was seen as a short-term fix, while the remaining two were viewed as having longer-term potential.

Additional discussion centered on the type of spa to be built. Recent acquisition of the Bliss spa brand for Starwood's W Hotels was an option, offering day spa amenities and an indulgence atmosphere. The second option was to remain a holistic resort spa with an emphasis on health and restoration. The third option was to become a destination spa with dedicated guest stays and week-long programs. Day spas are the fastest-growing category, with few destination spas.

The Phoenician management team, with assistance from Starwood Field Operations and Corporate offices, prepared an extensive analysis of strengths, weaknesses, opportunities, and threats to better understand the environment. The result of this analysis was used by the team to identify the set of activities necessary for each option. The Corporate Design and Construction group developed architectural and engineering plans, as

Work Breakdown Structure	Activity Time (days)	Activity Precedence Relationships
Project Conception		
A. Kick-off meeting	2	
B. Creation of spa specifications	30	A
Geotechnical Investigation		
C. Preliminary site characterizations	10	B
D. Subsurface investigation	10	C
E. Laboratory testing	5	D
F. Geologic hazard assessments	10	E
Design Development		
G. Initial designs	70	B
H. Preliminary zoning compliance plan	15	C, G
I. Final designs	18	H
J. Owner approval of designs	5	I
Documentation and Cost Estimation		
K. Construction documentation and landscape package	80	F, I
L. Acquisition of contractor estimates and bids	90	J, K
Decision		
M. Owner approval of one of the three projects	60	L

well as the work breakdown structure and diagrams showing the critical path for the possible project options. The work breakdown structure, activity times, and activity precedence relationships are shown in the table on the previous page.

QUESTIONS

1. Coordinating departments in a major project is always a challenge. Which departments within the Starwood organization likely played a role in each of the following project related activities?
   a. Defining and organizing the project
   b. Planning the project
   c. Monitoring and controlling the project

2. Many times, project decision makers do not rely solely on financial hurdles, such as return on investment or internal rates of return, but place a lot of emphasis on intangible factors. Which are the salient intangible factors associated with selecting one of the three options for the spa?

3. Timing is always a challenge in managing projects. Construct a network diagram for the spa selection process. How soon can The Phoenician management make a decision on the spa?

When the Phoenician, a luxury hotel in Phoenix, Arizona, sought to redesign its Center for Well-Being, its management team created a work breakdown structure in order to compare different project options and choose the best one.

CASE   The Pert Mustang

Roberts Auto Sales and Service (RASAS) consists of three car dealerships that sell and service several makes of American and Japanese cars, two auto parts stores, a large body shop and car painting business, and an auto salvage yard. Vicky Roberts, owner of RASAS, went into the car business when she inherited a Ford dealership from her father. She was able to capitalize on her knowledge and experience to build her business into the diversified and successful mini-empire it is today. Her motto, "Sell 'em today, repair 'em tomorrow!" reflects a strategy that she refers to in private as "Get 'em coming and going."

Roberts has always retained a soft spot in her heart for high-performance Mustangs and just acquired a 1965 Shelby Mustang GT 350 that needs a lot of restoration. She also notes the public's growing interest in the restoration of vintage automobiles. Roberts is thinking of expanding into the vintage car restoration business and needs help in assessing the feasibility of such a move. She wants to restore her 1965 Shelby Mustang to mint condition, or as close to mint condition as possible. If she decides to go into the car restoring business, she can use the Mustang as an exhibit in sales and advertising and take it to auto shows to attract business for the new shop.

Roberts believes that many people want the thrill of restoring an old car themselves, but they do not have the time to run down all the old parts. Still, others just want to own a vintage auto because it is different and many of them have plenty of money to pay someone to restore an auto for them.

Roberts wants the new business to appeal to both types of people. For the first group, she envisions serving as a parts broker for NOS ("new old stock"), new parts that were manufactured many years ago and are still packaged in their original cartons. It can be a time-consuming process to find the right part. RASAS could also machine new parts to replicate those that are hard to find or that no longer exist.

In addition, RASAS could assemble a library of parts and body manuals for old cars to serve as an information resource for do-it-yourself restorers. The do-it-yourselfers could come to RASAS for help in compiling parts lists, and RASAS could acquire the parts for them. For others, RASAS would take charge of the entire restoration.

Roberts asked the director of service operations to take a good look at her Mustang and determine what needs to be done to restore it to the condition it was in when it came from the factory more than 40 years ago. She

wants to restore this car in time to exhibit it at the Detroit Auto Show. If the car gets a lot of press, it will be a real public relations coup for RASAS—especially if Roberts decides to enter this new venture. Even if she does not, the car will be a showpiece for the rest of the business.

Roberts asked the director of service operations to prepare a report about what is involved in restoring the car and whether it can be done in time for the Detroit show in 45 working days using PERT/CPM. The parts manager, the body shop manager, and the chief mechanic have provided the following estimates of times and activities that need to be done, as well as cost estimates:

a. Order all needed material and parts (upholstery, windshield, carburetor, and oil pump). Time: 2 days. Cost (telephone calls and labor): $100.

b. Receive upholstery material for seat covers. Cannot be done until order is placed. Time: 30 days. Cost: $2,100.

c. Receive windshield. Cannot be done until order is placed. Time: 10 days. Cost: $800.

d. Receive carburetor and oil pump. Cannot be done until order is placed. Time: 7 days. Cost: $1,750.

e. Remove chrome from body. Can be done immediately. Time: 1 day. Cost: $200.

f. Remove body (doors, hood, trunk, and fenders) from frame. Cannot be done until chrome is removed. Time: 1 day. Cost: $300.

g. Have fenders repaired by body shop. Cannot be done until body is removed from frame. Time: 4 days. Cost: $1,000.

h. Repair doors, trunk, and hood. Cannot be done until body is removed from frame. Time: 6 days. Cost: $1,500.

i. Pull engine from chassis. Do after body is removed from frame. Time: 1 day. Cost: $200.

j. Remove rust from frame. Do after the engine has been pulled from the chassis. Time: 3 days. Cost: $900.

k. Regrind engine valves. Do after the engine has been pulled from the chassis. Time: 5 days. Cost: $1,000.

l. Replace carburetor and oil pump. Do after engine has been pulled from chassis and after carburetor and oil pump have been received. Time: 1 day. Cost: $200.

m. Rechrome the chrome parts. Chrome must have been removed from the body first. Time: 3 days. Cost: $210.

n. Reinstall engine. Do after valves are reground and carburetor and oil pump have been installed. Time: 1 day. Cost: $200.

o. Put doors, hood, and trunk back on frame. The doors, hood, and trunk must have been repaired first. The frame must have had its rust removed first. Time: 1 day. Cost: $240.

p. Rebuild transmission and replace brakes. Do so after the engine has been reinstalled and the doors, hood, and trunk are back on the frame. Time: 4 days. Cost: $2,000.

q. Replace windshield. Windshield must have been received. Time: 1 day. Cost: $100.

r. Put fenders back on. The fenders must have been repaired first, the transmission rebuilt, and the brakes replaced. Time: 1 day. Cost: $100.

s. Paint car. Cannot be done until the fenders are back on and windshield replaced. Time: 4 days. Cost: $1,700.

t. Reupholster interior of car. Must have received upholstery material first. Car must have been painted first. Time: 7 days. Cost: $2,400.

u. Put chrome parts back on. Car must have been painted and chrome parts rechromed first. Time: 1 day. Cost: $100.

v. Pull car to the Detroit Auto Show. Must have completed reupholstery of interior and have put the chrome parts back on. Time: 2 days. Cost: $1,000.

Roberts wants to limit expenditures on this project to what could be recovered by selling the restored car. She has already spent $50,000 to acquire the car. In addition, she wants a brief report on some of the aspects of the proposed business, such as how it fits in with RASAS's other businesses and what RASAS's operations task should be with regard to cost, quality, customer service, and flexibility.

In the restoration business there are various categories of restoration. A basic restoration gets the car looking great and running, but a mint condition restoration puts the car back in original condition—as it was "when it rolled off the line." When restored cars are resold, a car in mint condition commands a much higher price than one that is just a basic restoration. As cars are restored, they can also be customized. That is, something is put on the car that could not have been on the original. Roberts wants a mint condition restoration for her Mustang, without customization. (The proposed new business would accept any kind of restoration a customer wanted.)

The total budget cannot exceed $70,000 including the $50,000 Roberts has already spent. In addition, Roberts cannot spend more than $3,600 in any week given her present financial position. Even though much of the work will be done by Roberts's own employees, labor and materials costs must be considered. All relevant costs have been included in the cost estimates.

QUESTIONS

1. Using the information provided, prepare the report that Vicky Roberts requested, assuming that the project will begin immediately. Assume 45 working days are available to complete the project, including transporting the car to Detroit before the auto show begins. Your report should briefly discuss the aspects of the proposed new business, such as the competitive priorities that Roberts asked about.

2. Construct a table containing the project activities using the letter assigned to each activity, the time estimates, and the precedence relationships from which you will assemble the network diagram.

3. Draw a network diagram of the project similar to Figure 4. Determine the activities on the critical path and the estimated slack for each activity.

4. Prepare a project budget showing the cost of each activity and the total for the project. Can the project be completed within the budget? Will the project require more than $3,600 in any week? To answer this question, assume that activities B, C, and D must be paid for when the item is received (the earliest finish time for the activity). Assume that the costs of all other activities that span more than one week can be prorated. Each week contains five work days. If problems exist, how might Roberts overcome them?

Source: This case was prepared by and is used by permission of Dr. Sue P. Siferd, Professor Emerita, Arizona State University (Updated September, 2007).

Selected References

Goldratt, E. M. *Critical Chain.* Great Barrington, MA: North River, 1997.

Hartvigsen, David. *SimQuick: Process Simulation with Excel.* 2nd ed. Upper Saddle River, NJ: Prentice Hall, 2004.

Kerzner, Harold. *Advanced Project Management: Best Practices on Implementation,* 2nd ed. New York: John Wiley & Sons, 2004.

Kerzner, Harold. *Project Management: A Systems Approach to Planning, Scheduling, and Controlling,* 10th ed. New York: John Wiley & Sons, 2009.

Lewis, J. P. *Mastering Project Management,* 2nd ed. New York: McGraw-Hill, 2001.

Mantel Jr., Samuel J., Jack R. Meredith, Scott M. Shafer, and Margaret M. Sutton. *Project Management in Practice,* 3rd ed. New York: John Wiley & Sons, 2007.

Meredith, Jack R., and Samuel J. Mantel, *Project Management: A Managerial Approach,* 6th ed. New York: John Wiley & Sons, 2005.

Muir, Nancy C. *Microsoft Project 2007 for Dummies,* New York: John Wiley & Sons, 2006.

Nicholas, John M, and Herman Stein. *Project Management for Business, Engineering, and Technology,* 3rd ed. Burlington, MA: Butterworth-Heinemann, 2008.

"A Guide to Project Management Body of Knowledge," 2008. Available from the Project Management Institute at www.pmi.org.

Srinivasan, Mandyam, Darren Jones, and Alex Miller. "CORPS Capabilities." *APICS Magazine* (March 2005), pp. 46–50.

QUALITY AND
PERFORMANCE

A Baseline Engineer for Verizon readies his computer that will control a bank of cell phones
making and receiving calls on different networks. He travels through northern Virginia,
Washington, DC, and Maryland with a truck outfitted to test the services of Verizon and its
competitors to see where faults lie in Verizon's system.

Verizon Wireless

Anyone who owns a cell phone knows the agony of a dropped call. Did you
know that the reason for the dropped call may be the phone itself, and
not the strength of the signal? Verizon Wireless serves more than 62 million
customers in the United States and, along with the other major carriers, it knows
that if the phone does not work, the company, and not the manufacturer, will
likely take the blame from the customer. Verizon touts the reliability of its services
and can ill afford the failure of cell phones due to the quality of manufacture.
Verizon expects manufacturers such as Motorola, Samsung, and LG Electronics
to provide defect-free phones; however, experience has indicated that extensive
testing by Verizon employees is also needed.

In addition to a tear-down analysis that looks for weaknesses in a phone's
hardware and components, the device is tested for its ability to withstand
temperature extremes, vibration, and stress. Beyond these physical tests,
Verizon uses two approaches to assess a phone's capability to receive cellular
signals and clearly communicate to the caller. First, Verizon hires 98 test personnel who drive $300,000 specially equipped vans more than 1 million miles
a year to measure network performance using prospective new cell phones.
They make more than 3 million voice call attempts and 16 million data tests
annually. The tests check the coverage of the network as well as the capability
of the cell phones to pick up the signals and clearly communicate to the caller.
Second, Verizon uses Mr. Head, a robotic mannequin, who has a recorded
voice and is electronically equipped with a rubber ear that evaluates how well

From Chapter 5 of *Operations Management: Processes and Supply Chains*, Tenth Edition. Lee J. Krajewski, Larry
P. Ritzman, Manoj K. Malhotra. Copyright © 2013 by Pearson Education, Inc. All rights reserved.

the phone's mouthpiece transmits certain phonetics. Mr. Head utters what sounds like gibberish; however, it actually covers the range of sounds in normal speech patterns. Other systems monitor the tests and summarize results.

Some phones spend so much time in the test phase that ultimately they never make it to the market. Clearly, in those cases, the cost of poor quality to the manufacturer is very high.

Source: Amol Sharma, "Testing, Testing," *Wall Street Journal* (October 23, 2007); Janet Hefler, "Verizon Tester Checks Vineyard Networks," *The Martha's Vineyard Times* (August 30, 2007); Jon Gales, "Ride Along With a Verizon Wireless Test Man," *Mobile Tracker* (April 4, 2005) **http:// investor.verizon.com** (2007).

LEARNING GOALS *After reading this chapter, you should be able to:*

1. Define the four major costs of quality.
2. Describe the role of ethics in the quality of services and products.
3. Explain the basic principles of TQM programs.
4. Explain the basic principles of Six Sigma programs.
5. Describe how to construct control charts and use them to determine whether a process is out of statistical control.
6. Describe how to determine whether a process is capable of producing a service or product to specifications.

Creating Value through Operation Management

Using Operations to Compete
Project Management

Managing Processes

Process Strategy
Process Analysis
Quality and Performance
Capacity Planning
Constraint Management
Lean Systems

Managing Supply Chains

Supply Chain Inventory Management
Supply Chain Design
Supply Chain Location Decisions
Supply Chain Integration
Supply Chain Sustainability and Humanitarian Logistics
Forecasting
Operations Planning and Scheduling
Resource Planning

The challenge for businesses today is to satisfy their customers through the exceptional performance of their processes. Verizon Wireless is one example of a company that met the challenge by designing and managing processes that provide customers with total satisfaction. Evaluating process performance is important if this is to happen.

Evaluating process performance is also necessary for managing supply chains. For example, at Verizon Wireless, the process of delivering cell phone communications to the customer might be measured on the consistency of service and the sound quality of the voice transmissions. The procurement process, which involves selecting the suppliers for the cell phones and evaluating how they deliver their products, might be measured in terms of the quality of the cell phones delivered to Verizon, the on-time delivery performance of the suppliers, and the cost of the cell phones. Ultimately, the evaluation of the supply chain consisting of these two processes and many others will depend on how well it satisfies the customers of Verizon, who consider the value of the service to be how well it meets or exceeds expectations. The performance of these individual processes must be consistent with the performance measures for the supply chain.

Quality and Performance across the Organization

Quality and performance should be everybody's concern. Take for example QVC, a $7.4 billion televised shopping service. QVC airs 24 hours a day, all year round. QVC sells some 60,000 items ranging from jewelry, tools, cookware, clothing, and gourmet food to computers and annually ships more than 166 million packages worldwide.

QVC's processes, which span all the functional areas, spring into action with a customer order: Order taking and delivery date promising, billing, and order delivery all ensue once an order is placed. QVC operates four call centers that handle 179 million calls annually from customers who want to order something, complain about a problem, or just get product information. The call center representative's demeanor and skill are critical to achieving a successful customer encounter. QVC management keeps track of productivity, quality, and customer satisfaction measures for all processes. When the measures slip, problems are addressed aggressively. Knowing how to assess whether the process is performing well and when to take action are key skills QVC managers must have. In this chapter, we first address the costs of quality and then focus on Total Quality Management and Six Sigma, two philosophies and supporting tools that many companies embrace to evaluate and improve quality and performance.

Costs of Quality

When a process fails to satisfy a customer, the failure is considered a **defect**. For example, according to the California Academy of Family Physicians, defects for the processes in a doctor's practice are defined as "anything that happened in my office that should not have happened, and that I absolutely do not want to happen again." Obviously, this definition covers process failures that the patient sees, such as poor communication and errors in prescription dosages. It also includes failures the patient does not see, such as incorrect charting.

Many companies spend significant time, effort, and expense on systems, training, and organizational changes to improve the quality and performance of their processes. They believe that it is important to be able to gauge current levels of performance so that any process gaps can be determined. Gaps reflect potential dissatisfied customers and additional costs for the firm. Most experts estimate that the costs of quality range from 20 to 30 percent of gross sales. These costs can be broken down into four major categories: (1) prevention, (2) appraisal, (3) internal failure, and (4) external failure.

defect

Any instance when a process fails to satisfy its customer.

Prevention Costs

Prevention costs are associated with preventing defects before they happen. They include the costs of redesigning the process to remove the causes of poor performance, redesigning the service or product to make it simpler to produce, training employees in the methods of continuous improvement, and working with suppliers to increase the quality of purchased items or contracted services. In order to prevent problems from happening, firms must invest additional time, effort, and money.

prevention costs

Costs associated with preventing defects before they happen.

Appraisal Costs

Appraisal costs are incurred when the firm assesses the level of performance of its processes. As the costs of prevention increase and performance improves, appraisal costs decrease because fewer resources are needed for quality inspections and the subsequent search for causes of any problems that are detected.

appraisal costs

Costs incurred when the firm assess the performance level of its processes.

Internal Failure Costs

Internal failure costs result from defects that are discovered during the production of a service or product. Defects fall into two main categories: (1) *rework*, which is incurred if some aspect of a service must be performed again or if a defective item must be rerouted to some previous operation(s) to correct the defect; and (2) *scrap*, which is incurred if a defective item is unfit for further processing. For example, an analysis of the viability of acquiring a company might be sent back to the mergers and acquisitions department if an assessment of the company's history of environmental compliance is missing. The proposal for the purchase of the company may be delayed, which may result in the loss of the purchase opportunity.

internal failure costs

Costs resulting from defects that are discovered during the production of a service or product.

External Failure Costs

External failure costs arise when a defect is discovered after the customer receives the service or product. Dissatisfied customers talk about bad service or products to their friends, who in turn tell others. If the problem is bad enough, consumer protection groups may even alert the media. The potential impact on future profits is difficult to assess, but without doubt external failure costs erode market share and profits. Encountering defects and correcting them after the product is in the customer's hands is costly.

External failure costs also include warranty service and litigation costs. A **warranty** is a written guarantee that the producer will replace or repair defective parts or perform the service to the customer's satisfaction. Usually, a warranty is given for some specified period. For example, television repairs are usually guaranteed for 90 days and new automobiles for 5 years or 50,000 miles, whichever comes first. Warranty costs must be considered in the design of new services or products.

external failure costs

Costs that arise when a defect is discovered after the customer receives the service or product.

warranty

A written guarantee that the producer will replace or repair defective parts or perform the service to the customer's satisfaction.

Ethics and Quality

The costs of quality go beyond the out-of-pocket costs associated with training, appraisal, scrap, rework, warranties, litigation, or the lost sales from dissatisfied customers. There is a greater societal effect that must be factored into decision making involving the production of services or products, which often requires balancing the traditional measures of quality performance and the overall benefits to society. For example, in the health care industry, aiming for zero complications in cardiac surgery might sound good; however, if it comes at the cost of turning down high-risk patients, is society being served in the best way? Or, how much time, energy, and money should go into delivering vaccines or preventing complications? These are questions that often do not have clear answers.

Deceptive business practices are another source of concern for service or product quality. Deceptive business practice involves three elements: (1) the conduct of the provider is intentional and motivated by a desire to exploit the customer; (2) the provider conceals the truth based upon what is actually known to the provider; and (3) the transaction is intended to generate a disproportionate economic benefit to the provider at the expense of the customer. This behavior is unethical, diminishes the quality of the customers' experience, and may impose a substantial cost on society. Quality is all about increasing the satisfaction of customers. When a firm engages in unethical behavior and the customer finds out about it, the customer is unlikely to favorably assess the quality of his or her experience with that firm or to return as a customer.

Firms that produce better quality services or products can expect to earn a premium for that higher quality. They can also expect to grow and prosper over time because of their ability to create true value for customers. Firms that engage in deception, however, undermine the ability and competence of their employees and demean their relationship with external customers. The unfortunate message these firms send to their employees, who are also their internal customers, is that management views them as being less capable of producing quality services or products than their counterparts in ethical firms. Under these conditions employees are also less likely to be motivated to put forth their best effort. The message unethical firms send to their external customers is that their product or service cannot effectively compete with that of others and so they must engage in deception in order to be profitable. Employees of firms that attempt to profit by deceiving customers are less likely to create true value for customers through product or service improvements that can enhance the customers' experience. That erodes a firm's ability to compete now and in the future.

Ethical behavior falls on the shoulders of all employees of an organization. It is not ethical to knowingly deceive customers and pass defective services or products to internal or external customers. The well-being of all stakeholders, such as stockholders, customers, employees, partners, and creditors, should be considered.

The quality costs of prevention, assessment, internal failure, and external failure must be balanced with ethical considerations to arrive at the appropriate processes and approaches to manage them. Nonetheless, developing the cultural environment for ethical behavior is not cost-free. Employees must be educated in how ethics interfaces with their jobs. The firm may organize an ethics task force or an ethics public relations group to provide an interface between the firm and society. Documentation may be required. We now turn to a discussion of Total Quality Management and Six Sigma, two philosophies companies use to evaluate and improve quality and process performance along technical, service, and ethical dimensions.

total quality management (TQM)

A philosophy that stresses three principles for achieving high levels of process performance and quality: (1) customer satisfaction, (2) employee involvement, and (3) continuous improvement in performance.

quality

A term used by customers to describe their general satisfaction with a service or product.

Total Quality Management

Total quality management (TQM) is a philosophy that stresses three principles for achieving high levels of process performance and quality. These principles are related to (1) customer satisfaction, (2) employee involvement, and (3) continuous improvement in performance. As Figure 1 indicates, TQM also involves a number of other important elements. Service/product design and purchasing are covered later in this text. Here, we just focus on the three main principles of TQM.

Customer Satisfaction

Customers, internal or external, are satisfied when their expectations regarding a service or product have been met or exceeded. Often, customers use the general term **quality** to describe their level of satisfaction with a service or product. Quality has multiple dimensions in the mind of the customer. One or more of the following five definitions apply at any one time.

▲ FIGURE 1
TQM Wheel

Conformance to Specifications Although customers evaluate the service or product they receive, it is the processes that produced the service or product that are really being judged. In this case, a process failure would be the process's inability to meet certain advertised or implied performance standards. Conformance to specifications may relate to consistent quality, on-time delivery, or delivery speed.

Value Another way customers define quality is through value, or how well the service or product serves its intended purpose at a price customers are willing to pay. The service/product development process plays a role here, as do the firm's competitive priorities relating to top quality versus low-cost operations. The two factors must be balanced to produce value for the customer. How much value a service or product has in the mind of the customer depends on the customer's expectations before purchasing it.

Fitness for Use When assessing how well a service or product performs its intended purpose, the customer may consider the convenience of a service, the mechanical features of a product, or other aspects such as appearance, style, durability, reliability, craftsmanship, and serviceability. For example, you may define the quality of the entertainment center you purchased on the basis of how easy it was to assemble and its appearance and styling.

Support Often the service or product support provided by the company is as important to customers as the quality of the service or product itself. Customers get upset with a company if its financial statements are incorrect, responses to its warranty claims are delayed, its advertising is misleading, or its employees are not helpful when problems are incurred. Good support once the sale has been made can reduce the consequences of quality failures.

Psychological Impressions People often evaluate the quality of a service or product on the basis of psychological impressions: atmosphere, image, or aesthetics. In the provision of services where the customer is in close contact with the provider, the appearance and actions of the provider are especially important. Nicely dressed, courteous, friendly, and sympathetic employees can affect the customer's perception of service quality.

Call centers provide support for a firm's products or services as well as contribute to the psychological impression of the customer regarding the experience. Calls to the center are often monitored to ensure that the customer is satisfied.

Bernhard Classen/Alamy

Attaining quality in all areas of a business is a difficult task. To make things even more difficult, consumers change their perceptions of quality. In general, a business's success depends on the accuracy of its perceptions of consumer expectations and its ability to bridge the gap between those expectations and operating capabilities. Good quality pays off in higher profits. High-quality services and products can be priced higher and yield a greater return. Poor quality erodes the firm's ability to compete in the marketplace and increases the costs of producing its service or product. Managerial Practice 1 shows how Steinway & Sons balanced consumer expectations for high-end pianos with its capability to meet those expectations.

Employee Involvement

One of the important elements of TQM is employee involvement, as shown in Figure 1. A program in employee involvement includes changing organizational culture and encouraging teamwork.

Cultural Change One of the main challenges in developing the proper culture for TQM is to define *customer* for each employee. In general, customers are internal or external. *External customers* are the people or firms who buy the service or product. Some employees, especially those having little contact with external customers, may have difficulty seeing how their jobs contribute to the whole effort.

It is helpful to point out to employees that each employee also has one or more *internal customers*—employees in the firm who rely on the output of other employees. All employees must do a good job of serving their internal customers if external customers ultimately are to be satisfied. They will be satisfied only if each internal customer demands value be added that the external customer will recognize and pay for. The notion of internal customers applies to all parts of a firm and enhances cross-functional coordination. For example, accounting must prepare accurate and timely reports for management, and purchasing must provide high-quality materials on time for operations.

MANAGERIAL PRACTICE 1 — Quality and Performance at Steinway & Sons

A specialist adjusts the levers and dampers of a grand concert piano at the Steinway & Sons factory in Hamburg.

Christian Charisius/Reuters/Corbis

The first contestant in the Van Cliburn International Piano Competition is about to play Tchaikovsky Piano Concerto No. 1 before a packed audience in Fort Worth, Texas. The tension mounts as his fingers approach the keyboard of the Steinway & Sons grand concert piano; both the contestant and piano perform admirably much to the relief of the contestant and the operations manager of the concert. Why was the Steinway piano chosen for such a visible event? It is one of the highest-quality grand pianos you can buy. In addition, Steinway has a market share of over 95 percent in concert halls and it is the piano of choice for professional musicians from Van Cliburn to Billy Joel.

Steinway began operations in the 1880s. Today, the company blends the art of hand crafting, which uses methods essentially the same as when the company started, with twenty-first-century manufacturing technology to produce about 3,100 grand pianos a year. Some 12,000 parts are fashioned, mostly in-house, and assembled for each piano; it takes 9 months to a year compared to 20 days for a mass-produced piano. Eight different species of wood go into every grand piano, each selected for its physical properties and aesthetic characteristics. The craft-oriented production process is painstaking to ensure quality at each step. For example, each board for a piano is hand

selected for a given part. In a time-consuming process, craftsmen bend 17 laminations of the piano's hard maple rim into place with clamps. The Alaska Sitka spruce soundboard is hand-planed so it is arched, thicker at its center than its tapered edges, to withstand the 1,000 pounds of pressure from the more than 200 strings. The piano's "action," which contains keys (88 of them), whippens, shanks, and hammers, uses 100 parts, manufactured on numerical control machines, to sound each note and is pieced together at 30 different desks. Quality is checked at each operation to avoid passing defective parts downstream.

There are six characteristics of quality in Steinway pianos:

- **Sound** Tone and pitch contribute to the fullness and roundness of the sound from the piano. In a process called "voicing," minute adjustments are made to the felt pad of each hammer in the piano's action to either mellow the tone or increase its brilliance. Then a tone regulator listens to the piano's pitch and turns the tuning pins to adjust string tension. Steinways are world renowned for their sound; however, because of the natural characteristics of the wood, each piano will have its own personality.

- **Finish** Wood veneers are selected for their beauty. Boards not meeting standards are discarded, creating a large amount of scrap.

- **Feel** Each of the 88 keys must require the same amount of pressure to activate. In a process called "action weigh-off," lead is added to each key so that there is a consistent feel. Action parts are held to tolerances within +/–0.0005 inch.

- **Durability** The piano must have a long life and perform up to expectations throughout.

- **Image** There is a certain mystique associated with the Steinway brand. Some people attribute a cult-like experience to owning a Steinway.

- **Service** Steinway will go out of its way to service a piano that is inoperative, even to the extent of providing a loaner for a major concert.

The six characteristics link to four of our definitions of quality: (1) conformance to specifications (*feel*), (2) fitness for use (*sound, finish, durability*); (3) support (*service*); and (4) psychological impressions (*image*). As for value, our fifth definition of quality, Steinway grand pianos cost anywhere from $47,000 to $165,000 unless you want a nine-foot recreation of the famous Alma-Tadema piano built in 1887, in which case it will cost $675,000. Want to buy one?

Sources: Andy Serwer, "Happy Birthday, Steinway," *Fortune*, vol. 147, no. 5 (March 17, 2003), pp. 94–97; Leo O'Connor, "Engineering on a Grand scale," *Mechanical Engineering*, vol. 116, no. 10 (October, 1994), pp. 52–58; Steinway Musical Instruments, Inc. Annual Report 2006, **www.steinwaymusical.com**; **www.steinway.com/factory/tour.shtml**, 2007.

quality at the source

A philosophy whereby defects are caught and corrected where they were created.

teams

Small groups of people who have a common purpose, set their own performance goals and approaches, and hold themselves accountable for success.

In TQM, everyone in the organization must share the view that quality control is an end in itself. Errors or defects should be caught and corrected at the source, not passed along to an internal or external customer. For example, a consulting team should make sure its billable hours are correct before submitting them to the accounting department. This philosophy is called **quality at the source**. In addition, firms should avoid trying to "inspect quality into the product" by using inspectors to weed out unsatisfactory services or defective products after all operations have been performed. By contrast, in some manufacturing firms, workers have the authority to stop a production line if they spot quality problems.

Teams Employee involvement is a key tactic for improving processes and quality. One way to achieve employee involvement is by the use of **teams**, which are small groups of people who have a common purpose, set their own performance goals and approaches, and hold themselves accountable for success.

The three approaches to teamwork most often used are (1) problem-solving teams, (2) special-purpose teams, and (3) self-managed teams. All three use some amount of **employee empowerment**, which moves responsibility for decisions further down the organizational chart—to the level of the employee actually doing the job.

First introduced in the 1920s, *problem-solving teams*, also called **quality circles**, became popular in the late 1970s after the Japanese used them successfully. Problem-solving teams are small groups of supervisors and employees who meet to identify, analyze, and solve process and quality problems. Employees take more pride and interest in their work if they are allowed to help shape it. Although problem-solving teams can successfully reduce costs and improve quality, they die if management fails to implement many of the suggestions they generate.

An outgrowth of the problem-solving teams, **special-purpose teams** address issues of paramount concern to management, labor, or both. For example, management may form a special-purpose team to design and introduce new work policies or new technologies or to address customer service problems. Essentially, this approach gives workers a voice in high-level decisions. Special-purpose teams first appeared in the United States in the early 1980s.

The **self-managed team** approach takes worker participation to its highest level: A small group of employees work together to produce a major portion, or sometimes all, of a service or product. Members learn all the tasks involved in the operation, rotate from job to job, and take over managerial duties such as work and vacation scheduling, ordering supplies, and hiring. In some cases, team members design the process and have a high degree of latitude as to how it takes shape. Self-managed teams essentially change the way work is organized because employees have control over their jobs. Some self-managed teams have increased productivity by 30 percent or more in their firms.

Process measurement is the key to quality improvement. Here a quality inspector measures the diameter of holes in a machined part.

Continuous Improvement

Continuous improvement, based on a Japanese concept called *kaizen*, is the philosophy of continually seeking ways to improve processes. Continuous improvement involves identifying benchmarks of excellent practice and instilling a sense of employee ownership in the process. The focus of continuous improvement projects is to reduce waste, such as reducing the length of time required to process requests for loans at a bank, the amount of scrap generated at a milling machine, or the number of employee injuries at a construction site. The basis of the continuous improvement philosophy are the beliefs that virtually any aspect of a process can be improved and that the people most closely associated with a process are in the best position to identify the changes that should be made. The idea is not to wait until a massive problem occurs before acting.

Employees should be given problem-solving tools, such as the statistical process control (SPC) methods we discuss later in this chapter, and a sense of ownership of the process to be improved. A sense of operator ownership emerges when employees feel a responsibility for the processes and methods they use and take pride in the quality of the service or product they produce. It comes from participation on work teams and in problem-solving activities, which instill in employees a feeling that they have some control over their workplace and tasks.

Most firms actively engaged in continuous improvement train their work teams to use the **plan-do-study-act cycle** for problem solving. Another name for this approach is the Deming Wheel, named after the renowned statistician W. Edwards Deming who taught quality improvement techniques to the Japanese after World War II. Figure 2 shows this cycle, which lies at the heart of the continuous improvement philosophy. The cycle comprises the following steps:

1. *Plan.* The team selects a process (an activity, method, machine, or policy) that needs improvement. The team then documents the selected process, usually by analyzing related data; sets qualitative goals for improvement; and discusses various ways to achieve the goals. After assessing the benefits and costs of the alternatives, the team develops a plan with quantifiable measures for improvement.

2. *Do.* The team implements the plan and monitors progress. Data are collected continuously to measure the improvements in the process. Any changes in the process are documented, and further revisions are made as needed.

employee empowerment

An approach to teamwork that moves responsibility for decisions further down the organizational chart—to the level of the employee actually doing the job.

quality circles

Another name for problem-solving teams; small groups of supervisors and employees who meet to identify, analyze, and solve process and quality problems.

special-purpose teams

Groups that address issues of paramount concern to management, labor, or both.

self-managed team

A small group of employees who work together to produce a major portion, or sometimes all, of a service or product.

continuous improvement

The philosophy of continually seeking ways to improve processes based on a Japanese concept called *kaizen*.

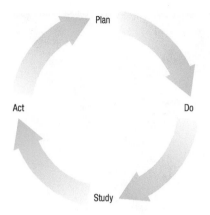

▲ FIGURE 2
Plan-Do-Study-Act Cycle

plan-do-study-act cycle

A cycle, also called the Deming Wheel, used by firms actively engaged in continuous improvement to train their work teams in problem solving.

Six Sigma

A comprehensive and flexible system for achieving, sustaining, and maximizing business success by minimizing defects and variability in processes.

▼ FIGURE 3
Six Sigma Approach Focuses on Reducing Spread and Centering the Process

3. *Study*. The team analyzes the data collected during the *do* step to find out how closely the results correspond to the goals set in the *plan* step. If major shortcomings exist, the team reevaluates the plan or stops the project.

4. *Act*. If the results are successful, the team documents the revised process so that it becomes the standard procedure for all who may use it. The team may then instruct other employees in the use of the revised process.

Problem-solving projects often focus on those aspects of processes that do not add value to the service or product. Value is added in processes such as machining a part or serving a customer through a Web page. No value is added in activities such as inspecting parts for defects or routing requests for loan approvals to several different departments. The idea of continuous improvement is to reduce or eliminate activities that do not add value and, thus, are wasteful.

Six Sigma

Six Sigma, which relies heavily on the principles of TQM, is a comprehensive and flexible system for achieving, sustaining, and maximizing business success by minimizing defects and variability in processes. Six Sigma has a different focus than TQM: It is driven by a close understanding of customer needs; the disciplined use of facts, data, and statistical analysis; and diligent attention to managing, improving, and reinventing business processes. Figure 3 shows how Six Sigma focuses on reducing variation in processes as well as centering processes on their target measures of performance. Either flaw—too much variation or an off-target process—degrades performance of the process. For example, a mortgage loan department of a bank might advertise loan approval decisions in 2 days. If the actual performance ranges from 1 day to 5 days, with an average of 2 days, those customers who had to wait longer than 2 days would be upset. Process variability causes customer dissatisfaction. Similarly, if actual performance consistently produced loan decisions in 3 days, all customers would be dissatisfied. In this case, the process is consistent, but off the target. Six Sigma is a rigorous approach to align processes with their target performance measures with low variability.

The name Six Sigma, originally developed by Motorola for its manufacturing operations, relates to the goal of achieving low rates of defective output by developing processes whose mean output for a performance measure is +/− six standard deviations (sigma) from the limits of the design specifications for the service or product. We will discuss variability and its implications on the capability of a process to perform at acceptable levels when we present the tools of statistical process control.

Although Six Sigma was rooted in an effort to improve manufacturing processes, credit General Electric with popularizing the application of the approach to non-manufacturing processes such as sales, human resources, customer service, and financial services. The concept of eliminating defects is the same, although the definition of "defect" depends on the process involved. For example, a human resource department's failure to meet a hiring target counts as a defect. Six Sigma has been successfully applied to a host of service processes, including financial services, human resource processes, marketing processes, and health care administrative processes.

Six Sigma Improvement Model

Figure 4 shows the Six Sigma Improvement Model, a five-step procedure that leads to improvements in process performance. The model bears a lot of similarity, the Blueprint for Process Analysis, for good reason: Both models strive for process improvement. Either model can be applied to projects involving incremental improvements to processes or to projects requiring major changes, including a redesign of an existing process or the development of a new process. The Six Sigma Improvement Model, however, is heavily reliant on statistical process control. The following steps comprise the model:

■ *Define*. Determine the characteristics of the process's output that are critical to customer satisfaction and identify any gaps between these characteristics and the

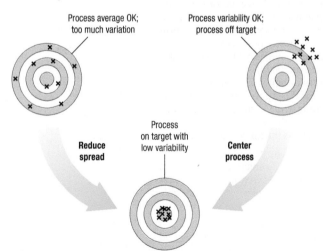

process's capabilities. Get a picture of the current process by documenting it using *flowcharts* and *process charts*.

- *Measure.* Quantify the work the process does that affects the gap. Select what to measure, identify data sources, and prepare a data collection plan.

- *Analyze.* Use the data on measures to perform process analysis, applying tools such as Pareto charts, scatter diagrams, and cause-and-effect diagrams and the statistical process control (SPC) tools in this chapter to determine where improvements are necessary. Whether or not major redesign is necessary, establish procedures to make the desired outcome routine.

- *Improve.* Modify or redesign existing methods to meet the new performance objectives. Implement the changes.

- *Control.* Monitor the process to make sure that high performance levels are maintained. Once again, data analysis tools such as Pareto charts, bar charts, scatter diagrams, as well as the statistical process control tools can be used to control the process.

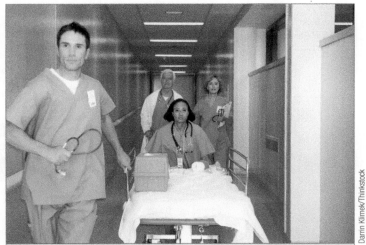
Hospital personnel rush to help a patient in an emergency. Six Sigma can be used to improve service processes in a hospital.

Successful users of Six Sigma have found that it is essential to rigorously follow the steps in the Six Sigma Improvement Model, which is sometimes referred to as the *DMAIC process* (whose name comes from using the first letter of each step in the model). To accomplish the goals of Six Sigma, employees must be trained in the "whys" and the "how-tos" of quality and what it means to customers, both internal and external. Successful firms using Six Sigma develop a cadre of internal teachers who then are responsible for teaching and assisting teams involved in a process improvement project. These teachers have different titles depending on their experience and level of achievement. **Green Belts** devote part of their time to teaching and helping teams with their projects and the rest of their time to their normally assigned duties. **Black Belts** are full-time teachers and leaders of teams involved in Six Sigma projects. Finally, **Master Black Belts** are full-time teachers who review and mentor Black Belts.

Acceptance Sampling

Before any internal process can be evaluated for performance, the inputs to that process must be of good quality. **Acceptance sampling**, which is the application of statistical techniques to determine if a quantity of material from a supplier should be accepted or rejected based on the inspection or test of one or more samples, limits the buyer's risk of rejecting good-quality materials (and unnecessarily delaying the production of goods or services) or accepting bad-quality materials (and incurring downtime due to defective materials or passing bad products to customers). Relative to the specifications for the material the buyer is purchasing, the buyer specifies an **acceptable quality level (AQL)**, which is a statement of the proportion of defective items (outside of specifications) that the buyer will accept in a shipment. These days, that proportion is getting very small, often measured in parts per ten-thousand. The idea of acceptance sampling is to take a sample, rather than testing the entire quantity of material, because that is often less expensive. Therein lies the risk—the sample may not be representative of the entire lot of goods from the supplier. The basic procedure is straightforward.

1. A random sample is taken from a large quantity of items and tested or measured relative to the specifications or quality measures of interest.

2. If the sample passes the test (low number of defects), the entire quantity of items is accepted.

3. If the sample fails the test, either (a) the entire quantity of items is subjected to 100 percent inspection and all defective items repaired or replaced or (b) the entire quantity is returned to the supplier.

In a supply chain, any company can be both a producer of goods purchased by another company and a consumer of goods or raw materials supplied by another company. Figure 5 shows

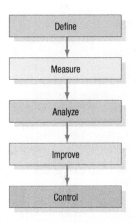

Define → **Measure** → **Analyze** → **Improve** → **Control**

▲ FIGURE 4
Six Sigma Improvement Model

Green Belt

An employee who achieved the first level of training in a Six Sigma program and spends part of his or her time teaching and helping teams with their projects.

Black Belt

An employee who reached the highest level of training in a Six Sigma program and spends all of his or her time teaching and leading teams involved in Six Sigma projects.

Master Black Belt

Full-time teachers and mentors to several Black Belts.

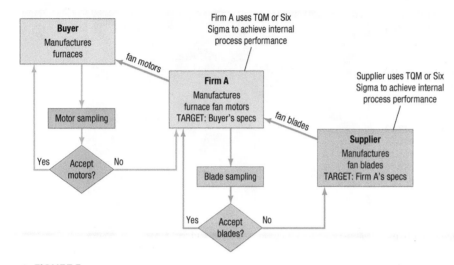

a flowchart of how acceptance sampling and internal process performance (TQM or Six Sigma) interface in a supply chain. From the perspective of the supply chain, the buyer's specifications for various dimensions of quality become the targets the supplier shoots for in a supply contract. The supplier's internal processes must be up to the task; TQM or Six Sigma can help achieve the desired performance. The buyer's sampling plan will provide a high probability of accepting AQL (or better). MyOMLab Supplement G, "Acceptance Sampling Plans," shows how to design an acceptance sampling plan that meets the level of risk desired.

▲ FIGURE 5
Interface of Acceptance Sampling and Process Performance Approaches in a Supply Chain

acceptable quality level (AQL)

The quality level desired by the consumer.

acceptance sampling

The application of statistical techniques to determine whether a quantity of material should be accepted or rejected based on the inspection or test of a sample.

statistical process control (SPC)

The application of statistical techniques to determine whether a process is delivering what the customer wants.

Statistical Process Control

Regardless of whether a firm is producing a service or a product, it is important to ensure that the firm's processes are providing the quality that customers want. A key element of TQM or Six Sigma is building the capability to monitor the performance of processes so that corrective action can be initiated in a timely fashion. Evaluating the performance of processes requires a variety of data gathering approaches. Think as checklists, histograms and bar charts, Pareto charts, scatter diagrams, cause-and-effect diagrams, and graphs. All of these tools can be used with TQM or Six Sigma. Here. we focus on the powerful statistical tools that can be used to monitor and manage repetitive processes.

Statistical process control (SPC) is the application of statistical techniques to determine whether a process is delivering what customers want. In SPC, tools called control charts are used primarily to detect defective services or products or to indicate that the process has changed and that services or products will deviate from their design specifications, unless something is done to correct the situation. SPC can also be used to inform management of improved process changes. Examples of process changes that can be detected by SPC include the following:

- A decrease in the average number of complaints per day at a hotel
- A sudden increase in the proportion of defective gear boxes
- An increase in the time to process a mortgage application
- A decline in the number of scrapped units at a milling machine
- An increase in the number of claimants receiving late payment from an insurance company

Let us consider the last situation. Suppose that the manager of the accounts payable department of an insurance company notices that the proportion of claimants receiving late payments rose from an average of 0.01 to 0.03. The first question is whether the rise is a cause for alarm or just a random occurrence. Statistical process control can help the manager decide whether further action should be taken. If the rise in the proportion is not just a random occurrence, the manager should seek explanations of the poor performance. Perhaps the number of claims significantly increased, causing an overload on the employees in the department. The decision might be to hire more personnel. Or perhaps the procedures being used are ineffective or the training of employees is inadequate. SPC is an integral part of TQM and Six Sigma.

Variation of Outputs

No two services or products are exactly alike because the processes used to produce them contain many sources of variation, even if the processes are working as intended. Nonetheless, it is important to minimize the variation in outputs because frequently variation is what the customer sees and feels. Suppose a physicians' clinic submits claims on behalf of its patients to a particular insurance company. In this situation, the physicians' clinic is the customer of the insurance company's bill payment process. In some cases, the clinic receives payment in 4 weeks, and in other cases 20 weeks. The time to process a request for payment varies because of the load on the insurance company's processes, the medical history of the patient, and the skills and attitudes of the employees. Meanwhile, the clinic must cover its expenses while it waits for payment. Regardless of whether the process is producing services or products, nothing can be done to eliminate variation in output completely; however, management should investigate the *causes* of the variation in order to minimize it.

Performance Measurements   Performance can be evaluated in two ways. One way is to measure **variables**—that is, service or product characteristics, such as weight, length, volume, or time, that can be *measured*. The advantage of using performance variables is that if a service or product misses its performance specifications, the inspector knows by how much. The disadvantage is that such measurements typically involve special equipment, employee skills, exacting procedures, and time and effort.

Another way to evaluate performance is to measure **attributes**; service or product characteristics that can be quickly *counted* for acceptable performance. This method allows inspectors to make a simple "yes/no" decision about whether a service or product meets the specifications. Attributes often are used when performance specifications are complex and measurement of variables is difficult or costly. Some examples of attributes that can be counted are the number of insurance forms containing errors that cause underpayments or overpayments, the proportion of airline flights arriving within 15 minutes of scheduled times, and the number of stove-top assemblies with spotted paint.

The advantage of counting attributes is that less effort and fewer resources are needed than for measuring variables. The disadvantage is that, even though attribute counts can reveal that process performance has changed, they do not indicate by how much. For example, a count may determine that the proportion of airline flights arriving within 15 minutes of their scheduled times declined, but the result does not show how much beyond the 15-minute allowance the flights are arriving. For that, the actual deviation from the scheduled arrival, a variable, would have to be measured.

Sampling   The most thorough approach to inspection is to inspect each service or product at each stage of the process for quality. This method, called *complete inspection*, is used when the costs of passing defects to an internal or external customer outweigh the inspection costs. Firms often use automated inspection equipment that can record, summarize, and display data. Many companies find that automated inspection equipment can pay for itself in a reasonably short time.

A well-conceived **sampling plan** can approach the same degree of protection as complete inspection. A sampling plan specifies a **sample size**, which is a quantity of randomly selected observations of process outputs, the time between successive samples, and decision rules that determine when action should be taken. Sampling is appropriate when inspection costs are high because of the special knowledge, skills, procedures, and expensive equipment that are required to perform the inspections, or because the tests are destructive.

Sampling Distributions   Relative to a performance measure, a process will produce output that can be described by a *process distribution*, with a mean and variance that will be known only with a complete inspection with 100 percent accuracy. The purpose of sampling, however, is to estimate a variable or attribute measure for the output of the process without doing a complete inspection. That measure is then used to assess the performance of the process itself. For example, the time required to process specimens at an intensive care unit lab in a hospital (a variable measure) will vary. If you measured the time to complete an analysis of a large number of patients and plotted the results, the data would tend to form a pattern that can be described as a process distribution. With sampling, we try to estimate the parameters of the process distribution using statistics such as the sample mean and the sample range or standard deviation.

1.   The *sample mean* is the sum of the observations divided by the total number of observations:

$$\bar{x} = \frac{\sum_{i=1}^{n} x_i}{n}$$

variables

Service or product characteristics, such as weight, length, volume, or time, that can be measured.

attributes

Service or product characteristics that can be quickly counted for acceptable performance.

sampling plan

A plan that specifies a sample size, the time between successive samples, and decision rules that determine when action should be taken.

sample size

A quantity of randomly selected observations of process outputs.

Wine production is an example of a situation where complete inspection is not an option. Here a quality inspector draws a sample of white wine from a stainless steel maturation tank.

where

$x_i =$ observation of a quality characteristic (such as time)

$n =$ total number of observations

$\bar{x} =$ mean

2. The *range* is the difference between the largest observation in a sample and the smallest. The *standard deviation* is the square root of the variance of a distribution. An estimate of the process standard deviation based on a sample is given by

$$\sigma = \sqrt{\frac{\sum_{i=1}^{n}(x_i - \bar{x})^2}{n-1}} \quad \text{or} \quad \sigma = \sqrt{\frac{\sum_{i=1}^{n}x^2 - \frac{\left(\sum_{i=1}^{n}x_i\right)^2}{n}}{n-1}}$$

where

$\sigma =$ standard deviation of a sample

$n =$ total number of observations in the sample

$\bar{x} =$ mean

$x_i =$ observation of a quality characteristic

Relatively small values for the range or the standard deviation imply that the observations are clustered near the mean.

These sample statistics have their own distribution, which we call a *sampling distribution*. For example, in the lab analysis process, an important performance variable is the time it takes to get results to the critical care unit. Suppose that management wants results available in an average of 25 minutes. That is, it wants the process distribution to have a mean of 25 minutes. An inspector periodically taking a sample of five analyses and calculating the sample mean could use it to determine how well the process is doing. Suppose that the process is actually producing the analyses with a mean of 25 minutes. Plotting a large number of these sample means would show that they have their own sampling distribution with a mean centered on 25 minutes, as does the process distribution mean, but with much less variability. The reason is that the sample means offset the highs and lows of the individual times in each sample. Figure 6 shows the relationship between the sampling distribution of sample means and the process distribution for the analysis times.

Some sampling distributions (e.g., for means with sample sizes of four or more and proportions with sample sizes of 20 or more) can be approximated by the normal distribution, allowing the use of the normal tables. For example, suppose you wanted to determine the probability that a sample mean will be more than 2.0 standard deviations higher than the process mean. For $z = 2.0$ standard deviations is 0.9772. Consequently, the probability is $1.0000 - 0.9772 = 0.0228$, or 2.28 percent. The probability that the sample mean will be more than 2.0 standard deviations lower than the process mean is also 2.28 percent because the normal distribution is symmetric to the mean. The ability to assign probabilities to sample results is important for the construction and use of control charts.

Common Causes   The two basic categories of variation in output include common causes and assignable causes. **Common causes of variation** are the purely random, unidentifiable sources of variation that are unavoidable with the current process. A process distribution can be characterized by its *location*, *spread*, and *shape*. Location is measured by the *mean* of the distribution, while spread is measured by the *range* or *standard deviation*. The shape of process distributions can be characterized as either symmetric or skewed. A *symmetric* distribution has the same number of observations above and below the mean. A *skewed* distribution has a greater number of observations either above or below the mean. If process variability results solely from common causes of variation, a typical assumption is that the distribution is symmetric, with most observations near the center.

Assignable Causes   The second category of variation, **assignable causes of variation**, also known as *special causes*, includes any variation-causing factors that can be identified and eliminated. Assignable causes of variation include an employee needing training or a machine needing repair. Let us return to the example of the lab analysis process. Figure 7 shows how assignable causes can change the distribution of output for the analysis process. The green curve is

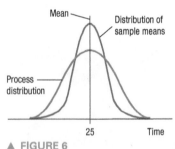

▲ **FIGURE 6**
Relationship Between the Distribution of Sample Means and the Process Distribution

common causes of variation

The purely random, unidentifiable sources of variation that are unavoidable with the current process.

assignable causes of variation

Any variation-causing factors that can be identified and eliminated.

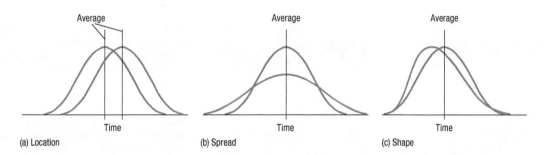

(a) Location   (b) Spread   (c) Shape

the process distribution when only common causes of variation are present. The **purple** curves depict a change in the distribution because of assignable causes. In Figure 7(a), the **purple** curve indicates that the process took more time than planned in many of the cases, thereby increasing the average time of each analysis. In Figure 7(b), an increase in the variability of the time for each case affected the spread of the distribution. Finally, in Figure 7(c), the **purple** curve indicates that the process produced a preponderance of the tests in less than average time. Such a distribution is skewed, or no longer symmetric to the average value. A process is said to be in statistical control when the location, spread, or shape of its distribution does not change over time. After the process is in statistical control, managers use SPC procedures to detect the onset of assignable causes so that they can be addressed.

▲ **FIGURE 7**
Effects of Assignable Causes on the Process Distribution for the Lab Analysis Process

control chart
A time-ordered diagram that is used to determine whether observed variations are abnormal.

Control Charts

To determine whether observed variations are abnormal, we can measure and plot the performance measure taken from the sample on a time-ordered diagram called a **control chart**. A control chart has a nominal value, or central line, which can be the process's historic average or a target that managers would like the process to achieve, and two control limits based on the sampling distribution of the quality measure. The control limits are used to judge whether action is required. The larger value represents the *upper control limit* (UCL), and the smaller value represents the *lower control limit* (LCL). Figure 8 shows how the control limits relate to the sampling distribution. A sample statistic that falls between the UCL and the LCL indicates that the process is exhibiting common causes of variation. A statistic that falls outside the control limits indicates that the process is exhibiting assignable causes of variation.

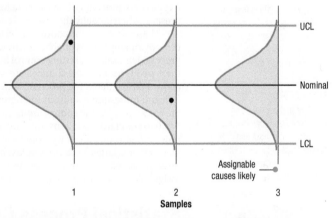

Assignable causes likely

1   2   3
Samples

▲ **FIGURE 8**
How Control Limits Relate to the Sampling Distribution: Observations from Three Samples

Observations falling outside the control limits do not always mean poor quality. For example, in Figure 8 the assignable cause may be a new billing process introduced to reduce the number of incorrect bills sent to customers. If the proportion of incorrect bills, that is, the performance measure from a sample of bills, falls *below* the LCL of the control chart, the new procedure likely changed the billing process for the better, and a new control chart should be constructed.

Managers or employees responsible for evaluating a process can use control charts in the following way:

1. Take a random sample from the process and calculate a variable or attribute performance measure.

2. If the statistic falls outside the chart's control limits or exhibits unusual behavior, look for an assignable cause.

3. Eliminate the cause if it degrades performance; incorporate the cause if it improves performance. Reconstruct the control chart with new data.

4. Repeat the procedure periodically.

Sometimes, problems with a process can be detected even though the control limits have not been exceeded. Figure 9 contains four examples of control charts. Chart (a) shows a process that is in statistical control. No action is needed. However, chart (b) shows a pattern called a *run* or a sequence of observations with a certain characteristic. A typical rule is to take remedial action

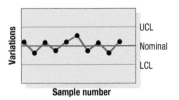

(a) Normal—No action

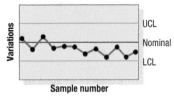

(b) Run—Take action

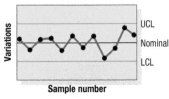

(c) Sudden change—Monitor

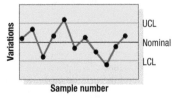

(d) Exceeds control limits—Take action

▲ FIGURE 9
Control Chart Examples

type I error

An error that occurs when the employee concludes that the process is out of control based on a sample result that falls outside the control limits, when in fact it was due to pure randomness.

type II error

An error that occurs when the employee concludes that the process is in control and only randomness is present, when actually the process is out of statistical control.

when five or more observations show a downward or upward trend, even if the points have not yet exceeded the control limits. Here, nine sequential observations are below the mean and show a downward trend. The probability is low that such a result could take place by chance.

Chart (c) shows that the process takes a sudden change from its normal pattern. The last four observations are unusual: The first drops close to the LCL, the next two rise toward the UCL, and the fourth remains above the nominal value. Managers or employees should monitor processes with such sudden changes even though the control limits have not been exceeded. Finally, chart (d) indicates that the process went out of control twice because two sample results fell outside the control limits. The probability that the process distribution has changed is high. We discuss more implications of being out of statistical control when we discuss process capability later in this chapter.

Control charts are not perfect tools for detecting shifts in the process distribution because they are based on sampling distributions. Two types of error are possible with the use of control charts. A **type I error** occurs when the conclusion is made that the process is out of control based on a sample result that falls outside the control limits, when in fact it was due to pure randomness. A **type II error** occurs when the conclusion is that the process is in control and only randomness is present, when actually the process is out of statistical control.

These errors can be controlled by the choice of control limits. The choice would depend on the costs of looking for assignable causes when none exist versus the cost of not detecting a shift in the process. For example, setting control limits at +/− three standard deviations from the mean reduces the type I error because chances are only 0.26 percent that a sample result will fall outside of the control limits unless the process is out of statistical control. However, the type II error may be significant; more subtle shifts in the nature of the process distribution will go undetected because of the wide spread in the control limits. Alternatively, the spread in the control limits can be reduced to +/− two standard deviations, thereby increasing the likelihood of sample results from a non-faulty process falling outside of the control limits to 4.56 percent. Now, the type II error is smaller, but the type I error is larger because employees are likely to search for assignable causes when the sample result occurred solely by chance. As a general rule, use wider limits when the cost for searching for assignable causes is large relative to the cost of not detecting a shift in the process distribution.

Statistical Process Control Methods

Statistical process control (SPC) methods are useful for both measuring the current process performance and detecting whether the process has changed in a way that will affect future performance. In this section, we first discuss mean and range charts for variable measures of performance and then consider control charts for attributes measures.

Control Charts for Variables

Control charts for variables are used to monitor the mean and the variability of the process distribution.

R-chart

A chart used to monitor process variability.

R-Chart A range chart, or **R-chart**, is used to monitor process variability. To calculate the range of a set of sample data, the analyst subtracts the smallest from the largest measurement in each sample. If any of the ranges fall outside the control limits, the process variability is not in control.

The control limits for the R-chart are

$$\text{UCL}_R = D_4\bar{R} \text{ and } \text{LCL}_R = D_3\bar{R}$$

where

$\bar{R}$ = average of several past R values and the central line of the control chart

D_3, D_4 = constants that provide three standard deviation (three-sigma) limits for a given sample size

Notice that the values for D_3 and D_4 shown in Table 1 change as a function of the sample size. Notice, too, that the spread between the control limits narrows as the sample size increases. This change is a consequence of having more information on which to base an estimate for the process range.

TABLE 1 | FACTORS FOR CALCULATING THREE-SIGMA LIMITS FOR THE $\bar{x}$-CHART AND R-CHART

Size of Sample (n)	Factor for UCL and LCL for $\bar{x}$-Chart (A_2)	Factor for LCL for R-Chart (D_3)	Factor for UCL for R-Chart (D_4)
2	1.880	0	3.267
3	1.023	0	2.575
4	0.729	0	2.282
5	0.577	0	2.115
6	0.483	0	2.004
7	0.419	0.076	1.924
8	0.373	0.136	1.864
9	0.337	0.184	1.816
10	0.308	0.223	1.777

Source: Reprinted with permission from *ASTM Manual on Quality Control of Materials*, copyright © ASTM International, 100 Barr Harbor Drive, West Conshohocken, PA 19428.

$\bar{x}$-Chart An $\bar{x}$-**Chart** (read "x-bar chart") is used to see whether the process is generating output, on average, consistent with a target value set by management for the process or whether its current performance, with respect to the average of the performance measure, is consistent with its past performance. A target value is useful when a process is completely redesigned and past performance is no longer relevant. When the assignable causes of process variability have been identified and the process variability is in statistical control, the analyst can then construct an $\bar{x}$-chart. The control limits for the $\bar{x}$-chart are

$$\text{UCL}_{\bar{x}} = \bar{\bar{x}} + A_2\bar{R} \quad \text{and} \quad \text{LCL}_{\bar{x}} = \bar{\bar{x}} - A_2\bar{R}$$

where

$\bar{\bar{x}} =$ central line of the chart, which can be either the average of past sample means or a target value set for the process

$A_2 =$ constant to provide three-sigma limits for the sample mean

The values for A_2 are contained in Table 1. Note that the control limits use the value of $\bar{R}$; therefore, the $\bar{x}$-chart must be constructed *after* the process variability is in control.

To develop and use $\bar{x}$- and R-charts, do the following:

Step 1. Collect data on the variable quality measurement (such as time, weight, or diameter) and organize the data by sample number. Preferably, at least 20 samples of size n should be taken for use in constructing a control chart.

Step 2. Compute the range for each sample and the average range, $\bar{R}$, for the set of samples.

Step 3. Use Table 1 to determine the upper and lower control limits of the R-chart.

Step 4. Plot the sample ranges. If all are in control, proceed to step 5. Otherwise, find the assignable causes, correct them, and return to step 1.

Step 5. Calculate $\bar{x}$ for each sample and determine the central line of the chart, $\bar{\bar{x}}$.

Step 6. Use Table 1 to determine the parameters for $\text{UCL}_{\bar{x}}$ and $\text{LCL}_{\bar{x}}$ and construct the $\bar{x}$-chart.

Step 7. Plot the sample means. If all are in control, the process is in statistical control in terms of the process average and process variability. Continue

$\bar{x}$-chart

A chart used to see whether the process is generating output, on average, consistent with a target value set by management for the process or whether its current performance, with respect to the average of the performance measure, is consistent with past performance.

An analyst measures the diameter of a part with a micrometer. After he measures the sample, he plots the range on the control chart.

to take samples and monitor the process. If any are out of control, find the assignable causes, address them, and return to step 1. If no assignable causes are found after a diligent search, assume that the out-of-control points represent common causes of variation and continue to monitor the process.

| EXAMPLE 1 | Using $\bar{x}$- and R-Charts to Monitor a Process |

MyOMLab

Active Model 5.1 in MyOMLab provides additional insight on the x-bar and R-charts and their uses for the metal screw problem.

MyOMLab

Tutor 5.1 in MyOMLab provides a new example to practice the use of x-bar and R-charts.

The management of West Allis Industries is concerned about the production of a special metal screw used by several of the company's largest customers. The diameter of the screw is critical to the customers. Data from five samples appear in the accompanying table. The sample size is 4. Is the process in statistical control?

SOLUTION

Step 1: For simplicity, we use only 5 samples. In practice, more than 20 samples would be desirable. The data are shown in the following table.

DATA FOR THE $\bar{x}$- AND R-CHARTS: OBSERVATIONS OF SCREW DIAMETER (IN.)

| Sample Number | Observations | | | | R | $\bar{x}$ |
	1	2	3	4		
1	0.5014	0.5022	0.5009	0.5027	0.0018	0.5018
2	0.5021	0.5041	0.5024	0.5020	0.0021	0.5027
3	0.5018	0.5026	0.5035	0.5023	0.0017	0.5026
4	0.5008	0.5034	0.5024	0.5015	0.0026	0.5020
5	0.5041	0.5056	0.5034	0.5047	0.0022	0.5045
				Average	0.0021	0.5027

Step 2: Compute the range for each sample by subtracting the lowest value from the highest value. For example, in sample 1 the range is $0.5027 - 0.5009 = 0.0018$ in. Similarly, the ranges for samples 2, 3, 4, and 5 are 0.0021, 0.0017, 0.0026, and 0.0022 in., respectively. As shown in the table, $\bar{R} = 0.0021$.

Step 3: To construct the R-chart, select the appropriate constants from Table 1 for a sample size of 4. The control limits are

$$UCL_R = D_4\bar{R} = 2.282(0.0021) = 0.00479 \text{ in.}$$

$$LCL_R = D_3\bar{R} = 0(0.0021) = 0 \text{ in.}$$

Step 4: Plot the ranges on the R-chart, as shown in Figure 10. None of the sample ranges falls outside the control limits. Consequently, the process variability is in statistical control. If any of the sample ranges fall outside of the limits, or an unusual pattern appears (see Figure 9), we would search for the causes of the excessive variability, address them, and repeat step 1.

FIGURE 10 ▶

Range Chart from the *OM Explorer* $\bar{x}$- and *R-Chart* Solver, Showing that the Process Variability Is In Control

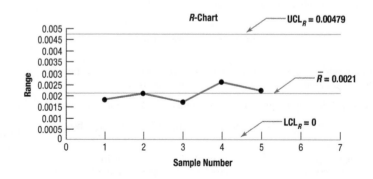

Step 5: Compute the mean for each sample. For example, the mean for sample 1 is

$$\frac{0.5014 + 0.5022 + 0.5009 + 0.5027}{4} = 0.5018 \text{ in.}$$

Similarly, the means of samples 2, 3, 4, and 5 are 0.5027, 0.5026, 0.5020, and 0.5045 in., respectively. As shown in the table, $\bar{\bar{x}} = 0.5027$.

Step 6: Now, construct the $\bar{x}$-chart for the process average. The average screw diameter is 0.5027 in., and the average range is 0.0021 in., so use $\bar{\bar{x}} = 0.5027$, $\bar{R} = 0.0021$, and A_2 from Table 1 for a sample size of 4 to construct the control limits:

$$\text{UCL}_{\bar{x}} = \bar{\bar{x}} + A_2\bar{R} = 0.5027 + 0.729(0.0021) = 0.5042 \text{ in.}$$

$$\text{LCL}_{\bar{x}} = \bar{\bar{x}} - A_2\bar{R} = 0.5027 - 0.729(0.0021) = 0.5012 \text{ in.}$$

Step 7: Plot the sample means on the control chart, as shown in Figure 11.

The mean of sample 5 falls above the UCL, indicating that the process average is out of statistical control and that assignable causes must be explored, perhaps using a cause-and-effect diagram.

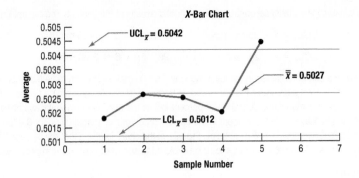

◀ **FIGURE 11**
The *x*-bar Chart from the *OM Explore $\bar{x}$-* and *R-Chart* Solver for the Metal Screw, Showing that Sample 5 Is Out of Control

DECISION POINT

A new employee operated the lathe machine that makes the screw on the day sample 5 was taken. To solve the problem, management initiated a training session for the employee. Subsequent samples showed that the process was back in statistical control.

If the standard deviation of the process distribution is known, another form of the $\bar{x}$-chart may be used:

$$\text{UCL}_{\bar{x}} = \bar{\bar{x}} + z\sigma_{\bar{x}} \quad \text{and} \quad \text{LCL}_{\bar{x}} = \bar{\bar{x}} - z\sigma_{\bar{x}}$$

where

$\sigma_{\bar{x}} = \sigma/\sqrt{n} =$ standard deviation of sample means

$\sigma =$ standard deviation of the process distribution

$n =$ sample size

$\bar{\bar{x}} =$ central line of the chart, which can be either the average of past sample means or a target value set for the process

$z =$ normal deviate (number of standard deviations from the average)

The analyst can use an R-chart to be sure that the process variability is in control before constructing the $\bar{x}$-chart. The advantage of using this form of the $\bar{x}$-chart is that the analyst can adjust the spread of the control limits by changing the value of z. This approach can be useful for balancing the effects of type I and type II errors.

| EXAMPLE 2 | Designing an $\bar{x}$-Chart Using the Process Standard Deviation |

The Sunny Dale Bank monitors the time required to serve customers at the drive-by window because it is an important quality factor in competing with other banks in the city. After analyzing the data gathered in an extensive study of the window operation, bank management determined that the mean time to process a customer at the peak demand period is 5 minutes, with a standard deviation of 1.5 minutes. Management wants to monitor the mean time to process a customer by periodically using a sample size of six customers. Assume that the process variability is in statistical control. Design an $\bar{x}$-chart that has a type I error of 5 percent. That is, set the control limits so that there is a 2.5 percent chance a sample result will fall below the LCL and a 2.5 percent chance that a sample result will fall above the UCL. After several weeks of sampling, two successive samples came in at 3.70 and 3.68 minutes, respectively. Is the customer service process in statistical control?

SOLUTION

$$\bar{\bar{x}} = 5.0 \text{ minutes}$$

$$\sigma = 1.5 \text{ minutes}$$

$$n = 6 \text{ customers}$$

$$z = 1.96$$

The process variability is in statistical control, so we proceed directly to the $\bar{x}$-chart. The control limits are

$$UCL_{\bar{x}} = \bar{\bar{x}} + z\sigma/\sqrt{n} = 5.0 + 1.96(1.5)/\sqrt{6} = 6.20 \text{ minutes}$$

$$LCL_{\bar{x}} = \bar{\bar{x}} - z\sigma/\sqrt{n} = 5.0 - 1.96(1.5)/\sqrt{6} = 3.80 \text{ minutes}$$

The value for z can be obtained in the following way. The normal distribution table (see Appendix 1) gives the proportion of the total area under the normal curve from $-\infty$ to z. We want a type I error of 5 percent, or 2.5 percent of the curve above the UCL and 2.5 percent below the LCL. Consequently, we need to find the z value in the table that leaves only 2.5 percent in the upper portion of the normal curve (or 0.9750 in the table). The value is 1.96. The two new samples are below the LCL of the chart, implying that the average time to serve a customer has dropped. Assignable causes should be explored to see what caused the improvement.

DECISION POINT

Management studied the time period over which the samples were taken and found that the supervisor of the process was experimenting with some new procedures. Management decided to make the new procedures a permanent part of the customer service process. After all employees were trained in the new procedures, new samples were taken and the control chart reconstructed.

Control Charts for Attributes

Two charts commonly used for performance measures based on attributes measures are the p- and c-chart. The p-chart is used for controlling the proportion of defects generated by the process. The c-chart is used for controlling the number of defects when more than one defect can be present in a service or product.

p-Charts The **p-chart** is a commonly used control chart for attributes. The performance characteristic is counted rather than measured, and the entire service or item can be declared good or defective. For example, in the banking industry, the attributes counted might be the number of nonendorsed deposits or the number of incorrect financial statements sent to customers. The method involves selecting a random sample, inspecting each item in it, and calculating the sample proportion defective, p, which is the number of defective units divided by the sample size.

Sampling for a p-chart involves a "yes/no" decision: The process output either is or is not defective. The underlying statistical distribution is based on the binomial distribution. However, for large sample sizes, the normal distribution provides a good approximation to it. The standard deviation of the distribution of proportion defectives, σ_p, is

$$\sigma_p = \sqrt{\bar{p}(1 - \bar{p})/n}$$

p-chart

A chart used for controlling the proportion of defective services or products generated by the process.

where

n = sample size
$\bar{p}$ = central line on the chart, which can be either the historical average population proportion defective or a target value

We can use σ_p to arrive at the upper and lower control limits for a p-chart:

$$\text{UCL}_p = \bar{p} + z\sigma_p \quad \text{and} \quad \text{LCL}_p = \bar{p} - z\sigma_p$$

where

z = normal deviate (number of standard deviations from the average)

The chart is used in the following way. Periodically, a random sample of size n is taken, and the number of defective services or products is counted. The number of defectives is divided by the sample size to get a sample proportion defective, p, which is plotted on the chart. When a sample proportion defective falls outside the control limits, the analyst assumes that the proportion defective generated by the process has changed and searches for the assignable cause. Observations falling below the LCL_p indicate that the process may actually have improved. The analyst may find no assignable cause because it is always possible that an out-of-control proportion occurred randomly. However, if the analyst discovers assignable causes, those sample data should not be used to calculate the control limits for the chart.

EXAMPLE 3	Using a *p*-Chart to Monitor a Process

The operations manager of the booking services department of Hometown Bank is concerned about the number of wrong customer account numbers recorded by Hometown personnel. Each week a random sample of 2,500 deposits is taken, and the number of incorrect account numbers is recorded. The results for the past 12 weeks are shown in the following table. Is the booking process out of statistical control? Use three-sigma control limits, which will provide a Type I error of 0.26 percent.

MyOMLab

Active Model 5.2 in MyOMLab provides additional insight on the *p*-chart and its uses for the booking services department.

MyOMLab

Tutor 5.2 in MyOMLab provides a new example to practice the use of the *p*-chart.

Sample Number	Wrong Account Numbers	Sample Number	Wrong Account Numbers
1	15	7	24
2	12	8	7
3	19	9	10
4	2	10	17
5	19	11	15
6	4	12	3
			Total 147

SOLUTION

Step 1: Using this sample data to calculate $\bar{p}$

$$\bar{p} = \frac{\text{Total defectives}}{\text{Total number of observations}} = \frac{147}{12(2,500)} = 0.0049$$

$$\sigma_p = \sqrt{\bar{p}(1-\bar{p})/n} = \sqrt{0.0049(1-0.0049)/2,500} = 0.0014$$

$$\text{UCL}_p = \bar{p} + z\sigma_p = 0.0049 + 3(0.0014) = 0.0091$$

$$\text{LCL}_p = \bar{p} - z\sigma_p = 0.0049 - 3(0.0014) = 0.0007$$

Step 2: Calculate each sample proportion defective. For sample 1, the proportion of defectives is 15/2,500 = 0.0060.

Step 3: Plot each sample proportion defective on the chart, as shown in Figure 12.

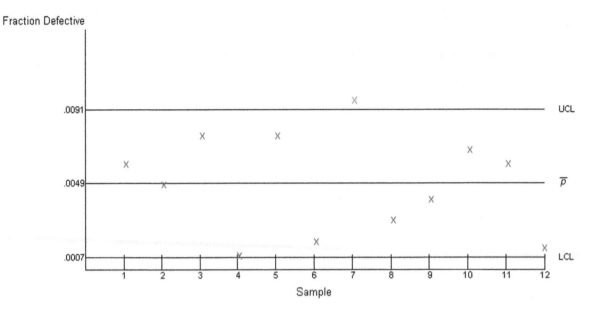

Fraction Defective

▲ **FIGURE 12**
The *p*-Chart from POM for Windows for Wrong Account Numbers, Showing that Sample 7 Is Out of Control

Sample 7 exceeds the UCL; thus, the process is out of control and the reasons for the poor performance that week should be determined.

DECISION POINT

Management explored the circumstances when sample 7 was taken. The encoding machine used to print the account numbers on the checks was defective that week. The following week the machine was repaired; however, the recommended preventive maintenance on the machine was not performed for months prior to the failure. Management reviewed the performance of the maintenance department and instituted changes to the maintenance procedures for the encoding machine. After the problem was corrected, an analyst recalculated the control limits using the data without sample 7. Subsequent weeks were sampled, and the booking process was determined to be in statistical control. Consequently, the *p*-chart provides a tool to indicate when a process needs adjustment.

c-chart

A chart used for controlling the number of defects when more than one defect can be present in a service or product.

***c*-Charts** Sometimes services or products have more than one defect. For example, a roll of carpeting may have several defects, such as tufted or discolored fibers or stains from the production process. Other situations in which more than one defect may occur include accidents at a particular intersection, bubbles in a television picture face panel, and complaints from a patron at a hotel. When management is interested in reducing the number of defects per unit or service encounter, another type of control chart, the ***c*-chart**, is useful.

The underlying sampling distribution for a *c*-chart is the Poisson distribution. The Poisson distribution is based on the assumption that defects occur over a continuous region on the surface of a product or a continuous time interval during the provision of a service. It further assumes that the probability of two or more defects at any one location on the surface or at any instant of time is negligible. The mean of the distribution is $\bar{c}$ and the standard deviation is $\sqrt{\bar{c}}$. A useful tactic is to use the normal approximation to the Poisson so that the central line of the chart is $\bar{c}$ and the control limits are

$$\mathrm{UCL}_c = \bar{c} + z\sqrt{\bar{c}} \quad \text{and} \quad \mathrm{LCL}_c = \bar{c} - z\sqrt{\bar{c}}$$

EXAMPLE 4	Using a *c*-Chart to Monitor Defects per Unit

The Woodland Paper Company produces paper for the newspaper industry. As a final step in the process, the paper passes through a machine that measures various product quality characteristics. When the paper production process is in control, it averages 20 defects per roll.

a. Set up a control chart for the number of defects per roll. For this example, use two-sigma control limits.
b. Five rolls had the following number of defects: 16, 21, 17, 22, and 24, respectively. The sixth roll, using pulp from a different supplier, had 5 defects. Is the paper production process in control?

MyOMLab

Tutor 5.3 in MyOMLab provides a new example to practice the use of the *c*-chart.

SOLUTION

a. The average number of defects per roll is 20. Therefore

$$UCL_c = \bar{c} + z\sqrt{\bar{c}} = 20 + 2(\sqrt{20}) = 28.94$$

$$LCL_c = \bar{c} - z\sqrt{\bar{c}} = 20 - 2(\sqrt{20}) = 11.06$$

The control chart is shown in Figure 13.

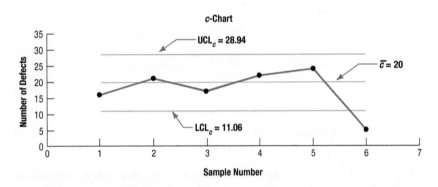

c-Chart

◄ **FIGURE 13**
The *c*-Chart from the *OM Explorer c-Chart* Solver for Defects per Roll of Paper

b. Because the first five rolls had defects that fell within the control limits, the process is still in control. The sixth roll's five defects, however, is below than the LCL, and therefore, the process is technically "out of control." The control chart indicates that something good has happened.

DECISION POINT

The supplier for the first five samples has been used by Woodland Paper for many years. The supplier for the sixth sample is new to the company. Management decided to continue using the new supplier for a while, monitoring the number of defects to see whether it stays low. If the number remains below the LCL for 20 consecutive samples, management will make the switch permanent and recalculate the control chart parameters.

Process Capability

Statistical process control techniques help managers achieve and maintain a process distribution that does not change in terms of its mean and variance. The control limits on the control charts signal when the mean or variability of the process changes. However, a process that is in statistical control may not be producing services or products according to their design specifications because the control limits are based on the mean and variability of the *sampling distribution*, not the design specifications. **Process capability** refers to the ability of the process to meet the design specifications for a service or product. Design specifications often are expressed as a **nominal value**, or target, and a **tolerance**, or allowance above or below the nominal value.

For example, the administrator of an intensive care unit lab might have a nominal value for the turnaround time of results to the attending physicians of 25 minutes and a tolerance of ±5 minutes because of the need for speed under life-threatening conditions. The tolerance gives an *upper specification* of 30 minutes and a *lower specification* of 20 minutes. The lab process must be capable of providing the results of analyses within these specifications; otherwise, it will produce a certain proportion of "defects." The administrator is also interested in detecting occurrences of turnaround times of less than 20 minutes because something might be learned that can be built into the lab process in the future. For the present, the physicians are pleased with results that arrive within 20 to 30 minutes.

nominal value

A target for design specifications.

process capability

The ability of the process to meet the design specifications for a service or product.

tolerance

An allowance above or below the nominal value.

Defining Process Capability

Figure 14 shows the relationship between a process distribution and the upper and lower specifications for the lab process turnaround time under two conditions. In Figure 14(a), the process is capable because the extremes of the process distribution fall within the upper and lower specifications. In Figure 14(b), the process is not capable because the lab process produces too many reports with long turnaround times.

FIGURE 14 ▶
The Relationship Between a
Process Distribution and Upper
and Lower Specifications

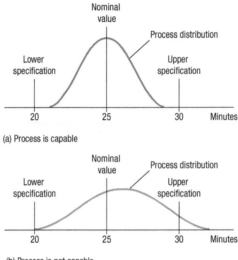

(a) Process is capable

(b) Process is not capable

Figure 14 shows clearly why managers are so concerned with reducing process variability. The less variability—represented by lower standard deviations—the less frequently bad output is produced. Figure 15 shows what reducing variability implies for a process distribution that is a normal probability distribution. The firm with two-sigma performance (the specification limits equal the process distribution mean ± 2 standard deviations) produces 4.56 percent defects, or 45,600 defects per million. The firm with four-sigma performance produces only 0.0063 percent defects, or 63 defects per million. Finally, the firm with six-sigma performance produces only 0.0000002 percent defects, or 0.002 defects per million.[1]

FIGURE 15 ▼
Effects of Reducing Variability on
Process Capability

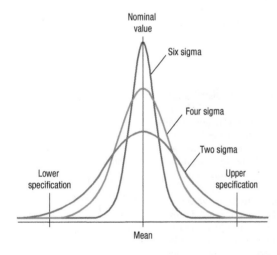

How can a manager determine quantitatively whether a process is capable? Two measures commonly are used in practice to assess the capability of a process: the process capability index and the process capability ratio.

Process Capability Index   The **process capability index**, C_{pk}, is defined as

$$C_{pk} = \text{Minimum of} \left[\frac{\bar{\bar{x}} - \text{Lower specification}}{3\sigma}, \frac{\text{Upper specification} - \bar{\bar{x}}}{3\sigma} \right]$$

where

$\sigma = $ standard deviation of the process distribution

The process capability index measures how well the process is centered as well as whether the variability is acceptable. As a general rule, most values of any process distribution fall within ± 3 standard deviations of the mean. Consequently, ± 3 standard deviations is used as the benchmark. Because the process capability index is concerned with how well the process distribution is centered relative to the specifications, it checks to see if the process average is at least three standard deviations

---

[1]Our discussion assumes that the process distribution has no assignable causes. Six Sigma programs, however, define defect performance with the assumption that the process average has moved 1.5 standard deviations. In such a case, there would be 3.4 defects per million. See **www.isixsigma.com** for the rationale behind that assumption.

from the upper and lower specifications. We take the minimum of the two ratios because it gives the *worst-case* situation.

The process capability index must be compared to a critical value to judge whether a process is capable. Firms striving to achieve three-sigma performance use a critical value for the ratio of 1.0. A firm targeting four-sigma performance will use 1.33 (or 4/3), a firm targeting five-sigma performance will use 1.67 (or 5/3), and a firm striving for six-sigma performance will use 2.00 (or 6/3). Processes producing services or products with less than three-sigma performance will have C_{pk} values less than 1.0.

If a process passes the process capability index test, we can declare the process is capable. Suppose a firm desires its processes to produce at the level of four-sigma performance. If C_{pk} is greater than or equal to the critical value of 1.33, we can say the process is capable. If C_{pk} is less than the critical value, either the process average is too close to one of the tolerance limits and is generating defective output, or the process variability is too large. To find out whether the variability is the culprit, we need another test.

Process Capability Ratio   If a process fails the process capability *index* test, we need a quick test to see if the process variability is causing the problem. If a process is *capable*, it has a process distribution whose extreme values fall within the upper and lower specifications for a service or product. For example, if the process distribution is normal, 99.74 percent of the values fall within ± 3 standard deviations. In other words, the range of values of the quality measure generated by a process is approximately 6 standard deviations of the process distribution. Hence, if a process is capable at the three-sigma level, the difference between the upper and lower specification, called the *tolerance width*, must be greater than 6 standard deviations. The **process capability ratio**, C_p, is defined as

$$C_p = \frac{\text{Upper specification} - \text{Lower specification}}{6\sigma}$$

Suppose management wants four-sigma capability in their processes, and a process just failed the process capability index test at that level. A C_p value of 1.33, say, implies that the variability of the process is at the level of four-sigma quality and that the process is capable of consistently producing outputs within specifications, assuming that the process is centered. Because C_p passed the test, but C_{pk} did not, we can assume that the problem is that the process is not centered adequately.

Using Continuous Improvement to Determine the Capability of a Process

To determine the capability of a process to produce outputs within the tolerances, use the following steps.

Step 1.   Collect data on the process output, and calculate the mean and the standard deviation of the process output distribution.

Step 2.   Use the data from the process distribution to compute process control charts, such as an $\bar{x}$- and an R-chart.

Step 3.   Take a series of at least 20 consecutive random samples of size n from the process and plot the results on the control charts. If the sample statistics are within the control limits of the charts, the process is in statistical control. If the process is not in statistical control, look for assignable causes and eliminate them. Recalculate the mean and standard deviation of the process distribution and the control limits for the charts. Continue until the process is in statistical control.

Step 4.   Calculate the process capability *index*. If the results are acceptable, the process is capable and document any changes made to the process; continue to monitor the output by using the control charts. If the results are unacceptable, calculate the process capability *ratio*. If the results are acceptable, the process variability is fine and management should focus on centering the process. If the results of the process capability ratio are unacceptable, management should focus on reducing the variability in the process until it passes the test. As changes are made, recalculate the mean and standard deviation of the process distribution and the control limits for the charts and return to step 3.

Quality Engineering

Successful quality performance is often more than process improvement; it also involves service/product design. Originated by Genichi Taguchi, **quality engineering** is an approach that involves

---

process capability index, C_{pk}

An index that measures the potential for a process to generate defective outputs relative to either upper or lower specifications.

process capability ratio, C_p

The tolerance width divided by six standard deviations.

quality engineering

An approach originated by Genichi Taguchi that involves combining engineering and statistical methods to reduce costs and improve quality by optimizing product design and manufacturing processes.

EXAMPLE 5	Assessing the Process Capability of the Intensive Care Unit Lab

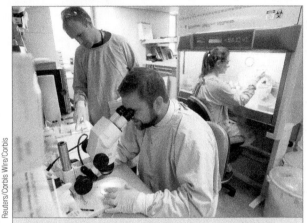

A doctor examines a specimen through his microscope in a lab at St. Vincent's Hospital.

The intensive care unit lab process has an average turnaround time of 26.2 minutes and a standard deviation of 1.35 minutes. The nominal value for this service is 25 minutes with an upper specification limit of 30 minutes and a lower specification limit of 20 minutes. The administrator of the lab wants to have four-sigma performance for her lab. Is the lab process capable of this level of performance?

SOLUTION

The administrator began by taking a quick check to see if the process is capable by applying the process capability index:

$$\text{Lower specification calculation} = \frac{26.2 - 20.0}{3(1.35)} = 1.53$$

$$\text{Upper specification calculation} = \frac{30.0 - 26.2}{3(1.35)} = 0.94$$

$$C_{pk} = \text{Minimum of } [1.53, 0.94] = 0.94$$

Since the target value for four-sigma performance is 1.33, the process capability index told her that the process was not capable. However, she did not know whether the problem was the variability of the process, the centering of the process, or both. The options available to improve the process depended on what is wrong.

She next checked the process variability with the process capability ratio:

$$C_p = \frac{30.0 - 20.0}{6(1.35)} = 1.23$$

The process variability did not meet the four-sigma target of 1.33. Consequently, she initiated a study to see where variability was introduced into the process. Two activities, report preparation and specimen slide preparation, were identified as having inconsistent procedures. These procedures were modified to provide consistent performance. New data were collected and the average turnaround was now 26.1 minutes with a standard deviation of 1.20 minutes. She now had the process variability at the four-sigma level of performance, as indicated by the process capability ratio:

$$C_p = \frac{30.0 - 20.0}{6(1.20)} = 1.39$$

However, the process capability index indicated additional problems to resolve:

$$C_{pk} = \text{Minimum of } \left[\frac{(26.1 - 20.0)}{3(1.20)}, \frac{(30.0 - 26.1)}{3(1.20)} \right] = 1.08$$

DECISION POINT

The lab process was still not at the level of four-sigma performance on turnaround time. The lab administrator searched for the causes of the off-center turnaround time distribution. She discovered periodic backlogs at a key piece of testing equipment. Acquiring a second machine provided the capacity to reduce the turnaround times to four-sigma capability.

MyOMLab

Active Model 5.3 in MyOMLab provides additional insight on the process capability problem at the intensive care unit lab.

MyOMLab

Tutor 5.4 in MyOMLab provides a new example to practice the process capability measures.

quality loss function

The rationale that a service or product that barely conforms to the specifications is more like a defective service or product than a perfect one.

combining engineering and statistical methods to reduce costs and improve quality by optimizing product design and manufacturing processes. Taguchi believes that unwelcome costs are associated with *any* deviation from a quality characteristic's target value. Taguchi's view is that the **quality loss function** is zero when the quality characteristic of the service or product is exactly on the target value, and that the quality loss function value rises exponentially as the quality characteristic gets closer to the specification limits. The rationale is that a service or product that barely conforms to the specifications is more like a defective service or product than a perfect one. Figure 16 shows Taguchi's quality loss function schematically. Taguchi concluded that managers should continually search for ways to reduce *all* variability from the target value in the production process and not be content with merely adhering to specification limits. See **http://elsmar.com/Taguchi.html** for a detailed discussion and animation of the Taguchi Loss Function.

International Quality Documentation Standards

Once a company has gone through the effort of making its processes capable, it must document its level of quality so as to better market its services or products. This documentation of quality is especially important in international trade. However, if each country had its own set of standards, companies selling in international markets would have difficulty complying with quality documentation standards in each country where they did business. To overcome this problem, the International Organization for Standardization devised a family of standards called ISO 9000 for companies doing business in the European Union. Subsequently, ISO 14000 was devised for environmental management systems and ISO 26000 for guidance on social responsibility.

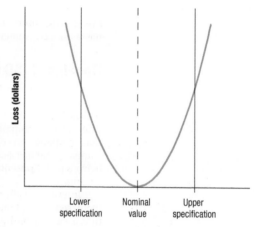

▲ FIGURE 16
Taguchi's Quality Loss Function

The ISO 9001:2008 Documentation Standards

ISO 9001:2008 is the latest update of the ISO 9000 standards governing documentation of a quality program. According to the International Organization for Standardization, the ISO 9001:2008 standards address *quality management* by specifying what the firm does to fulfill the customer's quality requirements and applicable regulatory requirements, while aiming to enhance customer satisfaction and achieve continual improvement of its performance in pursuit of these objectives. Companies become certified by proving to a qualified external examiner that they comply with all the requirements. Once certified, companies are listed in a directory so that potential customers can see which companies are certified and to what level. Compliance with ISO 9001:2008 standards says *nothing* about the actual quality of a product. Rather, it indicates to customers that companies can provide documentation to support whatever claims they make about quality. As of 2009, more than 1 million organizations worldwide have been certified in the ISO 9000 family of documentation standards.

ISO 9001:2008

A set of standards governing documentation of a quality program.

ISO 14000:2004 Environmental Management System

The **ISO 14000:2004** standards require documentation of a firm's environmental program. According to the International Organization for Standardization, the ISO 14000:2004 family addresses *environmental management* by specifying what the firm does to minimize harmful effects on the environment caused by its activities, and to achieve continual improvement of its environmental performance. The documentation standards require participating companies to keep track of their raw materials use and their generation, treatment, and disposal of hazardous wastes. Although not specifying what each company is allowed to emit, the standards require companies to prepare a plan for ongoing improvement in their environmental performance. ISO 14000:2004 covers a number of areas, including the following:

ISO 14000:2004

Documentation standards that require participating companies to keep track of their raw materials use and their generation, treatment, and disposal of hazardous wastes.

- *Environmental Management System.* Requires a plan to improve performance in resource use and pollutant output.
- *Environmental Performance Evaluation.* Specifies guidelines for the certification of companies.
- *Environmental Labeling.* Defines terms such as *recyclable, energy efficient,* and *safe for the ozone layer.*
- *Life-Cycle Assessment.* Evaluates the lifetime environmental impact from the manufacture, use, and disposal of a product.

To maintain their certification, companies must be inspected by outside, private auditors on a regular basis. As of 2010, more than 200,000 organizations in 155 countries have been certified for ISO 14000.

ISO 26000:2010 Social Responsibility Guidelines

The **ISO 26000:2010** guidelines, according to the International Organization for Standards, provide harmonized, globally relevant guidance on social responsibility for private and public sector organizations based on international consensus among experts. A firm does not get certified in ISO 26000; the guidelines are voluntary and are intended to promote best practice in ethical behavior in business. The seven core subjects of social responsibility covered in the guidelines are (1) human rights, (2) labor practices, (3) the environment, (4) fair operating practices,

ISO 26000:2010

International guidelines for organizational social responsibility.

(5) consumer issues, (6) community involvement and development, and (7) the organization. In this way the international community is encouraging ethical business behavior between businesses and consumers.

Benefits of ISO Certification

Completing the certification process can take as long as 18 months and involve many hours of management and employee time. The cost of certification can exceed $1 million for large companies. Despite the expense and commitment involved in ISO certification, it bestows significant external and internal benefits. The external benefits come from the potential sales advantage that companies in compliance have. Companies looking for a supplier will more likely select a company that has demonstrated compliance with ISO documentation standards, all other factors being equal. Consequently, more and more firms are seeking certification to gain a competitive advantage.

Internal benefits can be substantial. Registered companies report an average of 48 percent increased profitability and 76 percent improvement in marketing. The British Standards Institute, a leading third-party auditor, estimates that most ISO 9000-registered companies experience a 10 percent reduction in the cost of producing a product because of the quality improvements they make while striving to meet the documentation requirements. Certification in ISO 9001:2008 requires a company to analyze and document its procedures, which is necessary in any event for implementing continuous improvement, employee involvement, and similar programs. The guidelines and requirements of the ISO documentation standards provide companies with a jump-start in pursuing TQM programs.

Baldrige Performance Excellence Program

Regardless of where a company does business, it is clear that all organizations have to produce high-quality products and services if they are to be competitive. To emphasize that point, in August 1987 the U.S. Congress signed into law the Malcolm Baldrige National Quality Improvement Act, creating the Malcolm Baldrige National Quality Award, which is now entitled the **Baldrige Performance Excellence Program** (**www.quality.nist.gov**). Named for the late secretary of commerce, who was a strong proponent of enhancing quality as a means of reducing the trade deficit, the award promotes, recognizes, and publicizes quality strategies and achievements.

The application and review process for the Baldrige award is rigorous. However, the act of preparing the application itself is often a major benefit to organizations because it helps firms define what *quality* means for them. According to the U.S. Commerce Department's National Institute of Standards and Technology (NIST), investing in quality principles and performance excellence pays off in increased productivity, satisfied employees and customers, and improved profitability, both for customers and investors. The seven major criteria for the award are the following:

1. *Leadership.* Describes how senior leaders' actions guide and sustain the organization and how they communicate with the workforce and encourage high performance.

2. *Strategic Planning.* Describes how the organization establishes its strategy to address its strategic challenges, leverage its strategic advantages, and summarizes the organization's key strategic objectives and their related goals.

3. *Customer Focus.* Describes how the organization determines its service or product offerings and the mechanisms to support the customers' use of them.

4. *Measurement, Analysis, and Knowledge Management.* Describes how the organization measures, analyzes, reviews, and improves its performance through the use of data and information at all levels of the organization.

5. *Workforce Focus.* Describes how the organization engages, compensates, and rewards its workers and how they are developed to achieve high performance.

6. *Operations Focus.* Describes how the organization designs its work systems and determines its key processes to deliver customer value, prepare for potential emergencies, and achieve organizational success and sustainability.

7. *Results.* Describe the organization's performance and improvement in five categories: products and processes, customer focus, workforce focus, leadership and governance, and financial and market.

Customer satisfaction underpins these seven criteria. Criterion 7, Results, is given the most weight in selecting winners.

Baldrige Performance Excellence Program

A program named for the late secretary of commerce, Malcolm Baldrige, who was a strong proponent of enhancing quality as a means of reducing the trade deficit; organizations vie for an award that promotes, recognizes, and publicizes quality strategies and achievements.

LEARNING GOALS IN REVIEW

1 **Define the four major costs of quality.** See the section "Costs of Quality".

2 **Describe the role of ethics in the quality of services and products.** We explain how deceptive business practices can affect a customer's experiences and why the costs of quality should be balanced with ethical considerations in the section "Ethics and Quality".

3 **Explain the basic principles of TQM programs.** See the section "Total Quality Management". Focus on the five customer definitions of quality, Managerial Practice 1, which shows how one company matched processes to the five definitions, the importance of employee involvement, and how continuous improvement works. The key figures are Figures 1 and 2.

4 **Explain the basic principles of Six Sigma Programs.** We have summarized the essence of these important programs in the section "Six Sigma". Be sure to understand Figure 3, which shows the goals of Six Sigma, and Figure 4, which provides the improvement model. Figure 5 shows how TQM or Six Sigma works in a supply chain through the tactic of acceptance sampling.

5 **Describe how to construct control charts and use them to determine whether a process is out of statistical control.** See the section "Statistical Process Control". Understanding Figures 6 and 7 is key to understanding the methods to follow. The section "Statistical Process Control Methods", shows you how to determine if a process is in statistical control. Study Examples 1 to 5 as well as Solved Problems 1 to 3.

6 **Describe how to determine whether a process is capable of producing a service or product to specifications.** The major take-away in the chapter is found in the section "Process Capability". Be sure you understand Figures 4 and 5; study Example 5 and Solved Problem 4.

MyOMLab helps and assesses students with 16 problems on *x*-bar and *R*-bar Charts, *p*-charts, *c*-Charts, and Process Capability.

MyOMLab Resources	Titles	Link to the Book
Video	*Starwood: Process Performance and Quality*	Costs of Quality; Total Quality Management; Six Sigma
	Christchurch Parkroyal TQM	Costs of Quality; Total Quality Management
Active Model	5.1 *x*-bar and *R*-Charts	Control Charts for Variables; Example 1
	5.2 *p*-Chart	Control Charts for Attributes; Example 3
	5.3 Process Capability	Process Capability; Example 5
OM Explorer Solvers	*c*-Charts	Control Charts for Attributes; Example 4; Figure 13; Solved Problem 3
	p-Charts	Control Charts for Attributes; Example 3; Solved Problem 2
	Process Capability	Process Capability; Example 5; Solved Problem 4
	R- and *x*-bar Charts	Control Charts for Variables; Example 1; Figure 10 and Figure 11; Solved Problem 1
OM Explorer Tutors	5.1 *R*- and *x*-bar Charts	Control Charts for Variables; Example 1
	5.2 *p*-Charts	Control Charts for Attributes; Example 3
	5.3 *c*-Charts	Control Charts for Attributes; Example 4
	5.4 Process Capability	Process Capability; Example 5
POM for Windows	*p*-Charts	Control Charts for Attributes; Example 3; Figure 12; Solved Problem 2
	x-bar Charts	Control Charts for Variables; Example 1; Example 2; Solved Problem 1
	c-Charts	Control Charts for Attributes; Example 4; Solved Problem 3
	Process Capability	Process Capability; Example 5; Solved Problem 4
	Acceptance Sampling	Acceptance Sampling
SimQuick Simulation Exercises	Circuit Board Process	Six-Sigma Improvement Model

MyOMLab Resources	Titles	Link to the Book
Tutor Exercises	5.1 x-bar and R-Chart with Target Weight of 7.04 oz.	Control Charts for Variables
	5.2 p-Chart When Changes in Sample Values	Control Charts for Attributes
	5.3 Process Capability with a Change in Process Average and Variability	Process Capability
Virtual Tours	1. Steinway Factory, Verne O. Powell Flutes	Total Quality Management; Six Sigma
	2. Beach Beat Surfboards	Total Quality Management
MyOMLab Supplements	G. Acceptance Sampling Plans	Acceptance Sampling
Internet Exercise	1. National Institute of Standards and Technology, and International Organization for Standardization	Baldrige Performance Excellence Award International Quality Documentation Standards
	2. SAS Scandinavian Airline	Total Quality Management
	3. Jack in the Box	Customer Satisfaction
	4. Maybach	Customer Satisfaction
	5. Bureau of Transportation Statistics	Statistical Process Control
Key Equations		
Image Library		

Key Equations

1. Sample mean: $\bar{x} = \dfrac{\sum\limits_{i=1}^{n} x_i}{n}$

2. Standard deviation of a sample:

$$\sigma = \sqrt{\frac{\sum\limits_{i=1}^{n}(x_i - \bar{x})^2}{n-1}} \text{ or } \sigma = \sqrt{\frac{\sum\limits_{i=1}^{n} x_i^2 - \dfrac{(\sum x_i)^2}{n}}{n-1}}$$

3. Control limits for variable process control charts

   a. R-chart, range of sample:

   $$\text{Upper control limit} = \text{UCL}_R = D_4 \bar{R}$$
   $$\text{Lower control limit} = \text{LCL}_R = D_3 \bar{R}$$

   b. $\bar{x}$-chart, sample mean:

   $$\text{Upper control limit} = \text{UCL}_{\bar{x}} = \bar{\bar{x}} + A_2 \bar{R}$$
   $$\text{Lower control limit} = \text{LCL}_{\bar{x}} = \bar{\bar{x}} - A_2 \bar{R}$$

   c. When the standard deviation of the process distribution, σ, is known:

   $$\text{Upper control limit} = \text{UCL}_{\bar{x}} = \bar{\bar{x}} + z\sigma_{\bar{x}}$$
   $$\text{Lower control limit} = \text{LCL}_{\bar{x}} = \bar{\bar{x}} - z\sigma_{\bar{x}}$$

   where

   $$\sigma_{\bar{x}} = \frac{\sigma}{\sqrt{n}}$$

4. Control limits for attribute process control charts

 a. *p*-chart, proportion defective:

$$\text{Upper control limit} = \text{UCL}_p = \bar{p} + z\sigma_p$$
$$\text{Lower control limit} = \text{LCL}_p = \bar{p} - z\sigma_p$$

 where

$$\sigma_p = \sqrt{\bar{p}(1 - \bar{p})/n}$$

 b. *c*-chart, number of defects:

$$\text{Upper control limit} = \text{UCL}_c = \bar{c} + z\sqrt{\bar{c}}$$
$$\text{Lower control limit} = \text{LCL}_c = \bar{c} - z\sqrt{\bar{c}}$$

5. Process capability index:

$$C_{pk} = \text{Minimum of} \left[\frac{\bar{\bar{x}} - \text{Lower specification}}{3\sigma}, \frac{\text{Upper specification} - \bar{\bar{x}}}{3\sigma} \right]$$

6. Process capability ratio:

$$C_p = \frac{\text{Upper specification} - \text{Lower specification}}{6\sigma}$$

Key Terms

acceptable quality level (AQL)
acceptance sampling
appraisal costs
assignable causes of variation
attributes
Baldrige Performance Excellence
  Program
Black Belt
c-chart
common causes of variation
continuous improvement
control chart
defect
employee empowerment
external failure costs
Green Belt

internal failure costs
ISO 9001:2008
ISO 14000:2004
ISO 26000:2010
Master Black Belt
nominal value
p-chart
plan-do-study-act cycle
prevention costs
process capability
process capability index, C_{pk}
process capability ratio, C_p
quality
quality at the source
quality circles
quality engineering

quality loss function
R-chart
sample size
sampling plan
self-managed team
Six Sigma
special-purpose teams
statistical process control (SPC)
teams
tolerance
total quality management (TQM)
type I error
type II error
variables
warranty 159
x̄-chart

Solved Problem 1

The Watson Electric Company produces incandescent lightbulbs. The following data on the number of lumens for 40-watt lightbulbs were collected when the process was in control.

	OBSERVATION			
Sample	1	2	3	4
1	604	612	588	600
2	597	601	607	603
3	581	570	585	592
4	620	605	595	588
5	590	614	608	604

 a. Calculate control limits for an *R*-chart and an *x̄*-chart.

 b. Since these data were collected, some new employees were hired. A new sample obtained the following readings: 570, 603, 623, and 583. Is the process still in control?

SOLUTION

a. To calculate $\bar{x}$, compute the mean for each sample. To calculate R, subtract the lowest value in the sample from the highest value in the sample. For example, for sample 1,

$$\bar{x} = \frac{604 + 612 + 588 + 600}{4} = 601$$

$$R = 612 - 588 = 24$$

Sample	$\bar{x}$	R
1	601	24
2	602	10
3	582	22
4	602	32
5	604	24
Total	2,991	112
Average	$\bar{\bar{x}} = 598.2$	$\bar{R} = 22.4$

The R-chart control limits are

$$\text{UCL}_R = D_4\bar{R} = 2.282(22.4) = 51.12$$

$$\text{LCL}_R = D_3\bar{R} = 0(22.4) = 0$$

The $\bar{x}$-chart control limits are

$$\text{UCL}_{\bar{x}} = \bar{\bar{x}} + A_2\bar{R} = 598.2 + 0.729(22.4) = 614.53$$

$$\text{LCL}_{\bar{x}} = \bar{\bar{x}} - A_2\bar{R} = 598.2 - 0.729(22.4) = 581.87$$

b. First check to see whether the variability is still in control based on the new data. The range is 53 (or 623 − 570), which is outside the UCL for the R-chart. Since the process variability is out of control, it is meaningless to test for the process average using the current estimate for $\bar{R}$. A search for assignable causes inducing excessive variability must be conducted.

Solved Problem 2

The data processing department of the Arizona Bank has five data entry clerks. Each working day their supervisor verifies the accuracy of a random sample of 250 records. A record containing one or more errors is considered defective and must be redone. The results of the last 30 samples are shown in the table. All were checked to make sure that none was out of control.

Sample	Number of Defective Records	Sample	Number of Defective Records	Sample	Number of Defective Records	Sample	Number of Defective Records
1	7	9	6	17	12	24	7
2	5	10	13	18	4	25	13
3	19	11	18	19	6	26	10
4	10	12	5	20	11	27	14
5	11	13	16	21	17	28	6
6	8	14	4	22	12	29	11
7	12	15	11	23	6	30	9
8	9	16	8				
						Total	300

a. Based on these historical data, set up a *p*-chart using $z = 3$.

b. Samples for the next 4 days showed the following:

Sample	Number of Defective Records
Tues	17
Wed	15
Thurs	22
Fri	21

What is the supervisor's assessment of the data-entry process likely to be?

SOLUTION

a. From the table, the supervisor knows that the total number of defective records is 300 out of a total sample of 7,500 [or 30(250)]. Therefore, the central line of the chart is

$$\bar{p} = \frac{300}{7,500} = 0.04$$

The control limits are

$$UCL_p = \bar{p} + z\sqrt{\frac{\bar{p}(1 - \bar{p})}{n}} = 0.04 + 3\sqrt{\frac{0.04(0.96)}{250}} = 0.077$$

$$LCL_p = \bar{p} - z\sqrt{\frac{\bar{p}(1 - \bar{p})}{n}} = 0.04 - 3\sqrt{\frac{0.04(0.96)}{250}} = 0.003$$

b. Samples for the next 4 days showed the following:

Sample	Number of Defective Records	Proportion
Tues	17	0.068
Wed	15	0.060
Thurs	22	0.088
Fri	21	0.084

Samples for Thursday and Friday are out of control. The supervisor should look for the problem and, upon identifying it, take corrective action.

Solved Problem 3

The Minnow County Highway Safety Department monitors accidents at the intersection of Routes 123 and 14. Accidents at the intersection have averaged three per month.

a. Which type of control chart should be used? Construct a control chart with three-sigma control limits.

b. Last month, seven accidents occurred at the intersection. Is this sufficient evidence to justify a claim that something has changed at the intersection?

SOLUTION

a. The safety department cannot determine the number of accidents that did *not* occur, so it has no way to compute a proportion defective at the intersection. Therefore, the administrators must use a *c*-chart for which

$$UCL_c = \bar{c} + z\sqrt{\bar{c}} = 3 + 3\sqrt{3} = 8.20$$
$$LCL_c = \bar{c} - z\sqrt{\bar{c}} = 3 - 3\sqrt{3} = -2.196, \text{ adjusted to } 0$$

There cannot be a negative number of accidents, so the LCL in this case is adjusted to zero.

b. The number of accidents last month falls within the UCL and LCL of the chart. We conclude that no assignable causes are present and that the increase in accidents was due to chance.

Solved Problem 4

Pioneer Chicken advertises "lite" chicken with 30 percent fewer calories. (The pieces are 33 percent smaller.) The process average distribution for "lite" chicken breasts is 420 calories, with a standard deviation of the population of 25 calories. Pioneer randomly takes samples of six chicken breasts to measure calorie content.

a. Design an $\bar{x}$-chart using the process standard deviation. Use three-sigma limits.

b. The product design calls for the average chicken breast to contain 400 ± 100 calories. Calculate the process capability index (target = 1.33) and the process capability ratio. Interpret the results.

SOLUTION

a. For the process standard deviation of 25 calories, the standard deviation of the sample mean is

$$\sigma_{\bar{x}} = \frac{\sigma}{\sqrt{n}} = \frac{25}{\sqrt{6}} = 10.2 \text{ calories}$$

$$\text{UCL}_{\bar{x}} = \bar{\bar{x}} + z\sigma_{\bar{x}} = 420 + 3(10.2) = 450.6 \text{ calories}$$

$$\text{LCL}_{\bar{x}} = \bar{\bar{x}} - z\sigma_{\bar{x}} = 420 - 3(10.2) = 389.4 \text{ calories}$$

b. The process capability index is

$$C_{pk} = \text{Minimum of} \left[\frac{\bar{\bar{x}} - \text{Lower specification}}{3\sigma}, \frac{\text{Upper specification} - \bar{\bar{x}}}{3\sigma} \right]$$

$$= \text{Minimum of} \left[\frac{420 - 300}{3(25)} = 1.60, \frac{500 - 420}{3(25)} = 1.07 \right] = 1.07$$

The process capability ratio is

$$C_p = \frac{\text{Upper specification} - \text{Lower specification}}{6\sigma} = \frac{500 \text{ calories} - 300 \text{ calories}}{6(25)} = 1.33$$

Because the process capability ratio is 1.33, the process should be able to produce the product reliably within specifications. However, the process capability index is 1.07, so the current process is not centered properly for four-sigma performance. The mean of the process distribution is too close to the upper specification.

Discussion Questions

1. Consider Managerial Practice 1 and the discussion of Steinway's approach to achieving top quality. To get a better idea of the craft-oriented production process, visit **www.steinway.com/factory/tour.shtml**. However, Steinway also uses automation to produce the action mechanisms, a critical assembly in the grand pianos. Given the overall image of a Steinway piano, a very pricey hand-crafted object of beauty, what do you think of the use of automated equipment? Do you think it is a mistake to use automation in this way?

2. Recently, the Polish General Corporation, well-known for manufacturing appliances and automobile parts, initiated a $13 billion project to produce automobiles. A great deal of learning on the part of management and employees was required. Even though pressure was mounting to get a new product to market in early 2012, the production manager of the newly formed automobile division insisted on almost a year of trial runs before sales started because workers have to do their jobs 60 to 100 times before they can memorize the right sequence. The launch date was set for early 2013. What are the consequences of using this approach to enter the market with a new product?

3. Explain how unethical business practices degrade the quality of the experience a customer has with a service or product. How is the International Organization for Standardization trying to encourage ethical business behavior?

Problems

The OM Explorer and POM for Windows software is available to all students using the 10th edition of this text. Go to **www.pearsonhighered.com/krajewski** to download these computer packages. If you purchased MyOMLab, you also have access to Active Models software and significant help in doing the following problems. Check with your instructor on how best to use these resources. In many cases, the instructor wants you to understand how to do the calculations by hand. At the least, the software provides a check on your calculations. When calculations are particularly complex and the goal is interpreting the results in making decisions, the software replaces entirely the manual calculations. The software also can be a valuable resource well after your course is completed.

1. At Quickie Car Wash, the wash process is advertised to take less than 7 minutes. Consequently, management has set a target average of 390 seconds for the wash process. Suppose the average range for a sample of 9 cars is 10 seconds. Use Table 1 to establish control limits for sample means and ranges for the car wash process.

2. At Isogen Pharmaceuticals, the filling process for its asthma inhaler is set to dispense 150 milliliters (ml) of steroid solution per container. The average range for a sample of 4 containers is 3 ml. Use Table 1 to establish control limits for sample means and ranges for the filling process.

3. Garcia's Garage desires to create some colorful charts and graphs to illustrate how reliably its mechanics "get under the hood and fix the problem." The historic average for the proportion of customers that return for the same repair within the 30-day warranty period is 0.10. Each month, Garcia tracks 100 customers to see whether they return for warranty repairs. The results are plotted as a proportion to report progress toward the goal. If the control limits are to be set at two standard deviations on either side of the goal, determine the control limits for this chart. In March, 8 of the 100 customers in the sample group returned for warranty repairs. Is the repair process in control?

4. The Canine Gourmet Company produces delicious dog treats for canines with discriminating tastes. Management wants the box-filling line to be set so that the process average weight per packet is 45 grams. To make sure that the process is in control, an inspector at the end of the filling line periodically selects a random box of 10 packets and weighs each packet. When the process is in control, the range in the weight of each sample has averaged 6 grams.

   a. Design an R- and an $\bar{x}$-chart for this process.

   b. The results from the last 5 samples of 10 packets are

Sample	$\bar{x}$	R
1	44	9
2	40	2
3	46	5
4	39	8
5	48	3

   Is the process in control? Explain.

5. Aspen Plastics produces plastic bottles to customer order. The quality inspector randomly selects four bottles from the bottle machine and measures the outside diameter of the bottle neck, a critical quality dimension that determines whether the bottle cap will fit properly. The dimensions (in.) from the last six samples are

Sample	BOTTLE			
	1	2	3	4
1	0.594	0.622	0.598	0.590
2	0.587	0.611	0.597	0.613
3	0.571	0.580	0.595	0.602
4	0.610	0.615	0.585	0.578
5	0.580	0.624	0.618	0.614
6	0.585	0.593	0.607	0.569

   a. Assume that only these six samples are sufficient, and use the data to determine control limits for an R- and an $\bar{x}$-chart.

   b. Suppose that the specification for the bottle neck diameter is 0.600 ± 0.050 and the population standard deviation is 0.013 in. What is the Process Capability Index? The Process Capability Ratio?

   c. If the firm is seeking four-sigma performance, is the process capable of producing the bottle?

6. In an attempt to judge and monitor the quality of instruction, the administration of Mega-Byte Academy devised an examination to test students on the basic concepts that all should have learned. Each year, a random sample of 10 graduating students is selected for the test. The average score is used to track the quality of the educational process. Test results for the past 10 years are shown in Table 2.

   Use these data to estimate the center and standard deviation for this distribution. Then, calculate the two-sigma control limits for the process average. What comments would you make to the administration of the Mega-Byte Academy?

7. As a hospital administrator of a large hospital, you are concerned with the absenteeism among nurses' aides. The issue has been raised by registered nurses, who feel they often have to perform work normally done by their aides. To get the facts, absenteeism data were gathered for the last 3 weeks, which is considered a representative period for future conditions. After taking random samples of 64 personnel files each day, the following data were produced:

TABLE 2 | TEST SCORES ON EXIT EXAM

					STUDENT						
Year	1	2	3	4	5	6	7	8	9	10	Average
1	63	57	92	87	70	61	75	58	63	71	69.7
2	90	77	59	88	48	83	63	94	72	70	74.4
3	67	81	93	55	71	71	86	98	60	90	77.2
4	62	67	78	61	89	93	71	59	93	84	75.7
5	85	88	77	69	58	90	97	72	64	60	76.0
6	60	57	79	83	64	94	86	64	92	74	75.3
7	94	85	56	77	89	72	71	61	92	97	79.4
8	97	86	83	88	65	87	76	84	81	71	81.8
9	94	90	76	88	65	93	86	87	94	63	83.6
10	88	91	71	89	97	79	93	87	69	85	84.9

Day	Aides Absent	Day	Aides Absent
1	4	9	7
2	3	10	2
3	2	11	3
4	4	12	2
5	2	13	1
6	5	14	3
7	3	15	4
8	4		

Because your assessment of absenteeism is likely to come under careful scrutiny, you would like a type I error of only 1 percent. You want to be sure to identify any instances of unusual absences. If some are present, you will have to explore them on behalf of the registered nurses.

a. Design a *p*-chart.

b. Based on your *p*-chart and the data from the last 3 weeks, what can you conclude about the absenteeism of nurses' aides?

8. A textile manufacturer wants to set up a control chart for irregularities (e.g., oil stains, shop soil, loose threads, and tears) per 100 square yards of carpet. The following data were collected from a sample of twenty 100-square-yard pieces of carpet:

Sample	1	2	3	4	5	6	7	8	9	10
Irregularities	11	8	9	12	4	16	5	8	17	10
Sample	11	12	13	14	15	16	17	18	19	20
Irregularities	11	5	7	12	13	8	19	11	9	10

a. Using these data, set up a *c*-chart with $z = 3$.

b. Suppose that the next five samples had 15, 18, 12, 22, and 21 irregularities. What do you conclude?

9. The IRS is concerned with improving the accuracy of tax information given by its representatives over the telephone. Previous studies involved asking a set of 25 questions of a large number of IRS telephone representatives to determine the proportion of correct responses. Historically, the average proportion of correct responses has been 72 percent. Recently, IRS representatives have been receiving more training. On April 26, the set of 25 tax questions were again asked of 20 randomly selected IRS telephone representatives. The numbers of correct answers were 18, 16, 19, 21, 20, 16, 21, 16, 17, 10, 25, 18, 25, 16, 20, 15, 23, 19, 21, and 19.

a. What are the upper and lower control limits for the appropriate *p*-chart for the IRS? Use $z = 3$.

b. Is the tax information process in statistical control?

10. A travel agency is concerned with the accuracy and appearance of itineraries prepared for its clients. Defects can include errors in times, airlines, flight numbers, prices, car rental information, lodging, charge card numbers, and reservation numbers, as well as typographical errors. As the possible number of errors is nearly infinite, the agency measures the number of errors that do occur. The current process results in an average of three errors per itinerary.

a. What are the two-sigma control limits for these defects?

b. A client scheduled a trip to Dallas. Her itinerary contained six errors. Interpret this information.

11. Jim's Outfitters, Inc., makes custom fancy shirts for cowboys. The shirts could be flawed in various ways, including flaws in the weave or color of the fabric, loose buttons or decorations, wrong dimensions, and uneven stitches. Jim randomly examined 10 shirts, with the following results:

Shirt	Defects
1	8
2	0
3	7
4	12
5	5
6	10
7	2
8	4
9	6
10	6

a. Assuming that 10 observations are adequate for these purposes, determine the three-sigma control limits for defects per shirt.

b. Suppose that the next shirt has 13 flaws. What can you say about the process now?

12. The Big Black Bird Company produces fiberglass camper tops. The process for producing the tops must be controlled so as to keep the number of dimples low. When the process was in control, the following defects were found in 10 randomly selected camper tops over an extended period of time:

Top	Dimples
1	7
2	9
3	14
4	11
5	3
6	12
7	8
8	4
9	7
10	6

a. Assuming 10 observations are adequate for this purpose, determine the three-sigma control limits for dimples per camper top.

b. Suppose that the next camper top has 15 dimples. What can you say about the process now?

13. The production manager at Sunny Soda, Inc., is interested in tracking the quality of the company's 12-ounce bottle filling line. The bottles must be filled within the tolerances set for this product because the dietary information on the label shows 12 ounces as the serving size.

The design standard for the product calls for a fill level of 12.00 ± 0.10 ounces. The manager collected the following sample data (in fluid ounces per bottle) on the production process:

Sample	OBSERVATION			
	1	2	3	4
1	12.00	11.97	12.10	12.08
2	11.91	11.94	12.10	11.96
3	11.89	12.02	11.97	11.99
4	12.10	12.09	12.05	11.95
5	12.08	11.92	12.12	12.05
6	11.94	11.98	12.06	12.08
7	12.09	12.00	12.00	12.03
8	12.01	12.04	11.99	11.95
9	12.00	11.96	11.97	12.03
10	11.92	11.94	12.09	12.00
11	11.91	11.99	12.05	12.10
12	12.01	12.00	12.06	11.97
13	11.98	11.99	12.06	12.03
14	12.02	12.00	12.05	11.95
15	12.00	12.05	12.01	11.97

a. Are the process average and range in statistical control?

b. Is the process capable of meeting the design standard at four-sigma quality? Explain.

14. The Money Pit Mortgage Company is interested in monitoring the performance of the mortgage process. Fifteen samples of 5 completed mortgage transactions each were taken during a period when the process was believed to be in control. The times to complete the transactions were measured. The means and ranges of the mortgage process transaction times, measured in days, are as follows:

Sample	1	2	3	4	5	6	7	8	9	10	11	12	13	14	15
Mean	17	14	8	17	12	13	15	16	13	14	16	9	11	9	12
Range	6	11	4	8	9	14	12	15	10	10	11	6	9	11	13

Subsequently, samples of size 5 were taken from the process every week for the next 10 weeks. The times were measured and the following results obtained:

Sample	16	17	18	19	20	21	22	23	24	25
Mean	11	14	9	15	17	19	13	22	20	18
Range	7	11	6	4	12	14	11	10	8	6

a. Construct the control charts for the mean and the range, using the original 15 samples.

b. On the control charts developed in part (a), plot the values from samples 16 through 25 and comment on whether the process is in control.

c. In part (b), if you concluded that the process was out of control, would you attribute it to a drift in the mean, or an increase in the variability, or both? Explain your answer.

15. The Money Pit Mortgage Company of Problem 14 made some changes to the process and undertook a process capability study. The following data were obtained for 15 samples of size 5. Based on the individual observations, management estimated the process standard deviation to be 4.21 (days) for use in the process capability analysis. The lower and upper specification limits (in days) for the mortgage process times were 5 and 25.

Sample	1	2	3	4	5	6	7	8	9	10	11	12	13	14	15
Mean	11	12	8	16	13	12	17	16	13	14	17	9	15	14	9
Range	9	13	4	11	10	9	8	15	14	11	6	6	12	10	11

a. Calculate the process capability index and the process capability ratio values.

b. Suppose management would be happy with three-sigma performance. What conclusions is management likely to draw from the capability analysis? Can valid conclusions about the process be drawn from the analysis?

c. What remedial actions, if any, do you suggest that management take?

16. Webster Chemical Company produces mastics and caulking for the construction industry. The product is blended in large mixers and then pumped into tubes and capped. Management is concerned about whether the filling process for tubes of caulking is in statistical control. The process should be centered on 8 ounces per tube. Several samples of eight tubes were taken, each tube was weighed, and the weights in Table 3 were obtained.

a. Assume that only six samples are sufficient and develop the control charts for the mean and the range.

b. Plot the observations on the control chart and comment on your findings.

17. Management at Webster, in Problem 16, is now concerned as to whether caulking tubes are being properly capped. If a significant proportion of the tubes are not being sealed, Webster is placing its customers in a messy situation. Tubes are packaged in large boxes of 144. Several boxes are inspected, and the following numbers of leaking tubes are found:

Sample	Tubes	Sample	Tubes	Sample	Tubes
1	3	8	6	15	5
2	5	9	4	16	0
3	3	10	9	17	2
4	4	11	2	18	6
5	2	12	6	19	2
6	4	13	5	20	1
7	2	14	1	Total	72

Calculate p-chart three-sigma control limits to assess whether the capping process is in statistical control.

18. At Webster Chemical Company, lumps in the caulking compound could cause difficulties in dispensing a smooth bead from the tube. Even when the process is in control, an average of four lumps per tube of caulk will remain. Testing for the presence of lumps destroys the product, so an analyst takes random samples. The following results are obtained:

Tube No.	Lumps	Tube No.	Lumps	Tube No.	Lumps
1	6	5	6	9	5
2	5	6	4	10	0
3	0	7	1	11	9
4	4	8	6	12	2

Determine the c-chart two-sigma upper and lower control limits for this process. Is the process in statistical control?

TABLE 3 | OUNCES OF CAULKING PER TUBE

	TUBE NUMBER							
Sample	1	2	3	4	5	6	7	8
1	7.98	8.34	8.02	7.94	8.44	7.68	7.81	8.11
2	8.33	8.22	8.08	8.51	8.41	8.28	8.09	8.16
3	7.89	7.77	7.91	8.04	8.00	7.89	7.93	8.09
4	8.24	8.18	7.83	8.05	7.90	8.16	7.97	8.07
5	7.87	8.13	7.92	7.99	8.10	7.81	8.14	7.88
6	8.13	8.14	8.11	8.13	8.14	8.12	8.13	8.14

19. Janice Sanders, CEO of Pine Crest Medical Clinic, is concerned over the number of times patients must wait more than 30 minutes beyond their scheduled appointments. She asked her assistant to take random samples of 64 patients to see how many in each sample had to wait more than 30 minutes. Each instance is considered a defect in the clinic process. The table below contains the data for 15 samples.

Sample	Number of Defects
1	5
2	2
3	1
4	3
5	1
6	5
7	2
8	3
9	6
10	3
11	9
12	9
13	5
14	2
15	3

a. Assuming Janice Sanders is willing to use three-sigma control limits, construct a p-chart.

b. Based on your p-chart and the data in the table, what can you conclude about the waiting time of the patients?

20. Representatives of the Patriot Insurance Company take medical information over the telephone from prospective policy applicants prior to a visit to the applicant's place of residence by a registered nurse who takes vital sign measurements. When the telephone interview has incorrect or incomplete information, the entire process of approving the application is unnecessarily delayed and has the potential of causing loss of business. The following data were collected to see how many applications contain errors. Each sample has 200 randomly selected applications.

Sample	Defects	Sample	Defects
1	20	16	15
2	18	17	40
3	29	18	35
4	12	19	21
5	14	20	24
6	11	21	9
7	30	22	20
8	25	23	17
9	27	24	28
10	16	25	10
11	25	26	17
12	18	27	22
13	25	28	14
14	16	29	19
15	20	30	20

a. What are the upper and lower control limits of a p-chart for the number of defective applications? Use $z = 3$.

b. Is the process in statistical control?

21. The Digital Guardian Company issues policies that protect clients from downtime costs due to computer system failures. It is very important to process the policies quickly because long cycle times not only put the client at risk, they could also lose business for Digital Guardian. Management is concerned that customer service is degrading because of long cycle times, measured in days. The following table contains the data from five samples, each sample consisting of eight random observations.

Sample	OBSERVATION (DAYS)							
	1	2	3	4	5	6	7	8
1	13	9	4	8	8	15	8	6
2	7	15	8	10	10	14	10	15
3	8	11	4	11	8	12	9	15
4	12	7	12	9	11	8	12	8
5	8	12	6	12	11	5	12	8

a. What is your estimate of the process average?

b. What is your estimate of the average range?

c. Construct an R- and an $\bar{x}$-chart for this process. Are assignable causes present?

22. The Farley Manufacturing Company prides itself on the quality of its products. The company is engaged in competition for a very important project. A key element is a part that ultimately goes into precision testing equipment. The specifications are 8.000 ± 3.000 millimeters.

Management is concerned about the capability of the process to produce that part. The following data (shown below) were randomly collected during test runs of the process:

	OBSERVATION (MILLIMETERS)							
Sample	1	2	3	4	5	6	7	8
1	9.100	8.900	8.800	9.200	8.100	6.900	9.300	9.100
2	7.600	8.000	9.000	10.100	7.900	9.000	8.000	8.800
3	8.200	9.100	8.200	8.700	9.000	7.000	8.800	10.800
4	8.200	8.300	7.900	7.500	8.900	7.800	10.100	7.700
5	10.000	8.100	8.900	9.000	9.300	9.000	8.700	10.000

Assume that the process is in statistical control. Is the process capable of producing the part at the three-sigma level? Explain.

23. A critical dimension of the service quality of a call center is the wait time of a caller to get to a sales representative. Periodically, random samples of three customer calls are measured for time. The results of the last four samples are in the following table:

Sample	Time (Sec)		
1	495	501	498
2	512	508	504
3	505	497	501
4	496	503	492

a. Assuming that management is willing to use three-sigma control limits, and using only the historical information contained in the four samples, show that the call center access time is in statistical control.

b. Suppose that the standard deviation of the process distribution is 5.77. If the specifications for the access time are 500 ± 18 sec., is the process capable? Why or why not? Assume three-sigma performance is desired.

24. An automatic lathe produces rollers for roller bearings, and the process is monitored by statistical process control charts. The central line of the chart for the sample means is set at 8.50 and for the range at 0.31 mm. The process is in control, as established by samples of size 5. The upper and lower specifications for the diameter of the rollers are (8.50 + 0.25) and (8.50 − 0.25) mm, respectively.

a. Calculate the control limits for the mean and range charts.

b. If the standard deviation of the process distribution is estimated to be 0.13 mm, is the process capable of meeting specifications? Assume four-sigma performance is desired.

c. If the process is not capable, what percent of the output will fall outside the specification limits? (*Hint*: Use the normal distribution.)

Advanced Problems

25. Canine Gourmet Super Breath dog treats are sold in boxes labeled with a net weight of 12 ounces (340 grams) per box. Each box contains 8 individual 1.5-ounce packets. To reduce the chances of shorting the customer, product design specifications call for the packet-filling process average to be set at 43.5 grams so that the average net weight per box of 8 packets will be 348 grams. Tolerances are set for the box to weigh 348 ± 12 grams. The standard deviation for the *packet-filling* process is 1.01 grams. The target process capability ratio is 1.33. One day, the packet-filling process average weight drifts down to 43.0 grams. Is the packaging process capable? Is an adjustment needed?

26. The Precision Machining Company makes hand-held tools on an assembly line that produces one product every minute. On one of the products, the critical quality dimension is the diameter (measured in thousandths of an inch) of a hole bored in one of the assemblies. Management wants to detect any shift in the process average diameter from 0.015 in. Management considers the variance in the process to be in control. Historically, the average range has been 0.002 in., regardless of the process average. Design an $\bar{x}$-chart to control this process, with a center line at 0.015 in. and the control limits set at three sigmas from the center line.

Management provided the results of 80 minutes of output from the production line, as shown in Table 4. During these 80 minutes, the process average changed once. All measurements are in thousandths of an inch.

a. Set up an $\bar{x}$-chart with $n = 4$. The frequency should be sample four and then skip four. Thus, your first sample would be for minutes 1 − 4, the second would be for minutes 9 − 12, and so on. When would you stop the process to check for a change in the process average?

b. Set up an $\bar{x}$-chart with $n = 8$. The frequency should be sample eight and then skip four. When would you stop the process now? What can you say about the desirability of large samples on a frequent sampling interval?

27. Using the data from Problem 26, continue your analysis of sample size and frequency by trying the following plans.

a. Using the $\bar{x}$-chart for $n = 4$, try the frequency sample four, then skip eight. When would you stop the process in this case?

b. Using the $\bar{x}$-chart for $n = 8$, try the frequency sample eight, then skip eight. When would you consider the process to be out of control?

TABLE 4 | SAMPLE DATA FOR PRECISION MACHINING COMPANY

Minutes	Diameter (thousandths of an inch)											
1–12	15	16	18	14	16	17	15	14	14	13	16	17
13–24	15	16	17	16	14	14	13	14	15	16	15	17
25–36	14	13	15	17	18	15	16	15	14	15	16	17
37–48	18	16	15	16	16	14	17	18	19	15	16	15
49–60	12	17	16	14	15	17	14	16	15	17	18	14
61–72	15	16	17	18	13	15	14	14	16	15	17	18
73–80	16	16	17	18	16	15	14	17				

TABLE 5 | SAMPLE DATA FOR DATA TECH CREDIT CARD SERVICE

Samples	Number of Errors in Sample of 250									
1–10	3	8	5	11	7	1	12	9	0	8
11–20	3	5	7	9	11	3	2	9	13	4
21–30	12	10	6	2	1	7	10	5	8	4

c. Using your results from parts (a) and (b), determine what trade-offs you would consider in choosing between them.

28. The manager of the customer service department of Data Tech Credit Card Service Company is concerned about the number of defects produced by the billing process. Every day a random sample of 250 statements was inspected for errors regarding incorrect entries involving account numbers, transactions on the customer's account, interest charges, and penalty charges. Any statement with one or more of these errors was considered a defect. The study lasted 30 days and yielded the data in Table 5.

   a. Construct a p-chart for the billing process.

   b. Is there any nonrandom behavior in the billing process that would require management attention?

29. Red Baron Airlines serves hundreds of cities each day, but competition is increasing from smaller companies affiliated with major carriers. One of the key competitive priorities is on-time arrivals and departures. Red Baron defines *on time* as any arrival or departure that takes place within 15 minutes of the scheduled time. To stay on top of the market, management set the high standard of 98 percent on-time performance. The operations department was put in charge of monitoring the performance of the airline. Each week, a random sample of 300 flight arrivals and departures was checked for schedule performance. Table 6 contains the numbers of arrivals and departures over the last 30 weeks that did not meet Red Baron's definition of on-time service. What can you tell management about the quality of service? Can you identify any nonrandom behavior in the process? If so, what might cause the behavior?

30. Beaver Brothers, Inc., is conducting a study to assess the capability of its 150-gram bar soap production line. A critical quality measure is the weight of the soap bars after stamping. The lower and upper specification limits are 162 and 170 grams, respectively. As a part of an initial capability study, 25 samples of size 5 were collected by the quality assurance group and the observations in Table 7 were recorded.

After analyzing the data by using statistical control charts, the quality assurance group calculated the process capability ratio, C_p, and the process capability index, C_{pk}. It then decided to improve the stamping process, especially the feeder mechanism. After making all the changes that were deemed necessary, 18 additional samples were collected. The summary data for these samples are

$$\bar{\bar{x}} = 163 \text{ grams}$$

$$\bar{R} = 2.326 \text{ grams}$$

$$\sigma = 1 \text{ gram}$$

All sample observations were within the control chart limits. With the new data, the quality assurance group recalculated the process capability measures. It was pleased with the improved C_p but felt that the process should be centered at 166 grams to ensure that everything was in order. Its decision concluded the study.

   a. Draw the control charts for the data obtained in the initial study and verify that the process was in statistical control.

   b. What were the values obtained by the group for C_p and C_{pk} for the initial capability study? Comment on your findings and explain why further improvements were necessary.

   c. What are the C_p and C_{pk} after the improvements? Comment on your findings, indicating why the group decided to change the centering of the process.

   d. What are the C_p and C_{pk} if the process were centered at 166? Comment on your findings.

TABLE 6 | SAMPLE DATA FOR RED BARON AIRLINES

Samples	Number of Late Planes in Sample of 300 Arrivals and Departures									
1–10	3	8	5	11	7	2	12	9	1	8
11–20	3	5	7	9	12	5	4	9	13	4
21–30	12	10	6	2	1	8	4	5	8	2

TABLE 7 | SAMPLE DATA FOR BEAVER BROTHERS, INC.

Sample	OBS.1	OBS.2	OBS.3	OBS.4	OBS.5
1	167.0	159.6	161.6	164.0	165.3
2	156.2	159.5	161.7	164.0	165.3
3	167.0	162.9	162.9	164.0	165.4
4	167.0	159.6	163.7	164.1	165.4
5	156.3	160.0	162.9	164.1	165.5
6	164.0	164.2	163.0	164.2	163.9
7	161.3	163.0	164.2	157.0	160.6
8	163.1	164.2	156.9	160.1	163.1
9	164.3	157.0	161.2	163.2	164.4
10	156.9	161.0	163.2	164.3	157.3
11	161.0	163.3	164.4	157.6	160.6
12	163.3	164.5	158.4	160.1	163.3
13	158.2	161.3	163.5	164.6	158.7
14	161.5	163.5	164.7	158.6	162.5
15	163.6	164.8	158.0	162.4	163.6
16	164.5	158.5	160.3	163.4	164.6
17	164.9	157.9	162.3	163.7	165.1
18	155.0	162.2	163.7	164.8	159.6
19	162.1	163.9	165.1	159.3	162.0
20	165.2	159.1	161.6	163.9	165.2
21	164.9	165.1	159.9	162.0	163.7
22	167.6	165.6	165.6	156.7	165.7
23	167.7	165.8	165.9	156.9	165.9
24	166.0	166.0	165.6	165.6	165.5
25	163.7	163.7	165.6	165.6	166.2

Active Model Exercise

This Active Model appears in MyOMLab. It allows you to see the effects of sample size and z-values on control charts.

QUESTIONS

1. Has the booking process been in statistical control?

2. Suppose we use a 95 percent p-chart. How do the upper and lower control limits change? What are your conclusions about the booking process?

3. Suppose that the sample size is reduced to 2,000 instead of 2,500. How does this affect the chart?

4. What happens to the chart as we reduce the z-value?

5. What happens to the chart as we reduce the confidence level?

p-Chart

Reset Data	Questions

Number of samples	12
Sample size	2500
z value	3.0000
Confidence	99.73%

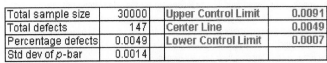

Total sample size	30000	Upper Control Limit	0.0091
Total defects	147	Center Line	0.0049
Percentage defects	0.0049	Lower Control Limit	0.0007
Std dev of p-bar	0.0014		

	# Defects	Fraction Defective
Sample 1	15	0.0060
Sample 2	12	0.0048
Sample 3	19	0.0076
Sample 4	2	0.0008
Sample 5	19	0.0076
Sample 6	4	0.0016
Sample 7	24	0.0096
Sample 8	7	0.0028
Sample 9	10	0.0040
Sample 10	17	0.0068
Sample 11	15	0.0060
Sample 12	3	0.0012

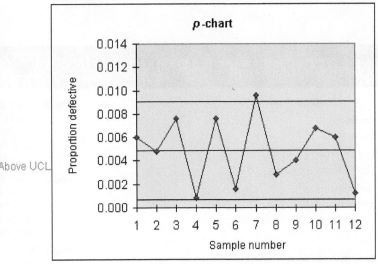

p-Chart Using Data from Example 3

VIDEO CASE — Process Performance and Quality at Starwood Hotels & Resorts

Starwood Hotels & Resorts is no stranger to quality measurement. In the most recent year, Starwood properties around the globe held 51 of approximately 700 spots on Condé Nast's Gold List of the world's best places to stay. Its spa and golf programs have consistently been ranked among the best in the world.

At Starwood, processes and programs are driven by the work of its team of Six Sigma experts, called Black Belts. Developed by Motorola more than 20 years ago, Six Sigma is a comprehensive and flexible system for achieving, sustaining, and maximizing business success by driving out defects and variability in a process. Starwood uses the five-step DMAIC process: (1) define, (2) measure, (3) analyze, (4) improve, and (5) control.

Clearly, understanding customer needs is paramount. To this end, Starwood collects data from customers on its Guest Satisfaction Index survey, called the "Voice of the Customer." The survey covers every department guests may have encountered during their stay, from the front desk and hotel room, to restaurants and concierge. Past surveys indicated that how well

problems were resolved during the guest stay was a key driver in high guest satisfaction scores. To increase its scores for problem resolution, the Sheraton brand of Starwood launched the Sheraton Service Promise program in the United States and Canada. The program was designed to give guests a single point of contact for reporting any problems. It was intended to focus associate (employee) attention on taking care of service issues during the guest's stay within 15 minutes of first receiving notice.

However, although scores did increase, they did not increase by enough. Consequently, Sheraton brought in its Six Sigma team to see what it could do. The team employed the basic Six Sigma model of define-measure-analyze-improve-control to guide its work. To define the problem, the Six Sigma team worked with data collected and analyzed by an independent survey organization, National Family Opinion. The study indicated that three key factors are needed in problem resolution: (1) speed, (2) empathy, and (3) efficiency. All three must be met in order for the guests to be satisfied and the Sheraton Service Promise fulfilled. Then, the team looked at the specific processes that affected performance: telephone operators' handling of requests, procedures for determining who to call, engineering workloads, and so on. The work identified in each area was measured. For example, call logs were established to track speed, empathy of associate handling the call, and efficiency of the staff charged with fixing the problem. The data collected were analyzed to determine why guests' problems were not resolved within the 15-minute standard. Pareto charts and other techniques were used for the analysis.

The final step involved control and monitoring to be sure that the improved processes developed by the Six Sigma team became part of the property's culture, and that they were not abandoned after the team's work was finished. Tracking continues for 12 to 18 months, with monthly feedback to the manager or department head responsible for the improvement of the Sheraton Service Promise program. The improvement effort also receives visibility through the company's intranet so the rest of the organization sees the benefits—including service levels and financial performance—and can use the experience to improve their own operations.

QUESTIONS

1. Implementing Six Sigma programs takes considerable time and commitment from an organization. In terms of top-down commitment, measurement systems to track progress, tough goal setting, education, communication, and customer priorities, evaluate the degree to which Starwood successfully addressed each with the redesign of the Sheraton Service Promise program.

2. How might the new Sheraton Service Promise process help Starwood avoid the four costs of poor process performance and quality (prevention, appraisal, internal failure, and external failure)?

3. Starwood is the first major hotel brand to commit to a dedicated Six Sigma program for improving quality. Why might an organization be reluctant to follow this type of formalized methodology? What other approaches could Starwood or its competitors use?

EXPERIENTIAL LEARNING

Statistical Process Control with a Coin Catapult

Exercise A: Control Charts for Variables

Materials

1 ruler

1 pen or pencil

1 coin (a quarter will do nicely)

1 yardstick

An exercise worksheet

Access to a calculator

Tasks

Divide into teams of two to four. If four people are on a team,

one person holds the yardstick and observes the action,

one person adjusts the catapult and launches the coin,

one person observes the maximum height for each trial, and

one person records the results.

If teams of fewer than four are formed, provide a support for the yardstick and combine the other tasks as appropriate.

Practice

To catapult the coin, put a pen or pencil under the 6-in. mark of the ruler. Put the coin over the 11-in. mark. Press both ends of the ruler down as far as they will go. Let the end that holds the coin snap up, catapulting the coin into the air. The person holding the yardstick should place the stick so that it is adjacent to, but does not interfere with, the trajectory of the coin. To observe the maximum height reached by the coin, the observer should stand back with his or her eye at about the same level as the top of the coin's trajectory. Practice until each person is comfortable with his or her role. The person operating the catapult should be sure that the pen or pencil fulcrum has not moved between shots and that the launch is done as consistently as possible.

Step 1: *Gather data.* Take four samples of five observations (launches) each. Record the maximum height reached by the coin in the first data table on the worksheet. When you have finished, determine the mean and range for each sample, and compute the mean of the means $\bar{\bar{x}}$ and the mean of the ranges $\bar{R}$.

Step 2: *Develop an R-chart.* Using the data gathered and the appropriate D_3 and D_4 values, compute the upper and lower three-sigma control limits for the range. Enter these values and plot the range for each of the four samples on the range chart on the worksheet. Be sure to indicate an appropriate scale for range on the y-axis.

Step 3: *Develop an $\bar{x}$-chart.* Now, using the data gathered and the appropriate value for A_2, compute the upper and lower three-sigma control limits for the sample means. Enter these values and plot the mean for each of the four samples on the $\bar{x}$-chart on the worksheet. Again, indicate an appropriate scale for the y-axis.

Step 4: *Observe the process.* Once a control chart has been established for a process, it is used to monitor the process and to identify when it is not running "normally." Collect two more samples of five trials each, as you did to collect the first set of data. Plot the range and the sample mean on the charts you constructed on the worksheet each time you collect a sample. What have you observed that affects the process? Does the chart indicate that the process is operating the way it did when you first collected data?

Step 5: *Observe a changed process.* Now change something (for instance, move the pencil out to the 8-in. mark). Collect data for samples 7 and 8. Plot the range and the sample mean on the charts you constructed on the worksheet as you complete each sample. Can you detect a change in the process from your control chart? If the process has changed, how sure are you that this change is real and not just due to the particular sample you chose?

Exercise B: Control Charts for Attributes

Materials

1 ruler

1 pen or pencil

1 coin (a quarter will do nicely)

1 paper or plastic cup (with a 4-in. mouth)

An exercise worksheet

Access to a calculator

Tasks

Divide into teams of two or three. If three people are on a team,

one person adjusts the catapult and launches the coin,

one person observes the results and fetches the coin, and

one person records the results.

If teams of two are formed, combine the tasks as appropriate.

Practice

The object is to flip a coin into a cup using a ruler. To catapult the coin, put a pen or pencil under the 6-in. mark of the ruler.

Put a coin over the 11-in. mark and let its weight hold that end of the ruler on the tabletop. Strike the raised end of the ruler with your hand to flip the coin into the air. Position a cup at the place where the coin lands so that on the next flip, the coin will land inside. You will have to practice several times until you find out how hard to hit the ruler and the best position for the cup. Be sure that the pen or pencil fulcrum has not moved between shots and that the launch is done as consistently as possible.

Step 1: *Gather data.* Try to catapult the coin into the cup 10 times for each sample. Record each trial in the data table on the worksheet as a hit (H) when the coin lands inside or a miss (M) when it does not. The proportion of misses will be the number of misses divided by the sample size, *n*, in this case 10. A miss is a "defect," so the proportion of misses is the proportion defective, *p*.

Step 2: *Develop a p-chart.* Compute the upper and lower three-sigma control limits for the average fraction defective. Plot these values and the mean for each of the four samples on the *p*-chart on the worksheet.

Step 3: *Observe the process.* Once a chart has been established for a process, it is used to monitor the process and to identify abnormal behavior. Exchange tasks so that someone else is catapulting the coin. After several practice launches, take four more samples of 10. Plot the proportion defective for this person's output. Is the process still in control? If it is not, how sure are you that it is out of control? Can you determine the control limits for a 95 percent confidence level? With these limits, was your revised process still in control?

Source: The basis for Exercise A was written by J. Christopher Sandvig, Western Washington University, as a variation of the "Catapulting Coins" exercise from *Games and Exercises for Operations Management* by Janelle Heinke and Larry Meile (Prentice Hall, 1995). Given these foundations, Larry Meile of Boston College wrote Exercise A. He also wrote Exercise B as a new extension.

Selected References

Babbar, Sunil. "Service Quality and Business Ethics," *International Journal of Service and Operations Management*, vol. 1, no. 3, 2005, pp. 203–219.

Babbar, Sunil. "Teaching Ethics for Quality as an Innovation in a Core Operations Management Course," *Decision Sciences Journal of Innovative Education*, vol. 8, no. 2, 2010, pp. 361–366.

Besterfield, Dale. *Quality Control*, 8th ed. Upper Saddle River, NJ: Prentice Hall, 2009.

Collier, David A. *The Service Quality Solution.* New York: Irwin Professional Publishing; Milwaukee: ASQC Quality Press, 1994.

Crosby, Philip B. *Quality Is Free: The Art of Making Quality Certain.* New York: McGraw-Hill, 1979.

Deming, W. Edwards. *Out of the Crisis.* Cambridge, MA: Massachusetts Institute of Technology Center for Advanced Engineering Study, 1986.

Duncan, Acheson J. *Quality Control and Industrial Statistics*, 5th ed. Homewood, IL: Irwin, 1986.

Feigenbaum, A.V. *Total Quality Control: Engineering and Management*, 3rd ed. New York: McGraw-Hill, 1983.

Hartvigsen, David. *SimQuick: Process Simulation with Excel*, 2nd ed. Upper Saddle River, NJ: Prentice Hall, 2004.

Hoyle, David. *ISO 9000*, 6th ed. Oxford: Butler-Heinemann, 2009.

Juran, J.M., and Frank Gryna, Jr. *Quality Planning and Analysis*, 2nd ed. New York: McGraw-Hill, 1980.

Kerwin, Kathleen. "When Flawless Isn't Enough." *Business Week* (December 8, 2003), pp. 80–82.

Lucier, Gregory T., and Sridhar Seshadri. "GE Takes Six Sigma Beyond the Bottom Line." *Strategic Finance* (May 2001), pp. 41–46.

Mitra, Amitava. *Fundamentals of Quality Control and Improvement*, 3rd ed. Hoboken, NJ: Wiley & Sons, 2008.

Pande, Peter S., Robert P. Neuman, and Roland R. Cavanagh. *The Six Sigma Way.* New York: McGraw-Hill, 2000.

Russell, J. P., and Dennis Arter. *ISO Lesson Guide to ISO 9001*, 3rd ed. Milwaukee: ASQC Quality Press, 2008.

Schwarz, Anne. "Listening to the Voice of the Customer Is the Key to QVC's Success." *Journal of Organizational Excellence* (Winter 2004), pp. 3–11.

Sester, Dennis. "Motorola: A Tradition of Quality." *Quality* (October 2001), pp. 30–34.

Yannick, Julliard. "Ethics Quality Management," *Techne' Journal*, vol. 8, no. 1 (Fall 2004), pp. 117–135.

VARLEY/SIPA/Newscom

Oil containment hard boom collecting foaming sea water at Queen Bess Island near Grand Isle, Louisiana

CONSTRAINT MANAGEMENT

British Petroleum Oil Spill in Gulf of Mexico

British Petroleum (BP) is one of the world's leading international oil, gas, and petrochemical products company, with operations in 29 countries, 79,000 employees, and 2010 sales of nearly $30 billion. It operates over 22,000 retail sites. On April 20, 2010, there was an explosion and fire on Transocean Ltd's Deepwater Horizon drilling rig that had been licensed to BP. It sank two days later in 5,000 feet of water, and released as many as 4.9 billion barrels of oil into the Gulf of Mexico before the damaged well was finally capped in mid-July 2010. The resulting oil spill closed down fisheries and threatened the delicate coastline and its fragile ecosystems. Pinnacle Strategies was one of the firms hired by BP to help in boosting the output of spill-fighting equipment like boats, ships, and rigs, as well as supplies of critical resources like containment booms, skimmers, and decontamination suits.

A boom is an inflatable floating device that can be used to trap oil downwind on a body of water. This oil can then be pumped into containers by skimming equipment. Limited production capacities of booms, however, represented a daunting challenge. Prestige Products in Walker, Michigan, could only make 500 feet of boom a day, whereas a single order of the size requested by BP would exceed the combined capacity of every boom manufacturer in the United States. Despite increasing the staff from 5 to 75 and raising production to 12,800 feet daily, the Prestige plant felt that it had reached its limit. That is where Ed Kincer from Pinnacle Strategies stepped in. He noticed that the boom was assembled in a flurry, with

From Chapter 7 of *Operations Management: Processes and Supply Chains*, Tenth Edition. Lee J. Krajewski, Larry P. Ritzman, Manoj K. Malhotra. Copyright © 2013 by Pearson Education, Inc. All rights reserved.

little to do in-between for several minutes. Cutters sliced boom by cutting one side, then walking 100 feet to cut the other side. Workers also sat idle while waiting for a welding machine. Waste occurred in the form of excessive walks, waiting for machines, and changing production rhythms. Kincer identified the constraints in the process, found ways to manage them, and more than tripled capacity. Prestige eventually ended up making more than a million feet of boom for BP.

Theory of constraints is the scientific approach that was used by Pinnacle to boost throughput for BP's other key suppliers as well. Kvichak Marine in Seattle quadrupled output of oil skimmers, while Illinois-based Elastec increased production from 4 skimmers a week to 26. Abasco, a Houston-based boom manufacturer, increased production by 20 percent due to rebalancing staff such that the welding operation kept going even during the breaks. At Supply Pro, a Texan manufacturer of absorbent boom, capacity increased several fold by using cellulose instead of scarce polypropylene. In six months, Pinnacle more than doubled the supply of skimmers, booms, and other critical resources by identifying bottlenecks at dozens of factories and working around them. These capacity enhancements throughout BP's supply chain ensured that lack of materials did not end up constraining the clean-up operations in the fight against the oil spill.

Source: Brown, A. "Theory of Constraints Tapped to Accelerate BP's Gulf of Mexico Cleanup." *Industry Week* (March 18, 2011); **http://www.newsweek.com/photo/2010/05/22/oil-spill-timeline.html**; **http://www.bp.com/**, May 5, 2011.

LEARNING GOALS *After reading this chapter, you should be able to:*

1. Explain the theory of constraints.
2. Understand linkage of capacity constraints to financial performance measures.
3. Identify bottlenecks.
4. Apply theory of constraints to product mix decisions.
5. Describe how to manage constraints in an assembly line.

constraint

Any factor that limits the performance of a system and restricts its output. In linear programming, a limitation that restricts the permissible choices for the decision variables.

bottleneck

A capacity constraint resource (CCR) whose available capacity limits the organization's ability to meet the product volume, product mix, or demand fluctuation required by the marketplace.

Suppose one of a firm's processes was recently reengineered, and yet results were disappointing. Costs were still high or customer satisfaction still low. What could be wrong? The answer might be constraints that remain in one or more steps in the firm's processes. A **constraint** is any factor that limits the performance of a system and restricts its output, while *capacity* is the maximum rate of output of a process or a system. When constraints exist at any step, as they did at suppliers of BP, capacity can become imbalanced—too high in some departments and too low in others. As a result, the overall performance of the system suffers.

Constraints can occur up or down the supply chain, with either the firm's suppliers or customers, or within one of the firm's processes like service/product development or order fulfillment. Three kinds of constraints can generally be identified: physical (usually machine, labor, or workstation capacity or material shortages, but could be space or quality), market (demand is less than capacity), or managerial (policy, metrics, or mind-sets that create constraints that impede work flow). A **bottleneck**[1] is a special type of a constraint that relates to the capacity shortage of a process, and is defined as any resource whose available capacity limits the organization's ability to meet the service or product volume, product mix, or fluctuating requirements demanded by the marketplace. A business system or a process would have at least one constraint or a bottleneck; otherwise, its output would be limited only by market demand. The experience of BP and other firms in the health care, banking, and manufacturing industries demonstrates how important managing constraints can be to an organization's future.

---

[1] Under certain conditions, a bottleneck is also called a *capacity constrained resource* (CCR). The process with the least capacity is called a bottleneck if its output is less than the market demand, or called a CCR if it is the least capable resource in the system but still has higher capacity than the market demand.

Managing Constraints across the Organization

Firms must manage their constraints and make appropriate capacity choices at the individual-process level, as well as at the organization level. Hence, this process involves inter-functional cooperation. Detailed decisions and choices made within each of these levels affect where resource constraints or bottlenecks show up, both within and across departmental lines. Relieving a bottleneck in one part of an organization might not have the desired effect unless a bottleneck in another part of the organization is also addressed. A bottleneck could be the sales department not getting enough sales or the loan department not processing loans fast enough. The constraint could be a lack of capital or equipment, or it could be planning and scheduling.

Managers throughout the organization must understand how to identify and manage bottlenecks in all types of processes, how to relate the capacity and performance measures of one process to another, and how to use that information to determine the firm's best service or product mix. This chapter explains how managers can best make these decisions.

Traffic bottleneck in Beijing, China.

The Theory of Constraints

The **theory of constraints (TOC)** is a systematic management approach that focuses on actively managing those constraints that impede a firm's progress toward its goal of maximizing profits and effectively using its resources. The theory was developed nearly three decades ago by Eli Goldratt, a well-known business systems analyst. It outlines a deliberate process for identifying and overcoming constraints. The process focuses not just on the efficiency of individual processes, but also on the bottlenecks that constrain the system as a whole. Pinnacle Strategies in the opening vignette followed this theory to improve BP's operations.

TOC methods increase the firm's profits more effectively by focusing on making materials flow rapidly through the entire system. They help firms look at the big picture—how processes can be improved to increase overall work flows, and how inventory and workforce levels can be reduced while still effectively utilizing critical resources. To do this, it is important to understand the relevant performance and capacity measures at the operational level, as well as their relationship to the more broadly understood financial measures at the firm level. These measures and relationships, so critical in successfully applying the principles of the TOC, are defined in Table 1.

theory of constraints (TOC)
A systematic management approach that focuses on actively managing those constraints that impede a firm's progress toward its goal.

Creating Value through Operations Management

Using Operations to Compete
Project Management

Managing Processes

Process Strategy
Process Analysis
Quality and Performance
Capacity Planning
Constraint Management
Lean Systems

Managing Supply Chains

Supply Chain Inventory Management
Supply Chain Design
Supply Chain Location Decisions
Supply Chain Integration
Supply Chain Sustainability and Humanitarian Logistics
Forecasting
Operations Planning and Scheduling
Resource Planning

TABLE 1 | HOW THE FIRM'S OPERATIONAL MEASURES RELATE TO ITS FINANCIAL MEASURES

Operational Measures	TOC View	Relationship to Financial Measures
Inventory (I)	All the money invested in a system in purchasing things that it intends to sell	A decrease in I leads to an increase in net profit, ROI, and cash flow.
Throughput (T)	Rate at which a system generates money through sales	An increase in T leads to an increase in net profit, ROI, and cash flows.
Operating Expense (OE)	All the money a system spends to turn inventory into throughput	A decrease in OE leads to an increase in net profit, ROI, and cash flows.
Utilization (U)	The degree to which equipment, space, or workforce is currently being used, and is measured as the ratio of average output rate to maximum capacity, expressed as a percentage	An increase in U at the bottleneck leads to an increase in net profit, ROI, and cash flows.

According to the TOC view, every capital investment in the system, including machines and work-in-process materials, represents inventory because they could all potentially be sold to make money. Producing a product or a service that does not lead to a sale will not increase a firm's throughput, but will increase its inventory and operating expenses. It is always best to manage the system so that utilization at the bottleneck resource is maximized in order to maximize throughput.

Key Principles of the TOC

The chief concept behind the TOC is that the bottlenecks should be scheduled to maximize their throughput of services or products while adhering to promised completion dates. The underlying assumption is that demand is greater or equal to the capacity of the process that produces the service or product, otherwise instead of internal changes, marketing must work towards promoting increasing its demand. For example, manufacturing a garden rake involves attaching a bow to the rake's head. Rake heads must be processed on the blanking press, welded to the bow, cleaned, and attached to the handle to make the rake, which is packaged and finally shipped to Sears, Home Depot, or Walmart, according to a specific delivery schedule. Suppose that the delivery commitments for all styles of rakes for the next month indicate that the welding station is loaded at 105 percent of its capacity, but that the other processes will be used at only 75 percent of their capacities. According to the TOC, the welding station is the bottleneck resource, whereas the blanking, cleaning, handle attaching, packaging, and shipping processes are nonbottleneck resources. Any idle time at the welding station must be eliminated to maximize throughput. Managers should therefore focus on the welding schedule.

Seven key principles of the TOC that revolve around the efficient use and scheduling of bottlenecks and improving flow and throughput are summarized in Table 2.

TABLE 2 | SEVEN KEY PRINCIPLES OF THE THEORY OF CONSTRAINTS

1. The focus should be on balancing flow, not on balancing capacity.

2. Maximizing the output and efficiency of every resource may not maximize the throughput of the entire system.

3. An hour lost at a bottleneck or a constrained resource is an hour lost for the whole system. In contrast, an hour saved at a nonbottleneck resource is a mirage because it does not make the whole system more productive.

4. Inventory is needed only in front of the bottlenecks in order to prevent them from sitting idle, and in front of assembly and shipping points in order to protect customer schedules. Building inventories elsewhere should be avoided.

5. Work, which can be materials, information to be processed, documents, or customers, should be released into the system only as frequently as the bottlenecks need it. Bottleneck flows should be equal to the market demand. Pacing everything to the slowest resource minimizes inventory and operating expenses.

6. Activating a nonbottleneck resource (using it for improved efficiency that does not increase throughput) is not the same as utilizing a bottleneck resource (that does lead to increased throughput). Activation of nonbottleneck resources cannot increase throughput, nor promote better performance on financial measures outlined in Table 1.

7. Every capital investment must be viewed from the perspective of its global impact on overall throughput (T), inventory (I), and operating expense (OE).

Reprinted Courtesy of Bal Seal Engineering, Inc. Copyright © Bal Seal Engineering, Inc. (2010). "Bal Seal" and "canted-coil" (list trademarks) are trademarks of Bal Seal Engineering, Inc. All rights reserved.

Bal Seal Engineering is a designer and manufacturer of custom seals and canted-coil™ springs for aerospace, automotive, transportation, medical and other industries. By applying many modern management principles including the theory of constraints (TOC), the company has been able to grow and improve customer satisfaction.

Practical application of the TOC involves the implementation of the following steps.

1. *Identify the System Bottleneck(s)*. For the rake example, the bottleneck is the welding station because it is restricting the firm's ability to meet the shipping schedule and, hence, total value-added funds. Other ways of identifying the bottleneck will be looked at in more detail a little later in this chapter.

2. *Exploit the Bottleneck(s)*. Create schedules that maximize the throughput of the bottleneck(s). For the rake example, schedule the welding station to maximize its utilization while meeting the shipping commitments to the extent possible. Also make sure that only good quality parts are passed on to the bottleneck.

3. *Subordinate All Other Decisions to Step 2*. Nonbottleneck resources should be scheduled to support the schedule of the bottleneck and not produce more than the bottleneck can handle. That is, the blanking press should not produce more than the welding station can handle, and the activities of the cleaning and subsequent operations should be based on the output rate of the welding station.

4. *Elevate the Bottleneck(s).* After the scheduling improvements in steps 1–3 have been exhausted and the bottleneck is still a constraint to throughput, management should consider increasing the capacity of the bottleneck. For example, if the welding station is still a constraint after exhausting schedule improvements, consider increasing its capacity by adding another shift or another welding machine. Other mechanisms are also available for increasing bottleneck capacity, and we address them a little later.

5. *Do Not Let Inertia Set In.* Actions taken in steps 3 and 4 will improve the welder throughput and may alter the loads on other processes. Consequently, the system constraint(s) may shift. Then, the practical application of steps 1–4 must be repeated in order to identify and manage the new set of constraints.

Because of its potential for improving performance dramatically, many manufacturers have applied the principles of the theory of constraints. All manufacturers implementing TOC principles can also dramatically change the mind-set of employees and managers. Instead of focusing solely on their own functions, they can see the "big picture" and where other improvements in the system might lie.

Identification and Management of Bottlenecks

Bottlenecks can both be internal or external to the firm, and typically represent a process, a step, or a workstation with the lowest capacity. **Throughput time** is the total elapsed time from the start to the finish of a job or a customer being processed at one or more workcenters. Where a bottleneck lies in a given service or manufacturing process can be identified in two ways. A workstation in a process is a bottleneck if (1) it has the highest total time per unit processed, or (2) it has the highest average utilization and total workload

throughput time

Total elapsed time from the start to the finish of a job or a customer being processed at one or more workcenters.

Managing Bottlenecks in Service Processes

Example 1 illustrates how a bottleneck step or activity can be identified for a loan approval process at a bank.

| EXAMPLE 1 | Identifying the Bottleneck in a Service Process |

Managers at the First Community Bank are attempting to shorten the time it takes customers with approved loan applications to get their paperwork processed. The flowchart for this process, consisting of several different activities, each performed by a different bank employee, is shown in Figure 1. Approved loan applications first arrive at activity or step 1, where they are checked for completeness and put in order. At step 2, the loans are categorized into different classes according to the loan amount and whether they are being requested for personal or commercial reasons. While credit checking commences at step 3, loan application data are entered in parallel into the information system for record-keeping purposes at step 4. Finally, all paperwork for setting up the new loan is finished at step 5. The time taken in minutes is given in parentheses.

Which single step is the bottleneck, assuming that market demand for loan applications exceeds the capacity of the process? The management is also interested in knowing the maximum number of approved loans this system can process in a 5-hour work day.

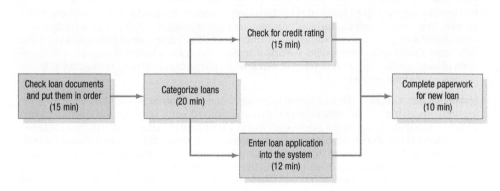

▲ FIGURE 1

Processing Credit Loan Applications at First Community Bank

SOLUTION

We define the bottleneck as step 2, which has the highest time per loan processed. The throughput time to complete an approved loan application is 15 + 20 + max (15, 12) + 10 = **60** minutes. Although we assume no waiting time in front of any step, in practice such a smooth process flow is not always the case. So the actual time taken for completing an approved loan will be longer than 60 minutes due to nonuniform arrival of applications, variations in actual processing times, and the related factors.

The capacity for loan completions is derived by translating the "minutes per customer" at the bottleneck step to "customer per hour." At First Community Bank, it is 3 customers per hour because the bottleneck step 2 can process only 1 customer every 20 minutes (60/3).

DECISION POINT

Step 2 is the bottleneck constraint. The bank will be able to complete a maximum of only 3 loan accounts per hour, or 15 new loan accounts in a 5-hour day. Management can increase the flow of loan applications by increasing the capacity of step 2 up to the point where another step becomes the bottleneck.

Todd Bigelow/Aurora Photos/Alamy

Due to constrained resources like doctors, nurses, and equipment, patients wait for medical care in a crowded waiting room at South Central Family Health Center in Los Angeles, California

A front-office process with high customer contact and divergence does not enjoy the simple line flows shown in Example 1. Its operations may serve many different customer types, and the demands on any one operation could vary considerably from one day to the next. However, bottlenecks can still be identified by computing the average utilization of each operation. However, the variability in workload also creates *floating bottlenecks*. One week the mix of work may make operation 1 a bottleneck, and the next week it may make operation 3 the bottleneck. This type of variability increases the complexity of day-to-day scheduling. In this situation, management prefers lower utilization rates, which allow greater slack to absorb unexpected surges in demand.

TOC principles outlined here are fairly broad-based and widely applicable. They can be useful for evaluating individual processes as well as large systems for both manufacturers as well as service providers. Service organizations, such as Delta Airlines, United Airlines, and major hospitals across the United States, including the U.S. Air Force health care system, use the TOC to their advantage.

Managing Bottlenecks in Manufacturing Processes

Bottlenecks can exist in all types of manufacturing processes, including the job process, batch process, line process, and continuous process. Since these processes differ in their design, strategic intent, and allocation of resources identification and management of bottlenecks will also differ accordingly with process type. We first discuss in this section issues surrounding management of bottlenecks in job and batch processes, while relegating constraint management in line processes for a later section.

Identifying Bottlenecks   Manufacturing processes often pose some complexities when identifying bottlenecks. If multiple services or products are involved, extra setup time at a workstation is usually needed to change over from one service or product to the next, which in turn increases the overload at the workstation being changed over. *Setup times* and their associated costs affect the size of the lots traveling through the job or batch processes. Management tries to reduce setup times because they represent unproductive time for workers or machines and thereby allow for smaller, more economic, batches. Nonetheless, whether setup times are significant or not, one way to identify a bottleneck operation is by its utilization. Example 2 illustrates how a bottleneck can be identified in a manufacturing setting where setups are negligible.

EXAMPLE 2	Identifying the Bottleneck in a Batch Process

Diablo Electronics manufactures four unique products (A, B, C, and D) that are fabricated and assembled in five different workstations (V, W, X, Y, and Z) using a small batch process. Each workstation is staffed by a worker who is dedicated to work a single shift per day at an assigned workstation. Batch setup times have been reduced to such an extent that they can be considered negligible. A flowchart denotes the path each product follows through the manufacturing process as shown in Figure 2, where each product's price, demand per week, and processing times per unit are indicated as well. Inverted triangles represent purchased parts and raw materials consumed per unit at different workstations. Diablo can make and sell up to the limit of its demand per week, and no penalties are incurred for not being able to meet all the demand.

Which of the five workstations (V, W, X, Y, or Z) has the highest utilization, and thus serves as the bottleneck for Diablo Electronics?

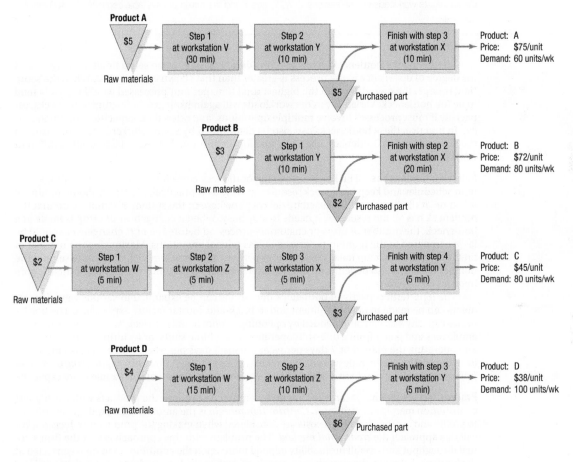

▲ **FIGURE 2**
Flowchart for Products A, B, C, and D

SOLUTION

Because the denominator in the utilization ratio is the same for every workstation, with one worker per machine at each step in the process, we can simply identify the bottleneck by computing aggregate workloads at each workstation.

The firm wants to satisfy as much of the product demand in a week as it can. Each week consists of 2,400 minutes of available production time. Multiplying the processing time at each station for a given product with the number of units demanded per week yields the workload represented by that product. These loads are summed across all products going through a workstation to arrive at the total load for the workstation, which is then compared with the others and the existing capacity of 2,400 minutes.

Workstation	Load from Product A	Load from Product B	Load from Product C	Load from Product D	Total Load (min)
V	60 × 30 = 1800	0	0	0	1,800
W	0	0	80 × 5 = 400	100 × 15 = 1,500	1,900
X	60 × 10 = 600	80 × 20 = 1,600	80 × 5 = 400	0	2,600
Y	60 × 10 = 600	80 × 10 = 800	80 × 5 = 400	100 × 5 = 500	2,300
Z	0	0	80 × 5 = 400	100 × 10 = 1,000	1,400

DECISION POINT
Workstation X is the bottleneck for Diablo Electronics because the aggregate workload at X is larger than the aggregate workloads of workstations V, W, Y, and Z and the maximum available capacity of 2,400 minutes per week.

Identifying the bottlenecks becomes considerably harder when setup times are lengthy and the degree of divergence in the process is greater than that shown in Example 2. When the setup time is large, the operation with the highest total time per unit processed would typically tend to be the bottleneck. Variability in the workloads will again likely create floating bottlenecks, especially if most processes involve multiple operations, and often their capacities are not identical. In practice, these bottlenecks can also be determined by asking workers and supervisors in the plant where the bottlenecks might lie and looking for piled up material in front of different workstations.

Relieving Bottlenecks The key to preserving bottleneck capacity is to carefully monitor short-term schedules and keep bottleneck resource as busy as is practical. Managers should minimize idle time at the bottlenecks, caused by delays elsewhere in the system and make sure that the bottleneck has all the resources it needs to stay busy. When a changeover or setup is made at a bottleneck, the number of units or customers processed before the next changeover should be large compared to the number processed at less critical operations. Maximizing the number of units processed per setup means fewer setups per year and, thus, less total time lost to setups. The number of setups also depends on the required product variety; more variety necessitates more frequent changeovers.

The long-term capacity of bottleneck operations can be expanded in various ways. Investments can be made in new equipment and in brick-and-mortar facility expansions. The bottleneck's capacity also can be expanded by operating it more hours per week, such as by hiring more employees and going from a one-shift operation to multiple shifts, or by hiring more employees and operating the plant 6 or 7 days per week versus 5 days per week. Managers also might relieve the bottleneck by redesigning the process, either through *process reengineering* or *process improvement*, or by purchasing additional machines or machines that can handle more capacity.

Product Mix Decisions Managers might be tempted to produce the products with the highest contribution margins or unit sales. *Contribution margin* is the amount each product contributes to profits and overhead; no fixed costs are considered when making the product mix decision. We call this approach the *traditional method*. The problem with this approach is that the firm's actual throughput and overall profitability depend more upon the contribution margin generated at the bottleneck than by the contribution margin of each individual product produced. We call this latter approach the *bottleneck method*. Example 3 illustrates both of these methods.

EXAMPLE 3	Determining the Product Mix Using Contribution Margin

The senior management at Diablo Electronics (see Exercise 2) wants to improve profitability by accepting the right set of orders, and so collected some additional financial data. Variable overhead costs are $8,500 per week. Each worker is paid $18 per hour and is paid for an entire week, regardless of how much the worker is used. Consequently, labor costs are fixed expenses. The plant operates one 8-hour shift per day, or 40 hours each week. Currently, decisions are made using the traditional method, which is to accept as much of the highest contribution margin product as possible (up to the limit of its demand), followed by the next highest contribution margin product, and so on until no more capacity is available. Pedro Rodriguez, the newly hired production supervisor, is knowledgeable about the theory of constraints and bottleneck-based scheduling.

He believes that profitability can indeed be improved if bottleneck resources were exploited to determine the product mix. What is the change in profits if, instead of the traditional method used by Diablo Electronics, the bottleneck method advocated by Pedro is used to select the product mix?

SOLUTION

Decision Rule 1: Traditional Method

Select the best product mix according to the highest overall contribution margin of each product.

Step 1: Calculate the contribution margin per unit of each product as shown here.

	A	B	C	D
Price	$75.00	$72.00	$45.00	$38.00
Raw material and purchased parts	−10.00	−5.00	−5.00	−10.00
= Contribution margin	$65.00	$67.00	$40.00	$28.00

When ordered from highest to lowest, the contribution margin per unit sequence of these products is B, A, C, D.

Step 2: Allocate resources V, W, X, Y, and Z to the products in the order decided in step 1. Satisfy each demand until the bottleneck resource (workstation X) is encountered. Subtract minutes away from 2,400 minutes available for each week at each stage.

Work Center	Minutes at the Start	Minutes Left After Making 80 B	Minutes Left After Making 60 A	Can Only Make 40 C	Can Still Make 100 D
V	2,400	2,400	600	600	600
W	2,400	2,400	2,400	2,200	700
X	2,400	800	200	0	0
Y	2,400	1,600	1,000	800	300
Z	2,400	2,400	2,400	2,200	1,200

The best product mix according to this traditional approach is then 60 A, 80 B, 40 C, and 100 D.

Step 3: Compute profitability for the selected product mix.

	Profits	
Revenue	(60 × $75) + (80 × $72) + (40 × $45) + (100 × $38)	= $15,860
Materials	(60 × $10) + (80 × $5) + (40 × $5) + (100 × $10)	= −$2,200
Labor	(5 workers) × (8 hours/day) × (5 days/week) × ($18/hour)	= −$3,600
Overhead		= −$8,500
Profit		= $1,560

Manufacturing the product mix of 60 A, 80 B, 40 C, and 100 D will yield a profit of $1,560 per week.

Decision Rule 2: Bottleneck Method

Select the best product mix according to the dollar contribution margin per minute of processing time at the bottleneck workstation X. This method would take advantage of the principles outlined in the theory of constraints and get the most dollar benefit from the bottleneck.

Step 1: Calculate the contribution margin/minute of processing time at bottleneck workstation X:

	Product A	Product B	Product C	Product D
Contribution margin	$65.00	$67.00	$40.00	$28.00
Time at bottleneck	10 minutes	20 minutes	5 minutes	0 minutes
Contribution margin per minute	$6.50	$3.35	$8.00	Not defined

When ordered from highest to lowest contribution margin/minute at the bottleneck, the manufacturing sequence of these products is D, C, A, B, which is reverse of the earlier order. Product D is scheduled first because it does not consume any resources at the bottleneck.

Step 2: Allocate resources V, W, X, Y, and Z to the products in the order decided in step 1. Satisfy each demand until the bottleneck resource (workstation X) is encountered. Subtract minutes away from 2,400 minutes available for each week at each stage.

Work Center	Minutes at the Start	Minutes Left After Making 100 D	Minutes Left After Making 80 C	Minutes Left After Making 60 A	Can Only Make 70 B
V	2,400	2,400	2,400	600	600
W	2,400	900	500	500	500
X	2,400	2,400	2,000	1,400	0
Y	2,400	1,900	1,500	900	200
Z	2,400	1,400	1,000	1,000	1,000

The best product mix according to this bottleneck-based approach is then 60 A, 70 B, 80 C, and 100 D.

Step 3: Compute profitability for the selected product mix.

	Profits	
Revenue	$(60 \times \$75) + (70 \times \$72) + (80 \times \$45) + (100 \times \$38)$	= $16,940
Materials	$(60 \times \$10) + (70 \times \$5) + (80 \times \$5) + (100 \times \$10)$	= −$2,350
Labor	(5 workers) × (8 hours/day) × (5 days/week) × ($18/hour)	= −$3,600
Overhead		= −$8,500
Profit		= $2,490

Manufacturing the product mix of 60 A, 70 B, 80 C, and 100 D will yield a profit of $2,490 per week.

DECISION POINT
By focusing on the bottleneck resources in accepting customer orders and determining the product mix, the sequence in which products are selected for production is reversed from **B, A, C, D** to **D, C, A, B**. Consequently, the product mix is changed from 60 A, 80 B, 40 C, and 100 D to 60 A, 70 B, 80 C, and 100 D. The increase in profits by using the bottleneck method is $930, ($2,490 − $1,560), or almost 60 percent over the traditional approach.

Linear programming could also be used to find the best product mix in Example 3. It must be noted, however, that the problem in Example 3 did not involve significant setup times. Otherwise, they must be taken into consideration for not only identifying the bottleneck, but also in determining the product mix. The experiential learning exercise of Min-Yo Garment Company at the end of this chapter provides an interesting illustration of how the product mix can be determined when setup times are significant. In this way, the principles behind the theory of constraints can be exploited for making better decisions about a firm's most profitable product mix.

drum-buffer-rope (DBR)

A planning and control system that regulates the flow of work-in-process materials at the bottleneck or the capacity constrained resource (CCR) in a productive system.

Drum-Buffer-Rope Systems **Drum-Buffer-Rope (DBR)** is a planning and control system based on the theory of constraints that is often used in manufacturing firms to plan and schedule production. It works by regulating the flow of work-in-process materials at the bottleneck or the capacity constrained resource (CCR). The bottleneck schedule is the *drum* because it sets the beat or the production rate for the entire plant and is linked to the market demand. The *buffer* is a time buffer that plans early flows to the bottleneck and thus protects it from disruption. It also ensures that the bottleneck is never starved for work. A finished-goods inventory buffer can also be placed in front of the shipping point in order to protect customer shipping schedules. Finally, the *rope* represents the tying of material release to the drum beat, which is the rate at which the bottleneck controls the throughput of the entire plant. It is thus a communication device to ensure that raw material is not introduced into the system at a rate faster than what the bottleneck can handle. Completing the loop, *buffer management* constantly monitors the execution of incoming bottleneck work. Working together, the drum, the buffer, and the rope can help managers create a production schedule that reduces lead times and inventories while simultaneously increasing throughput and on-time delivery.

To better understand the drum-buffer-rope system, consider the schematic layout shown in Figure 3. Process B, with a capacity of only 500 units per week, is the bottleneck because the upstream Process A and downstream Process C have capacities of 800 units per week and 700 units per week, respectively, and the market demand is 650 units per week, on average. In this case, because the capacity at process B is less than the market demand, it is the bottleneck. A constraint time buffer, which can be in the form of materials arriving earlier than needed, is placed right in front of the bottleneck (Process B). A shipping buffer, in the form of finished goods inventory, can also be placed prior to the shipping schedule in order to protect customer orders that are firm. Finally, a rope ties the material release schedule to match the schedule, or drum beat, at the bottleneck. The material flow is pulled forward by the drum beat prior to the bottleneck, while it is pushed downstream toward the customer subsequent to the bottleneck.

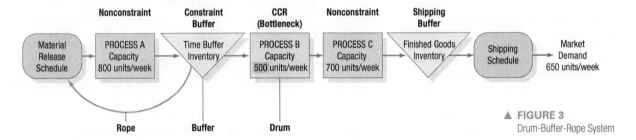

▲ FIGURE 3
Drum-Buffer-Rope System

DBR specifically strives to improve throughput by better utilizing the bottleneck resource and protecting it from disruption through the time buffer and protective buffer capacity elsewhere. So while the process batch in the DBR is any size that minimizes setups and improves utilization at the bottleneck, at nonconstrained resources the process batches are equal to what is needed for production at that time. The material can consequently be released in small batches known as transfer batches at the release point, which then combine at the constraint buffer to make a full process batch at the bottleneck. Transfer batches can be as small as one unit each, to allow a downstream workstation to start work on a batch before it is completely finished at the prior process. Using transfer batches typically facilitates a reduction in overall lead time.

DBR can be an effective system to use when the product the firm produces is relatively simple and the production process has more line flows. Planning is greatly simplified in this case and primarily revolves around scheduling the constrained resource and triggering other points to meet that bottleneck's schedule. Effectively implementing a DBR system requires an understanding of the TOC principles. However, such a system can be utilized in many different kinds of manufacturing and service organizations, either by itself or in conjunction with other planning and control systems. Managerial Practice 2 illustrates how the use of a DBR system improved the performance of the Marine Corps Maintenance Center in Albany, Georgia.

MANAGERIAL PRACTICE 1 — The Drum-Buffer-Rope System at a U.S. Marine Corps Maintenance Center

The U.S. Marine Corps Maintenance Center in Albany, Georgia, overhauls and repairs vehicles used by the corps, such as fuel tankers, trucks, earthmoving equipment, amphibious vehicles, and light armored vehicles. The overhaul process starts with the disassembly of each vehicle to determine the amount and nature of work that needs to be performed. The type and duration of the repair work can vary tremendously for even the same type of vehicle. Faced with such uncertainty, the Center was struggling until four years ago to complete its equipment repairs on time, and it had an increasing backlog to boot. For instance, the Center was able to repair only about 5 MK-48s (heavy-duty haulers) per month, when twice as many MK-48s—10 per month—typically needed repair. Different units of the corps were threatening to divert their orders to the private-sector repair companies.

TOC principles were used to identify the bottlenecks on the shop floor. After the Center's operations were studied in depth, however, contrary to everyone's expectations, it was discovered that more than enough capacity was available to repair and overhaul 10 MK-48s per month. The problem was not capacity; it was the Center's scheduling system. Products were being pushed onto the shop floor without regard for the status of the resources on the floor. Thus, what the Center had was a policy constraint related to the scheduling process, not an actual physical resource constraint.

In order to improve the Center's performance, its managers implemented a simplified form of a drum-buffer-rope system as shown in Figure 3. Since the Marine Corps Maintenance Center was not constrained by any internal resource, the drum in such a simplified system was based on firm orders. As orders came in, a quick check was done to measure the total load the Center's least-capable resource was handling. If the resource was not too heavily loaded, the order was accepted and released onto the shop floor for processing. The rope tied the shipping schedule directly to the material release schedule instead of the bottleneck schedule, and the only buffer maintained was the shipping buffer. Such a simplified DBR system did not require any specialized software. It focused simply on the market demand for repairs.

The Center's results following the change were impressive. Repair cycle times were reduced from an average of 167 days to 58 days, work-in-process levels were reduced from 550 percent of demand to 140 percent, and the cost to repair products went down by 25 to 30 percent due to an increased throughput. The Center's ability to repair MK-48s became much more flexible, too. In fact, it can now repair as many as 23 MK-48s per month. The Center is on schedule for 99 percent of the production lines where the TOC principles have been implemented, and the repair costs have decreased by 25 percent. Carrying out these simple improvements made the Albany Maintenance Center a world-class overhaul and repair operation.

Repairs to assault vehicles can vary tremendously at the U.S. Marine Corps Maintenance Center in Albany, Georgia. The center struggled to keep up with its repairs until managers implemented the simplified form of a drum-buffer-rope system. The result? Repair times fell from 167 days to just 58 days, on average.

Source: Mandyam Srinivasan, Darren Jones, and Alex Miller, "Applying Theory of Constraints Principles and Lean Thinking at the Marine Corps Maintenance Center," *Defense Acquisition Review Journal,* August–November 2004; M. Srinivasan, Darren Jones, and Alex Miller, "Corps Capabilities," APICS Magazine (March 2005), pp. 46–50.

Managing Constraints in a Line Process

Products created by a line process include the assembly of computers, automobiles, appliances, and toys. Such assembly lines can exist in providing services as well. For instance, putting together a standardized hamburger with a fixed sequence of steps is akin to operating an assembly line. While the product mix or demand volumes do not change as rapidly for line processes as for job or batch processes, the load can shift between work centers in a line as the end product being assembled is changed or the total output rate of the line is altered. Constraints arising out of such actions can be managed by balancing the workload between different stations in a line, which we explain next in greater detail.

Line Balancing

line balancing

The assignment of work to stations in a line process so as to achieve the desired output rate with the smallest number of workstations.

Line balancing is the assignment of work to stations in a line process so as to achieve the desired output rate with the smallest number of workstations. Normally, one worker is assigned to a station. Thus, the line that produces at the desired pace with the fewest workers is the most efficient one. Achieving this goal is much like the theory of constraints, because both approaches are concerned about bottlenecks. Line balancing differs in how it addresses bottlenecks. Rather than (1) taking on new customer orders to best use bottleneck capacity or (2) scheduling so that bottleneck resources are conserved, line balancing takes a third approach. It (3) creates workstations with workloads as evenly balanced as possible. It seeks to create workstations so that the capacity utilization for the bottleneck is not much higher than for the other workstations in the line. Another difference is that line balancing applies only to line processes that do assembly work, or to work that can be bundled in many ways to create the jobs for each workstation in the line. The latter situation can be found both in manufacturing and service settings.

Line balancing must be performed when a line is set up initially, when a line is rebalanced to change its hourly output rate, or when a product or process changes. The goal is to obtain workstations with well-balanced workloads (e.g., every station takes roughly 3 minutes per customer in a cafeteria line with different food stations).

work elements

The smallest units of work that can be performed independently.

immediate predecessors

Work elements that must be done before the next element can begin.

The analyst begins by separating the work into **work elements**, which are the smallest units of work that can be performed independently. The analyst then obtains the time standard for each element and identifies the work elements, called **immediate predecessors**, which must be done before the next element can begin.

Precedence Diagram Most lines must satisfy some technological precedence requirements; that is, certain work elements must be done before the next can begin. However, most lines also allow for some latitude and more than one sequence of operations. To help you better visualize immediate predecessors, let us run through the construction of a **precedence diagram**.[2] We denote the work elements by circles, with the time required to perform the work shown below each circle. Arrows lead from immediate predecessors to the next work element. Example 4 illustrates a manufacturing process, but a back office line-flow process in a service setting can be approached similarly.

precedence diagram

A diagram that allows one to visualize immediate predecessors better; work elements are denoted by circles, with the time required to perform the work shown below each circle.

EXAMPLE 4	**Constructing a Precedence Diagram**

Green Grass, Inc., a manufacturer of lawn and garden equipment, is designing an assembly line to produce a new fertilizer spreader, the Big Broadcaster. Using the following information on the production process, construct a precedence diagram for the Big Broadcaster.

Work Element	Description	Time (sec)	Immediate Predecessor(s)
A	Bolt leg frame to hopper	40	None
B	Insert impeller shaft	30	A
C	Attach axle	50	A
D	Attach agitator	40	B
E	Attach drive wheel	6	B
F	Attach free wheel	25	C
G	Mount lower post	15	C
H	Attach controls	20	D, E
I	Mount nameplate	18	F, G
		Total 244	

SOLUTION

Figure 4 shows the complete diagram. We begin with work element A, which has no immediate predecessors. Next, we add elements B and C, for which element A is the only immediate predecessor. After entering time standards and arrows showing precedence, we add elements D and E, and so on. The diagram simplifies interpretation. Work element F, for example, can be done anywhere on the line after element C is completed. However, element I must await completion of elements F and G.

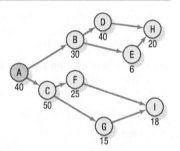

◄ **FIGURE 4**
Precedence Diagram for Assembling the Big Broadcaster

DECISION POINT

Management now has enough information to develop a line-flow layout that clusters work elements to form workstations, with a goal being to balance the workloads and, in the process, minimize the number of workstations required.

Desired Output Rate The goal of line balancing is to match the output rate to the staffing or production plan. For example, if the plan calls for 4,800 units or customers per week and the line operates 80 hours per week, the desired output rate ideally would be 60 units or customers (4,800/80) per hour. Matching output to the plan ensures on-time delivery and prevents buildup of unwanted inventory or customer delays. However, managers should avoid rebalancing a line too frequently because each time a line is rebalanced many workers' jobs on the line must be redesigned, temporarily hurting productivity and sometimes even requiring a new detailed layout for some stations.

---

[2]Precedence relationships and precedence diagrams are also important in the entirely different context of project management.

Cycle Time   After determining the desired output rate for a line, the analyst can calculate the line's cycle time. A line's **cycle time** is the maximum time allowed for work on a unit at each station.[3] If the time required for work elements at a station exceeds the line's cycle time, the station will be a bottleneck, preventing the line from reaching its desired output rate. The target cycle time is the reciprocal of the desired hourly output rate:

$$c = \frac{1}{r}$$

where

$$c = \text{cycle time in hours per unit}$$

$$r = \text{desired output rate in units per hour}$$

For example, if the line's desired output rate is 60 units per hour, the cycle time is $c = 1/60$ hour per unit, or 1 minute.

Theoretical Minimum   To achieve the desired output rate, managers use line balancing to assign every work element to a station, making sure to satisfy all precedence requirements and to minimize the number of stations, n, formed. If each station is operated by a different worker, minimizing n also maximizes worker productivity. Perfect balance is achieved when the sum of the work-element times at each station equals the cycle time, c, and no station has any idle time. For example, if the sum of each station's work-element times is 1 minute, which is also the cycle time, the line achieves perfect balance. Although perfect balance usually is unachievable in practice, owing to the unevenness of work-element times and the inflexibility of precedence requirements, it sets a benchmark, or goal, for the smallest number of stations possible. The **theoretical minimum (TM)** for the number of stations is

$$\text{TM} = \frac{\Sigma t}{c}$$

where

$$\Sigma t = \text{total time required to assemble each unit (the sum of all work-element standard times)}$$

$$c = \text{cycle time}$$

For example, if the sum of the work-element times is 15 minutes and the cycle time is 1 minute, $\text{TM} = 15/1$, or 15 stations. Any fractional values obtained for TM are rounded up because fractional stations are impossible.

Idle Time, Efficiency, and Balance Delay   Minimizing n automatically ensures (1) minimal idle time, (2) maximal efficiency, and (3) minimal balance delay. Idle time is the total unproductive time for all stations in the assembly of each unit:

$$\text{Idle time} = nc - \Sigma t$$

where

$$n = \text{number of stations}$$

$$c = \text{cycle time}$$

$$\Sigma t = \text{total standard time required to assemble each unit}$$

Efficiency is the ratio of productive time to total time, expressed as a percent:

$$\text{Efficiency (\%)} = \frac{\Sigma t}{nc}(100)$$

Balance delay is the amount by which efficiency falls short of 100 percent:

$$\text{Balance delay (\%)} = 100 - \text{Efficiency}$$

As long as c is fixed, we can optimize all three goals by minimizing n.

---

[3]Except in the context of line balancing, *cycle time* has a different meaning. It is the elapsed time between starting and completing a job. Some researchers and practitioners prefer the term *lead time*.

Skoda Automotive assembly line in Mlada Boleslav. Since 1991, Skoda has been a part of Volkswagen for over 20 years.

| EXAMPLE 5 | Calculating the Cycle Time, Theoretical Minimum, and Efficiency |

Green Grass's plant manager just received marketing's latest forecasts of Big Broadcaster sales for the next year. She wants its production line to be designed to make 2,400 spreaders per week for at least the next 3 months. The plant will operate 40 hours per week.

a. What should be the line's cycle time?

b. What is the smallest number of workstations that she could hope for in designing the line for this cycle time?

c. Suppose that she finds a solution that requires only five stations. What would be the line's efficiency?

MyOMLab

Tutor 7.1 in MyOMLab provides another example to calculate these line-balancing measures.

SOLUTION

a. First, convert the desired output rate (2,400 units per week) to an hourly rate by dividing the weekly output rate by 40 hours per week to get $r = 60$ units per hour. Then, the cycle time is

$$c = 1/r = 1/60 \text{ (hour/unit)} = 1 \text{ minute/unit} = 60 \text{ seconds/unit}$$

b. Now, calculate the theoretical minimum for the number of stations by dividing the total time, Σt, by the cycle time, $c = 60$ seconds. Assuming perfect balance, we have

$$TM = \frac{\Sigma t}{c} = \frac{244 \text{ seconds}}{60 \text{ seconds}} = 4.067 \text{ or } 5 \text{ stations}$$

c. Now, calculate the efficiency of a five-station solution, assuming for now that one can be found:

$$\text{Efficiency (\%)} = \frac{\Sigma t}{nc}(100) = \frac{244}{5(60)}(100) = 81.3\%$$

DECISION POINT

If the manager finds a solution with five stations that satisfies all precedence constraints, then that is the optimal solution; it has the minimum number of stations possible. However, the efficiency (sometimes called the *theoretical maximum efficiency*) will be only 81.3 percent. Perhaps the line should be operated less than 40 hours per week (thereby adjusting the cycle time) and the employees transferred to other kinds of work when the line does not operate.

Finding a Solution   Often, many assembly-line solutions are possible, even for such simple problems as Green Grass's. The goal is to cluster the work elements into workstations so that (1) the number of workstations required is minimized, and (2) the precedence and cycle-time requirements are not violated. The idea is to assign work elements to workstations subject to the precedence requirements so that the work content for the station is equal (or nearly so, but less than) the cycle time for the line. In this way, the number of workstations will be minimized.

Here we use the trial-and-error method to find a solution, although commercial software packages are also available. Most of these packages use different decision rules in picking which work element to assign next to a workstation being created. The ones used by POM for Windows are described in Table 3. The solutions can be examined for improvement, because there is no guarantee that they are optimal or even feasible. Some work elements cannot be assigned to the same station, some changes can be made to reduce the number of stations, or some shifts can provide better balance between stations.

TABLE 3 | HEURISTIC DECISION RULES IN ASSIGNING THE NEXT WORK ELEMENT TO A WORKSTATION BEING CREATED

Create one station at a time. For the station now being created, identify the unassigned work elements that qualify for assignment: They are candidates if

1. **All of their predecessors have been assigned to this station or stations already created.**

2. **Adding them to the workstation being created will not create a workload that exceeds the cycle time.**

Decision Rule	Logic
Longest work element	Picking the candidate with the longest time to complete is an effort to fit in the most difficult elements first, leaving the ones with short times to "fill out" the station.
Shortest work element	This rule is the opposite of the longest work element rule because it gives preference in workstation assignments to those work elements that are quicker. It can be tried because no single rule guarantees the best solution. It might provide another solution for the planner to consider.
Most followers	When picking the next work element to assign to a station being created, choose the element that has the most *followers* (due to precedence requirements). In Figure 4, item C has three followers (F, G, and I) whereas item D has only one follower (H). This rule seeks to maintain flexibility so that good choices remain for creating the last few workstations at the end of the line.
Fewest followers	Picking the candidate with the fewest followers is the opposite of the most followers rule.

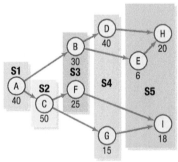

▲ FIGURE 5
Big Broadcaster Precedence
Diagram Solution

pacing

The movement of product from one station to the next as soon as the cycle time has elapsed.

Figure 5 shows a solution that creates just five workstations. We know that five is the minimum possible, because five is the theoretical minimum found in Example 5. All of the precedence and cycle-time requirements are also satisfied. Consequently, the solution is optimal for this problem. Each worker at each station must perform the work elements in the proper sequence. For example, workstation S5 consists of one worker who will perform work elements E, H, and I on each unit that comes along the assembly line. The processing time per unit is 44 seconds (6 + 20 + 18) which does not exceed the cycle time of 60 seconds (see Example 5). Furthermore, the immediate predecessors of these three work elements are assigned to this workstation or upstream workstations, so their precedence requirements are satisfied. The worker at workstation S5 can do element I at any time but will not start element H until element E is finished.

Managerial Considerations

In addition to balancing a line for a given cycle time, managers have four other considerations: (1) pacing, (2) behavioral factors, (3) number of models produced, and (4) different cycle times.

Pacing   The movement of product from one station to the next as soon as the cycle time has elapsed is called **pacing**. Pacing manufacturing processes allows materials handling to be automated and requires less inventory storage area. However, it is less flexible in handling unexpected delays that require either slowing down the entire line or pulling the unfinished work off the line to be completed later.

Behavioral Factors   The most controversial aspect of line-flow layouts is behavioral response. Studies show that installing production lines increases absenteeism, turnover, and grievances.

Paced production and high specialization (say, cycle times of less than 2 minutes) lower job satisfaction. Workers generally favor inventory buffers as a means of avoiding mechanical pacing. One study even showed that productivity increased on unpaced lines.

Number of Models Produced   A line that produces several items belonging to the same family is called a **mixed-model line**. In contrast, a single-model line produces one model with no variations. Mixed-model production enables a plant to achieve both high-volume production *and* product variety. However, it complicates scheduling and increases the need for good communication about the specific parts to be produced at each station.

mixed-model line

A production line that produces several items belonging to the same family.

Cycle Times   A line's cycle time depends on the desired output rate (or sometimes on the maximum number of workstations allowed). In turn, the maximum line efficiency varies considerably with the cycle time selected. Thus, exploring a range of cycle times makes sense. A manager might go with a particularly efficient solution even if it does not match the desired output rate. The manager can compensate for the mismatch by varying the number of hours the line operates through overtime, extending shifts, or adding shifts. Multiple lines might even be the answer.

LEARNING GOALS IN REVIEW

1 **Explain the theory of constraints.** Constraints or bottlenecks can exist in the form of internal resources or market demand in both manufacturing and service organizations, and in turn play an important role in determining system performance. See the section on "The Theory of Constraints (TOC)". Review opening vignette on BP Oil Spill clean-up for an application of TOC.

2 **Understand linkage of capacity constraints to financial performance measures.** Review and understand Table 1.

3 **Identify bottlenecks.** The TOC provides guidelines on how to identify and manage constraints. The section "Identification and Management of Bottlenecks," shows you how to identify bottlenecks in both service as well as manufacturing firms.

4 **Apply theory of constraints to product mix decisions.** Review Example 3 to understand how using a bottleneck based method for allocating resources and determining the product mix leads to greater profits.

5 **Describe how to manage constraints in an assembly line.** Assembly line balancing, as a special form of a constraint in managing a line process within both manufacturing and services, can also be an effective mechanism for matching output to a plan and running such processes more efficiently. The section "Managing Constraints in a Line Process," shows you how to balance assembly lines and create work stations. Review Solved Problem 2 for an application of line balancing principles.

MyOMLab helps you develop analytical skills and assesses your progress with multiple problems on processing time for average customer, bottleneck activity, maximum customers served at bottleneck per hour, average capacity of system, theoretical maximum of stations in an assembly line, longest work element decision rule, line's efficiency, and cycle time.

MyOMLab Resources	Titles	Link to the Book
Video	*Constraint Management at Southwest Airlines*	Managing Constraints Across the Organization; The Theory of Constraints
	1st Bank Villa Italia: Waiting Lines	Identification and Management of Bottlenecks
OM Explorer Solvers	Min-Yo Garment Company Spreadsheet	Estimate Capacity Requirements; Example 1; Managing Bottlenecks in Manufacturing Processes; Example 2
OM Explorer Tutors	7.1 Line Balancing	Line Balancing; Example 5; Solved Problem 2
POM for Windows	Line Balancing	Line Balancing; Example 5; Solved Problem 2
SimQuick Simulation Exercises	Simulating process of making jewelry boxes and making choice on investing in new machine	The Theory of Constraints; Example 1
Internet Exercise	Granite Rock and Chevron	The Theory of Constraints; Identification and Management of Bottlenecks
Key Equations		
Image Library		

Key Equations

1. Cycle time: $c = \dfrac{1}{r}$

2. Theoretical minimum number of workstations: $\text{TM} = \dfrac{\Sigma t}{c}$

3. Idle time: $nc - \Sigma t$

4. Efficiency(%): $\dfrac{\Sigma t}{nc}(100)$

5. Balance delay (%): $100 - \text{Efficiency}$

Key Terms

balance delay	immediate predecessors	theoretical minimum (TM)
bottleneck	line balancing	theory of constraints (TOC)
constraint	mixed-model line	throughput time
cycle time	pacing	work elements
drum-buffer-rope (DBR)	precedence diagram	

Solved Problem 1

Bill's Car Wash offers two types of washes: Standard and Deluxe. The process flow for both types of customers is shown in the following chart. Both wash types are first processed through steps A1 and A2. The Standard wash then goes through steps A3 and A4 while the Deluxe is processed through steps A5, A6, and A7. Both offerings finish at the drying station (A8). The numbers in parentheses indicate the minutes it takes for that activity to process a customer.

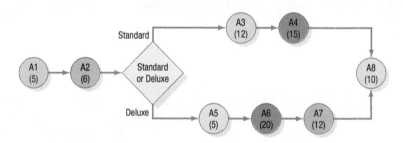

a. Which step is the bottleneck for the Standard car wash process? For the Deluxe car wash process?

b. What is the capacity (measured as customers served per hour) of Bill's Car Wash to process Standard and Deluxe customers? Assume that no customers are waiting at step A1, A2, or A8.

c. If 60 percent of the customers are Standard and 40 percent are Deluxe, what is the average capacity of the car wash in customers per hour?

d. Where would you expect Standard wash customers to experience waiting lines, assuming that new customers are always entering the shop and that no Deluxe customers are in the shop? Where would the Deluxe customers have to wait, assuming no Standard customers?

SOLUTION

a. Step A4 is the bottleneck for the Standard car wash process, and Step A6 is the bottleneck for the Deluxe car wash process, because these steps take the longest time in the flow.

b. The capacity for Standard washes is 4 customers per hour because the bottleneck step A4 can process 1 customer every 15 minutes (60/15). The capacity for Deluxe car washes is 3 customers per hour (60/20). These capacities are derived by translating the "minutes per customer" of each bottleneck activity to "customers per hour."

c. The average capacity of the car wash is $(0.60 \times 4) + (0.40 \times 3) = 3.6$ customers per hour.

d. Standard wash customers would wait before steps A1, A2, A3, and A4 because the activities that immediately precede them have a higher rate of output (i.e., smaller processing times). Deluxe wash customers would experience a wait in front of steps A1, A2, and A6 for the same reasons. A1 is included for both types of washes because the arrival rate of customers could always exceed the capacity of A1.

Solved Problem 2

A company is setting up an assembly line to produce 192 units per 8-hour shift. The following table identifies the work elements, times, and immediate predecessors:

Work Element	Time (Sec)	Immediate Predecessor(s)
A	40	None
B	80	A
C	30	D, E, F
D	25	B
E	20	B
F	15	B
G	120	A
H	145	G
I	130	H
J	115	C, I
	Total 720	

a. What is the desired cycle time (in seconds)?
b. What is the theoretical minimum number of stations?
c. Use trial and error to work out a solution, and show your solution on a precedence diagram.
d. What are the efficiency and balance delay of the solution found?

SOLUTION

a. Substituting in the cycle-time formula, we get

$$c = \frac{1}{r} = \frac{8 \text{ hours}}{192 \text{ units}}(3{,}600 \text{ seconds/hour}) = 150 \text{ seconds/unit}$$

b. The sum of the work-element times is 720 seconds, so

$$\text{TM} = \frac{\Sigma t}{c} = \frac{720 \text{ seconds/unit}}{150 \text{ seconds/unit-station}} = 4.8 \text{ or } 5 \text{ stations}$$

which may not be achievable.

c. The precedence diagram is shown in Figure 6. Each row in the following table shows work elements assigned to each of the five workstations in the proposed solution.

d. Calculating the efficiency, we get

$$\text{Efficiency} = \frac{\Sigma t}{nc}(100) = \frac{720 \text{ seconds/unit}}{5[150 \text{ seconds/unit}]} = 96\%$$

Thus, the balance delay is only 4 percent (100–96).

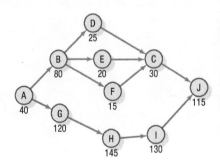

▲ FIGURE 6
Precedence Diagram

Station	Candidate(s)	Choice	Work-Element Time (Sec)	Cumulative Time (Sec)	Idle Time (c = 150 Sec)
S1	A	A	40	40	110
	B	B	80	120	30
	D, E, F	D	25	145	5
S2	E, F, G	G	120	120	30
	E, F	E	20	140	10
S3	F, H	H	145	145	5
S4	F, I	I	130	130	20
	F	F	15	145	5
S5	C	C	30	30	120
	J	J	115	145	5

Discussion Questions

1. Take a process that you encounter on a daily basis, such as the lunch cafeteria or the journey from your home to school/work, and identify the bottlenecks that limit the throughput of this process.

2. Using the same process as in question 1, identify conditions that would lead to the bottlenecks changing or shifting away from the existing bottleneck.

3. How could the efficiency of the redesigned process be improved further?

Problems

The OM Explorer and POM for Windows software is available to all students using the 10th edition of this text. Go to **www.pearsonhighered.com/krajewski** to download these computer packages. If you purchased MyOMLab, you also have access to Active Models software and significant help in doing the following problems. Check with your instructor on how best to use these resources. In many cases, the instructor wants you to understand how to do the calculations by hand. At the least, the software provides a check on your calculations. When calculations are particularly complex and the goal is interpreting the results in making decision, the software entirely replaces the manual calculations.

1. Bill's Barbershop has two barbers available to cut customers' hair. Both barbers provide roughly the same

experience and skill, but one is just a little bit slower than the other. The process flow in Figure 7 shows that all customers go through steps B1 and B2 and then can be served at either of the two barbers at step B3. The process ends for all customers at step B4. The numbers in parentheses indicate the minutes it takes that activity to process a customer.

a. How long does it take the average customer to complete this process?

b. What single activity is the bottleneck for the entire process?

c. How many customers can this process serve in an hour?

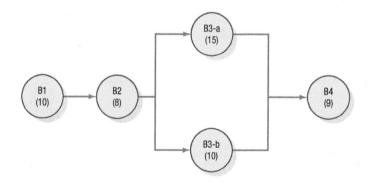

▲ FIGURE 7
Process Flow for Bill's Barbershop

2. Figure 8 details the process flow for two types of customers who enter Barbara's Boutique shop for customized dress alterations. After step T1, Type A customers proceed to step T2 and then to any of the three workstations at T3, followed by steps T4 and T7. After step T1, Type B customers proceed to step T5 and then steps T6 and T7. The numbers in parentheses are the minutes it takes to process a customer.

a. What is the capacity of Barbara's shop in terms of the numbers of Type A customers who can be served in an hour? Assume no customers are waiting at steps T1 or T7.

b. If 30 percent of the customers are Type A customers and 70 percent are Type B customers, what is the average capacity of Barbara's shop in customers per hour?

c. Assuming that the arrival rate is greater than five customers per hour, when would you expect Type A customers to experience waiting lines, assuming no Type B customers in the shop? Where would the Type B customers have to wait, assuming no Type A customers?

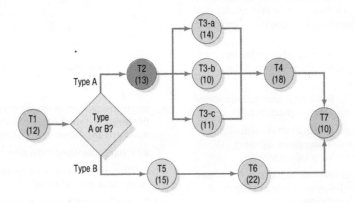

▲ FIGURE 8
Process Flow for Barbara's Boutique Customers

3. Canine Kernels Company (CKC) manufactures two different types of dog chew toys (A and B, sold in 1,000-count boxes) that are manufactured and assembled on three different workstations (W, X, and Y) using a small-batch process (see Figure 9). Batch setup times are negligible. The flowchart denotes the path each product follows through the manufacturing process, and each product's price, demand per week, and processing times per unit are indicated as well. Purchased parts and raw materials consumed during production are represented by inverted triangles. CKC can make and sell up to the limit of its demand per week; no penalties are incurred for not being able to meet all the demand. Each workstation is staffed by a worker who is dedicated to work on that workstation alone and is paid $6 per hour. Total labor costs per week are fixed. Variable overhead costs are $3,500/week. The plant operates one 8-hour shift per day, or 40 hours/week. Which of the three workstations, W, X, or Y, has the highest aggregate workload, and thus serves as the bottleneck for CKC?

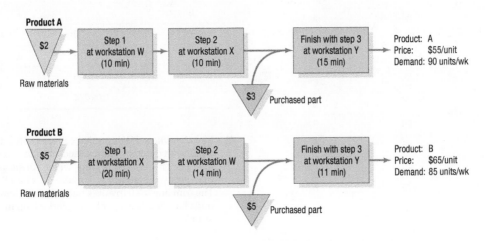

▲ FIGURE 9
Flowchart for Canine Kernels Company (CKC)

4. The senior management at Canine Kernels Company (CKC) is concerned with the existing capacity limitation, so they want to accept the mix of orders that maximizes the company's profits. Traditionally, CKC has utilized a method whereby decisions are made to produce as much of the product with the highest contribution margin as possible (up to the limit of its demand), followed by the next highest contribution margin product, and so on until no more capacity is available. Because capacity is limited, choosing the proper product mix is crucial. Troy Hendrix, the newly hired production supervisor, is an avid follower of the theory of constraints philosophy and the bottleneck method for scheduling. He believes that profitability can indeed be approved if bottleneck resources are exploited to determine the product mix.

   a. What is the profit if the traditional contribution margin method is used for determining CKC's product mix?

   b. What is the profit if the bottleneck method advocated by Troy is used for selecting the product mix?

   c. Calculate the profit gain, both in absolute dollars as well as in terms of percentage gains, by using TOC principles for determining product mix.

5. Use the longest work element rule to balance the assembly line described in the following table and Figure 10 so that it will produce 40 units per hour.

   a. What is the cycle time?

   b. What is the theoretical minimum number of workstations?

   c. Which work elements are assigned to each workstation?

   d. What are the resulting efficiency and balance delay percentages?

   e. Use the shortest work element rule to balance the assembly line. Do you note any changes in solution?

Work Element	Time (Sec)	Immediate Predecessor(s)
A	40	None
B	80	A
C	30	A
D	25	B
E	20	C
F	15	B
G	60	B
H	45	D
I	10	E, G
J	75	F
K	15	H, I, J
	Total 415	

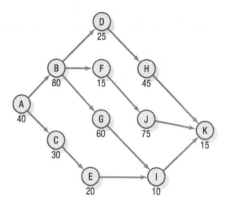

▲ FIGURE 10
Precedence Diagram

6. Johnson Cogs wants to set up a line to serve 60 customers per hour. The work elements and their precedence relationships are shown in the following table.

   a. What is the theoretical minimum number of stations?

   b. How many stations are required using the longest work element decision rule?

   c. Suppose that a solution requiring five stations is obtained. What is its efficiency?

Work Element	Time (Sec)	Immediate Predecessor(s)
A	40	None
B	30	A
C	50	A
D	40	B
E	6	B
F	25	C
G	15	C
H	20	D, E
I	18	F, G
J	30	H, I
	Total 274	

7. The *trim line* at PW is a small subassembly line that, along with other such lines, feeds into the final chassis line. The entire assembly line, which consists of more than 900 workstations, is to make PW's new E cars. The trim line itself involves only 13 work elements and must handle 20 cars per hour. Work-element data are as follows:

Work Element	Time (Sec)	Immediate Predecessor(s)
A	1.8	None
B	0.4	None
C	1.6	None
D	1.5	A
E	0.7	A
F	0.5	E
G	0.8	B
H	1.4	C
I	1.4	D
J	1.4	F, G
K	0.5	H
L	1.0	J
M	0.8	I, K, L

a. Draw a precedence diagram.

b. What cycle time (in minutes) results in the desired output rate?

c. What is the theoretical minimum number of stations?

d. Use the longest work element decision rule to balance the line and calculate the efficiency of your solution.

e. Use the most followers work element decision rule to balance the line and calculate the efficiency of your solution.

8. In order to meet holiday demand, Penny's Pie Shop requires a production line that is capable of producing 50 pecan pies per week, while operating only 40 hours per week. There are only 4 steps required to produce a single pecan pie with respective processing times of 5 min, 5 min, 45 min, and 15 min.

a. What should be the line's cycle time?

b. What is the smallest number of workstations Penny could hope for in designing the line considering this cycle time?

c. Suppose that Penny finds a solution that requires only four stations. What would be the efficiency of this line?

Advanced Problems

9. Melissa's Photo Studio offers both individual and group portrait options. The process flow diagram in Figure 11 shows that all customers must first register and then pay at one of two cashiers. Then, depending on whether they want a single or group portrait they go to different rooms. Finally, everyone picks up their own finished portrait.

a. How long does it take to complete the entire process for a group portrait?

b. What single activity is the bottleneck for the entire process, assuming the process receives equal amounts of both groups and individuals?

c. What is the capacity of the bottleneck for both groups and individuals?

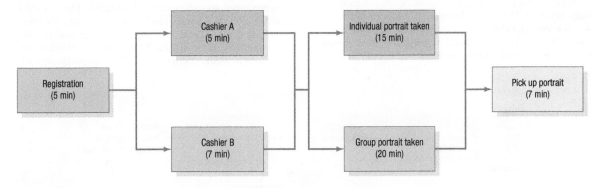

▲ FIGURE 11
Melissa's Photo Studio

10. Yost-Perry Industries (YPI) manufactures a mix of affordable guitars (A, B, C) that are fabricated and assembled at four different processing stations (W, X, Y, Z). The operation is a batch process with small setup times that can be considered negligible. The product information (price, weekly demand, and processing times) and process sequences are shown in Figure 12. Raw materials and purchased parts (shown as a per-unit consumption rate) are represented by inverted triangles. YPI is able to make and sell up to the limit of its demand per week with no penalties incurred for not meeting the full demand. Each workstation is staffed by one highly skilled worker who is dedicated to work on that workstation alone and is paid $15 per hour. The plant operates one 8-hour shift per day and operates on a 5-day work week (i.e., 40 hours of production per person per week). Overhead costs are $9,000/week. Which of the four workstations, W, X, Y, or Z, has the highest aggregate workload, and thus serves as the bottleneck for YPI?

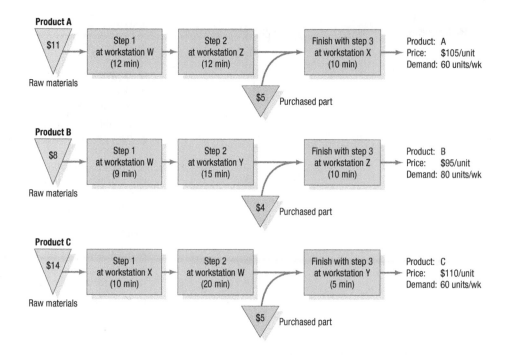

▶ FIGURE 12

Flowchart for Yost-Perry Industries (YPI)

11. Yost-Perry Industries' (YPI) senior management team wants to improve the profitability of the firm by accepting the right set of orders. Currently, decisions are made using the traditional method, which is to accept as much of the highest contribution margin product as possible (up to the limit of its demand), followed by the next highest contribution margin product, and so on until all available capacity is utilized. Because the firm cannot satisfy all the demand, the product mix must be chosen carefully. Jay Perry, the newly promoted production supervisor, is knowledgeable about the theory of constraints and the bottleneck-based method for scheduling. He believes that profitability can indeed be improved if bottleneck

resources are exploited to determine the product mix. What is the change in profits if, instead of the traditional method that YPI has used thus far, the bottleneck method advocated by Jay is used for selecting the product mix?

12. A.J.'s Wildlife Emporium manufactures two unique bird-feeders (Deluxe and Super Duper) that are manufactured and assembled in up to three different workstations (X, Y, Z) using a small batch process. Each of the products is produced according to the flowchart in Figure 13. Additionally, the flowchart indicates each product's price, weekly demand, and processing times per unit. Batch setup times are negligible. A.J. can make and sell up to the limit of its weekly demand and there are no penalties for

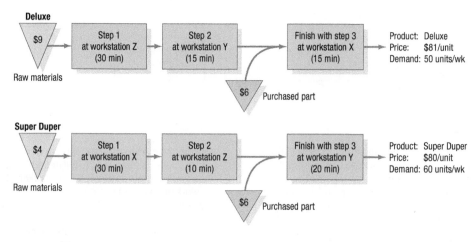

▲ FIGURE 13

A.J.'s Wildlife Emporium Flowchart

not being able to meet all of the demand. Each workstation is staffed by a worker who is dedicated to work on that workstation alone and is paid $16 per hour. The plant operates 40 hours per week, with no overtime. Overhead costs are $2,000 per week. Based on the information provided, as well as the information contained in the flowchart, answer the following questions.

a. Using the traditional method, which bases decisions solely on a product's contribution to profits and overhead, what is the optimal product mix and what is the overall profitability?

b. Using the bottleneck-based method, what is the optimal product mix and what is the overall profitability?

13. Cooper River Glass Works (CRGW) produces four different models of desk lamps as shown in Figure 14. The operations manager knows that total monthly demand exceeds the capacity available for production. Thus, she is interested in determining the product mix which will maximize profits. Each model's price, routing, processing times, and material cost is provided in Figure 14. Demand next month is estimated to be 200 units of model Alpha, 250 units of model Bravo, 150 units of model Charlie, and 225 units of model Delta. CRGW operates only one 8-hour shift per day and is scheduled to work 20 days next month (no overtime). Further, each station requires a 10 percent capacity cushion.

a. Which station is the bottleneck?

b. Using the traditional method, which bases decisions solely on a product's contribution to profits and overhead, what is the optimal product mix and what is the overall profitability?

c. Using the bottleneck-based method, what is the optimal product mix and what is the overall profitability?

14. The senior management at Davis Watercraft would like to determine if it is possible to improve firm profitability by changing their existing product mix. Currently, the product mix is determined by giving resource priority to the highest contribution margin watercraft. Davis Watercraft always has a contingent of 10 workers on hand; each worker is paid $25 per hour. Overhead costs are $35,000 per week. The plant operates 18 hours per day and 6 days per week. Labor is considered a fixed expense because workers are paid for their time regardless of their utilization. The production manager has determined that workstation 1 is the bottleneck. Detailed production information is provided below.

	Model		
	A	B	C
Price	$450	$400	$500
Material Cost	$50	$40	$110
Weekly Demand	100	75	40
Processing Time Station 1	60 min	0 min	30 min
Processing Time Station 2	0 min	0 min	60 min
Processing Time Station 3	10 min	60 min	0 min
Processing Time Station 4	20 min	30 min	40 min

a. Using the traditional method, which bases decisions solely on a product's contribution to profits and overhead, what is the product mix that yields the highest total profit? What is the resulting profit?

b. Using the bottleneck-based method, what is the product mix that yields the highest total profit? What is the resulting profit?

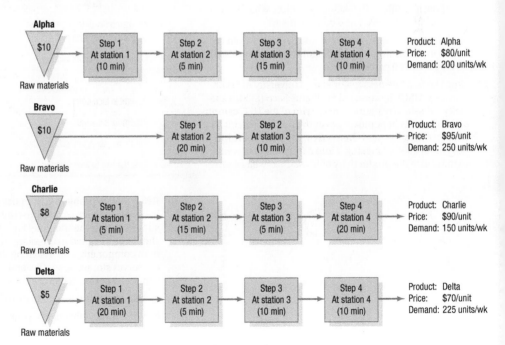

► **FIGURE 14**

Cooper River Glass Works Flowchart

15. A paced assembly line has been devised to manufacture calculators, as the following data show:

Station	Work Element Assigned	Work Element Time (min)
S1	A	2.7
S2	D, E	0.6, 0.9
S3	C	3.0
S4	B, F, G	0.7, 0.7, 0.9
S5	H, I, J	0.7, 0.3, 1.2
S6	K	2.4

   a. What is the maximum hourly output rate from this line? (*Hint*: The line can go only as fast as its slowest workstation.)

   b. What cycle time corresponds to this maximum output rate?

   c. If a worker is at each station and the line operates at this maximum output rate, how much idle time is lost during each 10-hour shift?

   d. What is the line's efficiency?

16. Jane produces custom greeting cards using six distinct work elements. She would like to produce 10 cards in each 8-hour card-making session. Figure 15 details each work element and its associated durations in minutes as well as their precedence relationships.

   a. What cycle time is required to satisfy the required output rate?

   b. What is the theoretical minimum number of workstations required?

   c. If Jane identifies a five-station solution, what is the associated efficiency and balance delay?

   d. If the cycle time increased by 100 percent, would the theoretical minimum number of workstations also increase by 100 percent?

17. Greg Davis, a business major at the University of South Carolina (USC), has opened Six Points Saco (SPS), a specialty subs–taco restaurant, at the rim of the USC campus. SPS has grown in popularity over the one year that it has been in operation, and Greg is trying to perfect the business model before making it into a franchise. He wants to maximize the productivity of his staff, as well as serve customers well in a timely fashion. One area of concern is the drive-thru operation during the 11:30 A.M. to 12:30 P.M. lunch hour.

The process of fulfilling an order involves fulfilling the tasks listed below.

Greg is interested in getting a better understanding of the staffing patterns that will be needed in order to operate his restaurant. After taking a course in operations management at the university, he knows that fulfilling a customer order at SPS is very similar to operating an assembly line. He has also used the POM for Windows software before, and wants to apply it for examining different demand scenarios for serving his customers.

   a. If all the seven tasks are handled by one employee, how many customers could be served per hour?

   b. If Greg wants to process 45 customers per hour, how many employees will he need during the peak period?

   c. With the number of employees determined in part b, what is the maximum number of customers who could be served every hour (i.e., what is the maximum output capacity)?

   d. Assuming that no task is assigned to more than one employee, what is the "maximum output capacity" from this assembly line? How many employees will be needed to actually accomplish this maximum output capacity?

   e. Beyond the output accomplished in part d, if Greg decides to add one additional worker to help out with a bottleneck task, where should he add that worker? With that addition, would he be able to process more customers per hour? If so, what is the new maximum output capacity for the drive-thru?

	Task	Time (Seconds)	Immediate Predecessors
A.	Take an order at the booth. Most orders are for a taco and a sub.	25	
B.	Collect money at the window.	20	A
C.	Gather drinks.	35	B
D.	Assemble taco order.	32	B
E.	Assemble sub order.	30	B
F.	Put drinks, taco, and sub in a bag.	25	C, D, E
G.	Give the bag to the customer.	10	F

18. Refer back to problem 7. Suppose that in addition to the usual precedence constraints, there are two zoning constraints within the trim line. First, work elements K and L should be assigned to the same station; both use a common component, and assigning them to the same station conserves storage space. Second, work elements H and J cannot be performed at the same station.

   a. Using trial and error, balance the line as best you can.

   b. What is the efficiency of your solution?

FIGURE 15 ▶
Precedence Diagram for
Custom Greeting Cards

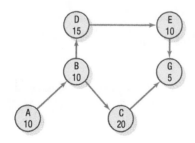

EXPERIENTIAL LEARNING | Min-Yo Garment Company

The Min-Yo Garment Company is a small firm in Taiwan that produces sportswear for sale in the wholesale and retail markets. Min-Yo's garments are unique because they offer fine embroidery and fabrics with a variety of striped and solid patterns. Over the 20 years of its existence, the Min-Yo Garment Company has become known as a quality producer of sports shirts with dependable deliveries. However, during that same period, the nature of the apparel industry has undergone change. In the past, firms could be successful producing standardized shirts in high volumes with few pattern or color choices and long production lead times. Currently, with the advent of regionalized merchandising and intense competition at the retail level, buyers of the shirts are looking for shorter lead times and much more variety in patterns and colors. Consequently, many more business opportunities are available today than ever before to a respected company such as Min-Yo.

Even though the opportunity for business success seemed bright, the management meeting last week was gloomy. Min-Yo Lee, president and owner of Min-Yo Garment, expressed concerns over the performance of the company: "We are facing strong competition for our products. Large apparel firms are driving prices down on high-volume licensed brands. Each day more firms enter the customized shirt business. Our profits are lower than expected, and delivery performance is deteriorating. We must reexamine our capabilities and decide what we can do best."

Products

Min-Yo has divided its product line into three categories: licensed brands, subcontracted brands, and special garments.

Licensed Brands

Licensed brands are brands that are owned by one company but, through a licensing agreement, are produced by another firm that also markets the brand in a specific geographic region. The licenser may have licensees all over the world. The licensee pays the licenser a fee for the privilege of marketing the brand in its region, and the licenser agrees to provide some advertising for the product, typically through media outlets that have international exposure. A key aspect of the licensing agreement is that the licensee must agree to provide sufficient quantities of product at the retail level. Running out of stock hurts the image of the brand name.

Currently, only one licensed brand is manufactured by Min-Yo. The brand, called the Muscle Shirt, is owned by a large "virtual corporation" in Italy that has no manufacturing facilities of its own. Min-Yo has been licensed to manufacture Muscle Shirts and sell them to large retail chains in Taiwan. The retail chains require prompt shipments at the end of each week. Because of competitive pressures from other licensed brands, low prices are important. Min-Yo sells each Muscle Shirt to retail chains for $6.

The demand for Muscle Shirts averages 900 shirts per week. The following demand for Muscle Shirts has been forecasted for the next 12 weeks.

Min-Yo's forecasts of Muscle Shirts are typically accurate to within ±200 shirts per week. If demand exceeds supply in any week, the excess demand is lost. No backorders are taken, and Min-Yo incurs no cost penalty for lost sales.

Subcontracted Brands

Manufacturers in the apparel industry often face uncertain demand. To maintain level production at their plants, many manufacturers seek subcontractors to produce their brands. Min-Yo is often considered a subcontractor because of its reputation in the industry. Although price is a consideration, the owners of subcontracted brands emphasize dependable delivery and the ability of the subcontractor to adjust order quantities on short notice.

Week	Demand	Week	Demand
1*	700	7	1,100
2	800	8	1,100
3	900	9	900
4	900	10	900
5	1,000	11	800
6	1,100	12	700

*In other words, the company expects to sell 700 Muscle Shirts at the end of week 1.

Currently, Min-Yo manufactures only one subcontracted brand, called the Thunder Shirt because of its bright colors. Thunder Shirts are manufactured to order for a company in Singapore. Min-Yo's price to this company is $7 per shirt. When orders are placed, usually twice a month, the customer specifies the delivery of certain quantities in each of the next 2 weeks. The last order the customer placed is overdue, forcing Min-Yo to pay a penalty charge. To avoid another penalty, 200 shirts must be shipped in week 1. The Singapore company is expected to specify the quantities it requires for weeks 2 and 3 at the beginning of week 1. The delivery schedule containing the orders for weeks 4 and 5 is expected to arrive at the beginning of week 3, and so on. The customer has estimated its average weekly needs for the year to be 200 shirts per week, although its estimates are frequently inaccurate.

Because of the importance of this large customer to Min-Yo and the lengthy negotiations of the sales department to get the business, management always tries to satisfy its needs. Management believes that if Min-Yo Garment ever refuses to accept an order from this customer, Min-Yo will lose the Thunder Shirt business. Under the terms of the sales contract, Min-Yo agreed to pay this customer $1 for every shirt not shipped on time for each week the shipment of the shirt is delinquent. Delinquent shipments must be made up.

Special Garments

Special garments are made only to customer order because of their low volume and specialized nature. Customers come to Min-Yo Garment to manufacture shirts for special promotions or special company occasions. Min-Yo's special garments are known as Dragon Shirts because of the elaborate embroidery and oriental flair of the designs. Because each shirt is made to a particular customer's specifications and requires a separate setup, special garments cannot be produced in advance of a firm customer order.

Although price is not a major concern for the customers of special garments, Min-Yo sells Dragon Shirts for $8 a shirt to ward off other companies seeking to enter the custom shirt market. Its customers come to Min-Yo because the company can produce almost any design with high quality and deliver an entire order on time. When placing an order for a Dragon Shirt, a customer specifies the design of the shirt (or chooses from Min-Yo's catalog), supplies specific designs for logos, and specifies the quantity of the order and the delivery date. In the past, management checked to see whether such an order would fit into the schedule, and then either accepted or rejected it on that basis. If Min-Yo accepts an order for delivery at the *end* of a certain week and fails to meet this commitment, it pays a penalty of $2 per shirt for each week delivery is delayed. This penalty is incurred weekly until the delinquent order is delivered. The company tried to forecast demand for specific designs of Dragon Shirts but has given up. Last week, Min-Yo had four Dragon Shirt opportunities of 50, 75, 200, and 60 units but chose not to accept any of the orders. Dragon Shirt orders in the past ranged from 50 units to 300 units with varying lead times.

Figure 16, Min-Yo's current open-order file, shows that in some prior week Min-Yo accepted an order of 400 Thunder Shirts for delivery last week. The open-order file is important because it contains the commitment management made to customers. Commitments are for a certain quantity and a date of delivery. As customer orders are accepted, management enters the quantity in the green cell representing the week that they are due. Because Dragon Shirts are unique unto themselves, they each have their own order number for future use. No Dragon Shirt orders appear in the open-order file because Min-Yo has not committed to any in the past several weeks.

Manufacturing

Process

The Min-Yo Garment Company has the latest process technology in the industry—a machine, called a garment maker, that is run by one operator on each of three shifts. This single machine process can make every garment Min-Yo produces; however, the changeover times consume a substantial amount of capacity. Company policy is to run the machine three shifts a day, five days a week. If business is insufficient to keep the machine busy, the workers are idle because Min-Yo is committed to never fire or lay off a worker. By the same token, the firm has a policy of never working on weekends. Thus, the capacity of the process is 5 days × 24 hours = 120 hours per week. The hourly wage is $10 per hour, so the firm is committed to a fixed labor cost of $10 × 120 = $1,200 per week. Once the machine has been set up to make a particular type of garment, it can produce

that garment at the rate of 10 garments per hour, regardless of type. The cost of the material in each garment, regardless of type, is $4. Raw materials are never a problem and can be obtained overnight.

Scheduling the Garment Maker

Scheduling at Min-Yo is done once each week, after production for the week has been completed and shipped, after new orders from customers have arrived, and before production for the next week has started. Scheduling results in two documents.

The first is a production schedule, shown in Figure 17. The schedule shows what management wants the garment maker process to produce in a given week. Two spreadsheet entries are required for each product that is to be produced in a given week. They are in the green shaded cells. The first is the production quantity. In Figure 17, the schedule shows that Min-Yo produced quantities of 800 units for Muscle and 200 units for Thunder last week. The second input is a "1" if the machine is to be set up for a given product or a "blank" if no changeover is required. Figure 17 shows that last week changeovers were required for the Muscle and Thunder production runs. The changeover information is important because, at the end of a week, the garment maker process will be set up for the last product produced. If the same product is to be produced first the following week, no new changeover will be required. Management must keep track of the sequence of production each week to take advantage of this savings. The only exception to this rule is Dragon Shirts, which are unique orders that always require a changeover. In week 0, Min-Yo did not produce any Dragon Shirts; however, it did produce 800 Muscle Shirts, followed by 200 Thunder Shirts. Finally, the spreadsheet calculates the hours required for the proposed

MIN-YO GARMENT COMPANY

<u>Open Order File</u> (Record of commitments)

Product	\multicolumn{10}{c}{Week Order is Due}									
	1	2	3	4	5	6	7	8	9	10
Thunder Orders	400									
Dragon Order 1										
Dragon Order 2										
Dragon Order 3										
Dragon Order 4										
Dragon Order 5										
Dragon Order 6										
Dragon Order 7										
Dragon Order 8										
Dragon Order 9										
Dragon Order 10										
Dragon Order 11										
Dragon Order 12										
Dragon Order 13										
Dragon Order 14										
Dragon Order 15										

▶ ▶| Intro / Open Order File / Week 1 / Week 2 / Week 3 / Week 4 / Week 5 / Week 6 / Week 7 / Week 8 / Week 9 / Week 10 / S|◀ ▶

▲ FIGURE 16

Min-Yo's Open Order File

Note: All orders are to be delivered at the end of the week indicated, after production for the week has been completed and before next week's production is started.

MIN-YO GARMENT COMPANY

PRODUCTION SCHEDULE

The two inputs to the Production Schedule table are:
1. The quantity you decide to produce this time period
2. Whether there is a setup/changover required (1 or 0)

PRODUCT	Changeover	Quantity		Changeover	Quantity		Changeover	Quantity
Muscle	1	800						
Hours		88						
Thunder	1	200						
Hours		30						
Dragon Order 1			Dragon Order 11			Dragon Order 21		
Dragon Order 2			Dragon Order 12			Dragon Order 22		
Dragon Order 3			Dragon Order 13			Dragon Order 23		
Dragon Order 4			Dragon Order 14			Dragon Order 24		
Dragon Order 5			Dragon Order 15			Dragon Order 25		
Dragon Order 6			Dragon Order 16			Dragon Order 26		
Dragon Order 7			Dragon Order 17			Dragon Order 27		
Dragon Order 8			Dragon Order 18			Dragon Order 28		
Dragon Order 9			Dragon Order 19			Dragon Order 29		
Dragon Order 10			Dragon Order 20			Dragon Order 30		
Total Dragon Hours		0						
Total Dragon Production		0						
Total Hours scheduled		118						

Is production within capacity?   Yes

▲ FIGURE 17
Min-Yo's Production Schedule

schedule. Changeover times for Muscle, Thunder, and Dragon Shirts are 8, 10, and 25 hours respectively. Because the garment maker process produces 10 garments per hour regardless of type, the production hours required for Muscle Shirts is $8 + 800/10 = 88$ hours, and the production hours for Thunder Shirts is $10 + 200/10 = 30$ hours, as shown in Figure 17. The total time spent on the garment maker process on all products in a week cannot exceed 120 hours. The spreadsheet will not allow you to proceed if this constraint is violated.

The second document is a weekly profit and loss (P&L) statement that factors in sales and production costs, including penalty charges and inventory carrying costs, as shown in Figure 18. The inventory carrying cost for *any type of product* is $0.10 per shirt per week left in inventory after shipments for the week have been made. The spreadsheet automatically calculates the P&L statement, which links to the open-order file and the production schedule, after the demand for Muscle Shirts is known. Figure 18 shows that the actual demand for Muscle Shirts last week was 750 shirts.

P&L STATEMENT

Product	Price	Beg Inv	Production	Available	Demand	Sales	End Inv	Inv/Past due costs
Muscle	$6	550	800	1350	750	4500	600	60
Thunder	$7		200	200	400	1400	-200	200
Dragon Orders	$8		0	0	0	0	0	0
Totals			1000			5900		260

		Current	Cumulative
Sales Total		$5,900	$5,900
Labor	$1,200		
Materials	$4,000		
Inv/Past due	$260		
Total Cost		$5,460	
Profit Contribution		$440	$440

▲ FIGURE 18
Min-Yo's P&L Schedule

Notes

- The past due quantity of shirts are those shirts not shipped as promised, and appear as a negative number in the "End Inv" column.

- Available = Beginning inventory + Production

- Sales = Demand × Price when demand < available; Available × Price, otherwise

- Inventory cost = $0.10 times number of shirts in inventory. Past due cost equals past due quantity times the penalty ($1 for Thunder Shirts; $2 for Dragon Shirts). These costs are combined in the "Inv/Past Due Costs" column.

The Simulation

At Min-Yo Garment Company, the executive committee meets weekly to discuss the new order possibilities and the load on the garment maker process. The executive committee consists of top management representatives from finance, marketing, and operations. You will be asked to participate on a team and play the role of a member of the executive committee in class. During this exercise, you must decide how far into the future to plan. Some decisions, such as the markets you want to exploit, are long-term in nature. Before class, you may want to think about the markets and their implications for manufacturing. Other decisions are short-term and have an impact on the firm's ability to meet its commitments. In class, the simulation will proceed as follows.

1. Use the Min-Yo Tables spreadsheet in OM Explorer in MyOMLab. It is found in the Solver menu, under Constraint Management. You will start by specifying the production schedule for week 1, based on the forecasts for week 1 in the case narrative for Muscle Shirts and additional information on new and existing orders for the customized shirts from your instructor. *You may assume that your managerial predecessors left the garment machine set up for Thunder Shirts.* The production schedule decision is to be made in collaboration with your executive committee colleagues in class.

2. When all the teams have finalized their production plans for week 1, the instructor will supply the actual demands for Muscle Shirts in week 1. Enter that quantity in the P&L statement in the spreadsheet for week 1.

3. After the P&L statement for week 1 is completed, the instructor will announce the new order requests for Thunder Shirts and Dragon Shirts to be shipped in week 2 and the weeks beyond.

4. You should look at your order requests, accept those that you want, and reject the rest. Add those that you accept for delivery in future periods to your open-order file. Enter the quantity in the cell representing the week the order is due. You are then irrevocably committed to them and their consequences.

5. You should then make out a new production schedule, specifying what you want your garment-maker process to do in the next week (it will be for week 2 at that time).

6. The instructor will impose a time limit for each period of the simulation. When the time limit for one period has been reached, the simulation will proceed to the next week. Each week the spreadsheet will automatically update your production and financial information in the Summary Sheet.

VIDEO CASE | Constraint Management at Southwest Airlines

What if you could take a commercial airline flight any time, and anywhere you wanted to go? Just show up at the airport without the need to consider time schedules or layovers. Aside from the potentially cost-prohibitive nature of such travel, there are also constraints in the airline system that preclude this kind of operation. From the lobby check-in process through to boarding at the gate and processing plane turnaround, the process of operating the airline is filled with constraints that must be managed in order for them to be successful and profitable. Flight schedules are tightly orchestrated and controlled, departure and arrival gates at airports are limited, and individual aircraft have seating capacities in each section of the plane, to name a few.

Southwest Airlines is one company that has figured out how to manage its constraints and generate positive customer experiences in the process. No other airline can claim the same level of profitability and customer satisfaction Southwest regularly achieves. What is its secret?

Talk to any loyal Southwest customer and you will hear rave reviews about its low fares, great customer service, and lack of assigned seating that gives customers a chance to choose who they sit next to onboard. From an operations perspective, it is much more than what the customer sees. Behind the scenes, operations managers carefully manage and execute—3,400 times a day in over 60 cities in the United States—a process designed to manage all potential bottleneck areas.

Southwest's famous rapid gate-turnaround of 25 minutes or less demonstrates how attention to the activities that ground operations must complete to clean, fuel, and prepare a plane for flight can become bottlenecks if not properly scheduled. In the terminal at the gate, passenger boarding also can be a bottleneck if the boarding process itself is not carefully managed. Since the individual mix of passengers present a different set of issues with each flight that often are not evident until the passengers actually arrive

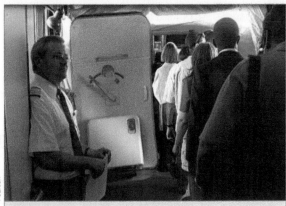

Passengers boarding a Southwest Airlines flight.

at the gate, ranging from families with kids and strollers to large quantities of carry-on bags and passengers needing wheelchair assistance, operations managers must be ready for any and all situations to avoid a boarding bottleneck while also assuring a pleasant and stress-free gate experience for all passengers.

In 2007, as part of the company's continuous improvement activities, Southwest focused its attention on the passenger boarding process to determine whether there was a better way to board. Its existing process consisted of three groups, A, B, C, with no assigned seating. Depending on passenger check-in and arrival time, passengers were given a spot in a group.

Those first to check-in received choice places in the A group. Last to check-in ended up in the C group, and usually had a choice of only middle seats in the back of the plane upon boarding. As passengers arrived at the gate, they queued up in their respective boarding group areas to await the boarding call.

Seven different alternate boarding scenarios were designed and tested. They included

- New family pre-boarding behind the "A" group of first-to-board passengers
- Family pre-boarding before anyone else, but seating choices limited on-board to behind the wing
- Six boarding groups (within A-B-C groups) instead of the original three A-B-C groups
- Assigned boarding gate line positions based on both boarding group and gate arrival time
- Single boarding chute at the gate, but up to nine groups all in one queue
- Boarding with a countdown clock to give customers an incentive to get in line and board quickly; incentives given out if everyone was on time
- Educational boarding video to make the boarding process fun, inform passengers how to board efficiently, and provide the company another way to promote its brand.

QUESTIONS

1. Analyze Southwest's passenger boarding process using the Theory of Constraints.
2. Which boarding scenario among the different ones proposed would you recommend for implementation? Why?
3. How should Southwest evaluate the gate boarding and plane turnaround process?
4. How will Southwest know that the bottleneck had indeed been eliminated after the change in the boarding process?

Selected References

Brown, A. "Theory of Constraints Tapped to Accelerate BP's Gulf of Mexico Cleanup." *Industry Week* (March 18, 2011).

Corominas, Albert, Rafael Pastor, and Joan Plans. "Balancing Assembly Line with Skilled and Unskilled Workers." *Omega*, vol. 36, no. 6 (2008), pp. 1126–1132.

Goldratt, E.M., and J. Cox. *The Goal*, 3rd rev. ed. New York: North River Press, 2004.

McClain, John O., and L. Joseph Thomas. "Overcoming the Dark Side of Worker Flexibility." *Journal of Operations Management*, vol. 21, (2003), pp. 81–92.

Srikanth, Mokshagundam L., and Michael Umble. *Synchronous Management: Profit-Based Manufacturing for the 21st Century*, vol. 1. Guilford, CT: Spectrum Publishing Company, 1997.

Srinivasan, Mandyam, Darren Jones, and Alex Miller. 2004. "Applying Theory of Constraints Principles and Lean Thinking at the Marine Corps Maintenance Center." *Defense Acquisition Rev. Quart.* (August–November 2004), pp. 134–145.

Srinivasan, Mandyam, Darren Jones, and Alex Miller. "Corps Capabilities." *APICS Magazine* (March 2005), pp. 46–50.

Steele, Daniel C., Patrick R. Philipoom, Manoj K. Malhotra, and Timothy D. Fry. "Comparisons Between Drum-Buffer-Rope and Material Requirements Planning: A Case Study." *International Journal of Production Research*, vol. 43, no. 15 (2005), pp. 3181–3208.

Umble, M., E. Umble, and S. Murakami. "Implementing Theory of Constraints in a Traditional Japanese Manufacturing Environment: The Case of Hitachi Tool Engineering." *International Journal of Production Research*, vol. 44, no. 15 (2006), pp. 1863–1880.

EVERETT KENNEDY BROWN/epa/Corbis

LEAN SYSTEMS

Panasonic company employees work on the disassembly line of CRT television sets at the company's Panasonic Eco Technology Center in Kato city, Hyogo prefecture, Japan. In conjunction with Panasonic's efforts to develop easy-to-recycle products, the company is also developing new recycling technologies and focusing on building lean operations. To prevent waste, an annual total of 30,700 tons of home appliances are recycled at the Panasonic facility, including 29,400 television units, 135,700 air conditioners, 173,300 washing machines and 149,100 refrigerators.

Panasonic Corporation

Panasonic Corporation, which was originally founded as Matsushita Corporation in 1918 to produce lamps, has grown to become one of the largest electronic manufacturing firms in the world. With over 384,000 employees and 680 consolidated companies, it is the largest producer in Japan of over 15,000 electronic products under the brand names of Panasonic, National, Quasar, and Technics, among others. Renowned for its global focus on efficiency and lean operations, its pursuit of excellence is exemplified nowhere better than at the Matsushita Electric Company's factory in Saga on Japan's southern island of Kyushu, where cordless phones, fax machines, and security cameras are made in record time by machines in a spotless facility.

Even though the plant's efficiency had doubled over a four-year span, managers saw opportunities for "trimming the fat" and improving further. The plant's conveyor belts were replaced by a cluster of robots that could seamlessly hand off work to one another, flexibly substitute for a broken robot, and synchronize production using software. As a result, throughput time declined from 2.5 days to 40 minutes, allowing the Saga plant to make twice as many phones per week, which in turn allowed a reduction in inventory because components such as chips and circuit boards spend much less time in the factory. Being able to make things faster means that the plant can quickly change the product mix even as customer demands shift and new products are introduced, thus allowing Panasonic to keep ahead of low cost rivals in Korea, China, and other Asian countries.

Panasonic has used the lessons learned from the Saga mother plant to change layouts and setups at six other plants in China, Malaysia, Mexico, and Great Britain.

From Chapter 8 of *Operations Management: Processes and Supply Chains,* Tenth Edition. Lee J. Krajewski, Larry P. Ritzman, Manoj K. Malhotra. Copyright © 2013 by Pearson Education, Inc. All rights reserved.

These plants have been able to similarly cut their inventories and improve productivity, even as ideas from local staff at each plant were incorporated into the change effort. The next sets of improvements are focused on breaking assembly lines into cells and better utilizing the idle robots. In addition, standardized circuit board designs that are common to a large variety of end products are being used in order to minimize the retooling of robots for every type of board. By relentlessly focusing on minimizing waste and continuously improving efficiency, Panasonic has posted record profit growths and has become a model for other electronic firms.

Source: Kenji Hall, "No One Does Lean like the Japanese," *Business Week* (July 10, 2006), pp. 40–41; http://panasonic.net/corporate/, April 25, 2011.

LEARNING GOALS *After reading this chapter, you should be able to:*

1. Describe how lean systems can facilitate the continuous improvement of processes.
2. Identify the characteristics and strategic advantages of lean systems.
3. Understand value stream mapping and its role in waste reduction.
4. Understand *kanban* systems for creating a production schedule in a lean system.
5. Explain the implementation issues associated with the application of lean systems.

Creating Value through Operations Management

Using Operations to Compete
Project Management

Managing Processes

Process Strategy
Process Analysis
Quality and Performance
Capacity Planning
Constraint Management
Lean Systems

Managing Supply Chains

Supply Chain Inventory Management
Supply Chain Design
Supply Chain Location Decisions
Supply Chain Integration
Supply Chain Sustainability and Humanitarian Logistics
Forecasting
Operations Planning and Scheduling
Resource Planning

Panasonic Corporation is a learning organization and an excellent example of an approach for designing supply chains known as **lean systems**, which allow firms like Panasonic to continuously improve its operations and spread the lessons learned across the entire corporation. Lean systems are operations systems that maximize the value added by each of a company's activities by removing waste and delays from them. They encompass the company's operations strategy, process design, quality management, constraint management, layout design, supply chain design, and technology and inventory management, and can be used by both service and manufacturing firms. Like a manufacturer, each service business takes an order from a customer, delivers the service, and then collects revenue. Each service business purchases services or items, receives and pays for them, and hires and pays employees. Each of these activities bears considerable similarity to those in manufacturing firms. They also typically contain huge amounts of waste. There are many ways to improve processes, regardless of whether they are manufacturing or nonmanufacturing processes. These same principles can be applied to make service processes lean, whether they are front-office, hybrid-office, or back-office designs. In this chapter we will explore how process improvement techniques can be used to make a firm lean.

We begin by discussing the continuous improvement aspect of lean systems, followed by a discussion of the characteristics of lean systems and the design of layouts needed to achieve these characteristics. We also address different types of lean systems used in practice, and some of the implementation issues that companies face.

Lean Systems across the Organization

Lean systems affect a firm's internal linkages between its core and supporting processes and its external linkages with its customers and suppliers. The design of supply chains using the lean systems approach is important to various departments and functional areas across the organization. Marketing relies on lean systems to deliver high-quality services or products on time and at reasonable prices. Human resources must put in place the right incentive systems that reward teamwork, and also recruit, train, and evaluate the employees needed to create a flexible workforce that can successfully operate a lean system. Engineering must design products that use more common parts, so that fewer setups are required and focused factories can be used. Operations is responsible for maintaining close ties with suppliers, designing the lean system, and using it in the production of services or goods. Accounting must adjust its billing and cost accounting practices to provide the support needed to manage lean systems. Finally, top management must embrace the lean philosophy and make it a part of organizational culture and learning, as was done by Panasonic in the opening vignette.

Continuous Improvement Using a Lean Systems Approach

One of the most popular systems that incorporate the generic elements of lean systems is the just-in-time (JIT) system. According to Taiichi Ohno, one of the earlier pioneers at Toyota Corporation, the **just-in-time (JIT) philosophy** is simple but powerful—*eliminate waste* or *muda* by cutting excess capacity or inventory and removing non-value-added activities. Table 1 shows the eight types of waste that often occur in firms in an interrelated fashion, and which must be eliminated in implementing lean systems.

The goals of a lean system are thus to eliminate these eight types of waste, produce services and products only as needed, and to continuously improve the value-added benefits of operations. A **JIT system** organizes the resources, information flows, and decision rules that enable a firm to realize the benefits of JIT principles.

lean systems
Operations systems that maximize the value added by each of a company's activities by removing waste and delays from them.

just-in-time (JIT) philosophy
The belief that waste can be eliminated by cutting unnecessary capacity or inventory and removing non-value-added activities in operations.

TABLE 1 | THE EIGHT TYPES OF WASTE OR MUDA[1]

Waste	Definition
1. Overproduction	Manufacturing an item before it is needed, making it difficult to detect defects and creating excessive lead times and inventory.
2. Inappropriate Processing	Using expensive high precision equipment when simpler machines would suffice. It leads to overutilization of expensive capital assets. Investment in smaller flexible equipment, immaculately maintained older machines, and combining process steps where appropriate reduce the waste associated with inappropriate processing.
3. Waiting	Wasteful time incurred when product is not being moved or processed. Long production runs, poor material flows, and processes that are not tightly linked to one another can cause over 90 percent of a product's lead time to be spent waiting.
4. Transportation	Excessive movement and material handling of product between processes, which can cause damage and deterioration of product quality without adding any significant customer value.
5. Motion	Unnecessary effort related to the ergonomics of bending, stretching, reaching, lifting, and walking. Jobs with excessive motion should be redesigned.
6. Inventory	Excess inventory hides problems on the shop floor, consumes space, increases lead times, and inhibits communication. Work-in-process inventory is a direct result of overproduction and waiting.
7. Defects	Quality defects result in rework and scrap, and add wasteful costs to the system in the form of lost capacity, rescheduling effort, increased inspection, and loss of customer good will.
8. Underutilization of Employees	Failure of the firm to learn from and capitalize on its employees' knowledge and creativity impedes long-term efforts to eliminate waste.

By spotlighting areas that need improvement, lean systems lead to continuous improvement in quality and productivity. The Japanese term for this approach to process improvement is *kaizen*. The key to *kaizen* is the understanding that excess capacity or inventory hides underlying problems with the processes that produce a service or product. Lean systems provide the mechanism for management to reveal the problems by systematically lowering capacities or inventories until the problems are exposed. For example, Figure 1 characterizes the philosophy behind continuous improvement with lean systems. In services, the water surface represents service system capacity, such as staff levels. In manufacturing, the water surface represents product and component inventory levels. The rocks represent problems encountered in the fulfillment of services or products. When the water surface is high enough, the boat passes over the rocks because the high level of capacity or inventory covers up problems. As capacity or inventory shrinks, rocks are exposed. Ultimately, the boat will hit a rock if the water surface falls far enough. Through lean systems, workers, supervisors, engineers, and analysts apply methods for continuous improvement to demolish the exposed rock. The coordination required to achieve smooth material flows in lean systems identifies problems in time for corrective action to be taken.

Maintaining low inventories, periodically stressing the system to identify problems, and focusing on the elements of the lean system lie at the heart of continuous improvement. For example, a Kawasaki plant in Lincoln, Nebraska, periodically cuts its safety stocks almost to zero. The problems at the plant are exposed, recorded, and later assigned to employees as improvement projects. After improvements are made, inventories are permanently cut to the new level.

JIT system
A system that organizes the resources, information flows, and decision rules that enable a firm to realize the benefits of JIT principles.

[1] David McBride, "The Seven Manufacturing Wastes," August 29, 2003, **http://www.emsstrategies.com** by permission of EMS Consulting Group, Inc. © 2003.

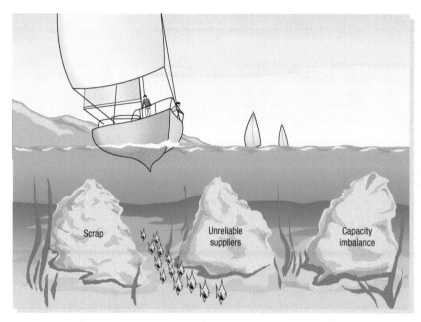

▲ FIGURE 1
Continuous Improvement with
Lean Systems

Many firms use this trial-and-error process to develop more efficient manufacturing operations. In addition, workers using special presses often fabricate parts on the assembly line in exactly the quantities needed. Service processes, such as scheduling, billing, order taking, accounting, and financial planning, can be improved with lean systems, too. In service operations, a common approach used by managers is to place stress on the system by reducing the number of employees doing a particular activity or series of activities until the process begins to slow or come to a halt. The problems can be identified, and ways for overcoming them explored. Other *kaizen* tactics can be used as well. Eliminating the problem of too much scrap might require improving the firm's work processes, providing employees with additional training, or finding higher-quality suppliers. Eliminating capacity imbalances might involve revising the firm's master production schedule and improving the flexibility of its workforce. Irrespective of which problem is solved, there are always new ones that can be addressed to enhance system performance.

Oftentimes, continuous improvement occurs with the ongoing involvement and input of new ideas from employees, who play an important role in implementing the JIT philosophy. In 2007 alone, about 740,000 corporate-wide improvement suggestions were received at Toyota. A large majority of them got implemented, and employees making those suggestions received rewards ranging from 500 yen (about $5) to upwards of 50,000 yen (about $500) depending upon their bottom line impact.

Supply Chain Considerations in Lean Systems

In this section, we discuss the two salient characteristics of lean systems that are related to creating and managing material flows in a supply chain: close supplier ties and small lot sizes.

Close Supplier Ties

Because lean systems operate with low levels of capacity slack or inventory, firms that use them need to have a close relationship with their suppliers. Supplies must be shipped frequently, have short lead times, arrive on schedule, and be of high quality. A contract might even require a supplier to deliver goods to a facility as often as several times per day.

The lean system philosophy is to look for ways to improve efficiency and reduce inventories throughout the supply chain. Close cooperation between companies and their suppliers can be a win–win situation for everyone. Better communication of component requirements, for example, enables more efficient inventory planning and delivery scheduling by suppliers, thereby improving supplier profit margins. Customers can then negotiate lower component prices. Close supplier relations cannot be established and maintained if companies view their suppliers as adversaries whenever contracts are negotiated. Rather, they should consider suppliers to be partners in a venture, wherein both parties have an interest in maintaining a long-term, profitable relationship. Consequently, one of the first actions undertaken when a lean system is implemented is to pare down the number of suppliers, and make sure they are located in close geographic proximity in order to promote strong partnerships and better synchronize product flows.

A particularly close form of supplier partnerships through lean systems is the JIT II system, which was conceived and implemented by Bose Corporation, a producer of high-quality professional sound and speaker systems. In a JIT II system, the supplier is brought into the plant to be an active member of the purchasing office of the customer. The *in-plant representative* is on site full-time at the supplier's expense and is empowered to plan and schedule the replenishment of materials from the supplier. Thus, JIT II fosters extremely close interaction with suppliers. The qualifications for a supplier to be included in the program are stringent.

In general, JIT II can offer benefits to both buyers and suppliers because it provides the organizational structure needed to improve supplier coordination by integrating the logistics, production, and purchasing processes together.

Small Lot Sizes

Lean systems use lot sizes that are as small as possible. A **lot** is a quantity of items that are processed together. Small lots have the advantage of reducing the average level of inventory relative to large lots. Small lots pass through the system faster than large lots since they do not keep materials waiting. In addition, if any defective items are discovered, large lots cause longer delays because the entire lot must be examined to find all the items that need rework. Finally, small lots help achieve a uniform workload on the system and prevent overproduction. Large lots consume large chunks of capacity at workstations and, therefore, complicate scheduling. Small lots can be juggled more effectively, enabling schedulers to efficiently utilize capacities.

Although small lots are beneficial to operations, they have the disadvantage of increased setup frequency. A *setup* is the group of activities needed to change or readjust a process between successive lots of items, sometimes referred to as a *changeover*. This changeover in itself is a process that can be made more efficient. Setups involve trial runs, and the material waste can be substantial as the machines are fine tuned for the new parts. Typically, a setup takes the same time regardless of the size of the lot. Consequently, many small lots, in lieu of several large lots, may result in waste in the form of idle employees, equipment, and materials. Setup times must be brief to realize the benefits of small-lot production.

Achieving brief setup times often requires close cooperation among engineering, management, and labor. For example, changing dies on large presses to form automobile parts from sheet metal can take 3 to 4 hours. At Honda's Marysville, Ohio, plant—where four stamping lines stamp all the exterior and major interior body panels for Accord production—teams worked on ways to reduce the changeover time for the massive dies. As a result, a complete change of dies for a giant 2,400-ton press now takes less than 8 minutes. The goal of **single-digit setup** means having setup times of less than 10 minutes. Some techniques used to reduce setup times at the Marysville plant include using conveyors for die storage, moving large dies with cranes, simplifying dies, enacting machine controls, using microcomputers to automatically feed and position work, and preparing for changeovers while a job currently in production is still being processed.

Process Considerations in Lean Systems

In this section, we discuss the following characteristics of lean systems: pull method of work flow, quality at the source, uniform workstation loads, standardized components and work methods, flexible workforce, automation, Five S (5S) practices, and total preventive maintenance (TPM).

Pull Method of Work Flow

Managers have a choice as to the nature of the material flows in a process or supply chain. Most firms using lean operations use the **pull method**, in which customer demand activates the production of a good or service. In contrast, a method often used in conventional systems that do not emphasize lean systems is the **push method**, which involves using forecasts of demand and producing the item before the customer orders it. To differentiate between these two methods, let us use a service example that involves a favorite pastime, eating.

For an illustration of the pull method, consider a five-star restaurant in which you are seated at a table and offered a menu of exquisite dishes, appetizers, soups, salads, and desserts. You can choose from filet mignon, porterhouse steak, yellow fin tuna, grouper, and lamb chops. Your choice of several salads is prepared at your table. Although some appetizers, soups, and desserts can be prepared in advance and brought to temperature just before serving, the main course and salads cannot. Your order for the salad and the main course signals the chef to begin preparing your specific requests. For these items, the restaurant is using the *pull method*. Firms using the pull method must be able to fulfill the customer's demands within an acceptable amount of time.

For an understanding of the push method, consider a cafeteria on a busy downtown corner. During the busy periods around 12 P.M. and 5 P.M. lines develop, with hungry patrons eager to eat and then move on to other activities. The cafeteria offers choices of chicken (roasted or deep fried), roast beef, pork chops, hamburgers, hot dogs, salad, soup (chicken, pea, and clam chowder), bread (three types), beverages, and desserts (pies, ice cream, and cookies). Close coordination is required between the cafeteria's "front office," where its employees interface with customers; and its "back office," the kitchen, where the food is prepared and then placed along the cafeteria's buffet line.

lot
A quantity of items that are processed together.

single-digit setup
The goal of having a setup time of less than 10 minutes.

pull method
A method in which customer demand activates production of the service or item.

push method
A method in which production of the item begins in advance of customer needs.

Diners fill their plates at a restaurant buffet. Because the food items must be prepared in advance, the restaurant uses a push method of work flow.

Because it takes substantial time to cook some of the food items, the cafeteria uses a *push method*. The cafeteria would have a difficult time using the pull method because it could not wait until a customer asked for an item before asking the kitchen to begin processing it. After all, shortages in food could cause riotous conditions (recall that customers are hungry), whereas preparing an excess amount of food will be wasteful because it will go uneaten. To make sure that neither of these conditions occurs, the cafeteria must accurately forecast the number of customers it expects to serve.

The choice between the push and pull methods is often situational. Firms using an assemble-to-order strategy sometimes use both methods: the push method to produce the standardized components and the pull method to fulfill the customer's request for a particular combination of the components.

Quality at the Source

Consistently meeting the customer's expectations is an important characteristic of lean systems. One way to achieve this goal is by adhering to a practice called *quality at the source*, which is a philosophy whereby defects are caught and corrected where they are created. The goal for workers is to act as their own quality inspectors and never pass on defective units to the next process. Automatically stopping the process when something is wrong and then fixing the problems on the line itself as they occur is also known as **jidoka**. *Jidoka* tends to separate worker and machine activities by freeing workers from tending to machines all the time, thus allowing them to staff multiple operations simultaneously. *Jidoka* represents a visual management system whereby status of the system in terms of safety, quality, delivery, and cost performance relative to the goals for a given fabrication cell or workstation in an assembly line is clearly visible to workers on the floor at all times.

An alternative to *jidoka* or quality at the source is the traditional practice of pushing problems down the line to be resolved later. This approach is often ineffective. For example, a soldering operation at the Texas Instruments antenna department had a defect rate that varied from 0 to 50 percent on a daily basis, averaging about 20 percent. To compensate, production planners increased the lot sizes, which only increased inventory levels and did nothing to reduce the number of defective items. The company's engineers then discovered through experimentation that gas temperature was a critical variable in producing defect-free items. They subsequently devised statistical control charts for the firm's equipment operators to use to monitor the temperature and adjust it themselves. Process yields immediately improved and stabilized at 95 percent, and Texas Instruments was eventually able to implement a lean system.

One successful approach for implementing quality at the source is to use **poka-yoke**, or mistake-proofing methods aimed at designing fail-safe systems that attack and minimize human error. *Poka-yoke* systems work well in practice. Consider, for instance, a company that makes modular products. The company could use the poka-yoke method by making different parts of the modular product in such a way that allows them to be assembled in only one way—the correct way. Similarly, a company's shipping boxes could be designed to be packed only in a certain way to minimize damage and eliminate all chances of mistakes. At Toyota plants, every vehicle being assembled is accompanied by an RFID chip containing information on how many nuts and bolts need to be tightened on that vehicle for an operation at a given workstation. A green light comes on when the right number of nuts have been tightened. Only then does the vehicle move forward on the assembly line.

Another tool for implementing quality at the source is *andon*, which is a system that gives machines and machine operators the ability to signal the occurrence of any abnormal condition such as tool malfunction, shortage of parts, or the product being made outside the desired specifications. It can take the form of audio alarms, blinking lights, LCD text displays, or chords that can be pulled by workers to ask for help or stop the production line if needed. Stopping a production line can, however, cost a company thousands of dollars each minute production is halted. Needless to say, management must realize the enormous responsibility this method puts on employees and must prepare them properly.

jidoka

Automatically stopping the process when something is wrong and then fixing the problems on the line itself as they occur.

poka-yoke

Mistake-proofing methods aimed at designing fail-safe systems that minimize human error.

Owen Franken/CORBIS

Uniform Workstation Loads

A lean system works best if the daily load on individual workstations is relatively uniform. Service processes can achieve uniform workstation loads by using reservation systems. For example, hospitals schedule surgeries in advance of the actual service so that the facilities and facilitating goods can be ready when the time comes. The load on the surgery rooms and surgeons can be evened out to make the best use of these resources. Another approach is to use differential pricing of the service to manage the demand for it. Uniform loads are the rationale behind airlines promoting weekend travel or red-eye flights that begin late in the day and end in the early morning. Efficiencies can be realized when the load on the firm's resources can be managed.

For manufacturing processes, uniform loads can be achieved by assembling the same type and number of units each day, thus creating a uniform daily demand at all workstations. Capacity planning, which recognizes capacity constraints at critical workstations, and line balancing are used to develop the master production schedule. For example, at Toyota the production plan may call for 4,500 vehicles per week for the next month. That requires two full shifts, 5 days per week, producing 900 vehicles each day, or 450 per shift. Three models are produced: Camry (C), Avalon (A), and Solara (S). Suppose that Toyota needs 200 Camrys, 150 Avalons, and 100 Solaras per shift to satisfy market demand. To produce 450 units in one shift of 480 minutes, the line must roll out a vehicle every 480/450 = 1.067 minutes. The 1.067 minutes, or 64 seconds, represents the **takt time** of the process, defined as the cycle time needed to match the rate of production to the rate of sales or consumption.

With traditional big-lot production, all daily requirements of a model are produced in one batch before another model is started. The sequence of 200 Cs, 150 As, and 100 Ss would be repeated once per shift. Not only would these big lots increase the average inventory level, but they also would cause lumpy requirements on all the workstations feeding the assembly line.

But there are other two options for devising a production schedule for the vehicles. These options are based on the Japanese concept of *heijunka*, which is the leveling of production load by both volume and product mix. It does not build products according to the actual flow of customer orders, but levels out the total volume of orders in a period so that the same amount and mix are being made each day.[2]

Let us explore two possible *heijunka* options. The first option uses leveled **mixed-model assembly**, producing a mix of models in smaller lots. Note that the production requirements at Toyota are in the ratio of 4 Cs to 3 As to 2 Ss, found by dividing the model's production requirements by the greatest common divisor, or 50. Thus, the Toyota planner could develop a production cycle consisting of 9 units: 4 Cs, 3 As, and 2 Ss. The cycle would repeat in 9(1.067) = 9.60 minutes, for a total of 50 times per shift (480 min/9.60 min = 50).

The second *heijunka* option uses a lot size of one, such as the production sequence of C–S–C–A–C–A–C–S–A repeated 50 times per shift. The sequence would achieve the same total output as the other options; however, it is feasible only if the setup

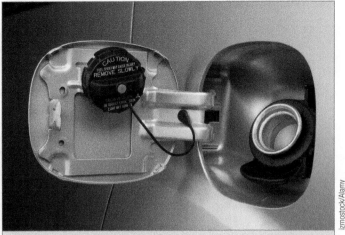

An example of poka-yoke is the design of new fuel doors in automobiles. They are mistake proof since the filling pipe insert keeps larger, leaded-fuel nozzle from being inserted. In addition, a gas cap tether does not allow the motorist to drive off without the cap, and is also fitted with a ratchet to signal proper tightness and prevent over-tightening.

takt time

Cycle time needed to match the rate of production to the rate of sales or consumption.

heijunka

The leveling of production load by both volume and product mix.

mixed-model assembly

A type of assembly that produces a mix of models in smaller lots.

Toyota Motor Manufacturing, Indiana (TMMI) is building the Sienna minivan and the Sequoia sport utility vehicle on a new mixed-model assembly line in the expanded plant.

---

[2]David McBride, "Heijunka, Leveling the Load," September 1, 2004, **http://www.emsstrategies.com**

times are brief. The sequence generates a steady rate of component requirements for the various models and allows the use of small lot sizes at the feeder workstations. Consequently, the capacity requirements at those stations are greatly smoothed. These requirements can be compared to actual capacities during the planning phase, and modifications to the production cycle, production requirements, or capacities can be made as necessary.

Standardized Components and Work Methods

In highly repetitive service operations, great efficiencies can be gained by analyzing work methods and documenting the improvements for all employees to use. For example, UPS consistently monitors its work methods, from sorting packages to delivering them, and revises them as necessary to improve service. In manufacturing, the standardization of components increases the total quantity that must be produced for that component. For example, a firm producing 10 products from 1,000 different components could redesign its products so that they consist of only 100 different components with larger daily requirements. Panasonic did similar standardization with its printed circuit boards in the opening vignette. Because the requirements per component increase, each worker performs a standardized task or work method more often each day. Productivity tends to increase because workers learn to do their tasks more efficiently with increased repetition. Standardizing components and work methods help a firm achieve the high-productivity, low-inventory objectives of a lean system.

Flexible Workforce

The role of workers is elevated in lean systems. Workers in flexible workforces can be trained to perform more than one job. A benefit of flexibility is the ability to shift workers among workstations to help relieve bottlenecks as they arise without the need for inventory buffers—an important aspect of the uniform flow of lean systems. Also, workers can step in and do the job for those who are on vacation or who are out sick. Although assigning workers to tasks they do not usually perform can temporarily reduce their efficiency, some job rotation tends to relieve boredom and refreshes workers. At some firms that have implemented lean systems, cross-trained workers may switch jobs every 2 hours.

The more customized the service or product is, the greater the firm's need for a multiskilled workforce. For example, stereo repair shops require broadly trained personnel who can identify a wide variety of component problems when the customer brings the defective unit into the shop and who then can repair the unit. Alternatively, back-office designs, such as the mail-processing operations at a large post office, have employees with more narrowly defined jobs because of the repetitive nature of the tasks they must perform. These employees do not have to acquire as many alternative skills. In some situations, shifting workers to other jobs may require them to undergo extensive, costly training.

Spirit AeroSystems' plant in Prestwick, Scotland, has seen some big changes. For one, it has invested in automation on the A320 production line.

Automation

Automation plays a big role in lean systems and is a key to low-cost operations. Money freed up because of inventory reductions or other efficiencies can be invested in automation to reduce costs. The benefits, of course, are greater profits, greater market share (because prices can be cut), or both. Automation can play a big role when it comes to providing lean services. For example, banks offer ATMs that provide various bank services on demand 24 hours a day. Automation should be planned carefully, however. Many managers believe that if some automation is good, more is better, which is not always the case. At times, humans can do some jobs better than robots and automated assembly systems.

Five S Practices

Five S (5S) is a methodology for organizing, cleaning, developing, and sustaining a productive work environment. It represents five related terms, each beginning with an *S*, that describe workplace practices conducive to visual controls and lean production. As shown in Figure 2, these five practices of sort, straighten, shine, standardize, and sustain build upon one another and are done systematically to achieve lean systems. These practices are interconnected, and are not something that can be done as a stand-alone program. As such, they serve as an enabler and an essential foundation of lean systems. Table 2 shows the terms[3] that represent the 5S and what they imply.

It is commonly accepted that 5S forms an important cornerstone of waste reduction and removal of unneeded tasks, activities, and materials. 5S practices can enable workers to visually see everything differently, prioritize tasks, and achieve a greater degree of focus. They can also be applied to a diverse range of manufacturing and service settings including organizing work spaces, offices, tool rooms, shop floors, and the like. Implementation of 5S practices have been shown to lead to lowered costs, improved on-time delivery and productivity, higher product quality, better use of floor space, and a safe working environment. It also builds the discipline needed to make the lean systems work well.

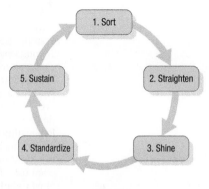

▲ FIGURE 2
5 S Practices

five S (5S)

A methodology consisting of five workplace practices—sorting, straightening, shining, standardizing, and sustaining—that are conducive to visual controls and lean production.

TABLE 2 | 5S DEFINED

5S Term	Definition
1. Sort	Separate needed items from unneeded items (including tools, parts, materials, and paperwork), and discard the unneeded.
2. Straighten	Neatly arrange what is left, with a place for everything and everything in its place. Organize the work area so that it is easy to find what is needed.
3. Shine	Clean and wash the work area and make it shine.
4. Standardize	Establish schedules and methods of performing the cleaning and sorting. Formalize the cleanliness that results from regularly doing the first three S practices so that perpetual cleanliness and a state of readiness are maintained.
5. Sustain	Create discipline to perform the first four S practices, whereby everyone understands, obeys, and practices the rules when in the plant. Implement mechanisms to sustain the gains by involving people and recognizing them through a performance measurement system.

Total Preventive Maintenance (TPM)

Because lean systems emphasize finely tuned flows of work and little capacity slack or buffer inventory between workstations, unplanned machine downtime can be disruptive. Total Preventive Maintenance (TPM), which is also sometimes referred to as total productive maintenance, can reduce the frequency and duration of machine downtime. After performing their routine maintenance activities, technicians can test other machine parts that might need to be replaced. Replacing parts during regularly scheduled maintenance periods is easier and quicker than dealing with machine failures during production. Maintenance is done on a schedule that balances the cost of the preventive maintenance program against the risks and costs of machine failure. Routine preventive maintenance is important for service businesses that rely heavily on machinery, such as the rides at Walt Disney World or Universal Studios.

Another tactic is to make workers responsible for routinely maintaining their own equipment, which will develop employee pride in keeping the machines in top condition. This tactic, however, typically is limited to general housekeeping chores, minor lubrication, and adjustments. Maintaining high-tech machines requires trained specialists. Nonetheless, performing even simple maintenance tasks goes a long way toward improving the performance of machines.

For long-term improvements, data can be collected for establishing trends in failure pattern of machines, which can subsequently be analyzed to establish better standards and procedures for preventive maintenance. The data can also provide failure history and costs incurred to maintain the systems.

---

[3]The Japanese words for these 5S terms are *seiri, seiton, seiso, seiketsu,* and *shitsuke,* respectively.

Toyota Production System

If you were to select one company that regularly invokes the above mentioned features of Lean Systems and also exemplifies excellence in automobile manufacturing, it would probably be Toyota. Despite its recent problems with quality and product recalls, as well as component shortages and delayed new model launches caused by the Japanese earthquake in March 2011, Toyota has become one of the largest car manufacturers in the world and also one of its most admired. Worldwide in its presence, Toyota has 12 manufacturing plants in North America alone producing over 1.5 million vehicles per year. Much of this success is attributed to the famed Toyota Production System (TPS), which is one of the most admired lean manufacturing systems in existence. Replicating the system, however, is fraught with difficulties. What makes the system tick, and why has Toyota been able to use it so successfully in many different plants?

Most outsiders see the TPS as a set of tools and procedures that are readily visible during a plant tour. Even though they are important for the success of the TPS, they are not the key. What most people overlook is that through the process of continuous improvement, Toyota built a learning organization over the course of 50 years. Lean systems require constant improvements to increase efficiency and reduce waste. Toyota's system stimulates employees to experiment to find better ways to do their jobs. In fact, Toyota sets up all of its operations as "experiments" and teaches employees at all levels how to use the scientific method of problem solving.

Four principles form the basis of the TPS. First, all work must be completely specified as to content, sequence, timing, and outcome. Detail is important; otherwise, a foundation for improvements is missing. Second, every customer–supplier connection must be direct, unambiguously specifying the people involved, the form and quantity of the services or goods to be provided, the way the requests are made by each customer, and the expected time in which the requests will be met. Customer–supplier connections can be internal (employee to employee) or external (company to company). Third, the pathway for every service and product must be simple and direct. That is, services and goods do not flow to the next available person or machine, but to a specific person or machine. With this principle, employees can determine, for example, whether a capacity problem exists at a particular workstation and then analyze ways to solve it.

The first three principles define the system in detail by specifying how employees do work, interact with each other, and how the work flows are designed. However, these specifications actually are "hypotheses" about the way the system should work. For example, if something goes wrong at a workstation enough times, the hypothesis about the methods the employee uses to do work is rejected. The fourth principle, then, is that any improvement to the system must be made in accordance with the scientific method, under the guidance of a teacher, at the lowest possible organizational level. The scientific method involves clearly stating a verifiable hypothesis of the form, "If we make the following specific changes, we expect to achieve this specific outcome." The hypothesis must then be tested under a variety of conditions. Working with a teacher, who is often the employees' supervisor, is a key to becoming a learning organization. Employees learn the scientific method and eventually become teachers of others. Finally, making improvements at the lowest level of the organization means that the employees who are actually doing the work are actively involved in making the improvements. Managers are advised only to coach employees—not to fix their problems for them.

These four principles are deceptively simple. However, they are difficult but not impossible to replicate. Those organizations that successfully implement them enjoy the benefits of a lean system that adapts to change. Toyota's lean system made it an innovative leader in the auto industry and served as an important cornerstone of its success.

House of Toyota

Taiichi Ohno and Eiji Toyoda created a graphic representation shown in Figure 3 to define the Toyota Production System (TPS) to its employees

Chang-Ran Kim/Reuters/Corbis

An employee helps assemble a vehicle in Toyota City, located in central Japan. Toyota's production system is among the most-admired lean manufacturing systems in the world.

and suppliers, and which is now known as the House of Toyota. It captures the four principles of TPS described above, and represents all the essential elements of lean systems that make the TPS work well. The house conveys stability. The roof, representing the primary goals of high quality, low cost, waste elimination, and short lead-times, is supported by the twin pillars of JIT and *jidoka*. Within JIT, TPS uses a pull system that focuses on one-piece work flow methods that can change and match the takt time of the process to the actual market demand because setup reductions and small changeover times are facilitated by cross-trained workers in cellular layouts. Implementing various tools of *jidoka* ensures that quality is built into the product rather than merely inspected at the end. Finally, within an environment of continuous improvement, operational stability to the House of Toyota is provided at the base by leveraging other lean concepts such as *heijunka*, standard work methods, 5S practices, total preventive maintenance, and elimination of waste throughout the supply chain within which the Toyota products flow to reach their eventual customers.

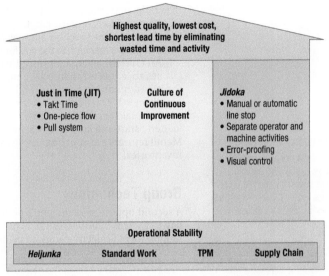

▲ FIGURE 3
House of Toyota[4]

Designing Lean System Layouts

Line flows are recommended in designing lean system layouts because they eliminate waste by reducing the frequency of setups. If volumes of specific products are large enough, groups of machines and workers can be organized into a line-flow layout to eliminate setups entirely. In a service setting, managers of back-office service processes can similarly organize their employees and equipment to provide uniform work flows through the process and, thereby, eliminate wasted employee time. Banks use this strategy in their check-processing operations, as does UPS in its parcel-sorting process.

When volumes are not high enough to justify dedicating a single line of multiple workers to a single customer type or product, managers still may be able to derive the benefits of line-flow layout—simpler materials handling, low setups, and reduced labor costs—by creating line-flow layouts in some portions of the facility. Two techniques for creating such layouts are one-worker, multiple-machines (OWMM) cells, and group technology (GT) cells.

one-worker, multiple-machines (OWMM) cell

A one-person cell in which a worker operates several different machines simultaneously to achieve a line flow.

▼ FIGURE 4
One-Worker, Multiple-Machines (OWMM) Cell

One Worker, Multiple Machines

If volumes are not sufficient to keep several workers busy on one production line, the manager might set up a line small enough to keep one worker busy. The **one-worker, multiple-machines (OWMM) cell** is a workstation in which a worker operates several different machines simultaneously to achieve a line flow. Having one worker operate several identical machines is not unusual. However, with an OWMM cell, several different machines are in the line.

Figure 4 illustrates a five-machine OWMM cell that is being used to produce a flanged metal part, with the machines encircling one operator in the center. (A U-shape also is common.) The operator moves around

---

[4]TBM Consulting Group; **http://www.tbmcg.com/about/ourroots/house_toyota.php**

the circle, performing tasks (typically loading and unloading) that have not been automated. Different products or parts can be produced in an OWMM cell by changing the machine setups. If the setup on one machine is especially time-consuming for a particular part, management can add a duplicate machine to the cell for use whenever that part is being produced.

An OWMM arrangement reduces both inventory and labor requirements. Inventory is cut because, rather than piling up in queues waiting for transportation to another part of the plant, materials move directly into the next operation. Labor is cut because more work is automated. The addition of several low-cost automated devices can maximize the number of machines included in an OWMM arrangement: automatic tool changers, loaders and unloaders, start and stop devices, and fail-safe devices that detect defective parts or products. Manufacturers are applying the OWMM concept widely because of their desire to achieve low inventories.

Group Technology

A second option for achieving line-flow layouts with low volume processes is **group technology (GT)**. This manufacturing technique creates cells not limited to just one worker and has a unique way of selecting work to be done by the cell. The GT method groups parts or products with similar characteristics into *families* and sets aside groups of machines for their production. Families may be based on size, shape, manufacturing or routing requirements, or demand. The goal is to identify a set of products with similar processing requirements and minimize machine changeover or setup. For example, all bolts might be assigned to the same family because they all require the same basic processing steps regardless of size or shape.

Once parts have been grouped into families, the next step is to organize the machine tools needed to perform the basic processes on these parts into separate cells. The machines in each cell require only minor adjustments to accommodate product changeovers from one part to the next in the same family. By simplifying product routings, GT cells reduce the time a job is in the shop. Queues of materials waiting to be worked on are shortened or eliminated. Frequently, materials handling is automated so that, after loading raw materials into the cell, a worker does not handle machined parts until the job has been completed.

Figure 5 compares process flows before and after creation of GT cells. Figure 5(a) shows a shop floor where machines are grouped according to function: lathing, milling, drilling, grinding, and assembly. After lathing, a part is moved to one of the milling machines, where it waits in line until it has a higher priority than any other job competing for the machine's capacity. When the milling operation on the part has been finished, the part is moved to a drilling machine, and so on. The queues can be long, creating significant time delays. Flows of materials are jumbled because the parts being processed in any one area of the shop have so many different routings.

By contrast, the manager of the shop shown in Figure 5(b) identified three product families that account for a majority of the firm's production. One family always requires two lathing operations followed by one operation at the milling machines. The second family always requires a milling operation followed by a grinding operation. The third family

group technology (GT)

An option for achieving line-flow layouts with low volume processes; this technique creates cells not limited to just one worker and has a unique way of selecting work to be done by the cell.

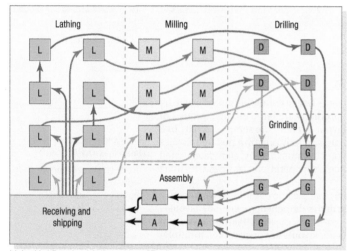

(a) Jumbled flows in a job shop without GT cells

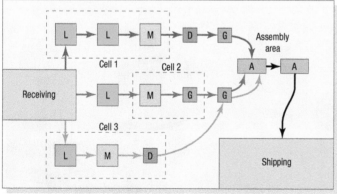

(b) Line flows in a job shop with three GT cells

▲ FIGURE 5

Process Flows Before and After the Use of GT Cells

Source: Mikell P. Groover. *Automation, Production Systems, and Computer-Aided Manufacturing.* 1st Edition, © 1980. Reprinted by permission of Pearson Education, Inc., Upper Saddle River, NJ.

requires the use of a lathe, a milling machine, and a drill press. For simplicity, only the flows of parts assigned to these three families are shown. The remaining parts are produced at machines outside the cells and still have jumbled routings. Some equipment might have to be duplicated, as when a machine is required for one or more cells and for operations outside the cells. However, by creating three GT cells, the manager has definitely created more line flows and simplified routings.

Value Stream Mapping

Value stream mapping (VSM) is a widely used qualitative lean tool aimed at eliminating waste or *muda*. Waste in many processes can be as high as 60 percent. Value stream mapping is helpful because it creates a visual "map" of every process involved in the flow of materials and information in a product's value chain. These maps consist of a *current state drawing*, a *future state drawing*, and an implementation plan. Value stream mapping spans the supply chain from the firm's receipt of raw materials or components to the delivery of the finished good to the customer. Thus, it tends to be broader in scope, displaying far more information than a typical process map or a flowchart used with Six Sigma process improvement efforts. Creating such a big picture representation helps managers identify the source of wasteful non-value-added activities.

Value stream mapping follows the steps shown in Figure 6. The first step is to focus on one product family for which mapping can be done. It is then followed by drawing a current state map of the existing production situation: Analysts start from the customer end and work upstream to draw the map by hand and record actual process times rather than rely on information not obtained by firsthand observation. Information for drawing the material and information flows can be gathered from the shop floor, including the data related to each process: cycle time (C/T), setup or changeover time (C/O), uptime (on-demand available machine time expressed as a percentage), production batch sizes, number of people required to operate the process, number of product variations, pack size (for moving the product to the next stage), working time (minus breaks), and scrap rate. Value stream mapping uses a standard set of icons for material flow, information flow, and general information (to denote operators, safety stock buffers, and so on). Even though the complete glossary is extensive, a representative set of these icons is shown in Figure 7. These icons provide a common language for describing in detail how a facility should operate to create a better flow.

value stream mapping (VSM)

A qualitative lean tool for eliminating waste or *muda* that involves a current state drawing, a future state drawing, and an implementation plan.

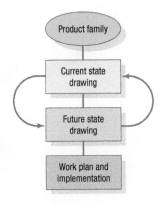

▲ FIGURE 6
Value Stream Mapping Steps
Source: Mike Rother and John Shook, *Learning to See* (Brookline, MA: The Lean Enterprise Institute, 2003), p. 9. Copyright © Lean Enterprise Institute, Inc. All right reserved, 2003. **www.lean.org**.

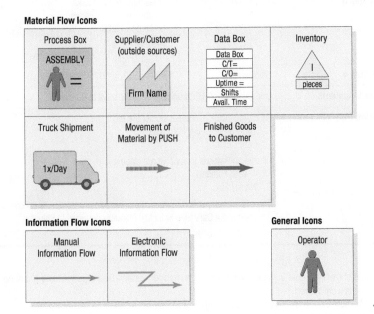

▲ FIGURE 7
Selected Set of Value Stream Mapping Icons

EXAMPLE 1	Determining the Value Stream Map, Takt Time, and Total Capacity

Jensen Bearings Incorporated, a ball bearing manufacturing company located in Lexington, South Carolina, receives raw material sheets from Kline Steel Company once a week every Monday for a product family of retainers (casings in which ball bearings are held), and then ships its finished product on a daily basis to a second-tier automotive manufacturing customer named GNK Enterprises. The product family of the bearing manufacturing company under consideration consists of two types of retainers—large (L) and small (S)—that are packaged for shipping in returnable trays with 60 retainers in each tray. The manufacturing process consists of a cell containing pressing operation, a piercing and forming cell, and a finish grind operation, after which the two types of retainers are staged for shipping. The information collected by the operations manager at Jensen Bearings Inc. is shown in Table 3.

TABLE 3 | OPERATIONS DATA FOR A FAMILY OF RETAINERS AT JENSEN BEARINGS, INC.

Overall Process Attributes	Average demand: 3,200/day (1,000 "L"; 2,200 "S") Batch size: 1000 Number of shifts per day: 1 Availability: 8 hours per shift with two 30-minute lunch breaks	
Process Step 1	Press	Cycle time = 3 seconds Setup time = 2 hours Up time = 90% Operators = 1 Every Part Every = 1 week WIP = 5 days of sheets (Before Press)
Process Step 2	Pierce & Form	Cycle time = 22 seconds Setup time = 30 minutes Up time = 100% Operators = 1 WIP = 1,000 "L," 1,250 "S" (Before Pierce & Form)
Process Step 3	Finish Grind	Cycle time = 35 seconds Setup time = 45 minutes Up time = 100% Operators = 1 WIP = 1,050 "L," 2,300 "S" (Before Finish Grind)
Process Step 4	Shipping	WIP = 500 "L," 975 "S" (After Finish Grind)
Customer Shipments	One shipment of 3,200 units each day in trays of 60 pieces	
Information Flow	All communications from customer are electronic: 180/90/60/30/day Forecasts Daily Order All communications to supplier are electronic 4-week Forecast Weekly Fax There is a weekly schedule manually delivered to Press, Pierce & Form, and Finish Grind and a Daily Ship Schedule manually delivered to Shipping All material is pushed	

a. Using data shown in Table 3; create a value stream map for Jensen Bearings Inc. and show how the data box values are calculated.
b. What is the takt time for this manufacturing cell?
c. What is the production lead time at each process in the manufacturing cell?
d. What is the total processing time of this manufacturing cell?
e. What is the capacity of this manufacturing cell?

SOLUTION

a. We use the VSM icons to illustrate in Figure 8 what a current state map would look like for Jensen Bearings Inc. The process characteristics and inventory buffers in front of each process are shown in the current state map of Figure 8. One worker occupies each station. However, what really sets the value stream maps apart from flowcharts is the inclusion of information flows at the top of Figure 8, which plan and coordinate all the process activities. The value stream maps are more comprehensive than process flowcharts, and meld together planning and control systems with detailed flowcharts to create a comprehensive supply chain view that includes both information and material flows between the firm and its suppliers and customers.

b. The cell's takt time is the rate at which the cell must produce units in order to match demand.

Daily Demand = [(1,000 + 2,200) pieces per week]/5 working days per week = 640 pieces per day

Daily Availability = (7 hours per day) × (3,600 seconds per hour) = 25,200 seconds per day

Takt Time = Daily Availability/Daily Demand = (25,200 seconds per day)/640 pieces per day = 39.375 seconds per piece

c. The production lead time (in days) is calculated by summing the inventory held between each processing step divided by daily demand.

Raw Material lead time = 5.0 days

WIP lead time between Press and Pierce & Form = (2,250/640) = 3.5 days

WIP lead time between Pierce & Form and Finish Grind = (3,350/640) = 5.2 days

WIP lead time between Finish Grind and Shipping = (1,475/640) = 2.3 days

Total Production Lead time = (5 + 3.5 + 5.2 + 2.3) = 16 days

d. The cycle time at each process is added to compute total processing time. The manufacturing cell's total processing time is (3 + 22 + 35) = 60 seconds.

e. The cell's capacity may be calculated by locating the bottleneck and computing the number of units that it can process in the available time per day at that bottleneck with the given batch size of 1,000 units.

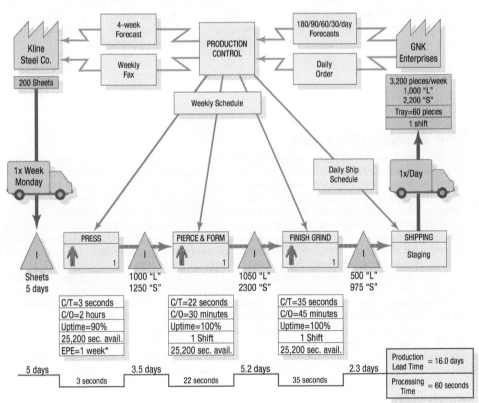

◀ **FIGURE 8**
Current State Map for a Family of Retainers at Jensen Bearings Incorporated

Capacity at Press	Capacity at Pierce & Form	Capacity at Finish Grind
Cycle time = 3 seconds	Cycle time = 22 seconds	Cycle time = 35 seconds
Setup Time = (2 hrs * 3,600 seconds per hour)/1000 units per batch = **7.2 seconds**	Setup Time = (30 minutes * 60 seconds per minute)/1000 units per batch = **1.8 seconds**	Setup Time = (45 minutes * 60 seconds per minute)/1,000 units per batch = **2.7 seconds**
Per Unit Processing Time = (3 + 7.2) = **10.2 seconds**	Per Unit Processing Time = (22 + 1.8) = **23.8 seconds**	Per Unit Processing Time = (35 + 2.7) = **37.7 seconds**

At a batch size of 1,000 units, Finish Grinding process is the bottleneck.

Availability at Grinding = 25,200 seconds per day

Time at bottleneck (with setup) = 37.7 seconds

Capacity (Availability/Time at bottleneck) = 25,200/37.7 = 668 units per day

DECISION POINT

Although the total processing time for each retainer is only 1 minute, it takes 16 days for the cumulative production lead time. Clearly *muda* or waste is present, and opportunities exist for reconfiguring the existing processes with the goal of eliminating inventories and reducing cumulative production lead time.

Once the current state map is done, the analysts can then use principles of lean systems to create a future state map with more streamlined product flows. The future state drawing highlights sources of waste and how to eliminate them. The developments of the current and future state maps are overlapping efforts. Finally, the last step is aimed at preparing and actively using an implementation plan to achieve the future state. It may take only a couple of days from the creation of a future state map to the point where implementation can begin for a single product family. At this stage, the future state map becomes a blueprint for implementing a lean system, and is fine-tuned as implementation progresses. As the future state becomes reality, a new future state map is drawn, thus denoting continuous improvement at the value stream level.

Unlike the theory of constraints which accepts the existing system bottlenecks and then strives to maximize the throughput given that set of constraint(s), value stream mapping endeavors to understand through current state and future state maps how existing processes can be altered to eliminate bottlenecks and other wasteful activities. The goal is to bring the production rate of the entire process closer to the customer's desired demand rate. The benefits of applying this tool to the waste-removal process include reduced lead times and work-in-process inventories, reduced rework and scrap rates, and lower indirect labor costs.

The *Kanban* System

kanban

A Japanese word meaning "card" or "visible record" that refers to cards used to control the flow of production through a factory.

One of the most publicized aspects of lean systems, and the TPS in particular, is the *kanban* system developed by Toyota. **Kanban**, meaning "card" or "visible record" in Japanese, refers to cards used to control the flow of production through a factory. In the most basic *kanban* system, a card is attached to each container of items produced. The container holds a given percent of the daily production requirements for an item. When the user of the parts empties a container, the card is removed from the container and put on a receiving post. The empty container is then taken to the storage area, and the card signals the need to produce another container of the part. When the container has been refilled, the card is put back on the container, which is then returned to a storage area. The cycle begins again when the user of the parts retrieves the container with the card attached.

Figure 9 shows how a single-card kanban system works when a fabrication cell feeds two assembly lines. As an assembly line needs more parts, the kanban card for those parts is taken to the receiving post, and a full container of parts is removed from the storage area. The receiving post accumulates cards for assembly lines and a scheduler sequences the production of replenishment parts. In this example, the fabrication cell will produce product 2 (red) before it produces product 1 (green). The cell consists of three different operations, but operation 2 has two workstations. Once production has been initiated in the cell, the product begins on operation 1, but could be routed to either of the workstations performing operation 2, depending on the workload at the time. Finally, the product is processed on operation 3 before being taken to the storage area.

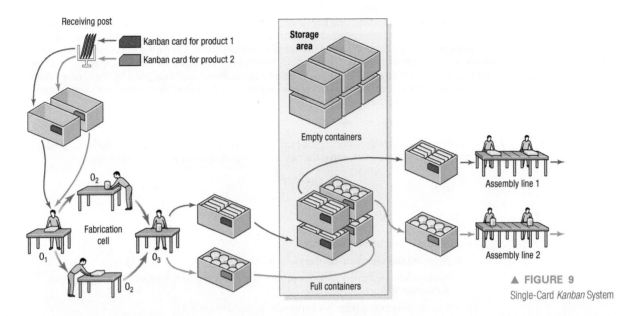

▲ **FIGURE 9**

Single-Card *Kanban* System

General Operating Rules

The operating rules for the single-card system are simple and are designed to facilitate the flow of materials while maintaining control of inventory levels.

1. Each container must have a card.

2. The assembly line always withdraws materials from the fabrication cell. The fabrication cell never pushes parts to the assembly line because, sooner or later, parts will be supplied that are not yet needed for production.

3. Containers of parts must never be removed from a storage area without a kanban first being posted on the receiving post.

4. The containers should always contain the same number of good parts. The use of nonstandard containers or irregularly filled containers disrupts the production flow of the assembly line.

5. Only nondefective parts should be passed along to the assembly line to make the best use of materials and worker's time. This rule reinforces the notion of building quality at the source, which is an important characteristic of lean systems.

6. Total production should not exceed the total amount authorized on the *kanbans* in the system.

Toyota uses a two-card system, based on a withdrawal card and a production-order card, to control inventory quantities more closely. The withdrawal card specifies the item and the quantity the user of the item should withdraw from the producer of the item, as well as the stocking locations for both the user and the producer. The production-order card specifies the item and the quantity to be produced, the materials required and where to find them, and where to store the finished item. Materials cannot be withdrawn without a withdrawal card, and production cannot begin without a production-order card. The cards are attached to containers when production commences. By manipulating the number of withdrawal and production cards in play at any time, management can control the flow of materials in the production system.

Determining the Number of Containers

The number of authorized containers in the TPS determines the amount of authorized inventory. Management must make two determinations: (1) the number of units to be held by each container, and (2) the number of containers flowing back and forth between the supplier station and the user station. The first decision amounts to determining the size of the production lot.

The number of containers flowing back and forth between two stations directly affects the quantities of work-in-process inventory, which includes any safety stock inventory to cover for unexpected requirements. The containers spend some time in production, in a line waiting, in a storage location, or in transit. The key to determining the number of containers required is to estimate the average lead time needed to produce a container of parts. The lead time is a function of the processing time per container at the supplier station, the waiting time during the production process, and the time required for materials handling. Little's Law, which says that the average work-in-process inventory (WIP) equals the average demand rate multiplied by the average time a unit spends in the manufacturing process, can be used to determine the number of containers needed to support the user station.

WIP = (average demand rate)(average time a container spends in the manufacturing process) + safety stock

In this application of determining the number of containers needed for a part, WIP is the product of κ, the number of containers, and c, the number of units in each container. Consequently,

$$\kappa c = \bar{d}(\bar{\omega} + \bar{\rho})(1 + \alpha)$$

$$\kappa = \frac{\bar{d}(\bar{\omega} + \bar{\rho})(1 + \alpha)}{c}$$

where

κ = number of containers for a part

$\bar{d}$ = expected daily demand for the part, in units

$\bar{\omega}$ = average waiting time during the production process plus materials handling time per container, in fractions of a day

$\bar{\rho}$ = average processing time per container, in fractions of a day

c = quantity in a standard container of the part

α = a policy variable that adds safety stock to cover for unexpected circumstances (Toyota uses a value of no more than 10 percent)

The number of containers must, of course, be an integer. Rounding κ up provides more inventory than desired, whereas rounding κ down provides less.

The container quantity, c, and the efficiency factor, α, are variables that management can use to control inventory. Adjusting c changes the size of the production lot, and adjusting α changes the amount of safety stock. The kanban system allows management to fine-tune the flow of

---

EXAMPLE 2 | **Determining the Appropriate Number of Containers**

Solver-Number of Containers
Enter data in yellow-shaded area.

Daily Expected Demand	2000
Quantity in Standard Container	22
Container Waiting Time (days)	0.06
Processing Time (days)	0.02
Policy Variable	10%
Containers Required	8

▲ FIGURE 10
OM Explorer Solver for
Number of Containers

The Westerville Auto Parts Company produces rocker-arm assemblies for use in the steering and suspension systems of four-wheel-drive trucks. A typical container of parts spends 0.02 day in processing and 0.08 day in materials handling and waiting during its manufacturing cycle. The daily demand for the part is 2,000 units. Management believes that demand for the rocker-arm assembly is uncertain enough to warrant a *safety stock* equivalent of 10 percent of its authorized inventory.

a. If each container contains 22 parts, how many containers should be authorized?

b. Suppose that a proposal to revise the plant layout would cut materials handling and waiting time per container to 0.06 day. How many containers would be needed?

Solution

a. If $\bar{d}$ = 2,000 units/day, $\bar{\rho}$ = 0.02 day, α = 0.10, $\bar{\omega}$ = 0.08 day and c = 22 units,

$$\kappa = \frac{2,000(0.08 + 0.02)(1.0)}{22} = \frac{220}{22} = 10 \text{ containers}$$

b. Figure 10 from OM Explorer shows that the number of containers drops to 8.

DECISION POINT

The average lead time per container is $\bar{\omega} + \bar{\rho}$. With a lead time of 0.10 day, 10 containers are needed. However, if the improved facility layout reduces the materials handling time and waiting time to $\bar{\omega}$ 0.06 day, only 8 containers are needed. The maximum authorized inventory of the rocker-arm assembly is κc units. Thus, in part (a), the maximum authorized inventory is 220 units, but in part (b), it is only 176 units. Reducing $\bar{\omega} + \bar{\rho}$ by 20 percent reduces the inventory of the part by 20 percent. Management must balance the cost of the layout change (a one-time charge) against the long-term benefits of inventory reduction.

materials in the system in a straightforward way. For example, removing cards from the system reduces the number of authorized containers of the part, thus reducing the inventory of the part. Thus. a major benefit is the simplicity of the system, whereby product mix or volume changes can easily be accomplished by adjusting the number of *kanbans* in the system.

Other *Kanban* Signals

Cards are not the only way to signal the need for more production of a part. Other, less formal methods are possible, including container and containerless systems.

Container System Sometimes, the container itself can be used as a signal device: An empty container signals the need to fill it. Unisys took this approach for low-value items. The amount of inventory of the part is adjusted by adding or removing containers. This system works well when the container is specially designed for a particular part and no other parts could accidentally be put in the container. Such is the case when the container is actually a pallet or fixture used to position the part during precision processing.

Containerless System Systems requiring no containers have been devised. In assembly-line operations, operators use their own workbench areas to put completed units on painted squares, one unit per square. Each painted square represents a container, and the number of painted squares on each operator's bench is calculated to balance the line flow. When the subsequent user removes a unit from one of the producer's squares, the empty square signals the need to produce another unit. McDonald's uses a containerless system. Information entered by the order taker at the cash register is transmitted to the cooks and assemblers, who produce the sandwiches requested by the customer.

Managerial Practice 1 illustrates how the University of Pittsburgh Medical Center Shadyside used principles of *kanban* systems, 5S methodology, cellular layouts, and continuous flow processes to significantly improve performance in its pathology department.

Operational Benefits and Implementation Issues

To gain competitive advantage and to make dramatic improvements, a lean system can be the solution. Lean systems can be an integral part of a corporate strategy based on speed because they cut cycle times, improve inventory turnover, and increase labor productivity. Recent studies also show that practices representing different components of lean systems such as JIT, TQM, Six Sigma, total preventive maintenance (TPM), and human resource management (HRM), individually as well as cumulatively, improve the performance of manufacturing plants as well as service facilities. Lean systems also involve a considerable amount of employee participation through small-group interaction sessions, which have resulted in improvements in many aspects of operations, not the least of which is service or product quality.

Even though the benefits of lean systems can be outstanding, problems can still arise after a lean system has long been operational and which was witnessed recently in product recalls and a perceived shift away from tightly controlled quality that has always been the standard at Toyota. In addition, implementing a lean system can take a long time. We address below some of the issues managers should be aware of when implementing a lean system.

Organizational Considerations

Implementing a lean system requires management to consider issues of worker stress, cooperation and trust among workers and management, and reward systems and labor classifications.

The Human Costs of Lean Systems Lean systems can be coupled with statistical process control (SPC) to reduce variations in output. However, this combination requires a high degree of regimentation and sometimes stresses the workforce. For example, in the Toyota Production System, workers must meet specified cycle times, and, with SPC, they must follow prescribed problem-solving methods. Such systems might make workers feel pushed and stressed, causing productivity losses or quality reductions. In addition, workers might feel a loss of some autonomy because of the close linkages in work flows between stations with little or no excess capacity or safety stocks. Managers can mitigate some of these effects by allowing for some slack in the system—either

A worker moves a stack of partially assembled athletic shoes from her stitching station at the New Balance factory in Skowhegan, Maine. She and five other members of her team have worked out a plan so that each person is cross-trained in another's skills. Similar ideas for improving proficiency, which are discussed during biweekly meetings with workers and supervisors, have led to improved performance at New Balance.

Robert F. Bukaty/ASSOCIATED PRESS

MANAGERIAL PRACTICE 1 — Lean Systems at the University of Pittsburgh Medical Center Shadyside

The University of Pittsburgh Medical Center (UPMC), comprising of 20 hospitals, serves more than 4 million people every year with 50,000 employees and 400 doctors' offices and outpatient sites. UPMC at Shadyside, a part of the UPMC system, is a 520-bed tertiary-care hospital with a medical staff of nearly 1,000 primary care physicians and specialists. Always seeking to improve, UPMC first applied principles of the Toyota Production System in 2001 in a 40-bed surgical unit and then systematized the concepts into a lean approach called the Clinical Design Initiative (CDI). This approach focuses on determining the root cause of a problem through direct observation, and then eliminating it by designing solutions that are visual, simple, and unambiguous. These solutions are then tested in a small area and improved until the desired clinical and cost outcomes, along with enhanced patient and staff satisfaction, are achieved. Once perfected, the improved process is rolled out to other areas of the hospital.

UPMC used the CDI methodology to speed up turnaround time in the pathology lab. The layout and work flows of the lab were based on a batch-and-queue push system that led to long lead times, complexity in tracking and moving large lots, delays in discovering quality problems, and high storage costs. Before making the transition to the lean system, UPMC ran a workshop on lean concepts for the staff members of the lab and followed it with a 5S exercise to better organize the department. Counter spaces were cleared so that the lab's equipment could be rearranged. Unneeded items were identified with red tags and removed. Visual controls were used to arrange the remaining items in a neat and easy-to-use manner.

The 5S exercise of cleaning house boosted staff morale. Kanban cards with reordering information were then attached to most items. Reordering supplies now takes only a few minutes a day. Stockouts and expensive rush orders have been eliminated and the overall inventory level of supplies has been reduced by 50 percent to 60 percent.

To move to a system based on line flows, equipment was moved around in the lab to create a cellular layout. The new arrangement allows tissue samples being processed to move through the lab cell from embedding,

After the pathology lab at the University of Pittsburgh Medical Center adopted a lean operations approach based on a line system versus a batch-and-queue system, the time it took to process samples dropped from days to just hours. Diagnoses were made more quickly as a result, and patients' stays at the hospital were shortened.

to cutting, to the oven, and slide staining. The samples move more quickly, and few or no samples end up waiting between steps. As a result, the overall time needed to prepare and analyze tissue samples fell from one or two days to less than a day. The reduction in turnaround time means doctors get pathology results quicker, which in turn speeds up diagnosis and leads to shorter stays for patients. Moreover, the lab does the same amount of work with 28 percent fewer people, and fewer errors because quality mistakes are discovered immediately.

Sources: "The Anatomy of Innovation," *Lean Enterprise Institute,* **www.lean.org**; **http://www.upmc.com**, April 25, 2011.

---

safety stock inventories or capacity slack—and by emphasizing work flows instead of worker pace. Managers also can promote the use of work teams and allow them to determine their task assignments within their domains of responsibility.

Cooperation and Trust In a lean system, workers and first-line supervisors must take on responsibilities formerly assigned to middle managers and support staff. Activities such as scheduling, expediting, and improving productivity become part of the duties of lower-level personnel. Consequently, the work relationships in the organization must be reoriented in a way that fosters cooperation and mutual trust between the workforce and management. However, this environment can be difficult to achieve, particularly in light of the historical adversarial relationship between the two groups.

Reward Systems and Labor Classifications In some instances, the reward system must be revamped when a lean system is implemented. At General Motors, for example, a plan to reduce stock at one plant ran into trouble because the production superintendent refused to cut back on the number of unneeded parts being made. Why? Because his or her salary was based on the plant's production volume.

The realignment of reward systems is not the only hurdle. Labor contracts traditionally crippled a company's ability to reassign workers to other tasks as the need arose. For example, a typical automobile plant in the United States has several unions and dozens of labor classifications.

Generally, the people in each classification are allowed to do only a limited range of tasks. In some cases, companies have managed to give these employees more flexibility by agreeing to other types of union concessions and benefits. In other cases, however, companies relocated their plants to take advantage of nonunion or foreign labor.

Process Considerations

Firms using lean systems typically have some dominant work flows. To take advantage of lean practices, firms might have to change their existing layouts. Certain workstations might have to be moved closer together, and cells of machines devoted to particular component families may have to be established. However, rearranging a plant to conform to lean practices can be costly. For example, many plants currently receive raw materials and purchased parts by rail, but to facilitate smaller and more frequent shipments, truck deliveries would be preferable. Loading docks might have to be reconstructed or expanded and certain operations relocated to accommodate the change in transportation mode and quantities of arriving materials.

Inventory and Scheduling

Manufacturing firms need to have stable master production schedules, short setups, and frequent, reliable supplies of materials and components to achieve the full potential of the lean systems concept.

Schedule Stability Daily production schedules in high-volume, make-to-stock environments must be stable for extended periods. At Toyota, the master production schedule is stated in fractions of days over a 3-month period and is revised only once a month. The first month of the schedule is frozen to avoid disruptive changes in the daily production schedule for each workstation; that is, the workstations execute the same work schedule each day of the month. At the beginning of each month, *kanbans* are reissued for the new daily production rate. Stable schedules are needed so that production lines can be balanced and new assignments found for employees who otherwise would be underutilized. Lean systems used in high-volume, make-to-stock environments cannot respond quickly to scheduling changes because little slack inventory or capacity is available to absorb these changes.

Setups If the inventory advantages of a lean system are to be realized, small lot sizes must be used. However, because small lots require a large number of setups, companies must significantly reduce setup times. Some companies have not been able to achieve short setup times and, therefore, have to use large-lot production, negating some of the advantages of lean practices. Also, lean systems are vulnerable to lengthy changeovers to new products because the low levels of finished goods inventory will be insufficient to cover demand while the system is down. If changeover times cannot be reduced, large finished goods inventories of the old product must be accumulated to compensate. In the automobile industry, every week that a plant is shut down for new-model changeover costs between $16 million and $20 million in pretax profits.

Purchasing and Logistics If frequent, small shipments of purchased items cannot be arranged with suppliers, large inventory savings for these items cannot be realized. For example, in the United States, such arrangements may prove difficult because of the geographic dispersion of suppliers.

The shipments of raw materials and components must be reliable because of the low inventory levels in lean systems. A plant can be shut down because of a lack of materials. Similarly, recovery becomes more prolonged and difficult in a lean system after supply chains are disrupted, which is what happened immediately after 9/11.

Process design and continuous improvement are key elements of a successful operations strategy. In this chapter we focused on lean systems as a directive for efficient process design and an approach to achieve continuous improvement. We showed how just-in-time systems (JIT), a popular lean systems approach, can be used for continuous improvement, and how a *kanban* system can be used to control the amount of work-in-process inventory. Transforming a current process design to one embodying a lean system's philosophy is a constant challenge for management, often fraught with implementation issues. However, the transformation can be facilitated by adopting appropriate management approaches as exemplified by firms like Panasonic and Toyota among others, and by using tools such as value stream mapping. The key point to remember is that the philosophy of lean systems, applicable at the process level, is also applicable at the supply chain level.

LEARNING GOALS IN REVIEW

1 Describe how lean systems can facilitate the continuous improvement of processes. See the section on "Continuous Improvement using a Lean Systems Approach". Review Figure 1 and the opening vignette on Panasonic Corporation.

2 Identify the characteristics and strategic advantages of lean systems. See the section on "Supply Chain Considerations in Lean Systems," and "Process Considerations in Lean Systems". The section on "Toyota Production System," illustrates how one firm implements Lean characteristics to gain strategic advantage over its competition.

3 Understand value stream mapping and its role in waste reduction. The section "Value Stream Mapping," shows you how to construct value stream maps and identify waste in the

processes. Review Example 1 for details on mapping and creating data boxes.

4 Understand *kanban* systems for creating a production schedule in a lean system. The section "The *Kanban* System," shows how firms like Toyota use simple visual systems to pull production and make exactly what the market demands. Example 2 shows how to calculate the number of *kanban* cards needed.

5 Explain the implementation issues associated with the application of lean systems. The section "Operational Benefits and Implementation Issues," reviews organizational and process considerations needed to successfully deploy lean systems and gain their benefits.

MyOMLab helps you develop analytical skills and assesses your progress with multiple problems on average cycle time, mixed model assembly, value stream mapping, number of containers, policy variable α, daily demand satisfied with given system, and authorized stock level.

MyOMLab Resources	Titles	Link to the Book
Video	*Lean Systems at Autoliv*	Lean Systems across the Organization; Process Considerations in Lean Systems; The Kanban System
	Versatile Buildings: Lean Systems	Continuous Improvement Using a Lean Systems Approach; Process Considerations in Lean Systems
OM Explorer Solvers	Number of Containers	The Kanban System; Example 2; Solved Problem 2
OM Explorer Tutors	8.1 Number of Containers	The Kanban System; Example 2; Solved Problem 2
Tutor Exercises	Number of Containers in Different Scenarios	The Kanban System; Example 2; Solved Problem 2
Virtual Tours	Workhorse Custom Chassis	Designing Lean System Layouts
	Rieger Orgelbau Pipe Organ Factory	Inventory and Scheduling
Internet Exercise	NUMMI, Yellow and Roadway (YRC)	Continuous Improvement Using a Lean Systems Approach
Key Equations		
Image Library		

Key Equation

Number of containers:

$$\kappa = \frac{\bar{d}(\bar{\omega} + \bar{\rho})(1 + \alpha)}{c}$$

Key Terms

five S (5S)
group technology
heijunka
jidoka
JIT system
just-in-time (JIT) philosophy

kanban
lean systems
lot
mixed-model assembly
one worker, multiple machines
(OWMM) cell

poka-yoke
pull method
push method
single-digit setup
takt time
value stream mapping (VSM)

Solved Problem 1

Metcalf, Inc. manufacturers engine assembly brackets for two major automotive customers. The manufacturing process for the brackets consists of a cell containing a forming operation, a drilling operation, a finish grinding operation, and packaging, after which the brackets are staged for shipping. The information collected by the operations manager at Metcalf, Inc. is shown in Table 4.

TABLE 4 | OPERATIONS DATA FOR BRACKETS AT METCALF, INC.

Overall Process Attributes	Average demand: 2700/day Batch size: 50 Number of shifts per day: 2 Availability: 8 hours per shift with a 30-minute lunch break	
Process Step 1	Forming	Cycle time = 11 seconds Setup time = 3 minutes Up time = 100% Operators = 1 WIP = 4000 units (Before Forming)
Process Step 2	Drilling	Cycle time = 10 seconds Setup time = 2 minutes Up time = 90% Operators = 1 WIP = 5,000 units (Before Drilling)
Process Step 3	Grinding	Cycle time = 17 seconds Setup time = 0 seconds Up time = 100% Operators = 1 WIP = 2,000 units (Before Grinding)
Process Step 4	Packaging	Cycle time = 15 seconds Setup time = 0 seconds Up time = 100% Operators = 1 WIP = 1,600 units (Before Packaging) WIP = 15,700 units (Before Shipping)
Customer Shipments	One shipment of 13,500 units each week	
Information Flow	All communications with customer are electronic There is a weekly order release to Forming All material is pushed	

a. Using data shown in Table 4; create a value stream map for Metcalf, Inc. and show how the data box values are calculated.

b. What is the takt time for this manufacturing cell?

c. What is the production lead time at each process in the manufacturing cell?

d. What is the total processing time of this manufacturing cell?

e. What is the capacity of this manufacturing cell?

SOLUTION

a. Figure 11, on the following page, shows the current value stream state map for Metcalf, Inc.

b. Daily Demand = 2,700 units per day

Daily Availability = (7.5 hours per day) × (3,600 seconds per hour) × (2 shifts per day) = 54,000 seconds per day

Takt Time = Daily Availability/Daily Demand = 54,000 seconds per day/2,700 pieces per day = 20 seconds per units

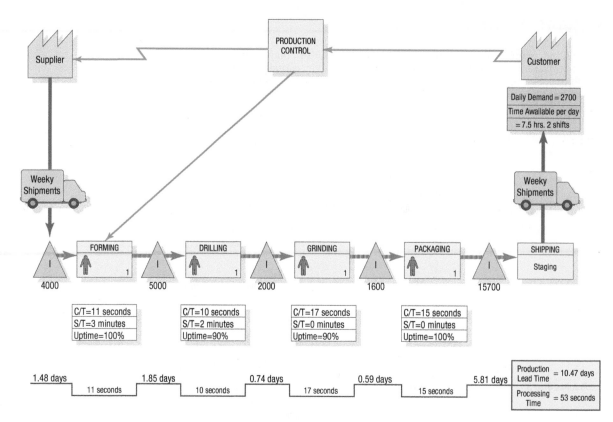

▲ FIGURE 11

Current State Value Stream
Map for Metcalf, Inc.

c. The production lead time (in days) is calculated by summing the inventory held between each processing step divided by daily demand.

Raw Material lead time = [4,000/2,700] = 1.48 days

WIP lead time between Forming and Drilling = [5,000/2,700] = 1.85 days

WIP lead time between Drilling and Grinding = [2,000/2,700] = 0.74 day

WIP lead time between Grinding and Packaging = [1,600/2,700] = 0.59 day

Finished Goods lead time before Shipping = [15,700/2,700] = 5.81 days

The cell's total production lead time is: 1.48 + 1.85 + 0.74 + 0.59 + 5.81 = 10.47 days

d. The manufacturing cell's total processing time is (11 + 10 + 17 + 15) = 53 seconds

e. The cell's capacity may be calculated by locating the bottleneck and computing the number of units that it can process in the available time per day at that bottleneck.

Capacity at Forming	Capacity at Drilling	Capacity at Grinding	Capacity at Packaging
Cycle time = 11 seconds	Cycle time = 10 seconds	Cycle time = 17 seconds	Cycle time = 15 seconds
Setup Time = (3 minutes * 60 seconds per minute)/ 50 units per batch = **3.6 seconds**	Setup Time = (2 minutes * 60 seconds per minute)/ 50 units per batch = **2.4 seconds**	Setup Time = **zero seconds**	Setup Time = **zero seconds**
Per Unit Processing Time = (11 + 3.6) = **14.6 seconds**	Per Unit Processing Time = (10 + 2.4) = **12.4 seconds**	Per Unit Processing Time = (17 + 0) = **17.0 seconds**	Per Unit Processing Time = (15 + 0) = **15.0 seconds**

At a batch size of 50 units, Finish Grinding process is the bottleneck

Availability at Grinding = 54,000 seconds per day

Time at bottleneck (with setup) = 17.0 seconds

Capacity (Availability/Time at bottleneck) = 54,000/17 = 3,176 units per day

Solved Problem 2

A company using a *kanban* system has an inefficient machine group. For example, the daily demand for part L105A is 3,000 units. The average waiting time for a container of parts is 0.8 day. The processing time for a container of L105A is 0.2 day, and a container holds 270 units. Currently, 20 containers are used for this item.

a. What is the value of the policy variable, α?

b. What is the total planned inventory (work-in-process and finished goods) for item L105A?

c. Suppose that the policy variable, α, was 0. How many containers would be needed now? What is the effect of the policy variable in this example?

SOLUTION

a. We use the equation for the number of containers and then solve for α:

$$\kappa = \frac{\bar{d}(\bar{\omega} + \bar{\rho})(1 + \alpha)}{c}$$

$$20 = \frac{3,000(0.8 + 0.2)(1 + \alpha)}{270}$$

and

$$(1 + \alpha) = \frac{20(270)}{3,000(0.8 + 0.2)} = 1.8$$

$$\alpha = 1.8 - 1 = 0.8$$

b. With 20 containers in the system and each container holding 270 units, the total planned inventory is $20(270) = 5,400$ units.

c. If $\alpha = 0$

$$\kappa = \frac{3,000(0.8 + 0.2)(1 + 0)}{270} = 11.11, \text{ or } 12 \text{ containers}$$

The policy variable adjusts the number of containers. In this case, the difference is quite dramatic because $\bar{\omega} + \bar{\rho}$ is fairly large and the number of units per container is small relative to daily demand.

Discussion Questions

1. Compare and contrast the following two situations:

   a. A company's lean system stresses teamwork. Employees feel more involved and, therefore, productivity and quality increase at the company. The problem is that workers also experience a loss of individual autonomy.

   b. A humanities professor believes that all students want to learn. To encourage students to work together and learn from each other—thereby increasing the involvement, productivity, and the quality of the learning experience—the professor announces that all students in the class will receive the same grade and that it will be based on the performance of the group.

2. Which elements of lean systems would be most troublesome for manufacturers to implement? Why?

3. List the pressures that lean systems pose for supply chains, whether in the form of process failures due to inventory shortages or labor stoppages, etc. Reflect on how these pressures may apply to a firm which is actually implementing lean philosophy in their operations.

4. Identify a service or a manufacturing process that you are familiar with, and draw a current state value stream map to depict its existing information and material flows.

Problems

The OM Explorer and POM for Windows software is available to all students using the 10th edition of this text. Go to **www.pearsonhighered.com/krajewski** to download these computer packages. If you purchased MyOMLab, you also have access to Active Models software and significant help in doing the following problems. Check with your instructor on how best to use these resources. In many cases, the instructor wants you to understand how to do the calculations by hand. At the least, the software provides a check on your calculations. When calculations are particularly complex and the goal is interpreting the results in making decisions, the software replaces entirely the manual calculations.

1. The Harvey Motorcycle Company produces three models: the Tiger, a sure-footed dirt bike; the LX2000, a nimble cafe racer; and the Golden, a large interstate tourer. This month's master production schedule calls for the production of 54 Goldens, 42 LX2000s, and 30 Tigers per 7-hour shift.

    a. What average cycle time is required for the assembly line to achieve the production quota in 7 hours?

    b. If mixed-model scheduling is used, how many of each model will be produced before the production cycle is repeated?

    c. Determine a satisfactory production sequence for the ultimate in small-lot production: one unit.

    d. The design of a new model, the Cheetah, includes features from the Tiger, LX2000, and Golden models. The resulting blended design has an indecisive character and is expected to attract some sales from the other models. Determine a mixed-model schedule resulting in 52 Goldens, 39 LX2000s, 26 Tigers, and 13 Cheetahs per 7-hour shift. Although the total number of motorcycles produced per day will increase only slightly, what problem might be anticipated in implementing this change from the production schedule indicated in part (b)?

2. A fabrication cell at Spradley's Sprockets uses the pull method to supply gears to an assembly line. George Jitson is in charge of the assembly line, which requires 500 gears per day. Containers typically wait 0.20 day in the fabrication cell. Each container holds 20 gears, and one container requires 1.8 days in machine time. Setup times are negligible. If the policy variable for unforeseen contingencies is set at 5 percent, how many containers should Jitson authorize for the gear replenishment system?

3. You are asked to analyze the *kanban* system of LeWin, a French manufacturer of gaming devices. One of the workstations feeding the assembly line produces part M670N. The daily demand for M670N is 1,800 units. The average processing time per unit is 0.003 day. LeWin's records show that the average container spends 1.05 days waiting at the feeder workstation. The container for M670N can hold 300 units. Twelve containers are authorized for the part. Recall that $\bar{\rho}$ is the average processing time per container, not per individual part.

    a. Find the value of the policy variable, α, that expresses the amount of implied safety stock in this system.

    b. Use the implied value of α from part (a) to determine the required reduction in waiting time if one container was removed. Assume that all other parameters remain constant.

4. An assembly line requires two components: gadjits and widjits. Gadjits are produced by center 1 and widjits by center 2. Each unit of the end item, called a jit-together, requires 3 gadjits and 2 widjits, as shown in Figure 12. The daily production quota on the assembly line is 800 jit-togethers.

    The container for gadjits holds 80 units. The policy variable for center 1 is set at 0.09. The average waiting time for a container of gadjits is 0.09 day, and 0.06 day is needed to produce a container. The container for widjits holds 50 units, and the policy variable for

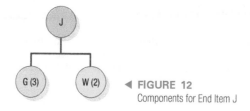

◀ FIGURE 12
Components for End Item J

center 2 is 0.08. The average waiting time per container of widgits is 0.14 day, and the time required to process a container is 0.20 day.

    a. How many containers are needed for gadjits?

    b. How many containers are needed for widjits?

5. Gestalt, Inc. uses a *kanban* system in its automobile production facility in Germany. This facility operates 8 hours per day to produce the Jitterbug, a replacement for the obsolete but immensely popular Jitney Beetle. Suppose that a certain part requires 150 seconds of processing at machine cell 33B and a container of parts average 1.6 hours of waiting time there. Management allows a 10 percent buffer for unexpected occurrences. Each container holds 30 parts, and 8 containers are authorized. How much daily demand can be satisfied with this system? (*Hint:* Recall that $\bar{\rho}$ is the average processing time per container, not per individual part.)

6. A U.S. Postal Service supervisor is looking for ways to reduce stress in the sorting department. With the existing arrangement, stamped letters are machine-canceled and loaded into tubs with 375 letters per tub. The tubs are then pushed to postal clerks, who read and key zip codes into an automated sorting machine at the rate of 1 tub per 375 seconds. To overcome the stress caused when the stamp canceling machine outpaces the sorting clerks, a pull system is proposed. When the clerks are ready to process another tub of mail, they will pull the tub from the canceling machine area. How many tubs should circulate between the sorting clerks and the canceling machine if 90,000 letters are to be sorted during an 8-hour shift, the safety stock policy variable, α, is 0.18, and the average waiting time plus materials handling time is 25 minutes per tub?

7. The production schedule at Mazda calls for 1,200 Mazdas to be produced during each of 22 production days in January and 900 Mazdas to be produced during each of 20 production days in February. Mazda uses a *kanban* system to communicate with Gesundheit, a nearby supplier of tires. Mazda purchases four tires per vehicle from Gesundheit. The safety stock policy variable, α, is 0.15. The container (a delivery truck) size is 200 tires. The average waiting time plus materials handling time is 0.16 day per container. Assembly lines are rebalanced at the beginning of each month. The average processing time per container in January is 0.10 day. February processing time will average 0.125 day per container. How many containers should be authorized for January? How many for February?

8. Jitsmart is a retailer of plastic action-figure toys. The action figures are purchased from Tacky Toys, Inc., and arrive in boxes of 48. Full boxes are stored on high shelves out of reach of customers. A small inventory is maintained

on child-level shelves. Depletion of the lower-shelf inventory signals the need to take down a box of action figures to replenish the inventory. A reorder card is then removed from the box and sent to Tacky Toys to authorize replenishment of a container of action figures. The average demand rate for a popular action figure, Agent 99, is 36 units per day. The total lead time (waiting plus processing) is 11 days. Jitsmart's safety stocky policy variable, α, is 0.25. What is the authorized stock level for Jitsmart?

9. Markland First National Bank of Rolla utilizes *kanban* techniques in its check processing facility. The following information is known about the process. Each *kanban* container can hold 50 checks and spends 24 minutes a day in processing and 2 hours a day in materials handling and waiting. Finally, the facility operates 24 hours per day and utilizes a policy variable for unforeseen contingencies of 0.25.

   a. If there are 20 *kanban* containers in use, what is the current daily demand of the check processing facility?

   b. If the *muda* or the waste in the system were eliminated completely, how many containers would then be needed?

Advanced Problems

10. The Farm-4-Less tractor company produces a grain combine (GC) in addition to both a large (LT) and small size tractor (SM). Its production manager desires to produce to customer demand using a mixed model production line. The current sequence of production, which is repeated 30 times during a shift, is SM-GC-SM-LT-SM-GC-LT-SM. A new machine is produced every 2 minutes. The plant operates two 8-hour shifts. There is no downtime because the 4 hours between each shift are dedicated to maintenance and restocking raw material. Based on this information, answer the following questions.

    a. How long does it take the production cycle to be completed?

    b. How many of each type of machine does Farm-4-Less produce in a shift?

11. Figure 13 provides a new current state value stream map for the family of retainers at the Jensen Bearings, Inc. firm described in Example 1. This map depicts the value stream after Kline Steel agrees to accept daily orders for steel sheets and also agrees to deliver the finished goods on a daily basis.

    Calculate each component of the new value stream's reduced lead time.

    a. How many days of raw material does the Bearing's plant now hold?

    b. How many days of work in process inventory is held between Press and Pierce & Form?

    c. How many days of work in process inventory is held between Pierce & Form and Finish Grind?

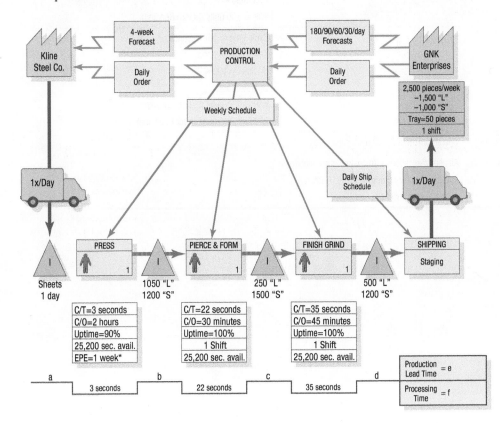

◀ **FIGURE 13**
New Current State Value Stream Map at Jensen Bearings, Inc.

d. How many days of work in process inventory is held between Finish Grind and Shipping?

e. What is the new value steam's production lead time?

f. What is the new value stream's processing time?

12. The manager at Ormonde, Inc. collected the value stream mapping data from the plant's most problematic manufacturing cell that fabricates parts for washing machines. This data is shown in Table 5. Using this data, calculate the current state performance of the cell and answer the following questions.

a. What is the cell's current inventory level?

b. What is the takt time for this manufacturing cell?

c. What is the production lead time at each process in the manufacturing cell?

d. What is the total processing time of this manufacturing cell?

e. What is the capacity of this manufacturing cell?

TABLE 5 | OPERATIONS DATA FOR ORMONDE, INC.

Overall Process Attributes	Average demand: 550/day Batch size: 20 Number of shifts per day: 3 Availability: 8 hours per shift with a 45-minute lunch break	
Process Step 1	Cutting	Cycle time = 120 seconds Setup time = 3 minutes Up time = 100% Operators = 1 WIP = 400 units (Before Cutting)
Process Step 2	Bending	Cycle time = 250 seconds Setup time = 5 minutes Up time = 99% Operators = 2 WIP = 500 units (Before Bending)
Process Step 3	Punching	Cycle time = 140 seconds Setup time = none Up time = 100% Operators = 1 WIP = 200 units (Before Punching) WIP = 1,000 units (After Punching)
Customer Shipments	One shipment of 2,750 units each week	
Information Flow	All communications with customer are electronic There is a weekly order release to Cutting All material is pushed	

VIDEO CASE | Lean Systems at Autoliv

Autoliv is a world-class example of lean manufacturing. This Fortune 500 company makes automotive safety components such as seat belts, airbags, and steering wheels, and has over 80 plants in more than 32 countries. Revenues in 2007 topped $6.7 billion. Autoliv's lean manufacturing environment is called the Autoliv Production System (APS), and is based on the principles of lean manufacturing pioneered by Toyota, one of the world's largest automobile manufacturers, and embodied in its Toyota Production System (TPS).

At the heart of Autoliv is a system that focuses on continuous improvement. Based on the "House of Toyota," Autoliv's Ogden, Utah, airbag module plant puts the concepts embodied in the house to work every day. The only difference between the Toyota house and the one at Autoliv is that the company has added a third pillar to its house to represent employee involvement in all processes because a culture of involvement, while the norm in Japan, is not always found in the United States.

Autoliv started its lean journey back in 1995. At that time, the Ogden plant was at manufacturing capacity with 22 work cells. Company managers acknowledge that, back then, Autoliv was "broken" and in need of significant and immediate change if it was to survive. This meant that everyone—from senior management to employees and suppliers—needed to be on-board with rebuilding the company. It was not that the company could not fulfill the needs of its automaker customers; however, with increasing demand for both reliable and cost-effective component supplies, pressure to change became obvious. Recognizing the value of Toyota's approach, senior management made the commitment to embark on its own journey to bring the transformative culture of lean manufacturing to Autoliv.

In 1998, *sensei* Takashi Harada arrived from Japan to spend three years teaching top company managers the principles, techniques, and culture of the lean system. This helped managers create an environment in which continuous improvement could be fostered and revered as an essential activity for long-term success. Because the environment was changing, it made it difficult at first for suppliers to meet Autoliv's constantly changing and unstable processes. It also made problems visible and forced the company to address and resolve the problems instead of finding ways to work around them as had been done in the past. Daily audits, monthly training, and more in-depth education programs were created to help focus attention on where changes needed to be made. Workers and management were organized into teams that were held accountable for common goals and tasked with working toward common success.

By 2004, the lean culture was integrated into the company, and it now hosts regular visits by other corporations who want to learn from Autoliv's journey and experiences. Compared to 1995, the space required for a typical work cell has been reduced by 88.5 percent, while the number of cells has grown over 400 percent. This has allowed Autoliv to dramatically increase its production capacity with minimal investment.

Lean concepts play out every day in the each plant. For example, everyone gathers at the start of the workday for pre-shift stretching and a brief meeting—this is part of the employee involvement pillar in the APS House. Then, workers head to one of 104 work cells on the plant floor. *Heijunka* Room team members deliver *heijunka* cards to each cell to communicate the work to be done in that cell. Lot sizes may vary with each card delivered to the cell. Everything the workers need to make the lot is in the cell and regularly replenished through the *kanban* card system. Every 24 minutes, another *heijunka* card comes to the cell to signal workers what they will build next. This is part of the JIT pillar in the house.

Since a culture of continuous improvement requires employees at every level to be responsible for quality, a worker may identify an "abnormal condition" during work execution that slows down the work of the cell, or

Autoliv employee folds an air bag in a Toyota-inspired production cell.

stops it altogether. This is embodied in the right pillar of the Toyota house—*jidoka*, which Autoliv interprets as "stop and fix." This is a rare occurrence, however, since both Autoliv and its suppliers are expected to deliver defect-free products. When a supplier is new, or has experienced quality issues, the supplier pays for inspection in Autoliv's receiving dock area until Autoliv is certain the supplier can meet quality expectations for all future deliveries. In this manner, workers in the cells know they can trust the integrity of the raw materials arriving through the *kanban* system into their cells for assembly. *Jidoka* may also come into play when a machine does not operate properly, or an employee notices a process that has deviated from the standard. When workers "stop and fix" a problem at the point of its creation, they save the company from added cost as well as lost confidence in the eyes of the customer.

To help focus worker efforts daily, Autoliv has a blue "communication wall" that everyone sees as they head to their work site. The wall contains the company's "policy deployment," which consists of company-wide goals for customer satisfaction, shareholder/financial performance, and safety and quality. The policy deployment begins with the company-wide goals, which then flow down to the plant level through the plant manager's goals, strategies, and actions for the facility. These linked activities assure that Autoliv achieves its goals. By communicating this information—and more—in a visual manner, the central pillar of the APS House is supported. Other visual communication and management methods are in place as well. For example, each cell has an overhead banner that states how that cell is doing each month in the areas of safety, quality, employee involvement, cost, and delivery. These all tie into the policy deployment shown on the communication wall.

Another visual communication method is to use a "rail" for the management of the *heijunka* cards in each cell. The rail has color-coded sections. As each card is delivered, it slides down a color-coded railing to the team. At the end nearest the cell, the rail is green, indicating that any cards that fall into this area can be completed within normal working hours. The middle of the rail is yellow, indicating overtime for the cell that day. The end is red, meaning weekend overtime is required to bring work processes back into harmony with customer demand. As a *heijunka* card slides down the rail, it stops when it hits the end or stacks up behind another card. If the cell is not performing at the required pace to meet customer demand, the cards will stack up on the rail and provide a very visual cue that the cell is not meeting expectations. This provides an opportunity for cell team members as well as management to implement immediate countermeasures to prevent required overtime if the situation is not remedied.

All aisles and walkways surrounding cells are to be clear of materials, debris, or other items. If anything appears in those areas, everyone can quickly see the abnormality. As team members work together to complete their day's work, the results of their efforts are displayed boldly on each cell's "communi-cube." This four-sided rotating display visually tells the story of the cell's productivity, quality, and 5S performance. The cube also contains a special section for the management of *kaizen* suggestions for the team itself. These *kaizens* enable the team to continuously improve the work environment as well as drive the achievement of team results.

Autoliv's lean journey embodied in the Autoliv Production System has led to numerous awards and achievement of its policy deployment goals. Product defects have been dramatically reduced, inventory levels are lower, and inventory turnover is approaching world-class levels of 50. Employee turnover is close to 5 percent, and remains well below that of other manufacturers in the industry. Yet the destination has not been reached. The company continues its emphasis on driving systemic improvement to avoid complacency and loss of competitive advantage. Best practices from sources beyond each immediate area of the organization are studied and integrated. And finding ways to engage and reward Autoliv's workforce in a maturing market is critical. Kaizen suggestions in the most recent year at the Ogden plant totaled 74,000, or nearly 60 per employee, indicating the culture of continuous improvement in Autoliv's APS House is alive and well.

QUESTIONS

1. Why is a visual management approach such an integral part of Autoliv's lean system?

2. Describe the JIT considerations presented in the chapter as they relate to Autoliv's manufacturing environment.

3. Which method of work flow is embodied in Autoliv's system? Why is this approach most suitable to its lean environment?

4. When Autoliv started its lean journey, a number of operational benefits and implementation issues had to be addressed. What were they, and how were they addressed?

CASE | Copper Kettle Catering

Copper Kettle Catering (CKC) is a full-service catering company that provides services ranging from box lunches for picnics or luncheon meetings to large wedding, dinner, or office parties. Established as a lunch delivery service for offices in 1972 by Wayne and Janet Williams, CKC has grown to be one of the largest catering businesses in Raleigh, North Carolina. The Williams's divide customer demand into two categories: *deliver only* and *deliver and serve*.

The deliver-only side of the business delivers boxed meals consisting of a sandwich, salad, dessert, and fruit. The menu for this service is limited to six sandwich selections, three salads or potato chips, and a brownie or fruit bar. Grapes and an orange slice are included with every meal, and iced tea can be ordered to accompany the meals. The overall level of demand for this service throughout the year is fairly constant, although the mix of menu items delivered varies. The planning horizon for this segment of the business is short: Customers usually call no more than a day ahead of time. CKC requires customers to call deliver-only orders in by 10:00 A.M. to guarantee delivery the same day.

The deliver-and-serve side of the business focuses on catering large parties, dinners, and weddings. The extensive range of menu items includes a full selection of hors d'oeuvres, entrées, beverages, and special-request items. The demand for these services is much more seasonal, with heavier demands occurring in the late spring–early summer for weddings and the late fall–early winter for holiday parties. However, this segment also has a longer planning horizon. Customers book dates and choose menu items weeks or months ahead of time.

CKC's food preparation facilities support both operations. The physical facilities layout resembles that of a job process. Five major work areas consist of a stove–oven area for hot food preparation, a cold area for salad preparation, an hors d'oeuvre preparation area, a sandwich preparation area, and an assembly area where deliver-only orders are boxed and deliver-and-serve orders are assembled and trayed. Three walk-in coolers store foods requiring refrigeration, and a large pantry houses nonperishable goods. Space limitations and the risk of spoilage limit the amount of raw materials and prepared food items that can be carried in inventory at any one time. CKC purchases desserts from outside vendors. Some deliver the desserts to CKC; others require CKC to send someone to pick up desserts at their facilities.

The scheduling of orders is a two-stage process. Each Monday, the Williamses develop the schedule of deliver-and-serve orders to be processed each day. CKC typically has multiple deliver-and-serve orders to fill each day of the week. This level of demand allows a certain efficiency in the preparation of multiple orders. The deliver-only orders are scheduled day to day, owing to the short-order lead times. CKC sometimes runs out of ingredients for deliver-only menu items because of the limited inventory space.

Wayne and Janet Williams have 10 full-time employees: 2 cooks and 8 food preparation workers, who also work as servers for the deliver-and-serve orders. In periods of high demand, the Williamses hire additional part-time servers. The position of cook is specialized and requires a high degree of training and skill. The rest of the employees are flexible and move between tasks as needed.

The business environment for catering is competitive. The competitive priorities are high-quality food, delivery reliability, flexibility, and cost—in that order. "The quality of the food and its preparation is paramount," states Wayne Williams. "Caterers with poor-quality food will not stay in business long." Quality is measured by both freshness and taste. Delivery reliability encompasses both on-time delivery and the time required to respond to customer orders (in effect, the order lead time). Flexibility focuses on both the range of catering requests that a company can satisfy and menu variety.

Recently, CKC began to notice that customers are demanding more menu flexibility and faster response times. Small specialty caterers who entered the market are targeting specific well-defined market segments. One example is a small caterer called Lunches-R-Us, which located a facility in the middle of a large office complex to serve the lunch trade and competes with CKC on cost.

Wayne and Janet Williams are impressed by the lean systems concept, especially the ideas related to increasing flexibility, reducing lead times, and lowering costs. They sound like what CKC needs to remain competitive. However, the Williamses wonder whether lean concepts and practices are transferable to a service business.

QUESTIONS

1. Are the operations of Copper Kettle Catering conducive to the application of lean concepts and practices? Explain.

2. What, if any, are the major barriers to implementing a lean system at Copper Kettle Catering?

3. What would you recommend that Wayne and Janet Williams do to take advantage of lean concepts in operating CKC?

Source: This case was prepared by Dr. Brooke Saladin, Wake Forest University, as a basis for classroom discussion. Copyright © Brooke Saladin. Used with permission.

Selected References

Ansberry, Clare. "Hurry-Up Inventory Method Hurts Where It Once Helped." *Wall Street Journal Online* (June 25, 2002).

Holweg, Matthias. "The Genealogy of Lean Production." *Journal of Operations Management*, vol. 25 (2007).

Klein, J. A. "The Human Costs of Manufacturing Reform." *Harvard Business Review* (March–April 1989).

Manufacturing Engineering Web site, www.mfgeng.com/5S.htm.

Mascitelli, Ron. "Lean Thinking: It's About Efficient Value Creation." *Target*, vol. 16, no. 2 (Second Quarter 2000).

McBride, David. "Toyota and Total Productive Maintenance." http://www.emsstrategies.com/dm050104article2.html; May 2004.

Millstein, Mitchell. "How to Make Your MRP System Flow." *APICS—The Performance Advantage* (July 2000).

Rother, Mike, and John Shook. *Learning to See*. Brookline, MA: The Lean Enterprise Institute, 2003.

Schaller, Jeff. "A 'Just Do It Now' Philosophy Rapidly Creates a Lean Culture, Produces Dramatic Results at Novametix Medical Systems." *Target*, vol. 18, no. 2 (Second Quarter 2002), .

Schonberger, Richard J. "Japanese Production Management: An Evolution—With Mixed Success." *Journal of Operations Management*, vol. 25 (2007).

Shah, Rachna, and Peter T. Ward. "Defining and Developing Measures of Lean Production." *Journal of Operations Management*, vol. 25 (2007).

Spear, Steven, and H. Kent Bowen. "Decoding the DNA of the Toyota Production System." *Harvard Business Review* (September–October 1999).

Spear, Steven J. "Learning to Lead at Toyota." *Harvard Business Review* (May 2004).

Stewart, Douglas M., and John R. Grout. "The Human Side of Mistake Proofing." *Production and Operations Management*, vol. 10, no. 4 (Winter 2001).

Tonkin, Lea. "System Sensor's Lean Journey." *Target*, vol. 18, no. 2 (Second Quarter 2002).

Womack, James P., and Daniel T. Jones. "Lean Consumption" *Harvard Business Review* (March 2005).

Paul J. Milette/Palm Beach Post/ZUMA Press/Newscom

SUPPLY CHAIN INVENTORY MANAGEMENT

An employee stacks a shipment of pet supplies at a new Walmart distribution center in Fort Pierce, Florida. The 1.2 million square foot facility will serve 45 Walmart stores on the east coast of Florida.

Inventory Management at Walmart

In the market for shaver blade replacements? A printer? First-aid supplies? Dog food? Hair spray? If so, you expect that the store you shop at will have what you want. However, making sure that the shelves are stocked with tens of thousands of products is no simple matter for inventory managers at Walmart, which has 8,800 Walmart stores and Sam's Club locations in 15 markets, employs more than 2 million associates, serves 200 million customers per week worldwide, and uses 100,000 suppliers. You can imagine in an operation this large that some things can get lost. Linda Dillman, then CIO at Walmart, recounts the story of the missing hair spray at one of the stores. The shelf needed to be restocked with a specific hair spray; however, it took three days to find the case in the backroom. Most customers will not swap hair sprays, so Walmart lost three days of sales on that product.

Knowing what is in stock, in what quantity, and where it is being held is critical to effective inventory management. Without accurate inventory information, companies can make major mistakes by ordering too much, not enough, or shipping products to the wrong location. Companies can have large inventories and still have stockouts of product because they have too much inventory of some products and not enough of others. Walmart, a $405 billion company with inventories in excess of $33 billion, is certainly aware of the potential benefits from improved inventory management and is constantly experimenting with ways to reduce inventory investment. Knowing when to replenish inventory stocks and

From Chapter 9 of *Operations Management: Processes and Supply Chains,* Tenth Edition. Lee J. Krajewski, Larry P. Ritzman, Manoj K. Malhotra. Copyright © 2013 by Pearson Education, Inc. All rights reserved.

inventory management

The planning and controlling of inventories in order to meet the competitive priorities of the organization.

lot size

The quantity of an inventory item management either buys from a supplier or manufactures using internal processes.

how much to order each time is critical when dealing with so much inventory investment. The application of technology is also important, such as using radio frequency identification (RFID) to track inventory shipments and stock levels at stores and warehouses throughout the supply chain. One handheld RFID reader could have found the missing case of hair spray in a few minutes.

Source: Laurie Sullivan, "Walmart's Way," Informationweek.com (September 27, 2004), pp. 36–50 Gus Whitcomb and Christi Gallagher, "Walmart Begins Roll-Out of Electronic Product Codes in Dallas/Fort Worth Area," **www.walmartstores.com** (February 2011), and Walmart 2010 Annual Report.

LEARNING GOALS *After reading this chapter, you should be able to:*

1 Identify the advantages, disadvantages, and costs of holding inventory.

2 Define the different types of inventory and the roles they play in supply chains.

3 Explain the basic tactics for reducing inventories in supply chains.

4 Determine the items deserving most attention and tightest inventory control.

5 Calculate the economic order quantity and apply it to various situations.

6 Determine the order quantity and reorder point for a continuous review inventory control system.

7 Determine the review interval and target inventory level for a periodic review inventory control system.

8 Define the key factors that determine the appropriate choice of an inventory system.

Creating Value through Operations Management

Using Operations to Compete
Project Management

Managing Processes

Process Strategy
Process Analysis
Quality and Performance
Capacity Planning
Constraint Management
Lean Systems

Managing Supply Chains

Supply Chain Inventory Management
Supply Chain Design
Supply Chain Location Decisions
Supply Chain Integration
Supply Chain Sustainability and Humanitarian Logistics
Forecasting
Operations Planning and Scheduling
Resource Planning

Inventory management, the planning and controlling of inventories in order to meet the competitive priorities of the organization, is an important concern for managers in all types of businesses. Effective inventory management is essential for realizing the full potential of any supply chain. The challenge is not to pare inventories to the bone to reduce costs or to have plenty around to satisfy all demands, but to have the right amount to achieve the competitive priorities of the business most efficiently. This type of efficiency can only happen if the right amount of inventory is flowing through the supply chain—through suppliers, the firm, warehouses or distribution centers, and customers. These decisions were so important for Walmart that it decided to use RFID to improve the information flows in the supply chain. Much of inventory management involves *lot sizing*, which is the determination of how frequently and in what quantity to order inventory. We make ample reference to the term **lot size**, which is the quantity of an inventory item management either buys from a supplier or manufactures using internal processes. In this chapter, we focus on the decision-making aspects of inventory management. We begin with an overview of the importance of inventory management to the organization and how to choose the items most deserving of management attention. We then introduce the basics of inventory decision making by exploring the economic order quantity and how it can be used to balance inventory holding costs with ordering costs. A major segment of the chapter is devoted to retail and distribution inventory control systems and how to use them.

Inventory Management across the Organization

Inventories are important to all types of organizations, their employees, and their supply chains. Inventories profoundly affect everyday operations because they must be counted, paid for, used in operations, used to satisfy customers, and managed. Inventories require an investment of funds, as does the purchase of a new machine. Monies invested in inventory are not available for investment in other things; thus, they represent a drain on the cash flows of an organization. Nonetheless, companies realize that the availability of products is a key selling point in many markets and downright critical in many more.

So, is inventory a boon or a bane? Certainly, too much inventory on hand reduces profitability, and too little inventory on hand creates shortages in the supply chain and ultimately damages customer confidence. Inventory management, therefore, involves trade-offs. Let us discover how companies can effectively manage inventories across the organization.

Inventory and Supply Chains

The value of inventory management becomes apparent when the complexity of the supply chain is recognized. The performance of numerous suppliers determines the inward flow of materials and services to a firm. The performance of the firm determines the outward flow of services or products to the next stage of the supply chain. The flow of materials, however, determines inventory levels. **Inventory** is a stock of materials used to satisfy customer demand or to support the production of services or goods. Figure 1 shows how inventories are created at one node in a supply chain through the analogy of a water tank. The flow of water into the tank raises the water level. The inward flow of water represents input materials, such as steel, component parts, office supplies, or a finished product. The water level represents the amount of inventory held at a plant, service facility, warehouse, or retail outlet. The flow of water from the tank lowers the water level in the tank. The outward flow of water represents the demand for materials in inventory, such as customer orders for a Huffy bicycle or service requirements for supplies such as soap, food, or furnishings. The rate of the outward flow also reflects the ability of the firm to match the demand for services or products. Another possible outward flow is that of scrap, which also lowers the level of useable inventory. Together, the difference between input flow rate and the output flow rate determines the level of inventory. Inventories rise when more material flows into the tank than flows out; they fall when more material flows out than flows in. Figure 1 also shows clearly why firms utilize Six Sigma and total quality management (TQM) to reduce defective materials: The larger the scrap flows, the larger the input flow of materials required for a given level of output.

A fundamental question in supply chain management is how much inventory to have. The answer to this question involves a tradeoff between the advantages and disadvantages of holding inventory. Depending on the situation, the pressures for having small inventories may or may not exceed the pressures for having large inventories.

inventory
A stock of materials used to satisfy customer demand or to support the production of services or goods.

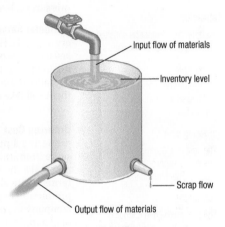

▲ **FIGURE 1**
Creation of Inventory

Pressures for Small Inventories

An inventory manager's job is to balance the advantages and disadvantages of both small and large inventories and find a happy medium between the two levels. The primary reason for keeping inventories small is that inventory represents a temporary monetary investment. As such, the firm incurs an opportunity cost, which we call the cost of capital, arising from the money tied up in inventory that could be used for other purposes. The **inventory holding cost** (or *carrying cost*) is the sum of the cost of capital plus the variable costs of keeping items on hand, such as storage and handling costs and taxes, insurance, and shrinkage costs. When these components change with inventory levels, so does the holding cost.

Companies usually state an item's holding cost per period of time as a percent of its value. The annual cost to maintain one unit in inventory typically ranges from 15 to 35 percent of its value. Suppose that a firm's holding cost is 20 percent. If the average value of total inventory is 20 percent of sales, the average annual cost to hold inventory is 4 percent [0.20(0.20)] of total sales. This cost is sizable in terms of gross profit margins, which often are less than 10 percent. Thus, the components of holding cost create pressures for small inventories.

inventory holding cost
The sum of the cost of capital and the variable costs of keeping items on hand, such as storage and handling, taxes, insurance, and shrinkage.

Cost of Capital The cost of capital is the opportunity cost of investing in an asset relative to the expected return on assets of similar risk. Inventory is an asset; consequently, we should use a cost measure that adequately reflects the firm's approach to financing assets. Most firms use the *weighted average cost of capital (WACC)*, which is the average of the required return on a firm's stock equity and the interest rate on its debt, weighted by the proportion of equity and debt in its portfolio. The cost of capital usually is the largest component of holding cost, as high as 15 percent of inventory value, depending on the particular capitalization portfolio of the firm. Firms typically update the WACC on an annual basis because it is used to make many financial decisions.

Storage and Handling Costs Inventory takes up space and must be moved into and out of storage. Storage and handling costs may be incurred when a firm rents space on either a long- or short-term basis. An inventory holding cost is incurred when a firm could use storage space productively in some other way.

Taxes, Insurance, and Shrinkage More taxes are paid if end-of-year inventories are high, and the cost of insuring the inventories increases, too. Shrinkage takes three forms. The first, *pilferage*, or theft of inventory by customers or employees, is a significant percentage of sales for some businesses. The second form of shrinkage, called *obsolescence*, occurs when inventory cannot be used or sold at full value, owing to model changes, engineering modifications, or unexpectedly low demand. Obsolescence is a big expense in the retail clothing industry. Drastic discounts on seasonal clothing frequently must be offered on many of these products at the end of a season. Finally, *deterioration* through physical spoilage or damage due to rough or excessive material handling results in lost value. Food and beverages, for example, lose value and might even have to be discarded when their shelf life is reached. When the rate of deterioration is high, building large inventories may be unwise.

Pressures for Large Inventories

Given the costs of holding inventory, why not eliminate it altogether? Let us look briefly at the pressures related to maintaining large inventories.

stockout

An order that cannot be satisfied, resulting in a loss of the sale.

backorder

A customer order that cannot be filled when promised or demanded but is filled later.

ordering cost

The cost of preparing a purchase order for a supplier or a production order for manufacturing.

setup cost

The cost involved in changing over a machine or workspace to produce a different item.

quantity discount

A drop in the price per unit when an order is sufficiently large.

raw materials (RM)

The inventories needed for the production of services or goods.

Customer Service Creating inventory can speed delivery and improve the firm's on-time delivery of goods. High inventory levels reduce the potential for stockouts and backorders, which are key concerns of wholesalers and retailers. A **stockout** is an order that cannot be satisfied, resulting in loss of the sale. A **backorder** is a customer order that cannot be filled when promised or demanded but is filled later. Customers do not like waiting for backorders to be filled. Many of them will take their business elsewhere. Sometimes, customers are given discounts for the inconvenience of waiting.

Ordering Cost Each time a firm places a new order, it incurs an **ordering cost**, or the cost of preparing a purchase order for a supplier or a production order for manufacturing. For the same item, the ordering cost is the same, regardless of the order size. The purchasing agent must take the time to decide how much to order and, perhaps, select a supplier and negotiate terms. Time also is spent on paperwork, follow-up, and receiving the item(s). In the case of a production order for a manufactured item, a blueprint and routing instructions often must accompany the order. However, the Internet streamlines the order process and reduces the costs of placing orders.

Setup Cost The cost involved in changing over a machine or workspace to produce a different item is the **setup cost.** It includes labor and time to make the changeover, cleaning, and sometimes new tools or equipment. Scrap or rework costs are also higher at the start of the production run. Setup cost also is independent of order size, which creates pressure to make or order a large supply of the items and hold them in inventory rather than order smaller batches.

Labor and Equipment Utilization By creating more inventory, management can increase workforce productivity and facility utilization in three ways. First, placing larger, less frequent production orders reduces the number of unproductive setups, which add no value to a service or product. Second, holding inventory reduces the chance of the costly rescheduling of production orders because the components needed to make the product are not in inventory. Third, building inventories improves resource utilization by stabilizing the output rate when demand is cyclical or seasonal. The firm uses inventory built during slack periods to handle extra demand in peak seasons. This approach minimizes the need for extra shifts, hiring, layoffs, overtime, and additional equipment.

Transportation Cost Sometimes, outbound transportation cost can be reduced by increasing inventory levels. Having inventory on hand allows more full-carload shipments to be made and minimizes the need to expedite shipments by more expensive modes of transportation. Inbound transportation costs can also be reduced by creating more inventory. Sometimes, several items are ordered from the same supplier. Placing these orders at the same time will increase inventories because some items will be ordered before they are actually needed; nonetheless, it may lead to rate discounts, thereby decreasing the costs of transportation and raw materials.

Metal saws, such as this one, require time to changeover from one product to the next. The depth and length of the cut must be adjusted and the blade itself may have to be changed.

GlowImages/Alamy

Payments to Suppliers A firm often can reduce total payments to suppliers if it can tolerate higher inventory levels. Suppose that a firm learns that a key supplier is about to increase its prices. In this case, it might be cheaper for the firm to order a larger quantity than usual—in effect delaying the price increase—even though inventory will increase temporarily. A firm can also take advantage of quantity discounts this way. A **quantity discount**, whereby the price per unit drops when the order is sufficiently large, is an incentive to order larger quantities.

Types of Inventory

Inventory exists in three aggregate categories that are useful for accounting purposes. **Raw materials (RM)** are the inventories needed for the production of services or goods. They are considered to be inputs to the transformation processes of the firm. **Work-in-process (WIP)** consists of items, such as components or assemblies, needed to produce a final product in manufacturing. WIP is also present in some service

Raw materials, work-in-process, and finished goods inventories can all be stocked in the same facility. Modern warehouses allow for efficient inventory access.

operations, such as repair shops, restaurants, check-processing centers, and package delivery services. **Finished goods (FG)** in manufacturing plants, warehouses, and retail outlets are the items sold to the firm's customers. The finished goods of one firm may actually be the raw materials for another.

Figure 2 shows how inventory can be held in different forms and at various stocking points. In this example, raw materials—the finished goods of the supplier—are held both by the supplier and the manufacturer. Raw materials at the plant pass through one or more processes, which transform them into various levels of WIP inventory. Final processing of this inventory yields finished goods inventory. Finished goods can be held at the plant, the distribution center (which may be a warehouse owned by the manufacturer or the retailer), and retail locations.

Another perspective on inventory is to classify it by how it is created. In this context, inventory takes four forms: (1) cycle, (2) safety stock, (3) anticipation, and (4) pipeline. They cannot be identified physically; that is, an inventory manager cannot look at a pile of widgets and identify which ones are cycle inventory and which ones are safety stock inventory. However, conceptually, each of the four types comes into being in an entirely different way. Once you understand these differences, you can prescribe different ways to reduce inventory, which we discuss in the next section.

work-in-process (WIP)

Items, such as components or assemblies, needed to produce a final product in manufacturing or service operations.

▼ **FIGURE 2**
Inventory of Successive Stocking Points

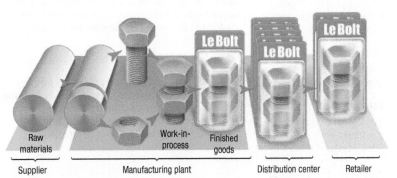

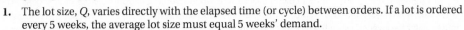

Raw materials | Work-in-process | Finished goods

Supplier | Manufacturing plant | Distribution center | Retailer

Cycle Inventory The portion of total inventory that varies directly with lot size is called **cycle inventory**. Determining how frequently to order, and in what quantity, is called **lot sizing**. Two principles apply.

1. The lot size, Q, varies directly with the elapsed time (or cycle) between orders. If a lot is ordered every 5 weeks, the average lot size must equal 5 weeks' demand.

2. The longer the time between orders for a given item, the greater the cycle inventory must be.

At the beginning of the interval, the cycle inventory is at its maximum, or Q. At the end of the interval, just before a new lot arrives, cycle inventory drops to its minimum, or 0. The average cycle inventory is the average of these two extremes:

$$\text{Average cycle inventory} = \frac{Q + 0}{2} = \frac{Q}{2}$$

finished goods (FG)

The items in manufacturing plants, warehouses, and retail outlets that are sold to the firm's customers.

cycle inventory

The portion of total inventory that varies directly with lot size.

lot sizing

The determination of how frequently and in what quantity to order inventory.

Pipeline inventories result from moving items and materials from one location to another. Because trains offer an economical way to transport large quantities of goods, they are a favorite choice to reduce the costs of pipeline inventories.

This formula is exact only when the demand rate is constant and uniform. However, it does provide a reasonably good estimate even when demand rates are not constant. Factors other than the demand rate (e.g., scrap losses) also may cause estimating errors when this simple formula is used.

Safety Stock Inventory   To avoid customer service problems and the hidden costs of unavailable components, companies hold safety stock. **Safety stock inventory** is surplus inventory that protects against uncertainties in demand, lead time, and supply changes. Safety stocks are desirable when suppliers fail to deliver either the desired quantity on the specified date or items of acceptable quality, or when manufactured items require significant amounts of scrap or rework. Safety stock inventory ensures that operations are not disrupted when such problems occur, allowing subsequent operations to continue.

To create safety stock, a firm places an order for delivery earlier than when the item is typically needed.[1] The replenishment order therefore arrives ahead of time, giving a cushion against uncertainty. For example, suppose that the average lead time from a supplier is 3 weeks, but a firm orders 5 weeks in advance just to be safe. This policy creates a safety stock equal to a 2 weeks' supply (5 − 3).

Anticipation Inventory   Inventory used to absorb uneven rates of demand or supply, which businesses often face, is referred to as **anticipation inventory**. Predictable, seasonal demand patterns lend themselves to the use of anticipation inventory. Uneven demand can motivate a manufacturer to stockpile anticipation inventory during periods of low demand so that output levels do not have to be increased much when demand peaks. Anticipation inventory also can help when suppliers are threatened with a strike or have severe capacity limitations.

Pipeline Inventory   Inventory that is created when an order for an item is issued but not yet received is called **pipeline inventory**. This form of inventory exists because the firm must commit to enough inventory (on-hand plus in-transit) to cover the lead time for the order. Longer lead times or higher demands per week create more pipeline inventory. As such, the average pipeline inventory between two stocking points can be measured as the average demand during lead time, $\overline{D}_L$, which is the average demand for the item per period ($\overline{d}$) multiplied by the number of periods in the item's lead time (L) to move between the two points, or

$$\text{Pipeline inventory} = \overline{D}_L = \overline{d}L$$

The equation assumes that both $\overline{d}$ and L are constants and that L is not affected by the order or lot size, Q. Changing an item's lot size does not directly affect the average level of the pipeline inventory. Nonetheless, the lot size can *indirectly* affect pipeline inventory if it is related to the lead time. In such a case, pipeline inventory will change depending on the relationship of L to Q. Example 1 shows how this can happen.

safety stock inventory

Surplus inventory that a company holds to protect against uncertainties in demand, lead time, and supply changes.

anticipation inventory

Inventory used to absorb uneven rates of demand or supply.

pipeline inventory

Inventory that is created when an order for an item is issued but not yet received.

EXAMPLE 1	Estimating Inventory Levels

MyOMLab

Tutor 9.1 in MyOMLab provides a new example to practice the estimation of inventory levels.

A plant makes monthly shipments of electric drills to a wholesaler in average lot sizes of 280 drills. The wholesaler's average demand is 70 drills a week, and the lead time from the plant is 3 weeks. The wholesaler must pay for the inventory from the moment the plant makes a shipment. If the wholesaler is willing to increase its purchase quantity to 350 units, the plant will give priority to the wholesaler and guarantee a lead time of only 2 weeks. What is the effect on the wholesaler's cycle and pipeline inventories?

---

[1]When orders are placed at fixed intervals, a second way to create safety stock is used. Each new order placed is larger than the quantity typically needed through the next delivery date.

Susan E. Benson/Stock Connection

SOLUTION

The wholesaler's current cycle and pipeline inventories are

$$\text{Cycle inventory} = \frac{Q}{2} = \frac{280}{2} = 140 \text{ drills}$$

$$\text{Pipeline inventory} = \overline{D}_L = \overline{d}L = (70 \text{ drills/week})(3 \text{ weeks}) = 210 \text{ drills}$$

Figure 3 shows the cycle and pipeline inventories if the wholesaler accepts the new proposal.

1. Enter the average lot size, average demand during a period, and the number of periods of lead time:

Average lot size	350
Average demand	70
Lead time	2

2. To compute cycle inventory, simply divide average lot size by 2. To compute pipeline inventory, multiply average demand by lead time:

Cycle inventory	175
Pipeline inventory	140

◀ **FIGURE 3**
Estimating Inventory Levels
Using Tutor 9.1

DECISION POINT

The effect of the new proposal on cycle inventories is to increase them by 35 units, or 25 percent. The reduction in pipeline inventories, however, is 70 units, or 33 percent. The proposal would reduce the total investment in cycle and pipeline inventories. Also, it is advantageous to have shorter lead times because the wholesaler only has to commit to purchases 2 weeks in advance, rather than 3 weeks.

Inventory Reduction Tactics

Managers always are eager to find cost-effective ways to reduce inventory in supply chains. Later in this chapter we examine various ways for finding optimal lot sizes. Here, we discuss something more fundamental—the basic tactics (which we call *levers*) for reducing inventory in supply chains. A primary lever is one that must be activated if inventory is to be reduced. A secondary lever reduces the penalty cost of applying the primary lever and the need for having inventory in the first place.

Cycle Inventory   The primary lever to reduce cycle inventory is simply to reduce the lot sizes of items moving in the supply chain. However, making such reductions in Q without making any other changes can be devastating. For example, setup costs or ordering costs can skyrocket. If these changes occur, two secondary levers can be used:

1. Streamline the methods for placing orders and making setups in order to reduce ordering and setup costs and allow Q to be reduced. This may involve redesigning the infrastructure for information flows or improving manufacturing processes.

2. Increase repeatability to eliminate the need for changeovers. **Repeatability** is the degree to which the same work can be done again. Repeatability can be increased through high product demand; the use of specialization; the devotion of resources exclusively to a product; the use of the same part in many different products; the use of *flexible automation*; the use of the *one-worker, multiple-machines* concept; or through *group technology*. Increased repeatability may justify new setup methods, reduce transportation costs, and allow quantity discounts from suppliers.

repeatability

The degree to which the same work can be done again.

Safety Stock Inventory   The primary lever to reduce safety stock inventory is to place orders closer to the time when they must be received. However, this approach can lead to unacceptable customer service unless demand, supply, and delivery uncertainties can be minimized. Four secondary levers can be used in this case:

1. Improve demand forecasts so that fewer surprises come from customers. Design the mechanisms to increase collaboration with customers to get advanced warnings for changes in demand levels.

2. Cut the lead times of purchased or produced items to reduce demand uncertainty. For example, local suppliers with short lead times could be selected whenever possible.

3. Reduce supply uncertainties. Suppliers are likely to be more reliable if production plans are shared with them. Put in place the mechanisms to increase collaboration with suppliers.

Surprises from unexpected scrap or rework can be reduced by improving manufacturing processes. Preventive maintenance can minimize unexpected downtime caused by equipment failure.

4. Rely more on equipment and labor buffers, such as capacity cushions and cross-trained workers. These buffers are important to businesses in the service sector because they generally cannot inventory their services.

Anticipation Inventory   The primary lever to reduce anticipation inventory is simply to match demand rate with production rate. Secondary levers can be used to even out customer demand in one of the following ways:

1. Add new products with different demand cycles so that a peak in the demand for one product compensates for the seasonal low for another.

2. Provide off-season promotional campaigns.

3. Offer seasonal pricing plans.

Pipeline Inventory   An operations manager has direct control over lead times but not demand rates. Because pipeline inventory is a function of demand during the lead time, the primary lever is to reduce the lead time. Two secondary levers can help managers cut lead times:

1. Find more responsive suppliers and select new carriers for shipments between stocking locations or improve materials handling within the plant. Improving the information system could overcome information delays between a distribution center and retailer.

2. Change Q in those cases where the lead time depends on the lot size.

ABC Analysis

stock-keeping unit (SKU)

An individual item or product that has an identifying code and is held in inventory somewhere along the supply chain.

ABC analysis

The process of dividing SKUs into three classes, according to their dollar usage, so that managers can focus on items that have the highest dollar value.

Thousands of items, often referred to as stock-keeping units, are held in inventory by a typical organization, but only a small percentage of them deserve management's closest attention and tightest control. A **stock-keeping unit (SKU)** is an individual item or product that has an identifying code and is held in inventory somewhere along the supply chain. **ABC analysis** is the process of dividing SKUs into three classes according to their dollar usage so that managers can focus on items that have the highest dollar value. This method is the equivalent of creating a *Pareto chart* except that it is applied to inventory rather than to process errors. As Figure 4 shows, class A items typically represent only about 20 percent of the SKUs but account for 80 percent of the dollar usage. Class B items account for another 30 percent of the SKUs but only 15 percent of the dollar usage. Finally, 50 percent of the SKUs fall in class C, representing a mere 5 percent of the dollar usage. The goal of ABC analysis is to identify the class A SKUs so management can control their inventory levels.

The analysis begins by multiplying the annual demand rate for an SKU by the dollar value (cost) of one unit of that SKU to determine its dollar usage. After ranking the SKUs on the basis of dollar usage and creating the Pareto chart, the analyst looks for "natural" changes in slope. The dividing lines in Figure 4 between classes are inexact. Class A SKUs could be somewhat higher or lower than 20 percent of all SKUs but normally account for the bulk of the dollar usage.

Class A SKUs are reviewed frequently to reduce the average lot size and to ensure timely deliveries from suppliers. It is important to maintain high inventory turnover for these items. By contrast, class B SKUs require an intermediate level of control. Here, less frequent monitoring of suppliers coupled with adequate safety stocks can provide cost-effective coverage of demands. For class C SKUs, much looser control is appropriate. While a stockout of a class C SKU can be as crucial as for a class A SKU, the inventory holding cost of class C SKUs tends to be low. These features suggest that higher inventory levels can be tolerated and that more safety stock and larger lot sizes may suffice for class C SKUs. See Solved Problem 2 for a detailed example of ABC analysis.

Creating ABC inventory classifications is useless unless inventory records are accurate. Technology can help; many companies are tracking inventory wherever it exists in the supply chain. Chips imbedded in product packaging contain information on the product and send signals that can be accessed by sensitive receivers and transmitted to a central location for processing. There are other, less sophisticated approaches of achieving accuracy that can be used. One way is to assign responsibility to specific employees for issuing and receiving materials and accurately reporting each transaction. Another method is to secure inventory behind locked doors or gates to prevent unauthorized

▼ FIGURE 4
Typical Chart Using ABC Analysis

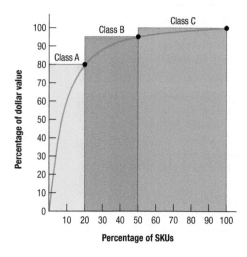

or unreported withdrawals. This method also guards against accidentally storing newly received inventory in the wrong locations, where it can be lost for months. **Cycle counting** can also be used, whereby storeroom personnel physically count a small percentage of the total number of SKUs each day, correcting errors that they find. Class A SKUs are counted most frequently. A final method, for computerized systems, is to make logic error checks on each transaction reported and fully investigate any discrepancies. The discrepancies can include (1) actual receipts when no receipts are scheduled, (2) disbursements that exceed the current on-hand inventory balance, and (3) receipts with an inaccurate (nonexistent) SKU number.

Now that we have identified the inventory items deserving of most attention, we devote the remainder of the chapter to the decisions of how much to order and when.

> **cycle counting**
> An inventory control method, whereby storeroom personnel physically count a small percentage of the total number of items each day, correcting errors that they find.

Economic Order Quantity

Supply chain managers face conflicting pressures to keep inventories low enough to avoid excess inventory holding costs but high enough to reduce ordering and setup costs. *Inventory holding cost* is the sum of the cost of capital and the variable costs of keeping items on hand, such as storage and handling, taxes, insurance, and shrinkage. *Ordering cost* is the cost of preparing a purchase order for a supplier or a production order for the shop, while *setup cost* is the cost of changing over a machine to produce a different item. In this section, we will address the *cycle inventory*, which is that portion of total inventory that varies directly with lot size. A good starting point for balancing these conflicting pressures and determining the best cycle-inventory level for an item is finding the **economic order quantity (EOQ)**, which is the lot size that minimizes total annual cycle-inventory holding and ordering costs. The approach to determining the EOQ is based on the following assumptions:

> **economic order quantity (EOQ)**
> The lot size that minimizes total annual inventory holding and ordering costs.

1. The demand rate for the item is constant (for example, always 10 units per day) and known with certainty.

2. No constraints are placed (such as truck capacity or materials handling limitations) on the size of each lot.

3. The only two relevant costs are the inventory holding cost and the fixed cost per lot for ordering or setup.

4. Decisions for one item can be made independently of decisions for other items. In other words, no advantage is gained in combining several orders going to the same supplier.

5. The lead time is constant (e.g., always 14 days) and known with certainty. The amount received is exactly what was ordered and it arrives all at once rather than piecemeal.

The economic order quantity will be optimal when all five assumptions are satisfied. In reality, few situations are so simple. Nonetheless, the EOQ is often a reasonable approximation of the appropriate lot size, even when several of the assumptions do not quite apply. Here are some guidelines on when to use or modify the EOQ.

- **Do not use the EOQ**
  - If you use the "make-to-order" strategy and your customer specifies that the entire order be delivered in one shipment
  - If the order size is constrained by capacity limitations such as the size of the firm's ovens, amount of testing equipment, or number of delivery trucks
- **Modify the EOQ**
  - If significant quantity discounts are given for ordering larger lots
  - If replenishment of the inventory is not instantaneous, which can happen if the items must be used or sold as soon as they are finished without waiting until the entire lot has been completed
- **Use the EOQ**
  - If you follow a "make-to-stock" strategy and the item has relatively stable demand
  - If your carrying costs per unit and setup or ordering costs are known and relatively stable

The EOQ was never intended to be an optimizing tool. Nonetheless, if you need to determine a reasonable lot size, it can be helpful in many situations.

Calculating the EOQ

We begin by formulating the total cost for any lot size Q for a given SKU. Next, we derive the EOQ, which is the Q that minimizes total annual cycle-inventory cost. Finally, we describe how to convert the EOQ into a companion measure, the elapsed time between orders.

When the EOQ assumptions are satisfied, cycle inventory behaves as shown in Figure 5. A cycle begins with Q units held in inventory, which happens when a new order is received. During the cycle, on-hand inventory is used at a constant rate and, because demand is known with certainty and the lead time is a constant, a new lot can be ordered so that inventory falls to 0 precisely when the new lot is received. Because inventory varies uniformly between Q and 0, the average cycle inventory equals half the lot size, Q.

FIGURE 5 ▶
Cycle-Inventory Levels

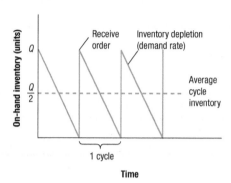

The annual holding cost for this amount of inventory, which increases linearly with Q, as Figure 6(a) shows, is

Annual holding cost = (Average cycle inventory)(Unit holding cost)

The annual ordering cost is

Annual ordering cost = (Number of orders/Year)(Ordering or setup cost)

The average number of orders per year equals annual demand divided by Q. For example, if 1,200 units must be ordered each year and the average lot size is 100 units, then 12 orders will be placed during the year. The annual ordering or setup cost decreases nonlinearly as Q increases, as shown in Figure 6(b), because fewer orders are placed.

FIGURE 6 ▶
Graphs of Annual
Holding, Ordering,
and Total Costs

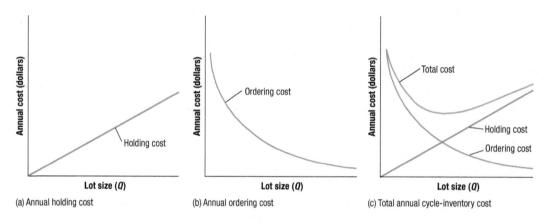

(a) Annual holding cost   (b) Annual ordering cost   (c) Total annual cycle-inventory cost

The total annual cycle-inventory cost,[2] as graphed in Figure 6(c), is the sum of the two cost components:

Total cost = Annual holding cost + Annual ordering or setup cost[3]

$$C = \frac{Q}{2}(H) + \frac{D}{Q}(S)$$

---

[2] Expressing the total cost on an annual basis usually is convenient (although not necessary). Any time horizon can be selected as long as D and H cover the same time period. If the total cost is calculated on a monthly basis, D must be monthly demand and H must be the cost of holding a unit for 1 month.

[3] The number of orders actually placed in any year is always a whole number, although the formula allows the use of fractional values. However, rounding is not needed because what is being calculated is an average for multiple years. Such averages often are nonintegers.

where

C = total annual cycle-inventory cost

Q = lot size, in units

H = cost of holding one unit in inventory for a year, often expressed as a percentage of the item's value

D = annual demand, in units per year

S = cost of ordering or setting up one lot, in dollars per lot

EXAMPLE 2	The Cost of a Lot-Sizing Policy

A museum of natural history opened a gift shop two years ago. Managing inventories has become a problem. Low inventory turnover is squeezing profit margins and causing cash-flow problems.

One of the top-selling SKUs in the container group at the museum's gift shop is a bird feeder. Sales are 18 units per week, and the supplier charges $60 per unit. The cost of placing an order with the supplier is $45. Annual holding cost is 25 percent of a feeder's value, and the museum operates 52 weeks per year. Management chose a 390-unit lot size so that new orders could be placed less frequently. What is the annual cycle-inventory cost of the current policy of using a 390-unit lot size? Would a lot size of 468 be better?

SOLUTION

We begin by computing the annual demand and holding cost as

$$D = (18 \text{ units/week})(52 \text{ weeks/year}) = 936 \text{ units}$$

$$H = 0.25(\$60/\text{unit}) = \$15$$

The total annual cycle-inventory cost for the current policy is

$$C = \frac{Q}{2}(H) + \frac{D}{Q}(S)$$

$$= \frac{390}{2}(\$15) + \frac{936}{390}(\$45) = \$2{,}925 + \$108 = \$3{,}033$$

The total annual cycle-inventory cost for the alternative lot size is

$$C = \frac{468}{2}(\$15) + \frac{936}{468}(\$45) = \$3{,}510 + \$90 = \$3{,}600$$

DECISION POINT

The lot size of 468 units, which is a half-year supply, would be a more expensive option than the current policy. The savings in ordering costs are more than offset by the increase in holding costs. Management should use the total annual cycle-inventory cost function to explore other lot-size alternatives.

Figure 7 displays the impact of using several Q values for the bird feeder in Example 2. Eight different lot sizes were evaluated in addition to the current one. Both holding and ordering costs were plotted, but their sum—the total annual cycle-inventory cost curve—is the important feature. The graph shows that the best lot size, or EOQ, is the lowest point on the total annual cost curve, or between 50 and 100 units. Obviously, reducing the current lot-size policy ($Q = 390$) can result in significant savings.

A more efficient approach is to use the EOQ formula:

$$\text{EOQ} = \sqrt{\frac{2DS}{H}}$$

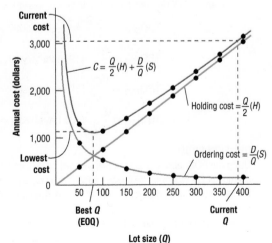

◀ **FIGURE 7**
Total Annual Cycle-Inventory Cost Function for the Bird Feeder

159

We use calculus to obtain the EOQ formula from the total annual cycle-inventory cost function. We take the first derivative of the total annual cycle-inventory cost function with respect to Q, set it equal to 0, and solve for Q. As Figure 7 indicates, the EOQ is the order quantity for which annual holding cost equals annual ordering cost. Using this insight, we can also obtain the EOQ formula by equating the formulas for annual ordering cost and annual holding cost and solving for Q. The graph in Figure 7 also reveals that when the annual holding cost for any Q exceeds the annual ordering cost, as with the 390-unit order, we can immediately conclude that Q is too high. A lower Q reduces holding cost and increases ordering cost, bringing them into balance. Similarly, if the annual ordering cost exceeds the annual holding cost, Q should be increased.

Sometimes, inventory policies are based on the time between replenishment orders, rather than on the number of units in the lot size. The **time between orders (TBO)** for a particular lot size is the average elapsed time between receiving (or placing) replenishment orders of Q units. Expressed as a fraction of a year, the TBO is simply Q divided by annual demand. When we use the EOQ and express time in terms of months, the TBO is

time between orders (TBO)

The average elapsed time between receiving (or placing) replenishment orders of Q units for a particular lot size.

$$TBO_{EOQ} = \frac{EOQ}{D} \text{ (12 months/year)}$$

In Example 3, we show how to calculate TBO for years, months, weeks, and days.

| EXAMPLE 3 | Finding the EOQ, Total Cost, and TBO |

MyOMLab

Tutor 9.2 in MyOMLab provides a new example to practice the application of the EOQ model.

MyOMLab

Active Model 9.1 in MyOMLab provides additional insight on the EOQ model and its uses.

FIGURE 8 ▶
Total Annual Cycle-Inventory Costs Based on EOQ Using Tutor 9.3

For the bird feeder in Example 2, calculate the EOQ and its total annual cycle-inventory cost. How frequently will orders be placed if the EOQ is used?

SOLUTION

Using the formulas for EOQ and annual cost, we get

$$EOQ = \sqrt{\frac{2DS}{H}} = \sqrt{\frac{2(936)(45)}{15}} = 74.94, \text{ or } 75 \text{ units}$$

Figure 8 shows that the total annual cost is much less than the $3,033 cost of the current policy of placing 390-unit orders.

Parameters

Current Lot Size (Q)	390	Economic Order Quantity	75
Demand (D)	936		
Order Cost (S)	$45		
Unit Holding Cost (H)	$15		

Annual Costs		**Annual Costs based on EOQ**	
Orders per Year	2.4	Orders per Year	12.48
Annual Ordering Cost	$108.00	Annual Ordering Cost	$561.60
Annual Holding Cost	$2,925.00	Annual Holding Cost	$562.50
Annual Inventory Cost	$3,033.00	Annual Inventory Cost	$1,124.10

When the EOQ is used, the TBO can be expressed in various ways for the same time period.

$$TBO_{EOQ} = \frac{EOQ}{D} = \frac{75}{936} = 0.080 \text{ year}$$

$$TBO_{EOQ} = \frac{EOQ}{D}(12 \text{ months/year}) = \frac{75}{936}(12) = 0.96 \text{ month}$$

$$TBO_{EOQ} = \frac{EOQ}{D}(52 \text{ weeks/year}) = \frac{75}{936}(52) = 4.17 \text{ weeks}$$

$$TBO_{EOQ} = \frac{EOQ}{D}(365 \text{ days/year}) = \frac{75}{936}(365) = 29.25 \text{ days}$$

DECISION POINT

Using the EOQ, about 12 orders per year will be required. Using the current policy of 390 units per order, an average of 2.4 orders will be needed each year (every 5 months). The current policy saves on ordering costs but incurs a much higher cost for carrying the cycle inventory. Although it is easy to see which option is best on the basis of total ordering and holding costs, other factors may affect the final decision. For example, if the supplier would reduce the price per unit for large orders, it may be better to order the larger quantity.

Managerial Insights from the EOQ

Subjecting the EOQ formula to *sensitivity analysis* can yield valuable insights into the management of inventories. Sensitivity analysis is a technique for systematically changing crucial parameters to determine the effects of a change. Table 1 shows the effects on the EOQ when we substitute different values into the numerator or denominator of the formula.

TABLE 1 | SENSITIVITY ANALYSIS OF THE EOQ

Parameter	EOQ	Parameter Change	EOQ Change	Comments
Demand	$\sqrt{\dfrac{2DS}{H}}$	↑	↑	Increase in lot size is in proportion to the square root of D.
Order/Setup Costs	$\sqrt{\dfrac{2DS}{H}}$	↓	↓	Weeks of supply decreases and inventory turnover increases because the lot size decreases.
Holding Costs	$\sqrt{\dfrac{2DS}{H}}$	↓	↑	Larger lots are justified when holding costs decrease.

As Table 1 shows, the EOQ provides support for some of the intuition you may have about inventory management. However, the effect of ordering or setup cost changes on inventories is especially important for *lean systems*. This relationship explains why manufacturers are so concerned about reducing setup time and costs; it makes small lot production economic. Actually, lean systems provide an environment conducive to the use of the EOQ. For example, yearly, monthly, daily, or hourly demand rates are known with reasonable certainty in lean systems, and the rate of demand is relatively uniform. Lean systems may have few process constraints if the firm practices *constraint management*. In addition, lean systems strive for constant delivery lead times and dependable delivery quantities from suppliers, both of which are assumptions of the EOQ. Consequently, the EOQ as a lot sizing tool is quite compatible with the principles of lean systems.

Inventory Control Systems

The EOQ and other lot-sizing methods answer the important question: *How much* should we order? Another important question that needs an answer is: *When* should we place the order? An inventory control system responds to both questions. In selecting an inventory control system for a particular application, the nature of the demands imposed on the inventory items is crucial. An important distinction between types of inventory is whether an item is subject to dependent or independent demand. Retailers, such as JCPenney, and distributors must manage **independent demand items**—that is, items for which demand is influenced by market conditions and is not related to the inventory decisions for any other item held in stock or produced. Independent demand inventory includes

- Wholesale and retail merchandise
- Service support inventory, such as stamps and mailing labels for post offices, office supplies for law firms, and laboratory supplies for research universities
- Product and replacement-part distribution inventories
- Maintenance, repair, and operating (MRO) supplies—that is, items that do not become part of the final service or product, such as employee uniforms, fuel, paint, and machine repair parts

Managing independent demand inventory can be tricky because demand is influenced by external factors. For example, the owner of a bookstore may not be sure how many copies of the latest best-seller novel customers will purchase during the coming month. As a result, the manager may decide to stock extra copies as a safeguard. Independent demand, such as the demand for various book titles, must be *forecasted*.

In this chapter, we focus on inventory control systems for independent demand items, which is the type of demand the bookstore owner, other retailers, service providers, and distributors face. Even though demand from any one customer is difficult to predict, low demand from some customers for a particular item often is offset by high demand from others. Thus, total demand for any independent demand item may follow a relatively smooth pattern, with some random fluctuations. *Dependent demand items* are those required as components or inputs to a service

independent demand items

Items for which demand is influenced by market conditions and is not related to the inventory decisions for any other item held in stock or produced.

Retailers typically face independent demands for their products. Here shoppers look for bargains at a JCPenney store in the Glendale Galleria in California.

Aurelia Ventura/La Opinion/Newscom

or product. Dependent demand exhibits a pattern very different from that of independent demand and must be managed with different techniques.

In this section, we discuss and compare two inventory control systems: (1) the continuous review system, called a *Q* system, and (2) the periodic review system, called a *P* system. We close with a look at hybrid systems, which incorporate features of both the *P* and *Q* systems.

Continuous Review System

A **continuous review (Q) system**, sometimes called a **reorder point (ROP) system** or *fixed order-quantity system*, tracks the remaining inventory of a SKU each time a withdrawal is made to determine whether it is time to reorder. In practice, these reviews are done frequently (e.g., daily) and often continuously (after each withdrawal). The advent of computers and electronic cash registers linked to inventory records has made continuous reviews easy. At each review, a decision is made about a SKU's inventory position. If it is judged to be too low, the system triggers a new order. The **inventory position (IP)** measures the SKU's ability to satisfy future demand. It includes **scheduled receipts (SR)**, which are orders that have been placed but have not yet been received, plus on-hand inventory (OH) minus backorders (BO). Sometimes. scheduled receipts are called **open orders**. More specifically,

$$\text{Inventory position} = \text{On-hand inventory} + \text{Scheduled receipts} - \text{Backorders}$$

$$IP = OH + SR - BO$$

When the inventory position reaches a predetermined minimum level, called the **reorder point (R)**, a fixed quantity *Q* of the SKU is ordered. In a continuous review system, although the order quantity *Q* is fixed, the time between orders can vary. Hence, *Q* can be based on the EOQ, a price break quantity (the minimum lot size that qualifies for a quantity discount), a container size (such as a truckload), or some other quantity selected by management.

Selecting the Reorder Point When Demand and Lead Time Are Constant To demonstrate the concept of a reorder point, suppose that the demand for feeders at the museum gift shop in Example 3 is always 18 per week, the lead time is a constant 2 weeks, and the supplier always ships the exact number ordered on time. With both demand and lead time constant, the museum's buyer can wait until the inventory position drops to 36 units, or (18 units/week) (2 weeks), to place a new order. Thus, in this case, the reorder point, *R*, equals the *total demand during lead time*, with no added allowance for safety stock.

Figure 9 shows how the system operates when demand and lead time are constant. The downward-sloping line represents the on-hand inventory, which is being depleted at a constant rate. When it reaches reorder point *R* (the horizontal line), a new order for *Q* units is placed. The on-hand inventory continues to drop throughout lead time *L* until the order is received. At that time, which marks the end of the lead time, on-hand inventory jumps by *Q* units. A new order arrives just when inventory drops to 0. The TBO is the same for each cycle.

The inventory position, IP, shown in Figure 9 corresponds to the on-hand inventory, except during the lead time. Just after a new order is placed, at the start of the lead time, IP increases by *Q*, as shown by the dashed line. The IP exceeds OH by this same margin

continuous review (Q) system

A system designed to track the remaining inventory of a SKU each time a withdrawal is made to determine whether it is time to reorder.

reorder point (ROP) system

See continuous review (*Q*) system.

inventory position (IP)

The measurement of a SKU's ability to satisfy future demand.

scheduled receipts (SR)

Orders that have been placed but have not yet been received.

open orders

See scheduled receipts (SR).

reorder point (R)

The predetermined minimum level that an inventory position must reach before a fixed quantity *Q* of the SKU is ordered.

FIGURE 9 ▶

Q System When Demand and Lead Time Are Constant and Certain

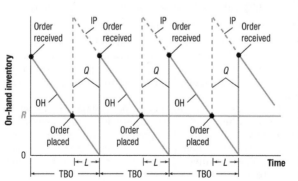

throughout the lead time.[4] At the end of the lead time, when the scheduled receipts convert to on-hand inventory, IP = OH once again. The key point here is to compare IP, not OH, with R in deciding whether to reorder. A common error is to ignore scheduled receipts or backorders.

EXAMPLE 4	**Placing a New Order When Demand and Lead Time Are Constant**

Demand for chicken soup at a supermarket is always 25 cases a day and the lead time is always 4 days. The shelves were just restocked with chicken soup, leaving an on-hand inventory of only 10 cases. No backorders currently exist, but there is one open order in the pipeline for 200 cases. What is the inventory position? Should a new order be placed?

SOLUTION

$$R = \text{Total demand during lead time} = (25)(4) = 100 \text{ cases}$$
$$IP = OH + SR - BO$$
$$= 10 + 200 - 0 = 210 \text{ cases}$$

DECISION POINT

Because IP exceeds R (210 versus 100), do not reorder. Inventory is almost depleted, but a new order need not be placed because the scheduled receipt is in the pipeline.

Selecting the Reorder Point When Demand Is Variable and Lead Time Is Constant   In reality demand is not always predictable. For instance, the museum's buyer knows that *average* demand is 18 feeders per week. That is, a variable number of feeders may be purchased during the lead time, with an average demand during lead time of 36 feeders (assuming that each week's demand is identically distributed and lead time is a constant 2 weeks). This situation gives rise to the need for safety stocks. Suppose that the museum's buyer sets R at 46 units, thereby placing orders before they typically are needed. This approach will create a safety stock, or stock held in excess of expected demand, of 10 units (46 − 36) to buffer against uncertain demand. In general

$$\text{Reorder point} = \text{Average demand during lead time} + \text{Safety stock}$$

$$= \bar{d}L + \text{safety stock}$$

where

$$\bar{d} = \text{average demand per week (or day or month)}$$

$$L = \text{constant lead tome in weeks (or days or months)}$$

Figure 10 shows how the Q system operates when demand is variable and lead time is constant. The wavy downward-sloping line indicates that demand varies from day to day. Its slope is steeper in the second cycle, which means that the demand rate is higher during this time period. The changing demand rate means that the time between orders changes, so $TBO_1 \neq TBO_2 \neq TBO_3$. Because of uncertain demand, sales during the lead time are unpredictable, and safety stock is added to hedge against lost sales. This addition is why R is higher in Figure 10 than in Figure 9. It also explains why the on-hand inventory usually does not drop to 0 by the time a replenishment order arrives. The greater the safety stock and thus the higher reorder point R, the less likely a stockout.

Because the average demand during lead time is variable, the real decision to be made when selecting R concerns the safety stock level. Deciding on a small or large safety stock is a trade-off between customer service and inventory holding costs. Cost minimization models can be used to find the best safety stock, but they require estimates of stockout and back-order costs, which are usually difficult to make with any precision because it is hard to estimate the effect of lost sales, lost customer confidence, future loyalty of customers, and market share because the customer went to a competitor. The usual approach for determining R is for management—based on

▼ **FIGURE 10**
Q System When Demand Is Uncertain

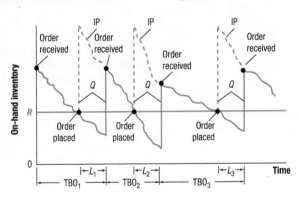

---

[4]A possible exception is the unlikely situation when more than one scheduled receipt is open at the same time because of long lead times.

judgment—to set a reasonable service-level policy for the inventory and then determine the safety stock level that satisfies this policy. There are three steps to arrive at a reorder point:

1. Choose an appropriate service-level policy.
2. Determine the distribution of demand during lead time.
3. Determine the safety stock and reorder point levels.

service level

The desired probability of not running out of stock in any one ordering cycle, which begins at the time an order is placed and ends when it arrives in stock.

cycle-service level

See service level.

protection interval

The period over which safety stock must protect the user from running out of stock.

Step 1: Service level policy   Select a **service level**, or **cycle-service level** (the desired probability of not running out of stock in any one ordering cycle), which begins at the time an order is placed and ends when it arrives in stock. The intent is to provide coverage over the **protection interval**, or the period over which safety stock must protect the user from running out of stock. For the Q system, the lead time is the protection interval. For example, in a bookstore the manager may select a 90 percent cycle-service level for a book. In other words, the probability is 90 percent that demand will not exceed the supply during the lead time. The probability of running short *during the protection interval*, creating a stockout or backorder, is only 10 percent $(100 - 90)$ in our example. This stockout risk, which occurs only during the lead time in the Q system, is greater than the overall risk of a stockout because the risk is nonexistent outside the ordering cycle.

Step 2: Distribution of demand during lead time   Determine the distribution of demand during lead time, which requires the specification of its mean and standard deviation. To translate a cycle-service level policy into a specific safety stock level, we must know how demand during the lead time is distributed. If demand and lead times vary little around their averages, the safety stock can be small. Conversely, if they vary greatly from one order cycle to the next, the safety stock must be large. Variability is measured by the distribution of demand during lead time. Sometimes, average demand during the lead time and the standard deviation of demand during the lead time are not directly available and must be calculated by combining information on the demand rate with information on the lead time. Suppose that lead time is constant and demand is variable, but records on demand are not collected for a time interval that is exactly the same as the lead time. The same inventory control system may be used to manage thousands of different SKUs, each with a different lead time. For example, if demand is reported *weekly*, these records can be used directly to compute the average and the standard deviation of demand during the lead time if the lead time is exactly 1 week. However, if the lead time is 3 weeks, the computation is more difficult.

We can determine the demand during the lead time distribution by making some reasonable assumptions. Suppose that the average demand, $\bar{d}$, is known along with the standard deviation of demand, σ_d, over some time interval such as days or weeks. Also, suppose that the probability distributions of demand for each time interval are identical and independent of each other. For example, if the time interval is a week, the probability distributions of demand are assumed to be the same each week (identical $\bar{d}$ and σ_d), and the total demand in 1 week does not affect the total demand in another week. Let L be the constant lead time, expressed in the same time units as the demand. Under these assumptions, average demand during the lead time will be the sum of the averages for each of the L identical and independent distributions of demand, or $\bar{d} + \bar{d} + \bar{d} + \ldots = \bar{d}L$. In addition, the variance of the distribution of demand during lead time will be the sum of the variances of the L identical and independent distributions of demand, or

$$\sigma_d^2 + \sigma_d^2 + \sigma_d^2 + \ldots = \sigma_d^2 L$$

Finally, the standard deviation of the distribution of demand during lead time is

$$\sigma_{dLT} = \sqrt{\sigma_d^2 L} = \sigma_d \sqrt{L}$$

Figure 11 shows how the demand distribution of the lead time is developed from the individual distributions of weekly demands, where $\bar{d} = 75$, $\sigma_d = 15$, and $L = 3$. In this example, average demand during the lead time is $(75)(3) = 225$ units and $\sigma_{dLT} = 15\sqrt{3} = 25.98$.

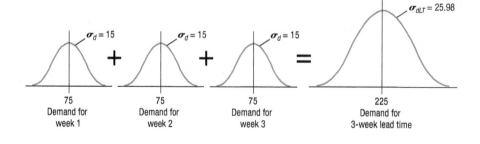

FIGURE 11 ▶
Development of Distribution of Demand During Lead Time

Step 3: Safety stock and reorder point When selecting the safety stock, the inventory planner often assumes that demand during the lead time is normally distributed, as shown in Figure 12.

The average demand during the lead time is the centerline of the graph, with 50 percent of the area under the curve to the left and 50 percent to the right. Thus, if a cycle-service level of 50 percent were chosen, the reorder point R would be the quantity represented by this centerline. Because R equals the average demand during the lead time plus the safety stock, the safety stock is 0 when R equals this average demand. Demand is less than average 50 percent of the time and, thus, having no safety stock will be sufficient only 50 percent of the time.

To provide a service level above 50 percent, the reorder point must be higher than the average demand during the lead time. As Figure 12 shows, that requires moving the reorder point to the right of the centerline so that more than 50 percent of the area under the curve is to the left of R. An 85 percent cycle-service level is achieved in Figure 12 with 85 percent of the area under the curve to the left of R (in blue) and only 15 percent to the right (in pink). We compute the safety stock as follows:

$$\text{Safety stock} = z\,\sigma_{dLT}$$

where

z = the number of standard deviations needed to achieve the cycle-service level

σ_{dLT} = standard deviation of demand during the lead time

The reorder point becomes

$$R = \overline{d}L + \text{safety stock}$$

The higher the value of z, the higher the safety stock and the cycle-service level should be. If $z = 0$, there is no safety stock, and stockouts will occur during 50 percent of the order cycles. For a cycle-service level of 85 percent, $z = 1.04$. Example 5 shows how to use the Normal Distribution appendix to find the appropriate z value, safety stock, and reorder point.

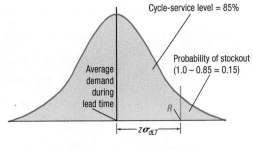

▲ **FIGURE 12**
Finding Safety Stock with Normal Probability Distribution for an 85 Percent Cycle-Service Level

EXAMPLE 5	Reorder Point for Variable Demand and Constant Lead Time

Let us return to the bird feeder in Example 3. The EOQ is 75 units. Suppose that the average demand is 18 units per week with a standard deviation of 5 units. The lead time is constant at 2 weeks. Determine the safety stock and reorder point if management wants a 90 percent cycle-service level.

SOLUTION
In this case, $\sigma_d = 5$, $\overline{d} = 18$ units, and $L = 2$ weeks, so $\sigma_{dLT} = \sigma_d\sqrt{L} = 5\sqrt{2} = 7.07$. Consult the body of the table in the Normal Distribution appendix for 0.9000, which corresponds to a 90 percent cycle-service level. The closest number is 0.8997, which corresponds to 1.2 in the row heading and 0.08 in the column heading. Adding these values gives a z value of 1.28. With this information, we calculate the safety stock and reorder point as follows:

$$\text{Safety stock} = z\sigma_{dLT} = 1.28(7.07) = 9.05, \text{ or } 9 \text{ units}$$
$$\text{Reorder point} = \overline{d}L + \text{Safety stock}$$
$$= 2(18) + 9 = 45 \text{ units}$$

DECISION POINT
The Q system for the bird feeder operates as follows: Whenever the inventory position reaches 45 units, order the EOQ of 75 units. Various order quantities and safety stock levels can be used in a Q system. For example, management could specify a different order quantity (because of shipping constraints) or a different safety stock (because of storage limitations).

MyOMLab
Tutor 9.3 in MyOMLab provides a new example to determine the safety stock and the reorder point for a Q system.

Selecting the Reorder Point When Both Demand and Lead Time Are Variable In practice, it is often the case that both the demand and the lead time are variable. Unfortunately, the equations for the safety stock and reorder point become more complicated. In the model below we make two simplifying assumptions. First, the demand distribution and the lead time distribution are measured in the same time units. For example, both demand and lead time are measured in weeks. Second, demand and lead time are *independent*. That is, demand per week is not affected by the length of the lead time.

$$\text{Safety stock} = z\sigma_{dLT}$$

$$R = (\text{Average weekly demand} \times \text{Average lead time in weeks}) + \text{Safety stock}$$

$$= \overline{d}\overline{L} + \text{Safety stock}$$

where

$$\overline{d} = \text{Average weekly (or daily or monthly) demand}$$
$$\overline{L} = \text{Average weekly (or daily or monthly) lead time}$$
$$\sigma_d = \text{Standard deviation of weekly (or daily or monthly) demand}$$
$$\sigma_{LT} = \text{Standard deviation of the lead time, and}$$
$$\sigma_{dLT} = \sqrt{\overline{L}\sigma_d^2 + \overline{d}^2\sigma_{LT}^2}$$

Now that we have determined the mean and standard deviation of the distribution of demand during lead time under these more complicated conditions, we can select the reorder point as we did before for the case where the lead time was constant.

| EXAMPLE 6 | Reorder Point for Variable Demand and Variable Lead Time |

The Office Supply Shop estimates that the average demand for a popular ball-point pen is 12,000 pens per week with a standard deviation of 3,000 pens. The current inventory policy calls for replenishment orders of 156,000 pens. The average lead time from the distributor is 5 weeks, with a standard deviation of 2 weeks. If management wants a 95 percent cycle-service level, what should the reorder point be?

SOLUTION

We have $\overline{d} = 12{,}000$ pens, $\sigma_d = 3{,}000$ pens, $\overline{L} = 5$ weeks, and $\sigma_{LT} = 2$ weeks.

$$\sigma_{dLT} = \sqrt{\overline{L}\sigma_d^2 + \overline{d}^2\sigma_{LT}^2} = \sqrt{(5)(3{,}000)^2 + (12{,}000)^2(2)^2} = 24{,}919.87 \text{ pens}$$

Consult the body of the Normal Distribution appendix for 0.9500, which corresponds to a 95 percent cycle-service level. That value falls exactly in the middle of the tabular values of 0.9495 (for a z value of 1.64) and 0.9505 (for a z value of 1.65). Consequently, we will use the more conservative value of 1.65. We calculate the safety stock and reorder point as follows:

$$\text{Safety stock} = z\sigma_{dLT} = (1.65)(24{,}919.87) = 41{,}117.79, \text{ or } 41{,}118 \text{ pens}$$

$$\text{Reorder point} = \overline{d}\overline{L} + \text{Safety stock} = (12{,}000)(5) + 41{,}118 = 101{,}118 \text{ pens}$$

DECISION POINT

Whenever the stock of ball-point pens drops to 101,118, management should place another replenishment order of 156,000 pens to the distributor.

Sometimes, the theoretical distributions for demand and lead time are not known. In those cases, we can use simulation to find the distribution of demand during lead time using discrete distributions for demand and lead times. Simulation can also be used to estimate the performance of an inventory system. More discussion, and an example, can be found in MyOMLab.

Two-Bin System The concept of a Q system can be incorporated in a **visual system**, that is, a system that allows employees to place orders when inventory visibly reaches a certain marker. Visual systems are easy to administer because records are not kept on the current inventory position. The historical usage rate can simply be reconstructed from past purchase orders. Visual systems are intended for use with low-value SKUs that have a steady demand, such as nuts and bolts or office supplies. Overstocking is common, but the extra inventory holding cost is minimal because the items have relatively little value.

MyOMLab

visual system

A system that allows employees to place orders when inventory visibly reaches a certain marker.

A visual system version of the Q system is the **two-bin system** in which a SKU's inventory is stored at two different locations. Inventory is first withdrawn from one bin. If the first bin is empty, the second bin provides backup to cover demand until a replenishment order arrives. An empty first bin signals the need to place a new order. Premade order forms placed near the bins let workers send one to purchasing or even directly to the supplier. When the new order arrives, the second bin is restored to its normal level and the rest is put in the first bin. The two-bin system operates like a Q system, with the normal level in the second bin being the re-order point R. The system also may be implemented with just one bin by marking the bin at the reorder point level.

two-bin system

A visual system version of the Q system in which a SKU's inventory is stored at two different locations.

Calculating Total Q System Costs   Total costs for the continuous review (Q) system is the sum of three cost components:

Total cost = Annual cycle inventory holding cost + annual ordering cost

+ annual safety stock holding cost

$$C = \frac{Q}{2}(H) + \frac{D}{Q}(S) + (H)(\text{Safety stock})$$

The annual cycle-inventory holding cost and annual ordering cost are the same equations we used for computing the total annual cycle-inventory cost in Example 2. The annual cost of holding the safety stock is computed under the assumption that the safety stock is on hand at all times. Referring to Figure 10 in each order cycle, we will sometimes experience a demand greater than the average demand during lead time, and sometimes we will experience less. On average over the year, we can assume the safety stock will be on hand. See Solved Problems 4 and 6 at the end of this chapter for an example of calculating the total costs for a Q system.

Periodic Review System

An alternative inventory control system is the **periodic review (P) system**, sometimes called a *fixed interval reorder system* or *periodic reorder system*, in which an item's inventory position is reviewed periodically rather than continuously. Such a system can simplify delivery scheduling because it establishes a routine. A new order is always placed at the end of each review, and the time between orders (TBO) is fixed at P. Demand is a random variable, so total demand between reviews varies. In a P system, the lot size, Q, may change from one order to the next, but the time between orders is fixed. An example of a periodic review system is that of a soft-drink supplier making weekly rounds of grocery stores. Each week, the supplier reviews the store's inventory of soft drinks and restocks the store with enough items to meet demand and safety stock require-ments until the next week.

Under a P system, four of the original EOQ assumptions are maintained: (1) no constraints are placed on the size of the lot, (2) the relevant costs are holding and ordering costs, (3) deci-sions for one SKU are independent of decisions for other SKUs, and (4) lead times are certain and supply is known. However, demand uncertainty is again allowed for. Figure 13 shows the peri-odic review system under these assumptions. The downward-sloping line again represents on-hand inventory. When the predetermined time, P, has elapsed since the last review, an order is placed to bring the inventory position, represented by the dashed line, up to the target inventory level, T. The lot size for the first review is Q_1, or the dif-ference between inventory position IP_1 and T. As with the continuous review system, IP and OH differ only during the lead time. When the order arrives at the end of the lead time, OH and IP again are identical. Figure 13 shows that lot sizes vary from one order cycle to the next. Because the inventory position is lower at the second review, a greater quantity is needed to achieve an inventory level of T.

Managerial Practice 1 shows how the use of periodic inventory review systems is important in supply chains in the chemical industry.

periodic review (P) sytem

A system in which an item's inventory position is reviewed periodically rather than continuously.

▼ **FIGURE 13**
P System When Demand Is Uncertain

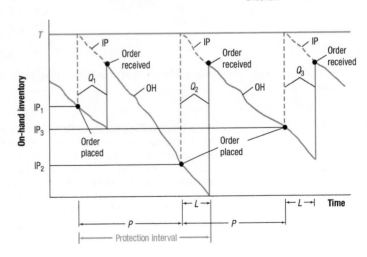

MANAGERIAL PRACTICE 1 — The Supply Chain Implications of Periodic Review Inventory Systems at Celanese

What do products such as paints, adhesives, coatings, plastics, medicines, cosmetics, detergents, textiles, or fragrances have in common? All of these products use acetic acid as a major component. Celanese, a $6.5 billion chemical company with $640 million in total inventories, is a major supplier of acetic acid in the world. The large investment in inventory forces Celanese to take a hard look at inventory policies for all products, including acetic acid. The key to successful management of the inventories was to acknowledge the interaction between the inventory policies at each stage of the supply chain with the realities of material flows and logistics in the chemical industry.

The supply chain for acetic acid is complex, involving 90 stages. For example, the supply chain is comprised of stages such as vendors supplying a liner to transport the acid, manufacturing sites producing the acid, transportation modes moving acid, warehouses storing it, and customer demand locations to which the acid is finally shipped. There are four manufacturing facilities, three in the United States and one in Singapore, each of which supplies several storage locations worldwide. Transportation stages correspond to rail, barges, trucks, and ocean vessels. Material typically moves in large quantities because of economies of scale and transportation schedules. Storage facilities may be supplied by multiple upstream facilities as well as the manufacturing plant itself.

The use of periodic review inventory systems at the storage and demand locations in this supply chain scenario makes sense for several reasons. First, the transportation modes have defined schedules of operation. Review periods at storage facilities reflect the schedule of the supplying transportation mode. Second, customer orders are typically batched and timed with weekly, bi-weekly, or monthly frequencies. Celanese often assigns customers and storage facilities specific days to place orders so that their own production

Large, fixed capacity modes of transportation require defined schedules of operation. Such a situation supports the use of periodic inventory systems. Here ocean vessels await loads of petro-chemicals at the Vopak terminal in the Port of Rotterdam.

schedules can be coordinated. Finally, the cyclic ordering is often a function of the capital intensity of the industry. Long production runs are scheduled to gain production efficiency; it is costly to set up the equipment for another product.

Specifying the best review period and target inventory levels for the various stages of the supply chain takes sophisticated mathematical models. Regardless of the effort required, it is important to recognize the implications of the supply chain when determining inventory policies.

Source: John M. Bossert and Sean P. Williams, "A Periodic-Review Modeling Approach for Guaranteed Service Supply Chains," *Interfaces*, Vol. 37, No. 5 (September/October 2007), pp 420–435; **http://finance.yahoo.com; www.Celanese.com**, 2008.

EXAMPLE 7 — Determining How Much to Order in a *P* System

A distribution center has a backorder for five 46-inch LCD TV sets. No inventory is currently on hand, and now is the time to review. How many should be reordered if $T = 400$ and no receipts are scheduled?

SOLUTION

$$IP = OH + SR - BO$$

$$= 0 + 0 - 5 = -5 \text{ sets}$$

$$T - IP = 400 - (-5) = 405 \text{ sets}$$

That is, 405 sets must be ordered to bring the inventory position up to *T* sets.

Selecting the Time between Reviews To run a *P* system, managers must make two decisions: the length of time between reviews, *P*, and the target inventory level, *T*. Let us first consider the time between reviews, *P*. It can be any convenient interval, such as each Friday or every other Friday. Another option is to base *P* on the cost trade-offs of the EOQ. In other words, *P* can be set equal to the average time between orders for the economic order quantity, or TBO_{EOQ}. Because demand is variable, some orders will be larger than the EOQ and some will be smaller. However, over an extended period of time, the average lot size should be close to the EOQ. If other models are used to determine the lot size, we divide the lot size chosen by the annual demand, *D*, and use this ratio as P. It will be expressed as the fraction of a year between orders, which can be converted into months, weeks, or days as needed.

Selecting the Target Inventory Level When Demand Is Variable and Lead Time Is Constant   Now, let us calculate the target inventory level, T, when demand is variable but the lead time is constant. Figure 13 reveals that an order must be large enough to make the inventory position, IP, last beyond the next review, which is P time periods away. The checker must wait P periods to revise, correct, and reestablish the inventory position. Then, a new order is placed, but it does not arrive until after the lead time, L. Therefore, as Figure 13 shows, a protection interval of $P + L$ periods is needed. A fundamental difference between the Q and P systems is the length of time needed for stockout protection. A Q system needs stockout protection only during the lead time because orders can be placed as soon as they are needed and will be received L periods later. A P system, however, needs stockout protection for the longer $P + L$ protection interval because orders are placed only at fixed intervals, and the inventory is not checked until the next designated review time.

As with the Q system, we need to develop the appropriate distribution of demand during the protection interval to specify the system fully. In a P system, we must develop the distribution of demand for $P + L$ time periods. The target inventory level T must equal the expected demand during the protection interval of $P + L$ periods, plus enough safety stock to protect against demand uncertainty over this same protection interval. We assume that lead time is constant and that demand in one period is independent of demand in the next period. Thus, the average demand during the protection interval is $\overline{d}(P + L)$, or

$$T = \overline{d}(P + L) + \text{Safety stock for the protection interval}$$

We compute safety stock for a P system much as we did for the Q system. However, the safety stock must cover demand uncertainty for a longer period of time. When using a normal probability distribution, we multiply the desired standard deviations to implement the cycle-service level, z, by the standard deviation of demand during the protection interval, σ_{P+L}. The value of z is the same as for a Q system with the same cycle-service level. Thus,

$$\text{Safety stock} = z\sigma_{P+L}$$

Based on our earlier logic for calculating σ_{dLT}, we know that the standard deviation of the distribution of demand during the protection interval is

$$\sigma_{P+L} = \sigma_d\sqrt{P + L}$$

Because a P system requires safety stock to cover demand uncertainty over a longer time period than a Q system, a P system requires more safety stock; that is, σ_{P+L} exceeds σ_{dLT}. Hence, to gain the convenience of a P system requires that overall inventory levels be somewhat higher than those for a Q system.

EXAMPLE 8	Calculating P and T

Again, let us return to the bird feeder example. Recall that demand for the bird feeder is normally distributed with a mean of 18 units per week and a standard deviation in weekly demand of 5 units. The lead time is 2 weeks, and the business operates 52 weeks per year. The Q system developed in Example 5 called for an EOQ of 75 units and a safety stock of 9 units for a cycle-service level of 90 percent. What is the equivalent P system? Answers are to be rounded to the nearest integer.

MyOMLab

Tutor 9.4 in MyOMLab provides a new example to determine the review interval and the target inventory for a P system.

SOLUTION

We first define D and then P. Here, P is the time between reviews, expressed in weeks because the data are expressed as demand *per week*:

$$D = (18 \text{ units/week})(52 \text{ weeks/year}) = 936 \text{ units}$$

$$P = \frac{\text{EOQ}}{D}(52) = \frac{75}{936}(52) = 4.2, \text{ or } 4 \text{ weeks}$$

With $\overline{d} = 18$ units per week, an alternative approach is to calculate P by dividing the EOQ by $\overline{d}$ to get 75/18 = 4.2, or 4 weeks. Either way, we would review the bird feeder inventory every 4 weeks. We now find the standard deviation of demand over the protection interval $(P + L = 6)$:

$$\sigma_{P+L} = \sigma_d\sqrt{P + L} = 52\sqrt{6} = 12.25 \text{ units}$$

Before calculating T, we also need a z value. For a 90 percent cycle-service level, $z = 1.28$ (see the Normal Distribution appendix). The safety stock becomes

$$\text{Safety stock} = z\sigma_{P+L} = 1.28(12.25) = 15.68, \text{ or } 16 \text{ units}$$

We now solve for T:

$$T = \text{Average demand during the protection interval} + \text{Safety stock}$$

$$= \bar{d}(P + L) + \text{Safety stock}$$

$$= (18 \text{ units/week})(6 \text{ weeks}) + 16 \text{ units} = 124 \text{ units}$$

DECISION POINT

Every 4 weeks we would order the number of units needed to bring inventory position IP (counting the new order) up to the target inventory level of 124 units. The P system requires 16 units in safety stock, while the Q system only needs 9 units. If cost were the only criterion, the Q system would be the choice for the bird feeder. As we discuss later, other factors may sway the decision in favor of the P system.

MyOMLab

single-bin system

A system of inventory control in which a maximum level is marked on the storage shelf or bin, and the inventor is brought up to the mark periodically.

Selecting the Target Inventory Level When Both Demand and Lead Time Are Variable   A useful approach for finding P and T in practice is simulation. Given discrete probability distributions for demand and lead time, simulation can be used to estimate the demand during the protection interval distribution. The *Demand During the Protection Interval Simulator* in OM Explorer can be used to determine the distribution. Once determined, the distribution can be used to select a value for T, given a desired cycle-service level. More discussion, and an example, can be found in MyOMLab.

Single-Bin System   The concept of a P system can be translated into a simple visual system of inventory control. In the **single-bin system**, a maximum level is marked on the storage shelf or bin, and the inventory is brought up to the mark periodically—say, once a week. The single bin may be, for example, a gasoline storage tank at a service station or a storage bin for small parts at a manufacturing plant.

Calculating Total P System Costs   The total costs for the P system are the sum of the same three cost elements for the Q system. The differences are in the calculation of the order quantity and the safety stock. As shown in Figure 13, the average order quantity will be the average consumption of inventory during the P periods between orders. Consequently, $Q = \bar{d}P$. Total costs for the P system are

$$C = \frac{\bar{d}P}{2}(H) + \frac{D}{\bar{d}P}(S) + (H)(\text{Safety stock})$$

See Solved Problem 5 at the end of this chapter for an example of calculating total P system costs.

Comparative Advantages of the Q and P Systems

Neither the Q nor the P system is best for all situations. Three P-system advantages must be balanced against three Q-system advantages. The advantages of one system are implicitly disadvantages of the other system.

The primary advantages of P systems are the following:

1. The system is convenient because replenishments are made at fixed intervals. Fixed replenishment intervals allow for standardized pickup and delivery times.

2. Orders for multiple items from the same supplier can be combined into a single purchase order. This approach reduces ordering and transportation costs and can result in a price break from the supplier.

3. The inventory position, IP, needs to be known only when a review is made (not continuously, as in a Q system). However, this advantage is moot for firms using computerized record-keeping systems, in which a transaction is reported upon each receipt or withdrawal. When inventory records are always current, the system is called a **perpetual inventory system**.

The primary advantages of Q systems are the following:

1. The review frequency of each SKU may be individualized. Tailoring the review frequency to the SKU can reduce total ordering and holding costs.

perpetual inventory system

A system of inventory control in which the inventory records are always current.

2. Fixed lot sizes, if large enough, can result in quantity discounts. The firm's physical limitations, such as its truckload capacities, materials handling methods, and shelf space might also necessitate a fixed lot size.

3. Lower safety stocks result in savings.

In conclusion, the choice between Q and P systems is not clear cut. Which system is better depends on the relative importance of its advantages in various situations.

Hybrid Systems

Various hybrid inventory control systems merge some but not all the features of the P and Q systems. We briefly examine two such systems: (1) optional replenishment and (2) base stock.

Optional Replenishment System   Sometimes called the optional review, min–max, or (s, S) system, the **optional replenishment system** is much like the P system. It is used to review the inventory position at fixed time intervals and, if the position has dropped to (or below) a predetermined level, to place a variable-sized order to cover expected needs. The new order is large enough to bring the inventory position up to a target inventory, similar to T for the P system. However, orders are not placed after a review unless the inventory position has dropped to the predetermined minimum level. The minimum level acts as the reorder point R does in a Q system. If the target is 100 and the minimum level is 60, the minimum order size is 40 (or $100 - 60$). Because continuous reviews need not be made, this system is particularly attractive when both review and ordering costs are high.

Base-Stock System   In its simplest form, the **base-stock system** issues a replenishment order, Q, each time a withdrawal is made, for the same amount as the withdrawal. This one-for-one replacement policy maintains the inventory position at a base-stock level equal to expected demand during the lead time plus safety stock. The base-stock level, therefore, is equivalent to the reorder point in a Q system. However, order quantities now vary to keep the inventory position at R at all times. Because this position is the lowest IP possible that will maintain a specified service level, the base-stock system may be used to minimize cycle inventory. More orders are placed, but each order is smaller. This system is appropriate for expensive items, such as replacement engines for jet airplanes. No more inventory is held than the maximum demand expected until a replacement order can be received.

optional replenishment system

A system used to review the inventory position at fixed time intervals and, if the position has dropped to (or below) a predetermined level, to place a variable-sized order to cover expected needs.

base-stock system

An inventory control system that issues a replenishment order, Q, each time a withdrawal is made, for the same amount of the withdrawal.

LEARNING GOALS IN REVIEW

1 **Identify the advantages, disadvantages, and costs of holding inventory.** We cover these important aspects of inventories in the section "Inventory and Supply Chains". Focus on the pressures for small or large inventories and Figure 1.

2 **Define the different types of inventory and the roles they play in supply chains.** The section "Types of Inventory," explains each type of inventory and provides an example in Figure 2. Example 1 and Solved Problem 1 show how to estimate inventory levels.

3 **Explain the basic tactics for reducing inventories in supply chains.** See the section "Inventory Reduction Tactics," for important approaches to managing inventory levels.

4 **Determine the inventory items deserving most attention and tightest inventory control.** The section "ABC Analysis," shows a simple approach to categorizing inventory items for ease of management oversight. Figure 4 has an example. Solved Problem 2 demonstrates the calculations.

5 **Calculate the economic order quantity and apply it to various situations.** See the section "Economic Order Quantity," for a complete discussion of EOQ model. Focus on Figures 5 through 7 to see how the EOQ model affects

inventory levels under the standard assumptions and how the EOQ provides the lowest cost solution. Review Examples 2 and 3 and Solved Problem 3 for help in calculating the total costs of various lot-size choices. Table 1 reveals important managerial insights from the EOQ.

6 **Determine the order quantity and reorder point for a continuous review inventory system.** The section "Continuous Review System," builds the essence of the Q system from basic principles to more-realistic assumptions. Be sure to understand Figures 10 and 12. Examples 4 through 6 and Solved Problems 4 and 6 show how to determine the parameters Q and R under various assumptions.

7 **Determine the review interval and target inventory level for a periodic review inventory control system.** We summarize the key concepts in the section "Periodic Review System,". Figure 13 shows how a P system operates while Examples 7 and 8 and Solved Problem 5 demonstrate how to calculate the parameters P and T.

8 **Define the key factors that determine the appropriate choice of an inventory system.** See the section "Comparative Advantages of the Q and P Systems".

MyOMLab helps you develop analytical skills and assesses your progress with multiple problems on cycle inventory, pipeline inventory, safety stock, inventory turns, weeks of supply, aggregate inventory value, time between orders, optimal order quantity, EOQ, optimal interval between orders, reorder point, demand during lead time, cycle-service level, target inventory *T*, and *P*.

MyOMLab Resources	Titles	Link to the Book
Video	*Inventory and Textbooks*	Entire chapter
Active Model	9.1 Economic Order Quantity	Economic Order Quantity; Example 3; Active Model Exercise
OM Explorer Solvers	Inventory Systems Designer	Inventory Control Systems; Example 3; Example 8; Solved Problem 3; Solved Problem 4; Solved Problem 5; Figure 15
	Demand During Protection Interval Simulator	Selecting the Reorder Point When Both Demand and Lead Time Are Variable; Selecting the Target Inventory Level When Both Demand and Lead Time Are Variable
	Q System Simulator	Continuous Review System
OM Explorer Tutors	9.1 Estimating Inventory Levels	Inventory and Supply Chains; Example 1; Figure 3; Solved Problem 1
	2 ABC Analysis	ABC Analysis; Solved Problem 2; Figure 14
	9.3 Finding EOQ and Total Cost	Economic Order Quantity; Example 3; Figure 8; Solved Problem 3
	9.4 Finding the Safety Stock and R	Continuous Review System; Example 5; Solved Problem 4
	9.5 Calculating *P* and *T*	Periodic Review System; Example 8; Solved Problem 5
POM for Windows	Economic Order Quantity (EOQ) Model	Economic Order Quantity; Example 3; Solved Problem 3
	ABC Analysis	ABC Analysis; Solved Problem 2
Tutor Exercises	9.1 Finding EOQ, Safety Stock, *R*, *P*, *T* at Bison College Bookstore	Economic Order Quantity; Inventory Control Systems
Tutorial on Inventory Management Systems	Using Simulation to Develop Inventory Management Systems	Selecting the Reorder Point When Demand and Lead Time Are Variable; Selecting the Target Inventory Level When Both Demand and Lead Time Are Variable
Advanced Problems	1. Office Supply Shop Simulation	Continuous Review System; Selecting the Reorder Point When Both Demand and Lead Time Are Variable
	2. Grocery Store Simulation	Periodic Review System; Selecting the Target Inventory Level when Both Demand and Lead Time Are Variable
	3. Floral Shop Simulation	Continuous Review System; Selecting the Reorder Point When Demand and Lead Time Are Variable
Virtual Tours	Stickley United Wood Treating	Inventory and Supply Chains Entire chapter
Internet Exercise	9.1 Round House	Inventory and Supply Chains
SimQuick Simulation Exercise	Inventory Control Systems	Continuous Review System; Periodic Review System
Key Equations		
Image Library		

Key Equations

1. Average cycle inventory: $\dfrac{Q}{2}$

2. Pipeline inventory: $\overline{D}_L = \overline{d}L$

3. Total annual cycle-inventory cost = Annual holding cost + Annual ordering or setup cost:

$$C = \frac{Q}{2}(H) + \frac{D}{Q}(S)$$

4. Economic order quantity:

$$EOQ = \sqrt{\frac{2DS}{H}}$$

5. Time between orders, expressed in weeks:

$$TBO_{EOQ} = \frac{EOQ}{D}(52 \text{ weeks/year})$$

6. Inventory position = On-hand inventory + Scheduled receipts − Backorders:

$$IP = OH + SR - BO$$

7. Continuous review system:

Protection interval = Lead time (L)

Standard deviation of demand during the lead time (constant L) $= \sigma_{dLT} = \sigma_d\sqrt{L}$

Standard deviation of demand during the lead time (variable L) =

$$\sigma_{dLT} = \sqrt{\overline{L}\sigma_d^2 + \overline{d}^2\sigma_{LT}^2}$$

Safety stock $= z\sigma_{dLT}$

Reorder point (R) for constant lead time $= \overline{d}L +$ Safety stock

Reorder point (R) for variable lead time $= \overline{d}\,\overline{L} +$ Safety stock

Order quantity $=$ EOQ

Replenishment rule: Order EOQ units when IP $\leq R$

Total Q system cost: $C = \dfrac{Q}{2}(H) + \dfrac{D}{Q}(S) + (H)(\text{Safety stock})$

8. Periodic review system:

Review interval = Time between orders $= P$

Protection interval = Time between orders + Lead time $= P + L$

Standard deviation of demand during the protection interval $\sigma_{P+L} = \sigma_d\sqrt{P + L}$

Safety stock $= z\sigma_{P+L}$

Target inventory level (T) = Average demand during the protection interval + Safety stock

$$= \overline{d}(P + L) + \text{Safety stock}$$

Order quantity = Target inventory level − Inventory position $= T - IP$

Replenishment rule: Every P time periods, order $T - IP$ units

Total P system cost: $C = \dfrac{\overline{d}P}{2}(H) + \dfrac{D}{\overline{d}P}(S) + (H)(\text{Safety stock})$

Key Terms

Solved Problem 1

A distribution center experiences an average weekly demand of 50 units for one of its items. The product is valued at $650 per unit. Inbound shipments from the factory warehouse average 350 units. Average lead time (including ordering delays and transit time) is 2 weeks. The distribution center operates 52 weeks per year; it carries a 1-week supply of inventory as safety stock and no anticipation inventory. What is the value of the average aggregate inventory being held by the distribution center?

SOLUTION

Type of Inventory	Calculation of Aggregate Average Inventory	
Cycle	$\dfrac{Q}{2} = \dfrac{350}{2}$	$=$ 175 units
Safety stock	1-week supply	$=$ 50 units
Anticipation	None	
Pipeline	$\bar{d}L = (50 \text{ units/week})(2 \text{ weeks})$	$=$ 100 units
	Average aggregate inventory	$=$ 325 units
	Value of aggregate inventory	$=$ $650(325)
		$=$ $211,250

Solved Problem 2

Booker's Book Bindery divides SKUs into three classes, according to their dollar usage. Calculate the usage values of the following SKUs and determine which is most likely to be classified as class A.

SOLUTION

The annual dollar usage for each SKU is determined by multiplying the annual usage quantity by the value per unit. As shown in Figure 14, the SKUs are then sorted by annual dollar usage, in declining order. Finally, A–B and B–C class lines are drawn roughly, according to the guidelines presented in the text. Here, class A includes only one SKU (signatures), which represents only 1/7, or 14 percent, of the SKUs but accounts for 83 percent of annual dollar usage. Class B includes the next two SKUs, which taken together represent 28 percent of the SKUs and account for 13 percent of annual dollar usage. The final four SKUs, class C, represent over half the number of SKUs but only 4 percent of total annual dollar usage.

SKU Number	Description	Quantity Used per Year	Unit Value ($)
1	Boxes	500	3.00
2	Cardboard (square feet)	18,000	0.02
3	Cover stock	10,000	0.75
4	Glue (gallons)	75	40.00
5	Inside covers	20,000	0.05
6	Reinforcing tape (meters)	3,000	0.15
7	Signatures	150,000	0.45

SKU Number	Description	Quantity Used per Year		Unit Value ($)		Annual Dollar Usage ($)
1	Boxes	500	×	3.00	=	1,500
2	Cardboard (square feet)	18,000	×	0.02	=	360
3	Cover stock	10,000	×	0.75	=	7,500
4	Glue (gallons)	75	×	40.00	=	3,000
5	Inside covers	20,000	×	0.05	=	1,000
6	Reinforcing tape (meters)	3,000	×	0.15	=	450
7	Signatures	150,000	×	0.45	=	67,500
					Total	81,310

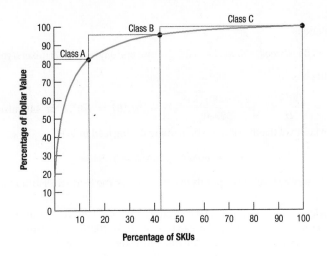

SKU #	Description	Qty Used/Year	Value	Dollar Usage	Pct of Total	Cumulative % of Dollar Value	Cumulative % of SKU	Class
7	Signatures	150,000	$0.45	$67,500	83.0%	83.0%	14.3%	A
3	Cover stock	10,000	$0.75	$7,500	9.2%	92.2%	28.6%	B
4	Glue	75	$40.00	$3,000	3.7%	95.9%	42.9%	B
1	Boxes	500	$3.00	$1,500	1.8%	97.8%	57.1%	C
5	Inside covers	20,000	$0.05	$1,000	1.2%	99.0%	71.4%	C
6	Reinforcing tape	3,000	$0.15	$450	0.6%	99.6%	85.7%	C
2	Cardboard	18,000	$0.02	$360	0.4%	100.0%	100.0%	C
Total				$81,310				

◀ FIGURE 14
Annual Dollar Usage for Class A, B, and C SKUs Using Tutor 9.2

Solved Problem 3

Nelson's Hardware Store stocks a 19.2 volt cordless drill that is a popular seller. Annual demand is 5,000 units, the ordering cost is $15, and the inventory holding cost is $4/unit/year.

a. What is the economic order quantity?

b. What is the total annual cost for this inventory item?

SOLUTION

a. The order quantity is

$$EOQ = \sqrt{\frac{2DS}{H}} = \sqrt{\frac{2(5,000)(\$15)}{\$4}} = \sqrt{37,500}$$

$$= 193.65, \text{ or } 194 \text{ drills}$$

b. The total annual cost is

$$C = \frac{Q}{2}(H) + \frac{D}{Q}(S) = \frac{194}{2}(\$4) + \frac{5,000}{194}(\$15) = \$774.60$$

Solved Problem 4

A regional distributor purchases discontinued appliances from various suppliers and then sells them on demand to retailers in the region. The distributor operates 5 days per week, 52 weeks per year. Only when it is open for business can orders be received. Management wants to reevaluate its current inventory policy, which calls for order quantities of 440 counter-top mixers. The following data are estimated for the mixer:

Average daily demand $(\bar{d}) = 100$ mixers

Standard deviation of daily demand $(\sigma_d) = 30$ mixers

Lead time $(L) = 3$ days

Holding cost $(H) = \$9.40/\text{unit/year}$

Ordering cost $(S) = \$35/\text{order}$

Cycle-service level $= 92$ percent

The distributor uses a continuous review (Q) system.

a. What order quantity Q, and reorder point, R, should be used?

b. What is the total annual cost of the system?

c. If on-hand inventory is 40 units, one open order for 440 mixers is pending, and no backorders exist, should a new order be placed?

SOLUTION

a. Annual demand is

$$D = (5 \text{ days/week})(52 \text{ weeks/year})(100 \text{ mixers/day}) = 26,000 \text{ mixers/year}$$

The order quantity is

$$EOQ = \sqrt{\frac{2DS}{H}} = \sqrt{\frac{2(26,000)(\$35)}{\$9.40}} = \sqrt{193,167} = 440.02, \text{ or } 440 \text{ mixers}$$

The standard deviation of the distribution of demand during lead time is

$$\sigma_{dLT} = \sigma_d\sqrt{L} = 30\sqrt{3} = 51.96$$

A 92 percent cycle-service level corresponds to $z = 1.41$ (see the Normal Distribution appendix). Therefore,

Safety stock $= z\sigma_{dLT} = 1.41(51.96 \text{ mixers}) = 73.26, \text{ or } 73 \text{ mixers}$

Average demand during the lead time $= \bar{d}L = 100(3) = 300 \text{ mixers}$

Reorder point $(R) = $ Average demand during the lead time $+$ Safety stock

$= 300 \text{ mixers} + 73 \text{ mixers} = 373 \text{ mixers}$

With a continuous review system, $Q = 440$ and $R = 373$.

b. The total annual cost for the Q systems is

$$C = \frac{Q}{2}(H) + \frac{D}{Q}(S) + (H) \text{ (Safety stock)}$$

$$C = \frac{440}{2}(\$9.40) + \frac{26,000}{440}(35) + (\$9.40)(73) = \$4,822.38$$

c. Inventory position = On-hand inventory + Scheduled receipts − Backorders

$$IP = OH + SR - BO = 40 + 440 - 0 = 480 \text{ mixers}$$

Because IP (480) exceeds R (373), do not place a new order.

Solved Problem 5

Suppose that a periodic review (P) system is used at the distributor in Solved Problem 4, but otherwise the data are the same.

a. Calculate the P (in workdays, rounded to the nearest day) that gives approximately the same number of orders per year as the EOQ.

b. What is the target inventory level, T? Compare the P system to the Q system in Solved Problem 4.

c. What is the total annual cost of the P system?

d. It is time to review the item. On-hand inventory is 40 mixers; receipt of 440 mixers is scheduled, and no backorders exist. How much should be reordered?

SOLUTION

a. The time between orders is

$$P = \frac{EOQ}{D}(260 \text{ days/year}) = \frac{440}{26,000}(260) = 4.4, \text{ or 4 days}$$

b. Figure 15 shows that $T = 812$ and safety stock $= (1.41)(79.37) = 111.91$, or about 112 mixers. The corresponding Q system for the counter-top mixer requires less safety stock.

c. The total annual cost of the P system is

$$C = \frac{\overline{d}P}{2}(H) + \frac{D}{\overline{d}P}(S) + (H)(\text{Safety stock})$$

$$C = \frac{(100)(4)}{2}(\$9.40) + \frac{26,000}{(100)(4)}(\$35) + (\$9.40)(1.41)(79.37)$$

$$= \$5,207.80$$

d. Inventory position is the amount on hand plus scheduled receipts minus backorders, or

$$IP = OH + SR - BO = 40 + 440 - 0 = 480 \text{ mixers}$$

The order quantity is the target inventory level minus the inventory position, or

$$Q = T - IP = 812 \text{ mixers} - 480 \text{ mixers} = 332 \text{ mixers}$$

An order for 332 mixers should be placed.

Continuous Review (Q) System	
z	1.41
Safety Stock	73
Reorder Point	373
Annual Cost	$4,822.38

Periodic Review (P) System	
Time Between Reviews (P)	4.00 Days
	☑ Enter manually
Standard Deviation of Demand During Protection Interval	79.37
Safety Stock	112
Average Demand During Protection Interval	700
Target Inventory Level (T)	812
Annual Cost	$5,207.80

◀ **FIGURE 15**
OM Explorer Solver for Inventory Systems

Solved Problem 6

Grey Wolf Lodge is a popular 500-room hotel in the North Woods. Managers need to keep close tabs on all room service items, including a special pine-scented bar soap. The daily demand for the soap is 275 bars, with a standard deviation of 30 bars. Ordering cost is $10 and the inventory holding cost is $0.30/bar/year. The lead time from the supplier is 5 days, with a standard deviation of 1 day. The lodge is open 365 days a year.

a. What is the economic order quantity for the bar of soap?

b. What should the reorder point be for the bar of soap if management wants to have a 99 percent cycle-service level?

c. What is the total annual cost for the bar of soap, assuming a Q system will be used?

SOLUTION

a. We have $D = (275)(365) = 100{,}375$ bars of soap; $S = \$10$; and $H = \$0.30$. The EOQ for the bar of soap is

$$EOQ = \sqrt{\frac{2DS}{H}} = \sqrt{\frac{2(100{,}375)(\$10)}{\$0.30}} = \sqrt{6{,}691{,}666.7}$$

$$= 2{,}586.83, \text{ or } 2{,}587 \text{ bars}$$

b. We have $\bar{d} = 275$ bars/day, $\sigma_d = 30$ bars, $\bar{L} = 5$ days, and $\sigma_{LT} = 1$ day.

$$\sigma_{dLT} = \sqrt{\bar{L}\sigma_d^2 + \bar{d}^2\sigma_{LT}^2} = \sqrt{(5)(30)^2 + (275)^2(1)^2} = 283.06 \text{ bars}$$

Consult the body of the Normal Distribution appendix for 0.9900, which corresponds to a 99 percent cycle-service level. The closest value is 0.9901, which corresponds to a z value of 2.33. We calculate the safety stock and reorder point as follows:

$$\text{Safety stock} = z\sigma_{dLT} = (2.33)(283.06) = 659.53, \text{ or } 660 \text{ bars}$$

$$\text{Reorder point} = \bar{d}\bar{L} + \text{Safety stock} = (275)(5) + 600 = 2{,}035 \text{ bars}$$

c. The total annual cost for the Q system is

$$C = \frac{Q}{2}(H) + \frac{D}{Q}(S) + (H)(\text{Safety stock})$$

$$= \frac{2{,}587}{2}(\$0.30) + \frac{100{,}375}{2{,}587}(\$10) + (\$0.30)(660) = \$974.05$$

Discussion Questions

1. What is the relationship between inventory and competitive priorities? Suppose that two competing manufacturers, Company H and Company L, are similar except that Company H has much higher investments in raw materials, work-in-process, and finished goods inventory than Company L. In which of the nine competitive priorities will Company H have an advantage?

2. Suppose that a large discount retailer with a lot of purchasing power in a supply chain requires that all suppliers incorporate a new information system that will reduce the cost of placing orders between the retailer and its suppliers as well as between the suppliers and their suppliers. Suppose also that order quantities and lead times are related; the smaller the order quantity the shorter the lead time from suppliers. Assume that all members of the supply chain use a continuous review system and EOQ order quantities. Explain the implications of the new information system for the supply chain in general and the inventory systems of the supply chain members in particular.

3. Will organizations ever get to the point where they will no longer need inventories? Why or why not?

Problems

The OM Explorer and POM for Windows software is available to all students using the 10th edition of this text. Go to **www.pearsonhighered.com/krajewski** to download these computer packages. If you purchased MyOMLab, you also have access to Active Models software and significant help in do-

ing the following problems. Check with your instructor on how best to use these resources. In many cases, the instructor wants you to understand how to do the calculations by hand. At the least, the software provides a check on your calculations. When calculations are particularly complex and the goal is interpreting the results in making decisions, the software replaces entirely the manual calculations.

1. A part is produced in lots of 1,000 units. It is assembled from 2 components worth $50 total. The value added in production (for labor and variable overhead) is $60 per unit, bringing total costs per completed unit to $110. The average lead time for the part is 6 weeks and annual demand is 3,800 units, based on 50 business weeks per year.

   a. How many units of the part are held, on average, in cycle inventory? What is the dollar value of this inventory?

   b. How many units of the part are held, on average, in pipeline inventory? What is the dollar value of this inventory? (*Hint:* Assume that the typical part in pipeline inventory is 50 percent completed. Thus, half the labor and variable overhead cost has been added, bringing the unit cost to $80, or $50 + $60/2.)

2. Prince Electronics, a manufacturer of consumer electronic goods, has five distribution centers in different regions of the country. For one of its products, a high-speed modem priced at $350 per unit, the average weekly demand at *each* distribution center is 75 units. Average shipment size to each distribution center is 400 units, and average lead time for delivery is 2 weeks. Each distribution center carries 2 weeks' supply as safety stock but holds no anticipation inventory.

   a. On average, how many dollars of pipeline inventory will be in transit to each distribution center?

   b. How much total inventory (cycle, safety, and pipeline) does Prince hold for all five distribution centers?

3. Terminator, Inc., manufactures a motorcycle part in lots of 250 units. The raw materials cost for the part is $150, and the value added in manufacturing 1 unit from its components is $300, for a total cost per completed unit of $450. The lead time to make the part is 3 weeks, and the annual demand is 4,000 units. Assume 50 working weeks per year.

   a. How many units of the part are held, on average, as cycle inventory? What is its value?

   b. How many units of the part are held, on average, as pipeline inventory? What is its value?

4. Oakwood Hospital is considering using ABC analysis to classify laboratory SKUs into three categories: those that will be delivered daily from their supplier (Class A items), those that will be controlled using a continuous review system (B items), and those that will be held in a two bin system (C items). The following table shows the annual dollar usage for a sample of eight SKUs. Rank the SKUs, and assign them to their appropriate category.

SKU	Dollar Value	Annual Usage
1	$0.01	1,200
2	$0.03	120,000
3	$0.45	100
4	$1.00	44,000
5	$4.50	900
6	$0.90	350
7	$0.30	70,000
8	$1.50	200

5. Southern Markets, Inc., is considering the use of ABC analysis to focus on the most critical SKUs in its inventory. Currently, there are approximately 20,000 different SKUs with a total dollar usage of $10,000,000 per year.

   a. What would you expect to be the number of SKUs and the total annual dollar usage for A items, B items and C items at Southern Markets, Inc.?

   b. The following table provides a random sample of the unit values and annual demands of eight SKUs. Categorize these SKUs as A, B, and C items.

SKU Code	Unit Value	Demand (Units)
A104	$2.10	2,500
D205	$2.50	30
X104	$0.85	350
U404	$0.25	250
L205	$4.75	20
S104	$0.02	4,000
X205	$0.35	1,020
L104	$4.25	50

6. Yellow Press, Inc., buys paper in 1,500-pound rolls for printing. Annual demand is 2,500 rolls. The cost per roll is $800, and the annual holding cost is 15 percent of the cost. Each order costs $50 to process.

   a. How many rolls should Yellow Press, Inc., order at a time?

   b. What is the time between orders?

7. Babble, Inc., buys 400 blank cassette tapes per month for use in producing foreign language courseware. The ordering cost is $12.50. Holding cost is $0.12 per cassette per year.

   a. How many tapes should Babble, Inc., order at a time?

   b. What is the time between orders?

8. At Dot Com, a large retailer of popular books, demand is constant at 32,000 books per year. The cost of placing an order to replenish stock is $10, and the annual cost of holding is $4 per book. Stock is received 5 working days after an order has been placed. No backordering is allowed. Assume 300 working days a year.

   a. What is Dot Com's optimal order quantity?

   b. What is the optimal number of orders per year?

   c. What is the optimal interval (in working days) between orders?

   d. What is demand during the lead time?

   e. What is the reorder point?

   f. What is the inventory position immediately after an order has been placed?

9. Leaky Pipe, a local retailer of plumbing supplies, faces demand for one of its SKUs at a constant rate of 30,000 units per year. It costs Leaky Pipe $10 to process an order to replenish stock and $1 per unit per year to carry the item in stock. Stock is received 4 working days after an order is placed. No backordering is allowed. Assume 300 working days a year.

a. What is Leaky Pipe's optimal order quantity?

b. What is the optimal number of orders per year?

c. What is the optimal interval (in working days) between orders?

d. What is the demand during the lead time?

e. What is the reorder point?

f. What is the inventory position immediately after an order has been placed?

10. Sam's Cat Hotel operates 52 weeks per year, 6 days per week, and uses a continuous review inventory system. It purchases kitty litter for $11.70 per bag. The following information is available about these bags.

Demand = 90 bags/week

Order cost = $54/order

Annual holding cost = 27 percent of cost

Desired cycle-service level = 80 percent

Lead time = 3 weeks (18 working days)

Standard deviation of *weekly* demand = 15 bags

Current on-hand inventory is 320 bags, with no open orders or backorders.

a. What is the EOQ? What would be the average time between orders (in weeks)?

b. What should R be?

c. An inventory withdrawal of 10 bags was just made. Is it time to reorder?

d. The store currently uses a lot size of 500 bags (i.e., $Q = 500$). What is the annual holding cost of this policy? Annual ordering cost? Without calculating the EOQ, how can you conclude from these two calculations that the current lot size is too large?

e. What would be the annual cost saved by shifting from the 500-bag lot size to the EOQ?

11. Consider again the kitty litter ordering policy for Sam's Cat Hotel in Problem 10.

a. Suppose that the weekly demand forecast of 90 bags is incorrect and actual demand averages only 60 bags per week. How much higher will total costs be, owing to the distorted EOQ caused by this forecast error?

b. Suppose that actual demand is 60 bags but that ordering costs are cut to only $6 by using the Internet to automate order placing. However, the buyer does not tell anyone, and the EOQ is not adjusted to reflect this reduction in S. How much higher will total costs be, compared to what they could be if the EOQ were adjusted?

12. In a Q system, the demand rate for strawberry ice cream is normally distributed, with an average of 300 pints *per week*. The lead time is 9 weeks. The standard deviation of *weekly* demand is 15 pints.

a. What is the standard deviation of demand during the 9-week lead time?

b. What is the average demand during the 9-week lead time?

c. What reorder point results in a cycle-service level of 99 percent?

13. Petromax Enterprises uses a continuous review inventory control system for one of its SKUs. The following information is available on the item. The firm operates 50 weeks in a year.

Demand = 50,000 units/year

Ordering cost = $35/order

Holding cost = $2/unit/year

Average lead time = 3 weeks

Standard deviation of weekly demand = 125 units

a. What is the economic order quantity for this item?

b. If Petromax wants to provide a 90 percent cycle-service level, what should be the safety stock and the reorder point?

14. In a continuous review inventory system, the lead time for door knobs is 5 weeks. The standard deviation of demand during the lead time is 85 units. The desired cycle-service level is 99 percent. The supplier of door knobs streamlined its operations and now quotes a one-week lead time. How much can safety stock be reduced without reducing the 99 percent cycle-service level?

15. In a two-bin inventory system, the demand for three-inch lag bolts during the 2-week lead time is normally distributed, with an average of 53 units per week. The standard deviation of weekly demand is 5 units.

a. What is the probability of demand exceeding the reorder point when the normal level in the second bin is set at 130 units?

b. What is the probability of demand exceeding the 130 units in the second bin if it takes 3 weeks to receive a replenishment order?

16. Nationwide Auto Parts uses a periodic review inventory control system for one of its stock items. The review interval is 6 weeks, and the lead time for receiving the materials ordered from its wholesaler is 3 weeks. Weekly demand is normally distributed, with a mean of 100 units and a standard deviation of 20 units.

a. What is the average and the standard deviation of demand during the protection interval?

b. What should be the target inventory level if the firm desires 97.5 percent stockout protection?

c. If 350 units were in stock at the time of a periodic review, how many units should be ordered?

17. In a P system, the lead time for a box of weed-killer is 2 weeks and the review period is 1 week. Demand during the protection interval averages 218 boxes, with a standard deviation of 40 boxes.

a. What is the cycle-service level when the target inventory is set at 300 boxes?

b. In the fall season, demand for weed-killer decreases but also becomes more highly variable. Assume that during the fall season, demand during the protection interval is expected to decrease to 180 boxes, but with a standard deviation of 50 boxes. What would be the cycle-service level if management keeps the target inventory level set at 300 boxes?

18. You are in charge of inventory control of a highly successful product retailed by your firm. Weekly demand for this item varies, with an average of 200 units and a standard deviation of 16 units. It is purchased from a wholesaler at a cost of $12.50 per unit. The supply lead time is 4 weeks. Placing an order costs $50, and the inventory carrying

rate per year is 20 percent of the item's cost. Your firm operates 5 days per week, 50 weeks per year.

a. What is the optimal ordering quantity for this item?

b. How many units of the item should be maintained as safety stock for 99 percent protection against stockouts during an order cycle?

c. If supply lead time can be reduced to 2 weeks, what is the percent reduction in the number of units maintained as safety stock for the same 99 percent stockout protection?

d. If through appropriate sales promotions, the demand variability is reduced so that the standard deviation of weekly demand is 8 units instead of 16, what is the percent reduction (compared to that in part [b]) in the number of units maintained as safety stock for the same 99 percent stockout protection?

19. Suppose that Sam's Cat Hotel in Problem 10 uses a P system instead of a Q system. The average daily demand is $\bar{d} = 90/6 = 15$ bags. and the standard deviation of

$daily$ demand is $\sigma_d = \dfrac{\sigma_{week}}{\sqrt{6}} = (15/\sqrt{6}) = 6.124$ bags.

a. What P (in working days) and T should be used to approximate the cost trade-offs of the EOQ?

b. How much more safety stock is needed than with a Q system?

c. It is time for the periodic review. How much kitty litter should be ordered?

20. Your firm uses a continuous review system and operates 52 weeks per year. One of the SKUs has the following characteristics.

Demand $(D) = 20,000$ units/year
Ordering cost $(S) = \$40/order$
Holding cost $(H) = \$2/unit/year$
Lead time $(L) = 2$ weeks
Cycle-service level $= 95$ percent

Demand is normally distributed, with a standard deviation of $weekly$ demand of 100 units.

Current on-hand inventory is 1,040 units, with no scheduled receipts and no backorders.

a. Calculate the item's EOQ. What is the average time, in weeks, between orders?

b. Find the safety stock and reorder point that provide a 95 percent cycle-service level.

c. For these policies, what are the annual costs of (i) holding the cycle inventory and (ii) placing orders?

d. A withdrawal of 15 units just occurred. Is it time to reorder? If so, how much should be ordered?

21. Your firm uses a periodic review system for all SKUs classified, using ABC analysis, as B or C items. Further, it uses a continuous review system for all SKUs classified as A items. The demand for a specific SKU, currently classified as an A item, has been dropping. You have been asked to evaluate the impact of moving the item from continuous review to periodic review. Assume your firm operates 52 weeks per year; the item's current characteristics are:

Demand $(D) = 15,080$ units/year
Ordering cost $(S) = \$125.00/order$

Holding cost $(H) = \$3.00/unit/year$
Lead time $(L) = 5$ weeks
Cycle-service level $= 95$ percent

Demand is normally distributed, with a standard deviation of weekly demand of 64 units.

a. Calculate the item's EOQ.

b. Use the EOQ to define the parameters of an appropriate continuous review and periodic review system for this item.

c. Which system requires more safety stock and by how much?

22. A company begins a review of ordering policies for its continuous review system by checking the current policies for a sample of SKUs. Following are the characteristics of one item.

Demand $(D) = 64$ units/week (Assume 52 weeks per year)
Ordering and setup cost $(S) = \$50/order$
Holding cost $(H) = \$13/unit/year$
Lead time $(L) = 2$ weeks
Standard deviation of $weekly$ demand $= 12$ units
Cycle-service level $= 88$ percent

a. What is the EOQ for this item?

b. What is the desired safety stock?

c. What is the reorder point?

d. What are the cost implications if the current policy for this item is $Q = 200$ and $R = 180$?

23. Using the same information as in Problem 22, develop the best policies for a periodic review system.

a. What value of P gives the same approximate number of orders per year as the EOQ? Round to the nearest week.

b. What safety stock and target inventory level provide an 88 percent cycle-service level?

24. Wood County Hospital consumes 1,000 boxes of bandages per week. The price of bandages is \$35 per box, and the hospital operates 52 weeks per year. The cost of processing an order is \$15, and the cost of holding one box for a year is 15 percent of the value of the material.

a. The hospital orders bandages in lot sizes of 900 boxes. What $extra$ cost does the hospital incur, which it could save by using the EOQ method?

b. Demand is normally distributed, with a standard deviation of weekly demand of 100 boxes. The lead time is 2 weeks. What safety stock is necessary if the hospital uses a continuous review system and a 97 percent cycle-service level is desired? What should be the reorder point?

c. If the hospital uses a periodic review system, with $P = 2$ weeks, what should be the target inventory level, T?

25. A golf specialty wholesaler operates 50 weeks per year. Management is trying to determine an inventory policy for its 1-irons, which have the following characteristics:
Demand $(D) = 2,000$ units/year
Demand is normally distributed
Standard deviation of $weekly$ demand $= 3$ units

Ordering cost = $40/order

Annual holding cost $(H) = $5/units

Desired cycle-service level = 90 percent

Lead time $(L) = 4$ weeks

a. If the company uses a periodic review system, what should P and T be? Round P to the nearest week.

b. If the company uses a continuous review system, what should R be?

26. Osprey Sports stocks everything that a musky fisherman could want in the Great North Woods. A particular musky lure has been very popular with local fishermen as well as those who buy lures on the Internet from Osprey Sports. The cost to place orders with the supplier is $30/order; the demand averages 4 lures per day, with a standard deviation of 1 lure; and the inventory holding cost is $1.00/lure/year. The lead time form the supplier is 10 days, with a standard deviation of 3 days. It is important to maintain a 97 percent cycle-service level to properly balance service with inventory holding costs. Osprey Sports is open 350 days a year to allow the owners the opportunity to fish for muskies during the prime season. The owners want to use a continuous review inventory system for this item.

a. What order quantity should be used?

b. What reorder point should be used?

c. What is the total annual cost for this inventory system?

27. The Farmer's Wife is a country store specializing in knickknacks suitable for a farm-house décor. One item experiencing a considerable buying frenzy is a miniature Holstein cow. Average weekly demand is 30 cows, with a standard deviation of 5 cows. The cost to place a replenishment order is $15 and the holding cost is $0.75/cow/year. The supplier, however, is in China. The lead time for new orders is 8 weeks, with a standard deviation of 2 weeks. The Farmer's Wife, which is open only 50 weeks a year, wants to develop a continuous review inventory system for this item with a cycle-service level of 90 percent.

a. Specify the continuous review system for the cows. Explain how it would work in practice.

b. What is the total annual cost for the system you developed?

Advanced Problems

It may be helpful to review MyOMLab Supplement E, "Simulation," before working Problem 29.

28. Muscle Bound is a chain of fitness stores located in many large shopping centers. Recently, an internal memo from the CEO to all operations personnel complained about the budget overruns at Muscle Bound's central warehouse. In particular, she said that inventories were too high and that the budget will be cut dramatically and proportionately equal for all items in stock. Consequently, warehouse management set up a pilot study to see what effect the budget cuts would have on customer service. They chose 5-pound barbells, which are a high volume SKU and consume considerable warehouse space. Daily demand for the barbells is 1,000 units, with a standard deviation of 150 units. Ordering costs are $40 per order. Holding costs are $2/unit/year. The supplier is located in the Philippines; consequently, the lead time is 35 days with a standard deviation of 5 days. Muscle Bound stores operate 313 days a year (no Sundays).

Suppose that the barbells are allocated a budget of $16,000 for total annual costs. If Muscle Bound uses a continuous review system for the barbells and cannot change the ordering costs and holding costs or the distributions of demand or lead time, what is the best cycle-service level management can expect from their system?

29. The Georgia Lighting Center stocks more than 3,000 lighting fixtures, including chandeliers, swags, wall lamps, and track lights. The store sells at retail, operates six days per week, and advertises itself as the "brightest spot in town." One expensive fixture is selling at an average rate of 5 units per day. The reorder policy is $Q = 40$ and $R = 15$. A new order is placed on the day the reorder point is reached. The lead time is 3 business days. For example, an order placed on Monday will be delivered on Thursday. Simulate the performance of this Q system for the next 3 weeks (18 workdays). Any stockouts result in lost sales (rather than backorders). The beginning inventory is 19 units, and no receipts are scheduled. Table 2 simulates the first week of operation. Extend Table 2 to simulate operations for the next 2 weeks if demand for the next 12 business days is 7, 4, 2, 7, 3, 6, 10, 0, 5, 10, 4, and 7.

a. What is the average daily ending inventory over the 18 days? How many stockouts occurred?

b. Simulate the inventory performance of the same item assuming a $Q = 30$, $R = 20$ system is used. Calculate the average inventory level and number of stockouts and compare with part (a).

TABLE 2 | FIRST WEEK OF OPERATION

Workday	Beginning Inventory	Orders Received	Daily Demand	Ending Inventory	Inventory Position	Order Quantity
1. Monday	19	—	5	14	14	40
2. Tuesday	14	—	3	11	51	—
3. Wednesday	11	—	4	7	47	—
4. Thursday	7	40	1	46	46	—
5. Friday	46	—	10	36	36	—
6. Saturday	36	—	9	27	27	—

Active Model Exercise

This Active Model appears in MyOMLab. It allows you to evaluate the sensitivity of the EOQ and associated costs to changes in the demand and cost parameters.

QUESTIONS

1. What is the EOQ and what is the lowest total cost?

2. What is the annual cost of holding inventory at the EOQ and the annual cost of ordering inventory at the EOQ?

3. From the graph, what can you conclude about the relationship between the lowest total cost and the costs of ordering and holding inventory?

4. How much does the total cost increase if the store manager orders twice as many bird feeders as the EOQ? How much does the total cost increase if the store manager orders half as many bird feeders as the EOQ?

5. What happens to the EOQ and the total cost when demand is doubled? What happens to the EOQ and the total cost when unit price is doubled?

6. Scroll through the lower order cost values and describe the changes to the graph. What happens to the EOQ?

7. Comment on the sensitivity of the EOQ model to errors in demand or cost estimates.

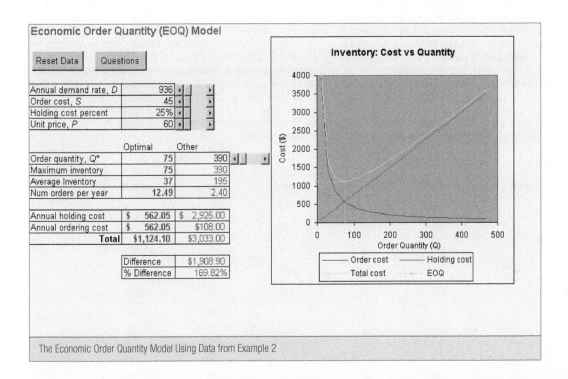

The Economic Order Quantity Model Using Data from Example 2

EXPERIENTIAL LEARNING | Swift Electronic Supply, Inc.

It was a typical fall afternoon in Southern California, with thousands of tourists headed to the beaches to have fun. About 40 miles away, however, Steven Holland, the CEO of the Swift Electronic Supply, Inc., faced a severe problem with Swift's inventory management.

An Intel veteran, Steven Holland worked in the electronic components distribution industry for more than 20 years. Seven years ago, he founded the Swift Electronic Supply, Inc., an electronic distributor. After several successful years, the company is now troubled with eroding profit margins. Recent economic downturns further worsened the situation. Factors such as the growth of B2B e-commerce, the globalization of markets, the increased popularity of value-added services, and ongoing consolidations among electronic distributors affect the future of Swift.

To reverse these influences, Holland talked to a prestigious local university. After consultation, Holland found the most effective way to increase

profitability is to cut inventory costs. As a starting point, he studied in detail a representative product, dynamic random access memory (DRAM), as the basis for his plan.

Industry and Company Preview

Owing to a boom in the telecommunications industry and the information technology revolution, electronics distributors experienced double-digit annual growth over the last decade. To cut the cost of direct purchasing forces, large component manufacturers such as Intel, Cisco, and Texas Instruments decided to outsource their procurement so that they could focus on product development and manufacturing. Therefore, independent electronic distributors like Swift started offering procurement services to these companies.

Swift serves component manufacturers in California and Arizona. Working as the intermediary between its customers and overseas original equipment manufacturers (OEMs), Swift's business model is quite simple. Forecasting customer demand, Swift places orders to a number of OEMs, stocks those products, breaks the quantities down, and delivers the products to its end customers.

Recently, due to more intense competition and declines in demand, Swift offered more flexible delivery schedules and was willing to accommodate small order quantities. However, customers can always shift to Swift's competitors should Swift not fulfill their orders. Steven Holland was in a dilemma: The intangible costs of losing customers can be enormous; however, maintaining high levels of inventory can also be costly.

Dram

Holland turned his attention to DRAM as a representative product. Previously, the company ordered a large amount every time it felt it was necessary. Holland's assistant developed a table (Table 3) that has 2 months of demand history. From Holland's experience, the demand for DRAM is relatively stable in the company's product line and it had no sales seasonality. The sales staff agrees that conditions in the current year will not be different from those of past years, and historical demand will be a good indicator of what to expect in the future.

The primary manufacturers of DRAM are those in Southeast Asia. Currently, Swift can purchase one unit of 128M DRAM for $10. After negotiation with a reputable supplier, Holland managed to sign a long-term agreement, which kept the price at $10 and allowed Swift to place orders at any time. The supplier also supplies other items in Swift's inventory. In addition, it takes the supplier of the DRAM 2 days to deliver the goods to Swift's warehouse using air carriers.

When Swift does not have enough inventory to fill a customer's order, the sales are lost; that is, Swift is not able to backorder the shortage because its customers fill their requirements through competitors. The customers will accept partial shipments, however.

It costs Swift $200 to place an order with the suppliers. This amount covers the corresponding internal ordering costs and the costs of delivering the products to the company. Holland estimates that the cost of lost sales amounts to $2 per unit of DRAM. This rough estimate includes the loss of profits, as well as the intangible damage to customer goodwill.

To simplify its inventory management system, Swift has a policy of maintaining a cycle-service level of 95 percent. The holding cost per day per unit is estimated to be 0.5 percent of the cost of goods, regardless of the product. Inventory holding costs are calculated on the basis of the ending inventory each day. The current balance is 1,700 units of DRAM in stock.

The daily purchasing routine is as follows. Orders are placed at the *beginning* of the day, before Swift is open for customer business. The orders arrive at the beginning of the day, 2 days later, and can be used for sales that day. For example, an order placed at the beginning of day 1 will arrive at Swift before Swift is open for business on day 3. The actual daily demand is always recorded at the *end* of the day, after Swift has closed for customer business. All cost computations are done at the end of the day after the total demand has been recorded.

TABLE 3 | HISTORICAL DEMAND DATA FOR THE DRAM (UNITS)

Day	Demand	Day	Demand	Day	Demand
1	869	21	663	41	959
2	902	22	1,146	42	703
3	1,109	23	1,016	43	823
4	947	24	1,166	44	862
5	968	25	829	45	966
6	917	26	723	46	1,042
7	1,069	27	749	47	889
8	1,086	28	766	48	1,002
9	1,066	29	996	49	763
10	929	30	1,122	50	932
11	1,022	31	962	51	1,052
12	959	32	829	52	1,062
13	756	33	862	53	989
14	882	34	793	54	1,029
15	829	35	1,039	55	823
16	726	36	1,009	56	942
17	666	37	979	57	986
18	879	38	976	58	736
19	1,086	39	856	59	1,009
20	992	40	1,036	60	852

Simulation

Holland believes that simulation is a useful approach to assess various inventory control alternatives. The historical data from Table 3 could be used to develop attractive inventory policies. The table was developed to record various costs and evaluate different alternatives. An example showing some recent DRAM inventory decisions is shown in Table 4.

1. Design a new inventory system for Swift Electronic Supply, Inc., using the data provided.

2. Provide the rationale for your system, which should include the decision rules you would follow to determine how much to order and when.

3. Simulate the use of your inventory system and record the costs. Develop a table such as Table 4 to record your results. Your instructor will provide actual demands on a day-to-day basis during the simulation.

TABLE 4 | EXAMPLE SIMULATION

Day	1	2	3	4	5	6	7	8	9	10
Beginning inventory position	1,700	831	1,500	391	3,000	3,232	2,315			
Number ordered	1,500		3,000	1,200			1,900			
Daily demand	869	902	1,109	947	968	917	1,069			
Day-ending inventory	831	−71	391	−556	2,032	2,315	1,246			
Ordering costs ($200 per order)	200		200	200			200			
Holding costs ($0.05 per piece per day)	41.55	0.00	19.55	0.00	101.60	115.75	62.30			
Shortage costs ($2 per piece)	0	142	0	1,112	0	0	0			
Total cost for day	241.55	142.00	219.55	1,312.00	101.60	115.75	262.30			
Cumulative cost from last day	0.00	241.55	383.55	603.10	1,915.10	2,016.70	2,132.45			
Cumulative costs to date	241.55	383.55	603.10	1,915.10	2,016.70	2,132.45	2,394.75			

CASE Parts Emporium

Parts Emporium, Inc., is a wholesale distributor of automobile parts formed by two disenchanted auto mechanics, Dan Block and Ed Spriggs. Originally located in Block's garage, the firm showed slow but steady growth for 7 years before it relocated to an old, abandoned meat-packing warehouse on Chicago's South Side. With increased space for inventory storage, the company was able to begin offering an expanded line of auto parts. This increased selection, combined with the trend toward longer car ownership, led to an explosive growth of the business. Fifteen years later, Parts Emporium was the largest independent distributor of auto parts in the north central region.

Recently, Parts Emporium relocated to a sparkling new office and warehouse complex off Interstate 55 in suburban Chicago. The warehouse space alone occupied more than 100,000 square feet. Although only a handful of new products have been added since the warehouse was constructed, its utilization increased from 65 percent to more than 90 percent of capacity. During this same period, however, sales growth stagnated. These conditions motivated Block and Spriggs to hire the first manager from outside the company in the firm's history.

It is June 6, Sue McCaskey's first day in the newly created position of materials manager for Parts Emporium. A recent graduate of a prominent business school, McCaskey is eagerly awaiting her first real-world problem. At approximately 8:30 A.M., it arrives in the form of status reports on inventory and orders shipped. At the top of an extensive computer printout is a handwritten note from Joe Donnell, the purchasing manager: "Attached you will find the inventory and customer service performance data. Rest assured that the individual inventory levels are accurate because we took a complete physical inventory count at the end of last week. Unfortunately, we do not keep compiled records in some of the areas as you requested. However, you are welcome to do so yourself. Welcome aboard!"

A little upset that aggregate information is not available, McCaskey decides to randomly select a small sample of approximately 100 items and compile inventory and customer service characteristics to get a feel for the "total picture." The results of this experiment reveal to her why Parts Emporium decided to create the position she now fills. It seems that the inventory is in all the wrong places. Although an *average* of approximately 60 days of inventory is on hand, the firm's customer service is inadequate. Parts Emporium tries to backorder the customer orders not immediately filled from stock, but some 10 percent of demand is being lost to competing distributorships. Because stockouts are costly, relative to inventory holding costs, McCaskey believes that a cycle-service level of at least 95 percent should be achieved.

McCaskey knows that although her influence to initiate changes will be limited, she must produce positive results immediately. Thus, she decides to concentrate on two products from the extensive product line: the EG151 exhaust gasket and the DB032 drive belt. If she can demonstrate significant gains from proper inventory management for just two products, perhaps Block and Spriggs will give her the backing needed to change the total inventory management system.

The EG151 exhaust gasket is purchased from an overseas supplier, Haipei, Inc. Actual demand for the first 21 weeks of this year is shown in the following table:

Week	Actual Demand	Week	Actual Demand
1	104	12	97
2	103	13	99
3	107	14	102
4	105	15	99
5	102	16	103
6	102	17	101
7	101	18	101
8	104	19	104
9	100	20	108
10	100	21	97
11	103		

A quick review of past orders, shown in another document, indicates that a lot size of 150 units is being used and that the lead time from Haipei is fairly constant at 2 weeks. Currently, at the end of week 21, no inventory is on hand, 11 units are backordered, and the company is awaiting a scheduled receipt of 150 units.

The DB032 drive belt is purchased from the Bendox Corporation of Grand Rapids, Michigan. Actual demand so far this year is shown in the following table:

Week	Actual Demand	Week	Actual Demand
11	18	17	50
12	33	18	53
13	53	19	54
14	54	20	49
15	51	21	52
16	53		

Because this product is new, data are available only since its introduction in week 11. Currently, 324 units are on hand, with no backorders and no scheduled receipts. A lot size of 1,000 units is being used, with the lead time fairly constant at 3 weeks.

The wholesale prices that Parts Emporium charges its customers are $12.99 for the EG151 exhaust gasket and $8.89 for the DB032 drive belt. Because no quantity discounts are offered on these two highly profitable items, gross margins based on current purchasing practices are 32 percent of the wholesale price for the exhaust gasket and 48 percent of the wholesale price for the drive belt.

Parts Emporium estimates its cost to hold inventory at 21 percent of its inventory investment. This percentage recognizes the opportunity cost of tying money up in inventory and the variable costs of taxes, insurance, and shrinkage. The annual report notes other warehousing expenditures for utilities and maintenance and debt service on the 100,000-square-foot warehouse, which was built for $1.5 million. However, McCaskey reasons that these warehousing costs can be ignored because they will not change for the range of inventory policies that she is considering.

Out-of-pocket costs for Parts Emporium to place an order with suppliers are estimated to be $20 per order for exhaust gaskets and $10 per order for drive belts. On the outbound side, the company can charge a delivery fee. Although most customers pick up their parts at Parts Emporium, some orders are delivered to customers. To provide this service, Parts Emporium contracts with a local company for a flat fee of $21.40 per order, which is added to the customer's bill. McCaskey is unsure whether to increase the ordering costs for Parts Emporium to include delivery charges.

QUESTIONS

1. Put yourself in Sue McCaskey's position and prepare a detailed report to Dan Block and Ed Spriggs on managing the inventory of the EG151 exhaust gasket and the DB032 drive belt. Be sure to present a proper inventory system and recognize all relevant costs.

2. By how much do your recommendations for these two items reduce annual cycle inventory, stockout, and ordering costs?

Selected References

Arnold, Tony J.R., Stephen Chapman, and Lloyd M. Clive. *Introduction to Materials Management*, 7th ed. Upper Saddle River, NJ: Prentice Hall, 2012.

Axsäter, Sven. *Inventory Control*, 2nd ed. New York: Springer Science + Business Media, LLC, 2006.

Bastow, B. J. "Metrics in the Material World." *APICS—The Performance Advantage* (May 2005), pp. 49–52 .

Benton, W.C. *Purchasing and Supply Chain Management*, 2nd ed. New York: McGraw-Hill, 2010.

Callioni, Gianpaolo, Xavier de Montgros, Regine Slagmulder, Luk N. Van Wassenhove, and Linda Wright. "Inventory-Driven Costs." *Harvard Business Review* (March 2005), pp. 135–141 .

Cannon, Alan R., and Richard E. Crandall. "The Way Things Never Were." *APICS—The Performance Advantage* (January 2004), pp. 32–35.

Hartvigsen, David. *SimQuick: Process Simulation with Excel*, 2nd ed. Upper Saddle River, NJ: Prentice Hall, 2004.

Operations Management Body of Knowledge. Falls Church, VA: American Production and Inventory Control Society, 2009.

Timme, Stephen G., and Christine Williams-Timme. "The Real Cost of Holding." *Supply Chain Management Review* (July/August 2003), pp. 30–37.

Walters, Donald. *Inventory Control and Management*, 2nd ed. West Sussex, England: John Wiley and Sons, Ltd, 2003.

NORMAL DISTRIBUTION

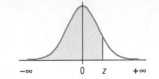

	.00	.01	.02	.03	.04	.05	.06	.07	.08	.09
.0	.5000	.5040	.5080	.5120	.5160	.5199	.5239	.5279	.5319	.5359
.1	.5398	.5438	.5478	.5517	.5557	.5596	.5636	.5675	.5714	.5753
.2	.5793	.5832	.5871	.5910	.5948	.5987	.6026	.6064	.6103	.6141
.3	.6179	.6217	.6255	.6293	.6331	.6368	.6406	.6443	.6480	.6517
.4	.6554	.6591	.6628	.6664	.6700	.6736	.6772	.6808	.6844	.6879
.5	.6915	.6950	.6985	.7019	.7054	.7088	.7123	.7157	.7190	.7224
.6	.7257	.7291	.7324	.7357	.7389	.7422	.7454	.7486	.7517	.7549
.7	.7580	.7611	.7642	.7673	.7704	.7734	.7764	.7794	.7823	.7852
.8	.7881	.7910	.7939	.7967	.7995	.8023	.8051	.8078	.8106	.8133
.9	.8159	.8186	.8212	.8238	.8264	.8289	.8315	.8340	.8365	.8389
1.0	.8413	.8438	.8461	.8485	.8508	.8531	.8554	.8577	.8599	.8621
1.1	.8643	.8665	.8686	.8708	.8729	.8749	.8770	.8790	.8810	.8830
1.2	.8849	.8869	.8888	.8907	.8925	.8944	.8962	.8980	.8997	.9015
1.3	.9032	.9049	.9066	.9082	.9099	.9115	.9131	.9147	.9162	.9177
1.4	.9192	.9207	.9222	.9236	.9251	.9265	.9279	.9292	.9306	.9319
1.5	.9332	.9345	.9357	.9370	.9382	.9394	.9406	.9418	.9429	.9441
1.6	.9452	.9463	.9474	.9484	.9495	.9505	.9515	.9525	.9535	.9545
1.7	.9554	.9564	.9573	.9582	.9591	.9599	.9608	.9616	.9625	.9633
1.8	.9641	.9649	.9656	.9664	.9671	.9678	.9686	.9693	.9699	.9706
1.9	.9713	.9719	.9726	.9732	.9738	.9744	.9750	.9756	.9761	.9767
2.0	.9772	.9778	.9783	.9788	.9793	.9798	.9803	.9808	.9812	.9817
2.1	.9821	.9826	.9830	.9834	.9838	.9842	.9846	.9850	.9854	.9857
2.2	.9861	.9864	.9868	.9871	.9875	.9878	.9881	.9884	.9887	.9890
2.3	.9893	.9896	.9898	.9901	.9904	.9906	.9909	.9911	.9913	.9916
2.4	.9918	.9920	.9922	.9925	.9927	.9929	.9931	.9932	.9934	.9936
2.5	.9938	.9940	.9941	.9943	.9945	.9946	.9948	.9949	.9951	.9952
2.6	.9953	.9955	.9956	.9957	.9959	.9960	.9961	.9962	.9963	.9964
2.7	.9965	.9966	.9967	.9968	.9969	.9970	.9971	.9972	.9973	.9974
2.8	.9974	.9975	.9976	.9977	.9977	.9978	.9979	.9979	.9980	.9981
2.9	.9981	.9982	.9982	.9983	.9984	.9984	.9985	.9985	.9986	.9986
3.0	.9987	.9987	.9987	.9988	.9988	.9989	.9989	.9989	.9990	.9990
3.1	.9990	.9991	.9991	.9991	.9992	.9992	.9992	.9992	.9993	.9993
3.2	.9993	.9993	.9994	.9994	.9994	.9994	.9994	.9995	.9995	.9995
3.3	.9995	.9995	.9995	.9996	.9996	.9996	.9996	.9996	.9996	.9997
3.4	.9997	.9997	.9997	.9997	.9997	.9997	.9997	.9997	.9997	.9998

From Appendix 1 of *Operations Management: Processes and Supply Chains,* Tenth Edition. Lee J. Krajewski, Larry P. Ritzman, Manoj K. Malhotra. Copyright © 2013 by Pearson Education, Inc. All rights reserved.

ANN E. GRAY
JAMES LEONARD

Process Fundamentals

Imagine that upon graduation you take a job managing a large bakery supplying supermarket chains with products ranging from breads to pies. Your mission is to improve the profitability of the operation. How will you start? Well, first, you will have to develop a good understanding of the current operation, the activities that take place to transform flour, water, yeast, and other ingredients into baked goods, and the effort involved in each activity—such as the labor, materials, and equipment required at each step. You will also need to understand the different products the bakery offers, and the reason that customers buy them from you and not your competitors. Do you have lower prices, faster delivery, higher quality, or a better product line that allows your customers to buy all their bakery needs from one source? Only after understanding the physical process itself, how it links to the performance of the bakery, and the level of performance required by customers, can you begin to look for opportunities to improve the bakery's profitability.

The goal of this overview is to provide tools that can help you understand operations, not just for a bakery, of course, but any type of operation. These tools are important not only for improving operations, but also for the daily management of an operation, or for the design of a new operation.

This overview begins by discussing the activities that take place in a "process". Analytical tools such as the process flow diagram are provided to help you walk into a new operation, such as your bakery, and understand how each of the process steps fits together. You'll be introduced to the types of management choices for designing, operating, and improving processes. Next, measures of the performance of a process and basic process analysis, the method used to determine what and how much a process is capable of producing, are introduced. You'll see how different types of processes can be used to make the same product, and how managers choose which process to use. Finally, the note focuses briefly on the complexity stemming from uncertainty and variability in the process, factors that make managing operations particularly difficult.

Elements of a Process

Throughout this course you will hear the terms "process," "operation," and "operating system." These will be used to mean any part of an organization that takes inputs and transforms them into outputs of greater value to the organization than the original inputs. In most situations we will focus on a subset of the entire organization—a single process that transforms a set of inputs into useful

Professor Ann E. Gray and Research Associate James Leonard prepared this note as the basis for class discussion. It is a rewritten version of an earlier note by Professor Paul W. Marshall, "A Note on Process Analysis," HBS No. 675-038.

Copyright © 1995-1997, 1999, 2007 President and Fellows of Harvard College. To order copies or request permission to reproduce materials, call 1-800-545-7685, write Harvard Business School Publishing, Boston, MA 02163, or go to http://www.hbsp.harvard.edu. No part of this publication may be reproduced, stored in a retrieval system, used in a spreadsheet, or transmitted in any form or by any means—electronic, mechanical, photocopying, recording, or otherwise—without the permission of Harvard Business School.

outputs. When talking about a set of processes, and in some cases the entire organization involved in transforming inputs into outputs, we will use the somewhat broader terms "operation" or "operating system."

Consider some examples of processes. An automobile assembly plant takes raw materials in the form of parts, components, and subassemblies. These materials, along with labor, capital, and energy, are transformed into automobiles. The transformation process is an assembly process and the output is an automobile. A restaurant takes inputs in the form of unprocessed or semiprocessed agricultural products. To these, labor (a cook and a server, for example), capital equipment (such as refrigerators and stoves), and energy (usually gas and/or electricity) are added, and the output is a meal.

Both of the processes mentioned above have physical products as an output. However, the output of some operating systems is a service. Consider an airline. The inputs are capital equipment in the form of airplanes and ground equipment; labor in the form of flight crews, ground crews, and maintenance crews; and energy in the form of fuel and electricity. These are transformed into a service, namely, a means of transportation between widely separated points. Processes with a service output also include those found in a hospital, or in an insurance company. In a hospital, capital, labor, and energy are applied to another input, patients, in order to transform them into healthier or more comfortable people.

More formally, *a process is a collection of tasks, connected by flows of goods and information, that transforms various inputs into more valuable outputs.* People, machines, and procedures are generally involved in the transformation. In order to understand a process it is useful to have a simple method of describing the process and some standard definitions for its components. A convenient way to describe an operating system is a *process flow diagram.*

Returning to our bakery example, let's assume there are two distinct production lines in the bakery for making bread. Flour, yeast, and water enter at the left and are converted into loaves of bread through mixing, proofing (letting the dough rise), baking, and packaging. This is a bit of a simplification, but we'll use it for illustration. There are two mixers, two proofers, and two ovens organized so that the ingredients mixed on the first mixer are automatically fed into the first proofer, and then sent to the first oven. All of the baked loaves of bread are packaged on the same packaging line. **Figure 1** shows the process flow diagram for the bakery.

Tasks in this process are shown as small rectangles, flows as arrows, and the storage of goods as inverted triangles. We see two identical *parallel lines* for mixing, proofing, and baking. Within each line, the tasks of mixing, proofing, and baking are defined as being in a *series* relationship, because one step cannot start until the previous one is complete. The maximum capacity of the two parallel lines would be found by adding the capacity of each line. Work-in-Process Inventory (WIP) is shown before packaging because, at times, the bakery may produce different types of bread at the same time, one on each line, yet only one type can be packaged at a time. If there were parallel packaging lines, there may not be the need for holding WIP between baking and packaging except, perhaps, to allow the bread time to cool. Once packaged, the bread moves into Finished Goods Inventory, and from there is transported to grocery store customers.

2

Figure 1   Process Flow Diagram for Bread-Making with Two Parallel Baking Lines

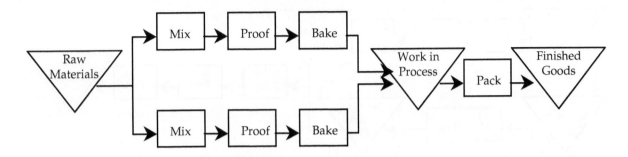

If the mixers, proofers, and ovens were not set up as two distinct lines, and the product could flow from *each* mixer to *either* proofer, and then to *either* oven, we would draw the process as in **Figure 2**. In this case, it is the individual *tasks* that operate in parallel, instead of two distinct parallel lines. (The distinction between these configurations will become important when performing a more detailed process analysis to determine the *capacity* of the system.)

Figure 2   Process Flow Diagram for Bread-Making with Two Mixers, Proofers, and Ovens

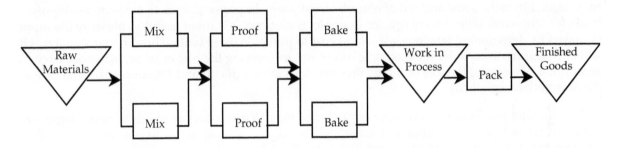

We may also want to show on a process flow diagram tasks that are performed in parallel but which must *both* be completed before the process can continue. For example, our bakery makes filled croissants in addition to breads. For these, the mixing, proofing, rolling, and cutting of the pastry take place in parallel with the mixing of the filling as shown in **Figure 3**. All these tasks must be completed before the croissants can be filled and baked. Proofing the dough takes longer than any of the other pastry-making steps. Proofing also takes longer than mixing the filling. This means that the rate at which filling and folding takes place is limited by the rate at which the *dough*, not the filling, is ready. And the rate at which the dough is ready is limited by the rate at which proofing takes place. It is the rate of the proofing step, the longest task, that defines how much bread can be made per hour.

Note that the nature of the parallel activities for making croissants is different from that of the two bread lines working in parallel as in **Figure 1**. To determine the capacity of the bread-making operation up until the dough is baked, we *add* the capacity of each of the parallel bread lines. To determine the capacity of croissant-making, however, we would take the *minimum* of the capacity of the two different parallel processes, in this case, the capacity of pastry making. This is because the output of the two lines must be *combined* to make the final product. We will revisit this issue in Section 1.2, when we do a formal capacity analysis.

Figure 3   Process Flow Diagram for Croissant-Making

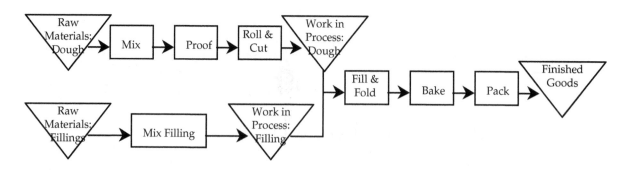

Once a process has been described using a process flow diagram, its components must be analyzed in order to draw some conclusions about its *performance* as a whole. In the following sections we will discuss each component of the process—the inputs, outputs, tasks, flows, and storage of goods—and begin to develop measurement and analysis methods along the way.

Inputs

The inputs to a process can be divided into at least four categories: labor, materials, energy, and capital. To analyze an operating system we must measure these inputs and determine the amount of each needed to make some amount of output. Usually we use physical units to measure the inputs—hours for labor and joules for energy, for example. Sometimes it is more useful to measure the input in dollars by determining how much it would cost to purchase these units. Thus, in many analyses it will be necessary to consider the economic conditions influencing the cost of labor, materials, energy, and capital. Measuring the cost of inputs thus becomes more difficult and requires additional care as the time horizon lengthens.

Determining how much of any input is needed to make a given output entails varying degrees of difficulty. Some inputs (e.g., labor and materials) are fully consumed to produce an output and thus are easy to assign to that unit of output. For example, it is easy to measure how much energy the oven uses to bake a batch of bread. Other inputs, however, are utilized in the production of an output, but are not fully consumed—the oven itself, for instance. The capital input is often the most difficult of the four categories to assign to a specific output because it is almost impossible to measure how much capital is consumed at any point in time. Generally accepted accounting rules are often used to allocate fixed costs, such as capital, to each unit of output.

Outputs

The output of a process is either a good or a service. The process flow diagram in **Figure 1** shows that the product is stored in Finished Goods Inventory (FGI) before leaving the system. In some organizations the finished goods inventory is kept apart from the operating system producing the good and is managed separately. Sometimes, the finished goods inventory does not exist at all: the process produces the output directly for distribution. In fact, this is an important characteristic of most processes providing services. It is often not easy (or possible) to store it for later distribution.

4

Although it is a simple matter to count the number of loaves of bread produced by the bakery, or to count the number of patients served by a hospital, it may not be simple to place a value on this output. The question of valuing the outputs can be approached from an economic point of view if a market will place a value on the output through the pricing mechanism. So, if we know the revenue that can be obtained from selling the good or service, that should serve as a measure of its value. For this reason, we must have a good understanding of the economic environment within which the process exists. Thus, "What are the market conditions?" and "What is the competition doing?" are important questions to address when analyzing a process.

For a new product, or one that has some improved characteristics, however, the question of what price *will be* paid for the output is difficult to answer unless some other information is known about the output. Here, we will consider three output characteristics: the *cost* of providing the output, the *quality* of the output, and the *timeliness* of the output. Often none of these measures is easily obtained, but they can serve as a checklist in our analysis of operating systems. If we are going to consider making a new type of bread, or increasing the quality of the bread, we may not know the price we can get for it. However, we do know that to value the new product, it is important to take into account the new product's characteristics, market conditions (is there an oversupply of specialty or high-end breads?), and the competitive situation (should we match the price of a competitor's similar product?).

Tasks, Flows, and Storage

So far we have discussed what goes into and what comes out of a process. We must also understand what goes on inside a process. The specifics of every process are different, but there are three general categories for all activities within the process: tasks, flows, and storage.

A task typically involves the addition of some input that makes the product or service more nearly like the desired output. Some examples of tasks are (1) operating a drill press to change a piece of metal; (2) inspecting a part to make sure it meets some standard; (3) flying an airplane; and (4) anesthetizing a patient before an operation. A task quite often takes the form of added labor and capital; in processes with some form of automation, capital and/or material may be substituted for labor in a task.

There are two types of flows to be considered in each process: the flow of goods and the flow of information. **Figure 4** depicts a process flow diagram with the flow of information shown explicitly— the flow of physical goods is indicated by solid lines and the information flow by broken lines.

Figure 4   Information and Physical Process Flow Diagram for the Bread-Making Process

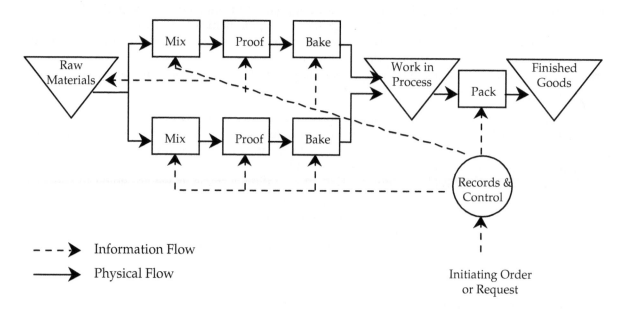

- - - ➤   Information Flow

———➤   Physical Flow

Initiating Order
or Request

Information flows in the bread-making process depicted in **Figure 4** are quite simple; they take the form of recipes and production orders. The list of ingredients and quantities for the type of bread that will be made next must go the operators or material handlers in charge of getting the raw material ingredients to each mixer. Information on mixing times and methods must go to the operators of the mixers, and baking temperatures and times must go to operators of the ovens. We will also have to inform packaging of what types and quantities of breads will be arriving to the packaging area so that they can set up their equipment with the correct bags.

In some types of operations, the information flows take place with the physical flows, often in the form of a routing slip attached to a single product or a batch of products. The analogy here would be the entire recipe and the production order moving with the bread. The oven operator, for instance, would receive baking instructions with the proofed dough as it arrives at the oven. If the operator could not or would not need to adjust the oven in advance, not providing this information in advance would not cause any production delay and would simplify the information flows. Other information that might be included on the routing slip includes the packaging lines that the loaves should be sent to (if there are multiple packaging lines), the appropriate bags to use for packaging, the supermarket name and location, the delivery date and time, and possibly even the truck into which the finished product should be loaded.

When the information does not physically move through the process with the goods, the worker may need to go to a central location to obtain the information before performing the task, or the worker may have the necessary information at the workstation or in his or her head. In analyzing a process it is often important to consider the information flows in addition to the physical flow of goods or services.

Storage (the holding of inventory) is the last of the three activities within a process we will define. Storage occurs when no task is being performed and the good or service is not being transported. In **Figures 1 - 4** we have shown the storage of goods as inverted triangles. While the bakery is operating, there will usually be work-in-process inside the mixers, proofers, and ovens, at the packaging machines, as well as some work-in-process inventory between each step, and raw materials and finished goods inventory in the warehouse. If there is no storage between two connected tasks there must be a planned continuous flow between these tasks to allow the receiving task to operate continuously. **Figures 1** and **2** show only one work-in-process storage, whereas **Figure 3** shows two. In many processes that are considered continuous, there are at least a few units of work-in-process inventory on a rack or chute waiting to be fed into a machine. Although technically these units are in storage and could be depicted on the process flow diagram as inverted triangles between processing steps, when these units represent just a few minutes of processing time they are often left off of the diagram.

It is also possible, and in fact necessary, to store information. This storage is shown as a circle in **Figure 4**, with an arrow coming in from the environment to start the process. In this case, there are two kinds of information: records and control. The term *records* typically refers to general instructions, such as blueprints and instructions of how a product should be made (i.e., the "recipe"). These records are product-specific. Records may also be machine-specific, tracking repair and preventative maintenance histories, for example. The term *control* usually refers to information specific to a given order, such as the order quantity, customer name or number, due date and routing procedure for the order, or special instructions that make the order different from the generally accepted procedures explained in the records.

Measuring the Performance of a Process

So far we have defined the process in general terms and given names to various components of the process, namely the *inputs*, the *outputs*, and the *tasks*, *flows*, and *storage* within the process. We have also noted that the process does not exist in isolation. Economic conditions influence the values of inputs and outputs, and the state of technology influences the nature of the tasks and flows. Using these concepts as a base, we can now explore some process characteristics, concentrating on four: *capacity*, *efficiency*, *flexibility*, and *quality*.

Capacity

Capacity is the maximum rate of output from the process and is measured in units of output per unit of time: a steel mill, for instance, can produce some number of tons of steel per year, or an insurance office can process some number of claims per hour. *Capacity is easy to define and hard to measure*. It is often possible to determine the *theoretical capacity* of a process—the most output it could generate under ideal conditions over some period of time. For planning purposes and management decisions, however, it is more useful to know the *effective capacity* of a process. And to measure effective capacity, we must know a great deal about the process, carefully analyzing the particular situation at hand.

Managers often believe that the capacity of a process is an absolute fixed quantity. This is rarely true. The capacity of a process can change for many reasons, and we will encounter several cases where this is a key factor. The steel mill, for instance, may be designed for some ideal capacity, but its effective capacity may be different due to a variety of internal and external factors, and management decisions. The nature and availability of the raw materials being utilized, the mix of products being produced, the quantity and nature of the labor input, and the number of shifts of operation will all impact the effective capacity. The yield of the process is also important. In most instances, the rate of *good* units produced is the relevant capacity measure.

Efficiency

Efficiency is a measure that relates the amount or value of the output of the process to the amount or value of the input. "Efficiency" is widely used to measure physical processes. Every engine has an efficiency, expressed as a ratio of output energy to input energy. So, an engine with 75% efficiency can deliver 75% of the input energy as useful output energy. The energy efficiency of physical systems cannot exceed 100%; the useful output energy is always less than the energy input. This is not generally true of economic processes, however. For example, if the process is going to generate sufficient resources to support its own continued operation, the *value* of the output should exceed the value of the input. If we measure the value of output by the revenues it will bring in the market, and if we measure the value of inputs by their costs, the measure of efficiency is profit, i.e., revenue minus cost. Thus, the profit is the value of output minus the value of input. Profit, however, is a very simplistic definition of efficiency; measuring efficiency is generally much more complex.

In some cases, the price received for the product is not a good representation of the economic value of the output. In certain markets, for example, it may be possible initially for a company to sell a product of low quality at a standard price. Over time, however, the company's reputation may be hurt by doing this, and *all* of the company's products, not just the low quality product, might become less desired by the market. The long-term loss in revenue should have been considered when establishing the cost and quality level of the original product. When determining the efficiency of a process as measured by profitability, it is important to look at long-run profits, not just the profit generated from any short-run action.

Utilization is another common measure. Utilization is the ratio of the input the process actually used in creating the output to the amount of that input available for use. In a labor-intensive process, for instance, direct labor utilization is often an efficiency measure. If, say, 100 workers are employed in a given process, and during an eight-hour shift 700 hours of labor were consumed in the actual manufacture of product, then the direct labor utilization during that shift was 87.5% ([700 hours/(100 X 8 hours)] = 0.875). In a similar way, to measure capital efficiency, companies often pay a great deal of attention to machine utilization, which measures the percentage of time machinery is used. Typically, this includes machine setup time as well as the time the machine is actively producing output.

In a small bakery where workers mix the dough, form loaves, and move the product from one step to another by hand, labor utilization is a critical measure of bakery performance. In an automated bakery, machine utilization may be more relevant.

Flexibility

A third characteristic we want to consider in analyzing a process is its *flexibility*. This is a measure of how long it would take to change the process so that it could produce a different output, or could use a different set of inputs. Flexibility, which allows a process to respond to changes in its environment, is also the least precise and hardest to define of the characteristics we have considered thus far. Flexibility must often be described in qualitative terms; doing so, however, does not make it any less important to managers.

Returning to our bakery, its flexibility may be described by the different types of bread that can be produced on a given line, or whether pastry products can also be made on the same line as bread products. Another type of flexibility may further be measured by the time required to switch the line from producing one type of product to another.[1]

Quality

Like flexibility, *quality* may be described in different ways. Product quality can be evaluated using external measures—comparing the product with others available in the marketplace—or using internal measures—comparing individual units with one another or with the product design specification. External quality measures generally assess how well the product design satisfies the wants and needs of customers. Product performance, features, reliability, durability, serviceability, and design aesthetics may all be components of product quality. Internal measures of product quality generally assess whether individual units meet design specifications.

In addition to designing, measuring and controlling *product* quality, a manufacturer also designs, measures and controls *process* quality. In order to produce a product with certain specifications, the process must be operating within certain tolerances. Process measures, such as the temperature in a kiln or the amount of force applied by a punch press, are generally used in assessing process quality. Any piece of processing equipment has specific capabilities defined by the range of process specifications it is able to achieve. A piece of equipment may not be able to perform a certain type of operation, such as grinding a piece of metal to a certain smoothness, if doing so requires operating outside this range or it may not be able to *consistently* perform the operation properly. In other circumstances, the equipment is capable of consistently operating within certain specifications, but is not operating consistently within these specifications because of poor equipment control. Both the design of the process and the way in which the process is operated are important determinants of process, and thus, product quality[2].

Within the plant, the impact of poor quality can be increased scrap, rework, yield losses resulting in lost capacity, downtime, additional testing, and lost management and worker time. If poor quality product leaves the factory, the impact can include a loss of goodwill toward the company and its brands, time and cost responding to customer complaints, and repair costs.

Process Terminology and Process Analysis

As the new manager of the bakery, once you understand its products and the process steps, and you have created a process flow diagram, you will want to determine the capacity of your operation. To do this, let's further simplify the bread-making example, as illustrated in **Figure 5**. Here, there are two steps required to prepare bread. The first is bread-making, which includes preparing the dough and baking the loaves, and the second is packaging the loaves. There is only a single line for mixing, proofing, and baking, and it is illustrated by one box representing the entire bread-making line.

---

[1] A more detailed description of different types of process flexibility and how they can be managed can be found in: Upton, David, "The Management of Manufacturing Flexibility," *California Management Review*, Winter, 1994, or Upton, David, "What really makes factories flexible?," *Harvard Business Review*, July–August, 1995.

[2] A more detailed description of different measures of quality can be found in: Garvin, David A., "Competing on the eight dimensions of quality," *Harvard Business Review*, November-December, 1987, or Garvin, David A., and Artemis March, "A Note on Quality: The Views of Deming, Juran, and Crosby," Harvard Business School Note 9-687-001, 1987.

9

Figure 5

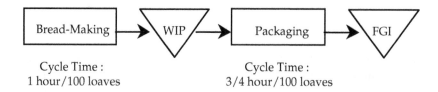

Based on the size of the mixers in the bakery, bread is made in batches of 100 loaves each. Bread-making completes a batch of 100 loaves every hour; thus, one hour is the bread-making *cycle time* for a batch of 100 loaves. Although packaging needs only 3/4 of an hour to place the 100 loaves in bags (its cycle time), the rate at which the entire process can operate is paced by bread-making. Thus, over the course of a day, packaging will incur *idle time* during the 1/4 hour periods in which the next batch of bread is still being made but packaging has already completed bagging the previous batch. Bread-making is the *bottleneck* of the operation. The cycle time for the entire process is 1 hour, the maximum of the cycle times of the two operations in series. Given the cycle time for the entire process, we can determine its *capacity*. Simply put, if the cycle time is 1 hour per 100 loaves, the line has a capacity of 100 loaves per hour, the inverse of the cycle time. To determine the daily capacity, we would need to know the number of hours the bakery is in operation per day. With any of these terms of measurement, it is important to be very explicit about the units (i.e., loaves per hour, minutes per loaf), particularly when performing calculations.

To perform our analysis of the capacity of the bread-making line above, we introduced some new terms and concepts. While we have provided formal definitions below, we must also stress that **calculating these measures requires close attention to the specifics of a particular process.** In addition, **different firms sometimes define these terms in different ways** for their own internal use. This variation is reflected in some of our case materials. However, for the purposes of class discussion, it makes sense to try to adhere to a common vocabulary.

Cycle Time (CT): The cycle time of a process is the average time between completion of successive units. In other words, cycle time answers the question, "How often does a unit complete the process?" Cycle time can be similarly defined for portions of a process. The cycle time of a particular task in a process reflects the average time between finishing the task for one unit and finishing the task for the next unit.

Sometimes a process is not operated at its maximum production rate. In those instances, you may need to distinguish between the rate at which units *can* complete the process (the minimum cycle time of the process) and the rate at which they actually *do* complete the process (the actual cycle time).

Bottleneck: The bottleneck of a process is the factor which limits production. Usually, we will speak of the task with the longest cycle time as a bottleneck, such as bread-making in **Figure 5**. In other situations, the available labor may be the bottleneck. In some settings, information, raw materials flow, or even a specific order may be a bottleneck. Just as the neck of a bottle limits the rate at which the liquid inside can be poured, a process bottleneck limits how quickly products can move through the process, and thus determines the process *cycle time*. The bottleneck may shift depending on what products are being produced or what labor or equipment is available at any point in time. Because bottlenecks pace a process and limit its *capacity*, they are important focal points for management attention.

Idle Time: Idle time refers to the time when useful work is not being performed; the term can be applied to a worker or to a machine. Time spent waiting to receive or deliver a unit is idle time unless there is some other useful task to be performed in the interim. Idle time can be present even in a perfectly balanced process. A worker in the packaging department, for example, may merely load twenty loaves of bread on a machine and then stand by while it bags the bread. This time might be idle time for the worker (unless he or she is *needed* to monitor the equipment's performance), while it is not idle time for the packaging machine. In **Figure 5**, the packaging machine will be idle 1/4 of the time.

Capacity: Capacity is a measure of how much can be produced or serviced in a specified period of time, e.g., tons per day, parts per minute, customers per hour. The capacity of a process is determined by the process bottleneck. Capacity utilization is a measure of how much output was actually achieved relative to capacity (how much output could have been achieved in an ideal situation). If the capacity of a process is 500 units per day and on a given day 480 are produced, then on that day capacity utilization was 96% (480 units/500 units = 0.96). We may speak of the capacity of a task, a machine, a worker, a work area, or of an entire process.[3] Cycle time and capacity are closely related. If the cycle time of a task is 30 minutes per unit, then the capacity of that task is 2 units per hour.

Capacity seems a straightforward measure, and for a specific task producing a specific product it often will be. But finding relevant capacity measures for an entire process can be complicated. In many cases, the system capacity will depend on the size and mix of products and order sizes. And because the capacity of an entire process is affected by product mix, staffing, labor contract issues, maintenance time, etc., the effective capacity and capacity utilization will depend upon the way the process is managed.

Suppose we have two lines for bread-making, as shown in **Figure 6**.

Figure 6

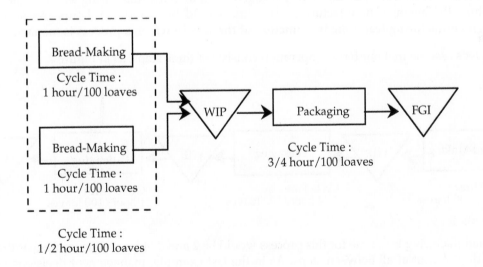

Cycle Time :
1/2 hour/100 loaves

---

[3] Companies such as Toyota Motor Manufacturing ensure that capacity exceeds customer requirements by calculating the *takt time*. This is determined by taking the time available to produce a certain product and dividing by customer demand for that product. The result, the takt time, is the production rate necessary to meet demand, and, if possible, a process should be designed with this takt time in mind. (For example, if an assembly line is available for 16 hours (960 minutes) per day and customer demand is 1,000 cars per day, the takt time is 0.96 minutes per car.)

Although the cycle time for each bread-making line is 1 hour/100 loaves, the cycle time of the two lines together is 1/2 hour/100 loaves or, equivalently, 0.005 hour/loaf. Because the packaging line takes 3/4 hour to bag 100 loaves (or 0.0075 hour/loaf), *it* becomes the bottleneck of the process. If both bread-making and packaging were operated for the same number of hours each day, we would not make bread at its maximum cycle time rate because we would not have the capacity to package it. There is, therefore, an *imbalance* in the cycle times of the two parts of the process. If, however, we could operate packaging for three shifts and bread-making for two shifts each day, then the daily capacity of each would be identical. To do this requires building up a shift's-worth of inventory each day as work-in-process that packaging would then bag during the third shift.

Balance/Imbalance: If every step in a process had the same cycle time (and performed consistently at that precise cycle time, with no variability), then the process would be in perfect balance. This is virtually never achieved in practice, however. The processes shown in **Figures 5 and 6** are both imbalanced. If a system is not perfectly balanced there will be potential *idle time* at the non-bottleneck parts of the process. Although the cycle times are imbalanced in **Figure 6**, we can balance the daily capacity at each of the two steps by adjusting the hours worked per day in each step.

For the processes above, we might want to know the *manufacturing lead time*—how long it takes to actually make and pack a batch of 100 loaves. For the process in **Figure 5**, the manufacturing lead time is 1 and 3/4 hours, as long as packaging begins immediately once the 100 loaves are made. The manufacturing lead time for the process in **Figure 6**, however, depends upon how the process is managed. Let's assume that we operate both steps in the process (bread-making and packaging) for the same number of hours per day. If we start a new batch every 3/4 hour, alternating between bread-making lines, each of these batches will be able to proceed directly to packaging, resulting in a manufacturing lead time of 1 and 3/4 hours. We could start a new batch on both bread-making lines at the same time, every 1 and 1/2 hours (any more rapidly would mean that we would be producing more bread than we could package). While one batch would move immediately to packaging, for a manufacturing lead time of 1 and 3/4 hours, the other would have to wait the 3/4 hour for the first batch and would then take 3/4 hour to be packaged, for a total manufacturing lead time of 2 and 1/2 hours. Thus, the average manufacturing lead time would be 2 and 1/8 hours. **As seen by this example, manufacturing lead time is a function of the way in which a process is managed.**

Now, let's assume that our bakery operation consists of three steps, as in **Figure 7**.

Figure 7

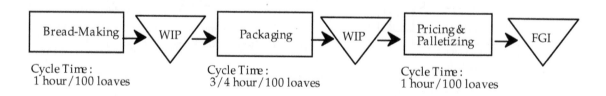

The manufacturing lead time for this process would be 2 and 3/4 hours, assuming that the batches of bread do not wait at all between steps. As in the last example, management decisions regarding scheduling could affect the lead time. If, for example, each step began operation at the same time, every hour on the hour, then packaged bread would wait for 1/4 hour before pricing and palletizing and the manufacturing lead time would be 3 hours. In this situation there would probably be no reason to follow this policy, but for many assembly lines the units are transferred by conveyor from one step to the next, and movement of the conveyor is paced by the slowest step in the process.

So far, we have not considered the direct impact of work-in-process on manufacturing lead time. In the bakery described by **Figure 7**, bread may not flow immediately from one step to the next. If, occasionally, a batch of bread does not bake properly, management may choose to keep an inventory buffer of one batch between steps to minimize disruptions. If there is a bad batch of bread, then, the packaging line would *not* have to shut down and, an hour later, be restarted. It would simply use up the batch in the buffer. Suppose we manage the process so that every step begins operation every hour on the hour. Then, a policy of keeping one batch of work-in-process as a buffer between steps would add 2 hours to the usual manufacturing lead time. To see this, imagine following a small amount of flour through the entire process. After being made into bread, it now waits 1 hour for the batch ahead of it before moving into packaging. After packaging, it then waits 1 hour until the batch ahead of it is completely priced and palletized.

Another reason why there may be work-in-process between steps is because it may take some time to move the bread between steps, either manually or on a conveyor. This time would also add to the manufacturing lead time.

Manufacturing lead time (MLT) **(also called** *throughput time (TPT))*: Manufacturing lead time refers to the length of time spent in the process. For a single task the cycle time and manufacturing lead time may be equal if only one station is performing the task. When a process involves multiple tasks or steps, the concepts of cycle and manufacturing lead time are quite different. Cycle time refers to how often a unit "drops off" the end of the process whereas manufacturing lead time refers to how long that unit takes between entering and leaving the process, including any in-process storage or transport time.

If units must wait between steps, the manufacturing lead time for a process may be far greater than the sum of the processing times of its individual tasks. Units may wait as work-in-process inventory between tasks, either while other batches are being processed, or while other units in their own batch are processed. Idle time may also add to the manufacturing lead time. This often occurs when a line is imbalanced but is paced by a conveyor at the speed of the slowest task, resulting in idle time between most steps of the process.

Lot Size (also called Batch Size): Most processes produce more than one product type. Suppose a process produced three products: P1, P2, and P3. The process could produce one unit of P1, then one unit of P2, then one unit of P3, then one unit of P1 and so on until we had 100 units each of P1, P2, and P3. Alternatively the process could produce 100 units of P1 before beginning production on 100 units of P2. In the first case, the lot size is equal to one unit; in the second case, the lot size is 100 units. If time must be expended setting up the equipment to make the transition from producing P1 to producing P2, then these two different lot sizes will result in quite different throughput and cycle times. The lot size, then, is number of units of a particular product type that will be produced before beginning production of another product type. Different product types in the same plant may have different lot sizes.

The size of a lot, or batch, may be constrained by physical limitations such as, in our bakery example, the size of the mixers or ovens. It may be determined by the size of an order (e.g., a customer orders 300 units of a special part). Or, the lot size may be strictly a management decision. A company making three colors of telephones, for instance, may choose to mold 1,000 plastic casings of each color before changing over to another color.

Setup Time/Run Time: Setup time refers to the time spent arranging tools, changing dies, setting machine speeds, cleaning equipment, etc., in preparation for the beginning of work on a specific type of product. Depending on the type of process, it might be necessary to spend from a few minutes to a few hours setting up to make the process ready for the transition from producing one product type to producing another product type. Setup time does not necessarily mean idle time for the task or process, however. It may be possible for a worker to do much of the setup for the production of a second product type "off-line" during the production of the first product type. This minimizes the amount of machine capacity lost due to setups. For our purposes, *setup time* refers to any time that is necessary for production but *is independent of the number of units to be produced*. In this respect, for production of a given lot, the setup time is fixed and the run time is proportional to the lot size. This is a useful distinction. Long setup times, for example, may make it attractive to produce in large lot sizes because the fixed cost of the set up can be spread over a larger production volume.

Run time per unit is the amount of time actually spent manufacturing the item (or performing the service) independent of the time required to set up the equipment. If units in a lot are processed sequentially, the run time per lot is the run time per unit multiplied by the number of units in a lot (i.e., the time the units in the particular lot are actually "running" on the equipment). This simple calculation is more complicated, however, if the equipment produces in batches, like an oven or kiln, or if there are multiple equipment stations involved.

Returning to the concept of manufacturing lead time (throughput time), if we were to follow a unit from when it first enters a process until it leaves, some of this time it would be worked on (run time), it may spend some of the time waiting for a machine to be set-up (setup time), and some of the time the unit would be waiting due to imbalance in the processing steps, due to machine downtime, or due to time spent as WIP inventory waiting for other products to be completed.

In addition to measures of cycle time, capacity, and manufacturing lead time, to evaluate a process you may also want to know the direct labor content and the direct labor utilization.

Direct Labor Content: Different organizations and disciplines use the term "direct labor content" in different ways. For our purposes, "direct labor content" refers to the actual amount of work "contained" in the product. Returning to the process in **Figure 5**, let's say that for a batch of 100 loaves, while the packaging equipment has a cycle time of 3/4 hour, the packaging operator spends only 40 minutes in activities such as loading the loaves onto the machines, setting up the right bags on each machine, and making any necessary machine adjustments. The direct labor content in packaging would be 40 minutes/100 loaves or 0.4 minutes/loaf. For the total direct labor content of the bread, the direct labor content of bread-making would need to be included. Indirect labor hours (maintenance, materials handling, management, etc.) are not included in the calculation of direct labor content. Setup time may or may not be included in direct labor content. Exactly what goes into direct labor content varies by firm, but, generally, setups performed by dedicated setup workers are not included because those workers are usually classified as indirect labor, and setups done by operators on their own machines are included, because these workers are classified as direct labor.

Note that direct labor content is not the same as direct labor cost. "Content" refers to the work done in actually manufacturing the product or performing the service (or setting up to do so), not to the wages paid. Labor cost differs from labor content due to imbalance, vacation pay, paid breaks, etc. Recall that the process cycle time in **Figure 5** is 1 hour/100 loaves. Even if the packaging operator is busy for only 40 minutes of every hour, the operator is paid for an entire hour. Thus, *idle time* adds to labor cost but does not affect labor content.

Direct Labor Utilization: Rather than measure idle time or direct labor content in minutes, it is often more useful to talk in percentage terms. Direct labor utilization is a measure of the percentage of time that workers are actually working on a product or performing a service, i.e.:

$$\text{Direct Labor Utilization} = \frac{\text{Direct labor content}}{\text{Total available labor time}}$$

Total available labor time consists of both direct labor content and any idle time. In the example above, direct labor utilization in packaging is 67% ([40 minutes/60 minutes] X 100). Part of the reason that the utilization is not 100% is due to the imbalance between packaging and bread-making (this accounts for 15 minutes of idle time per hour), while part (5 minutes of idle time per hour) is due to the work design (driven by the level of mechanization) in the packaging operation. If there are as many packaging operators as bread-making operators, and if the bread-making operators are 100% utilized, the overall direct labor utilization would be the average of the two numbers, or 83%.

All of this discussion has assumed that yields are 100%, i.e., that every unit that starts through the process goes all the way through every step of the process without mishap. The presence of rejects and/or rework complicates the analysis, of course. The impact of defects resulting in yields of less than 100% will be explored in subsequent modules.

When calculating process performance measures, carefully consider the details of the process and the managerial question you are seeking to answer. A good conceptual understanding of the terms in this overview will guide you in applying them to new environments and new types of decisions.

So far we have described some of the physical attributes of operating systems and how to measure their performance. We now turn to the decisions made in the management of operating systems.

Management Decisions

There are three general categories of decisions that must be made to manage an operation. First, is the *design* of the operation, and of the distinct processes that constitute the operation. Second, is the ongoing set of decisions—the *operating decisions*—that determine what is made at any point in time. Finally, there are *process improvement* decisions, which may be made, for example, to increase the output, lower cost, or improve the range of products that can be produced. You will be exposed to an extensive range of management decisions through the cases in this course, going far beyond the list below.

Design Choices. To start a new operation, the type of process must be selected. Although a high-volume continuous line might be chosen for a large bakery that makes only breads, a smaller, more flexible set of mixers and ovens might be chosen for a bakery making a wide variety of small batches of specialty breads, pies, cookies, cakes, rolls, and croissants. After selecting a general process type, the actual technology must also be chosen. The choice of process is likely to limit somewhat the choice of technology. When purchasing a high-volume continuous line, a firm is likely to have the option of selecting a much higher degree of automation than if purchasing individual machines designed for lower volumes and a wider variety of products. Other design choices include specifying the capacity of the operation, with an eye to future sales forecasts and the cost of adding capacity later to meet those forecasts. The way that the equipment is situated in the space available—the process layout—must also be determined, in conjunction with the pattern of material and information flows.

The choices made in designing a particular process determine in large part the inputs needed to provide the process outputs. It also determines in large part the range of outputs possible. As a simple example, consider two alternatives for providing copies of some information, one using a printing press and the other using a copier. The press involves several tasks to produce the information such as typesetting, proofreading, and press operation. The copier, on the other hand, requires only an operator and an original document containing the information and requires no setup activity. The cost of providing copies is different for each type of process. The printing press has a much higher setup cost but each additional copy is very cheap. Thus, for large numbers of copies the press has an economic advantage.

Ongoing Operating Decisions. Once an operation is up and running, the main management tasks are often order selection, scheduling, setting batch size, and inventory management. The bakery's manager(s) would need to determine, for example, when to make whole-wheat bread and when to make raisin bread over the coming week, how much of each to make, whether to take an order from a new grocery store, and how much inventory to hold as raw materials, work-in-process, and finished goods. Although these decisions for a bakery may seem relatively straightforward, the complexity increases with the number of different products, the lack of excess capacity available, the number of different customers and their requirements, and the cost of holding inventory.

Process Improvement Decisions. Managers can decide to physically alter the process by changing technology or adding machines or workers. They can redesign the physical or information flows, or change the design of individual tasks, or improve the methods by which the process is managed. These decisions are much like design decisions, but the existing system puts additional costs and constraints on the changes that can be made. The objective of process improvements may be to improve the cost, quality, or timeliness of the output. It may also be to make the process more flexible, allowing entirely new outputs to be made.

Management Complexity

Variability and uncertainty in the inputs, in the transformation process itself, in the outputs, or in demand increase the complexity of managing an operation. This can be illustrated using our bakery example. The simplest bakery produces one type of bread on a single line. No routing or product mix decisions need to be made, and very little information needs to be managed. The primary management tasks involve fixing any problems that arise, scheduling overtime if necessary, and looking for ways to improve the efficiency of the process or the quality of the bread.

Once there is variability in the process, it becomes more difficult to manage. One source of variability may be the inputs. If the flour purchased from different vendors is slightly different, methods must be in place to make the necessary adjustments in the quantities used, the mixing and proofing times, or the baking time. This may require more sophisticated control of equipment and additional quality control activities. It also requires an information system in place to inform operators (and the machines, directly, if the system is automated) of the composition of the flour being used and how to adjust for it. The bakery may also want to track the use of the different flour in such a way that they could determine if the differences in the flours lead to any additional customer complaints. This would place an additional burden on the information system.

Also, the more types of bread that the bakery makes, i.e., the higher the variability in outputs, the more difficult it is to manage. A bakery making 16 different types of bread has to schedule the process so that each type is made in the right amount, and demand is met. In addition, a set-up is involved in switching the machines from making one type of bread to another. The mixers will have to be cleaned and the oven temperature may need to be reset. Moreover, variability in demand also adds to the complexity of managing the bakery. If bread demand is seasonal, even if that demand is perfectly predictable, many more loaves will have to be produced during certain months of the year—and that may entail increasing the number of workers for that period or scheduling overtime.

In our discussion so far, the factors adding to management complexity have all been sources of *variability*, that is, changes that are known and anticipated. But *uncertainty* in inputs, in the process

16

itself, in outputs or in demand also leads to management complexity. Thus, in the bakery, it may happen that, owing to incomplete mixing or to fluctuations in the temperature in different parts of the oven, for example, not all the bread that comes out of the oven is good. Uncertainty in the subsequent yield of the process—not knowing exactly how many good loaves you will get from a given amount of dough—makes the scheduling task much more difficult. It also will probably require additional labor to sort out the bad bread, and may require that yield information be kept so that scheduling can be adjusted as necessary to ensure that demand is met. Uncertainty in demand also adds to management complexity. Inventory is often used to make it easier to fill demand when uncertainty exists in yield and/or demand. But inventory may be costly to hold, and can also increase management complexity because it, too, must be managed.

As you analyze new case situations, consider what it is that makes the management task complex in the different environments presented. Look for ways to eliminate the sources of complexity or to simplify the task of managing it.

Summary

In the bakery example presented here, we have not tried to address a management problem. In any real case it is clear that the nature of the problem should guide your analysis. Instead, we have tried to show the first two of several steps that might be useful in an analysis designed to address a management issue. These steps are summarized below.

1. Define the process—determine the tasks and the flows of information and goods. Also, determine where inventory is kept in the process. This effort can be recorded in a process flow diagram.

2. Determine the capacity or range of capacities for the process. This will require an analysis of each task and a comparison of how these tasks are balanced. In addition, determine the effect of inventory in the system on the capacity of tasks and flows. Inventories may allow the process to operate out of balance for some time, but in the long run the capacity of the process is limited by the capacity of its slowest task.

In many instances you will also need to determine the cost of inputs and relate these costs to the value of the output in some market by comparing the cost, quality, and timeliness of this output to the needs of the market.

We've seen that we cannot fully describe a process simply by the physical tasks, but that we need to consider management decisions ranging from how information is used to how work is scheduled in the process.

Glossary of TOM Terms

Manufacturing Lead Time (MLT)   The amount of time each unit spends in the manufacturing process (sometimes called Throughput Time). This includes time spent actively being worked upon at each step of the process as well as any time spent waiting between steps. The concept of a lead time applies to the total time spent in any process in which the start and finish are well-defined events. We can talk about lead times, for example, in service operations, or in the entire order-to-delivery process.

Cycle Time (CT)   Average time between completion of successive units. It is directly related to the output rate. A process with an output rate of 4 units per hour has a cycle time of 15 minutes.

Work-in-Process (WIP)   Number of units in the process at any point in time. If the process includes buffer inventories between steps, then the work-in-process is the total number of units being worked upon as well as waiting in inventory between steps. The units in inventory are usually referred to as Work-in-process *inventory*, to distinguish them from raw materials inventory or finished goods inventory.

Bottleneck   The production resource that limits the capacity of the overall process. This is usually the production equipment at the step with the lowest overall capacity, i.e., the longest cycle time. In some situations, the bottleneck resource may be labor available at a particular step or steps.

Capacity   The maximum rate of output of a process, measured in units of output per unit of time. The unit of time may be of any length: a year, a day, a shift, or a minute.

Utilization   Ratio of the input actually used over the amount of the input available. Labor utilization is the ratio of the actual labor time spent processing to the total amount of labor time available. Differences between the two can be due to inefficiencies in the process that lead to lost working time, as well as to imbalances in the cycle times at each step of the process that lead to idle time of workers at some steps while those at others are working. Capacity utilization is the ratio of the capacity actually used (i.e., the output of the process) to the total capacity available.

Process Flow Diagram   Diagram depicting the activities in a process and the flows between them. While most process flow diagrams focus on the physical processing of goods, information processing may also be depicted.

Lot Size (also called Batch Size)   Number of units of a particular product type that is produced before beginning production of another product type.

Note: In all of the above definitions, a "process" may refer to the complete production process, such as the making of bread from start to finish, or to a segment of the complete process, such as the packaging process.

Source: Adapted from Professor W. Bruce Chew, "A Glossary of TOM Terms," HBS No. 687-019.

Index

Page references followed by "f" indicate illustrated figures or photographs; followed by "t" indicates a table.